"*Acid Test* is a superb book. The people Tom Shroder introduces us to are across-the-board fascinating, the reporting he's done is deep and persuasive, and the writing is dazzling. Best of all, though, is what any open-minded reader will feel after finishing *Acid Test*: In a world of hurt, here is a new version of hope."

—David Finkel, Pulitzer Prize–winning author of
The Good Soldiers and *Thank You for Your Service*

"Tom Shroder's *Acid Test* is an inspiring and profoundly hopeful book."

—Wade Davis, author of *The Serpent and the Rainbow*

"Tom Shroder has written a book that is at once captivating and utterly surprising, with mind-blowing revelations of a lost history. The scourge of war and trauma and the mysteries of human consciousness fill virtually every one of the gripping chapters. With its impressive research, masterful storytelling, and, ultimately, the possibility of hope and healing, *Acid Test* is destined to be an important book."

—Brigid Schulte, author of *Overwhelmed*

"*Acid Test* is a trip of a different kind. Tom Shroder makes the hunt for relief from modern wars' biggest killers—depression and post-traumatic stress disorder—come alive in bright, unforgettable colors, characters, and emotions."

—Dana Priest, Pulitzer Prize–winning investigative
reporter and coauthor of *Top Secret America*

"*Acid Test* is a breath of fresh air after half a century of general hysteria, misinformation, confusion, and questionable decisions of scientific, political, and legal authorities concerning psychedelic substances. Tom Shroder's fascinating, well-researched, and clearly written account of psychedelic history, from the discovery of LSD to the current worldwide renaissance of interest in these remarkable substances and revival of research in this area, is a tour de force. Most important—socially, economically, and politically—is the book's focus on the psychedelic newcomer MDMA (Ecstasy). The pilot studies of this substance suggest that it might play an important role in helping to solve the formidable problem of PTSD that kills more American soldiers than the weapons of enemies."

—Stanislav Grof, MD, author of *LSD Psychotherapy*,
The Ultimate Journey, and *Psychology of the Future*

"Tom Shroder weaves together three compelling stories with such mastery that *Acid Test* reads like a first-rate novel. The book is that much more intriguing and consequential, though, because the stories are true and the subject matter—the healing of post-traumatic stress—of great currency and importance. We need to know how to treat the trauma that afflicts most of the world or we're in deep trouble."

—Richard Rockefeller, former chairman of
the US Advisory Board of Doctors Without Borders

"*Acid Test* represents such a critical contribution to our societal awareness, one that I am honored to wholeheartedly support. Faced with the challenge to alleviate the suffering of today's combat veterans, we must open ourselves to considering new modalities, revisiting therapeutic agents criminalized by fear and ideology, and harnessing the power of healing rituals and ancient wisdom. Put politics and preconceptions aside; open your mind; read this book; follow the data; and speak truth to power so that scientific rigor and emerging knowledge can lead the way. We owe our fellow humans no less."

—Loree Sutton, psychiatrist, retired US Army Brigadier General and founding director of the Defense Centers of Excellence for Psychological Health and Traumatic Brain Injury

"Shroder filters the psychedelic world [and] presents a compelling case for supporting responsible, rigorous research of psychedelic compounds. . . . Empty your mind of any preconceptions about psychedelic drugs and enjoy a fascinating trip through the politics, science, history, and promise of these controversial chemical compounds." —*Booklist*, starred review

"This clear-eyed account [explores] both the complex history of the issue and the current thinking on the use of LSD, Ecstasy, and other psychotropic substances for healing troubled minds. . . . Occasionally, the stories are amusing . . . often, they're moving. . . . A perceptive criticism of the failings of America's war on drugs, and Shroder delivers an important historical perspective on a highly controversial issue in modern medicine." —*Kirkus Reviews*

"Shroder both informs readers about the drugs' shadowy pasts and provides insight into the future of mental health." —*Publishers Weekly*

ALSO BY TOM SHRODER

Old Souls

The Most Famous Writer Who Ever Lived

ACID TEST

HOW A DARING GROUP OF
PSYCHONAUTS REDISCOVERED
THE POWER OF LSD, MDMA,
AND OTHER PSYCHEDELIC
DRUGS TO HEAL ADDICTION,
DEPRESSION, ANXIETY,
AND TRAUMA

TOM SHRODER

PLUME

This book is dedicated to

all the men and women we've left behind,

wounded, on life's battlefields.

PLUME
an imprint of Penguin Random House LLC
penguinrandomhouse.com

First published in the United States by Blue Rider Press,
an imprint of Penguin Random House LLC, 2014

First Plume printing 2015

Grateful acknowledgment is made to reprint the following:

Image on page 391 copyright Nicholas Blackston.
"The Guest House" by Jalal al-Din Rumi. Used with permission
of Coleman Barks, Maypop Books.

"Fidelity"
Written by Regina Spektor
© 2006 Soviet Kitsch Music. All rights administered by Sony / ATV Music Publishing LLC,
424 Church Street, Suite 1200, Nashville, TN 37219.
All rights reserved. Used by permission.

The Library of Congress has catalogued the Blue Rider Press hardcover edition as follows:
Shroder, Tom.
Acid test : LSD, Ecstasy, and the power to heal / Tom Shroder.
p.   cm.
ISBN 978-0-399-16279-4 (hc.)
ISBN 978-0-14-751637-4 (pbk.)
1. LSD (Drug)—Therapeutic use.   2. Ecstasy (Drug)—Therapeutic use.   3. Hallucinogenic
drugs—Therapeutic use.   4. Post-traumatic stress disorder—Treatment.   5. Mental
illness—Treatment.   6. Post-traumatic stress disorder—Patients—United States—Biography.
7. Mentally ill—United States—Biography.   I. Title.
RC483.5.L9S57   2014   2014016115
615.7'883—dc23

Printed in the United States of America
ScoutAutomatedPrintCode

Original hardcover design by Meighan Cavanaugh

CONTENTS

INTRODUCTION

Reading Tom Shroder's *Acid Test: LSD, Ecstasy, and the Power to Heal*, in 2014, when it first was completed, was a revelation. Initially, I gained tremendous insight into the underlying motivations and perspectives of other experts in my field who were profiled in the book. Even those like Dr. Michael Mithoefer, the lead psychiatrist at the Multidisciplinary Association for Psychedelic Studies (MAPS), and his co-therapist wife, Annie, whom I'd worked closely with for fourteen years. Especially revealing was Tom's portrait of former Marine Nick Blackston, a study participant with war-related post-traumatic stress disorder (PTSD), whose profound and moving story I got to know in a fuller way since, unless subjects in our studies choose to reach out, I'm shielded from personal information.

After I'd completed reading *Acid Test*, I was quietly elated. Through Tom's evocative description of each of our histories, and the central influences on our lives, the decades-long story of psychedelic therapy—from its accidental inception in a Swiss lab nearly eighty years ago to our thirty-year struggle to make it available to millions in need of healing—has been artfully woven together into a larger historical and cultural story that reads like a page-turning novel. I felt that people from all parts of our society and all political perspectives would react favorably to Tom's way of telling the larger narrative of counterculture and culture; of war, violence, and trauma; and of psychedelic therapy and healings. At the outset, I knew that, given the long history of stigma surrounding psychedelic drugs, it was a risk opening our full stories, personal and professional, to a mainstream journalist. But with the finished book in my hands, I knew that Tom's personal, intimate, and in-depth look into the lives of Michael and Annie and Nick and I had turned out to be a gamble worth taking.

As it turned out, *Acid Test* broke new ground in the public debate, followed by *Changing Our Minds: Psychedelic Sacraments and the New Psychotherapy* by journalist Don Lattin; and then by Michael Pollan's *How to Change Your Mind: What the New Science of Psychedelics Teaches Us About Consciousness, Dying, Addiction, Depression, and Transcendence.* These books would help open American minds to the healing potential of psychedelic therapies, safely administered through treatment protocols developed over half a century. Reading *Acid Test* seven years ago, I wouldn't have dared to hope that by 2017 the FDA would have designated MDMA a breakthrough therapy for PTSD, and then later add psilocybin for treatment-resistant depression (TRD) and major depressive disorder (MDD) to that designation. Nor would I have expected that that the pharmaceutical arm of our nonprofit MAPS, the MAPS Public Benefit Corporation (MAPS PBC), would be joined by more than a hundred for-profit psychedelic companies of all kinds, including several publicly traded ones with over $1 billion valuations and even one over $2 billion. MAPS, with its early sponsorship of MDMA-assisted therapy for PTSD, is the only psychedelic company in the final stage of FDA drug development research in Phase 3, with one successful Phase 3 study completed and the second underway. With about $115 million in total donations in MAPS's thirty-five years, and lots of hard work from more than a hundred staff and trained therapists, we've built public value well in excess of $1 billion. This value is based on the potential of MAPS to obtain FDA approval—extremely likely at this point—for the prescription use of MDMA-assisted therapy in the healing of millions of people with PTSD in somewhat similar ways as Nick's dramatic healing described in *Acid Test*.

Nick was one of the first of now over forty-five veterans who have been treated with MDMA-assisted therapy in MAPS's studies. When *Acid Test* was first published, MAPS had been working fruitlessly since 1990 to start research into MDMA-assisted therapy for PTSD inside the Department of Veterans' Affairs (VA) system. I would not have predicted that at the time this new edition of *Acid Test* is published, the VA would finally have permitted research into MDMA-assisted therapy for PTSD within its branches in Loma Linda, California; the Bronx, New York; and, soon, Portland, Oregon—or that these VAs and MAPS would have signed a formal agreement to cooperate in research and development. While these studies are still funded by philanthropists, and not the VA, that too could change in the foreseeable future. There is now even a strong possibility that active-duty soldiers with PTSD will be permitted by the Department of Defense to volunteer for treatment at our Expanded Access/Compassionate Use sites.

Astonishingly, Texas has allocated funding for a study of psilocybin-assisted therapy for PTSD to take place inside the Houston VA, and the Texas Legislature is considering funding for an MDMA-assisted therapy arm of that study to compare both to psilocybin-assisted therapy and treatment as usual. But most unexpected of all is that Harvard University—where Timothy Leary, Richard Alpert/Ram Dass, and Ralph Metzner helped start the psychedelic sixties through their psilocybin research there from 1960 to 1963; and then, after leaving Harvard, contributed to the psychedelic counterculture and the resulting backlash—has now created the Center for the Neuroscience of Psychedelics at Massachusetts General Hospital, one of the world's top hospitals for psychiatric care and research, which is affiliated with Harvard Medical School.

The breakthroughs and developments described above are all the more astounding given that at the time of *Acid Test*'s initial publication, despite the extremely positive results of early clinical trials, the future of psychedelic therapy was still very much in doubt. The prejudice against it remained a formidable obstacle.

Much has changed since *Acid Test* was first published. The prejudice against psychedelic research has largely subsided and been replaced by enthusiasm with public and bipartisan support, due to the potent combination of books like *Acid Test* educating the general public and the publication of high-quality scientific papers on clinical trials with extremely promising results. The FDA-regulated scientific research into MDMA-assisted therapy for PTSD, so compellingly described in *Acid Test*, culminated in a successfully completed Phase 3 study, with the outstanding data published in *Nature Medicine*, one of the world's highest-ranked medical journals. Phase 3 is the final stage of research to develop data on a drug's safety and efficacy for review by the FDA for possible approval for prescription use. MAPS's second confirmatory Phase 3 study is underway and scheduled for completion by October 2022. If the results of MAPS's second Phase 3 study are even half as good as the results of the first completed Phase 3 study, FDA approval for prescription use is likely before the end of 2023.

Though just a distant hope in 2014 when *Acid Test* was published, MAPS is now starting new research into MDMA-assisted therapy for PTSD at nine sites in six countries—England, the Netherlands, Germany, the Czech Republic, Norway, and Portugal—with the research to be reviewed by the European Medicines Agency (EMA) and the United Kingdom's Medicines and Healthcare Products Regulatory Agency, and possible approval for prescription use near the end of 2024. MAPS is also involved in research into MDMA-assisted therapy for PTSD in Australia and Brazil, and is seeking to start additional studies in many different countries to obtain global access to the healing potential of MDMA-assisted therapy for PTSD.

MAPS, the FDA, and the Drug Enforcement Administration have already engaged in preliminary discussions on how MDMA-assisted therapy for PTSD might be regulated should approval be granted for prescription use. The therapeutic approach described in *Acid Test* is a combination of psychotherapy and MDMA. MAPS has proposed that all therapists who will be permitted to treat patients in the future be required to go through a MAPS-authorized training program in the therapy used in the Phase 3 studies. Post-approval, therapists can modify the therapeutic approach they use, but they will need to have learned the approach that was used in the Phase 3 studies. MDMA itself will only be permitted to be administered under direct supervision of trained therapists, and only in clinical settings with no take-home medications. Prescriptions for MDMA will involve specialty pharmacies who ship the medicine directly to the prescribers and not to the patients.

At the time *Acid Test* was first published, there were fewer than twenty-five therapists trained by MAPS. Since then, MAPS has substantially enlarged our therapist-training program. Our online program with one hundred hours of content has just completed training a cohort of over 300 therapists from around the world, with a new cohort enrolling over 520 therapists. Our goal over the next seven years is to train 25,000 therapists, just in the United States, capable of delivering one million therapy sessions, pending FDA approval, between the end of 2023 and the end of 2029.

At the time of the publication of this new edition of *Acid Test*, there are estimated to be over 1,000 clinics providing the psychedelic ketamine and/or its chemically related cousin, esketamine, for depression and other indications. Although regulatory approval was provided for esketamine for depression as a medicine by itself without therapy, many of these clinics provide ketamine-assisted therapy, which is reported to work much better than ketamine alone. Therapists at these clinics are also interested in learning to provide MDMA-assisted therapy, psilocybin-assisted therapy, and other psychedelics that become approved over time. By 2033, a decade after the likely FDA-approval of MDMA-assisted therapy for PTSD, there could be over 6,000 psychedelic therapy clinics just in the United States alone.

Medical research and use lead the way and help catalyze drug-policy reform. In May 2019, Denver was the first city in the United States to make psilocybin mushrooms the lowest drug-enforcement priority. MAPS is training Denver police in psychedelic harm-reduction techniques to prepare them if they encounter people who are having difficult psychedelic experiences, to avoid escalation of the difficult trip, tranquilization, arrest, and hospitalization. There are now a growing number of cities and states that have decriminalized psychedelics. In 2020, Oregon voters passed the Oregon Psilocybin Initiative, which will legalize access statewide to psilocybin-assisted therapy for medical conditions and also for spiritual uses and personal growth, with therapist-training programs and special certifications to be regulated by the state.

The rapid growth of psychedelic research and treatment between the initial publication of *Acid Test* and this new edition suggests that progress may be more rapid than we currently anticipate, though of course it's also the case that progress could be impeded by unexpected resistance that we don't currently see coming. Around 2035, after a decade or so of the growth of psychedelic clinics, I predict we'll see the legalization of psychedelics for personal use outside of medicine and religion in a context I'm calling licensed legalization. This would involve educational requirements to obtain licenses and the possibility of revoking licenses for a period of time if people misbehave under the influence of a drug, with this licensed legalization eventually including all drugs. Around

2050, there could be a significant minority of mentally healthy and spiritualized people to form the core of an evolved humanity based on mass mental health capable of addressing the challenges we face as a species.

MAPS is now expanding our membership base in a program of monthly donors we call Team Psychedelic. We're also preparing for the world's largest psychedelic conference, which we are calling Psychedelic Science 2023/Psychedelic City, to take place June 18–25, 2023, in Denver, with potentially 10,000 attendees.

As you prepare to read *Acid Test*, it's important that you know that Nick is doing great, has not relapsed, and still no longer suffers from PTSD. Michael and I, and over a hundred MAPS staff, and over seventy-five therapists working on our research studies, still have lots of work to do to actually obtain FDA, Health Canada, Israeli Ministry of Health, and EMA approvals for prescription use, and then to globalize patient access and reform drug policy. If you are so inspired, you can join us in building toward this future vision, initially by reading *Acid Test*.

Rick Doblin, PhD
September 2021

FOREWORD

In 1975 I was a twenty-one-year-old college journalist, home on spring break in Sarasota, Florida, when I noticed a blurb in the local newspaper about a charismatic hippie with a pet wolf who was building himself a spectacular house in the woods near town. I decided to go out and see it for myself. I don't remember anything about the blurb. I doubt it mentioned anything about the influence of psychedelic drugs in this project. But I am guessing that I inferred it, because while I didn't much care about techniques of home building—nor would my college-student readers—I was extremely interested in the implications of the psychedelic experience.

I'm looking at a taped-together, Xeroxed copy of the story that resulted from that visit. Still no mention of drugs, but there it is between the lines. I wrote about the philosophy of the young builder, a guy named Rick Doblin, just a year older than me. It was about trying to live authentically, guided by an inner light rather than society's preconceived ideas; consciously working to discover and create his own destiny rather than trudging along the rutted tracks set before him.

These were the kinds of notions floating around a certain subculture in those days; it was evident in the woodland home itself, with its giant, rainbow-themed, spiritually suggestive stained-glass window. Maybe we discussed psychedelics, maybe we didn't. But they were in the air.

I myself was not entirely unfamiliar. Under the influence of the psilocybin mushrooms my friends and I had learned to pluck from cow dung in the rural fields not far from campus, then boil into tea and drink, I had seen the world—and myself—from a novel vantage point. It was like being able, for a few precious hours, to climb above your life and view it from on high, a perspective every bit as revealing as seeing a too-familiar landscape from the top of a mountain. Instead of individual cornstalks or oak trees or buildings, you saw checkerboard patterns of fields, serpentine forests following the course of a river, villages arrayed around ascending spires of churches. You saw, for once, how it all fit together.

One experience stands out in my memory, because it is something that I have carried with me, every day since, for four decades. As the drug took effect, instead of feeling the usual lift, I grew increasingly entangled by anxiety. I began to obsess about an ethical problem I was struggling with, which generalized to feelings of inadequacy in life overall and my inability to find solutions.

The more I struggled against these feelings, the weightier and more intractable they seemed. And then suddenly I had a vision: I saw myself with my arms wrapped around a boulder. I could feel its weight, almost unbearable to hold, and yet I was clinging to it. I knew that the heavy stone consisted of all my doubts and anxieties, and as I desperately clutched it to my chest, I saw in a flash that part of me *chose* to be anxious—as a way to avoid making choices and evade responsibility for them. To be free of that awful weight, all I had to do was open my arms, which I did. The stone simply dropped away.

Ever since, although it has rarely been easy, I've been able to see negative emotions, on a profound level, as a choice, and the will to let them go as something I could develop, like a muscle. The more I practiced, the better I got, and I no longer needed the mushrooms to do it.

There wasn't a moment I decided to stop doing psychedelic drugs. When I left the college environment they became less available, and I gained more responsibilities—a job, a family, a professional reputation—all of which made any illegal activity, and the potential health risks, unacceptable. But I never lost my interest in those psychedelic experiences, or forgot their profundity, and the lasting good they did me.

Ten years after graduation, I had become an editor at the *Miami Herald* Sunday magazine, *Tropic*, when I noticed a story in the Tampa newspaper about a perennial college student who was promoting the party drug Ecstasy as a breakthrough in psychotherapy. I did a double take: it was Rick Doblin, the hippie with the house in the woods, the same guy I had written about a decade earlier. I assigned a *Herald* feature writer to do a cover story on him. We headlined it: "A Timothy Leary for the '80s."

Twenty years passed. Now I was editor of *The Washington Post Magazine*, and once again an article that spoke to my lingering interest in the possible positive effects of psychedelics caught my eye. This time it was in the *New York Times*, about Harvard initiating a study testing the use of MDMA—Ecstasy—to treat anxiety and depression in terminal cancer patients. The man sponsoring the study: a very sophisticated-sounding Harvard Kennedy School PhD named Rick Doblin—*the hippie in the woods*.

I got a phone number and Rick answered. When I told him my name, he laughed. He not only remembered me and the two stories from twenty and thirty years earlier, he still had copies of them both. And just that morning, he told me, he'd held up the "Tim Leary" cover of *Tropic* at a board meeting of the Multidisciplinary Association for Psychedelic Studies (MAPS), his nonprofit organization, to demonstrate how completely he'd remade his image, from a rebellious hippie to the sponsor of cutting-edge scientific research in some of the nation's more conservative institutions.

This time I wrote the story myself, focusing on the MAPS-sponsored research a psychiatrist named Michael Mithoefer was conducting in Charleston, South Carolina, treating with MDMA-assisted psychotherapy mostly female victims of sexual abuse. The story appeared in *The Washington Post Magazine* in November 2007, and much of it has been adapted here in chapter forty-two.

I was pleased enough with the piece as published, but I felt it barely scratched the surface, both because of rapidly accumulating developments in psychedelic research and because I sensed that the significance of any given study could not be fully assessed without a deeper understanding of the people behind the studies, not to mention the century-long struggle of Western culture to come to grips with these powerful and, in some ways, profoundly threatening drugs.

This is what I have attempted in *Acid Test*. Whatever success I have had I owe entirely to the openness and honesty of the principal characters. Those people listed in the acknowledgments have granted me access to scores of records and privileged documents and agreed to sit for what amounted to a combined total of more than a hundred hours of interviews, unflinchingly answering the most intimate and sensitive questions, revealing things that were personally painful and might very well expose them to negative judgments or significantly complicate their lives.

Their reasons for agreeing to all the above are transparent. They accepted my contention that the full and complete disclosure of all the information surrounding the use and abuse of psychedelic drugs, the history of psychedelic therapy, the motivations of the researchers, and the experiences of the subjects is the best argument for continued and extended support of rigorous and responsible investigation.

I owe a special debt to those among them who have undergone

clinical trials to treat debilitating post-traumatic stress, a disorder that makes it particularly difficult and potentially painful to open up. In particular, I am indebted to Donna Kilgore, Tony Macie, and, above all, Nicholas Blackston. They all spent hours reviewing their case histories with me, leaving nothing off the record, as well as giving me permission to listen to or watch voluminous audio- and videotapes of their therapeutic sessions. It is hard to imagine a more naked vulnerability than allowing an outsider to witness hours spent delving into your deepest, most charged and haunting intimacies explored under the powerful effect of MDMA. Yet, these people made that sacrifice willingly, for no other reason than a sense of duty. They felt the therapy benefited them and quite possibly saved their lives, and they believed sharing their stories might help make the therapy available to others.

I am moved and awed by their courage.

1.

ALBERT

(ST. ALBERT'S FIRE)

M any years later, as Albert Hofmann wrote of the discovery that made him famous, he recalled the distant May morning when he experienced a phenomenon that bizarrely foreshadowed his extraordinary career.

"There are experiences that most of us are hesitant to speak about," he wrote, "because they do not conform to everyday reality and defy rational explanation. These are not particular external occurrences, but rather events of our inner lives, which are generally dismissed as figments of the imagination and barred from our memory. Suddenly the familiar view of our surroundings is transformed in a strange, delightful, or alarming way: it appears to us in a new light, takes on a special meaning. Such an experience can be as light and fleeting as a breath of air, or it can imprint itself deeply upon our minds."

On this particular Monday morning, walking along a forest path near Baden, Switzerland ("I can still point to the exact spot where it occurred," he would exult more than half a century later), what Hofmann encountered was definitely of the latter variety.

As he walked through the greening spring woodland, "all at once everything appeared in an uncommonly clear light. Was this something

I had simply failed to notice before? Was I suddenly discovering the spring forest as it actually looked? It shone with the most beautiful radiance, speaking to the heart, as though it wanted to encompass me in its majesty. I was filled with an indescribable sensation of joy, oneness, and blissful security."

He gaped, transfixed for an immeasurable moment, then watched, helpless, as the preternatural light slowly receded into mundanity. He felt spent, at once deflated and transformed.

"How could a vision that was so real and convincing, so directly and deeply felt—how could it end so soon? And how could I tell anyone about it, as my overflowing joy compelled me to do, since I knew there were no words to describe what I had seen?"

This was only the first of young Albert's several similar encounters with the ineffable, and through them he became convinced of "the existence of a miraculous, powerful, unfathomable reality that was hidden from everyday sight."

He felt moved to express the wonder of what he'd seen through art or poetry, but bitter attempts to do so persuaded him he was no artist, and never would be. "I was often troubled in those days," he wrote, "knowing that I was not cut out to be a poet or artist. I assumed I would have to keep these experiences to myself, important as they were to me."

So instead he became a chemist, working with tubes and flasks and Bunsen burners in cramped, poorly equipped, badly ventilated laboratories of the early twentieth century, using techniques that had advanced little in a hundred years. In short, he descended into the atomistic materialism of the science of his era, far from his youthful visions, and marching ever further away.

It is great irony, then, or fate, that following this contrary path led him, purely by chance, to discover an astoundingly potent drug that did far more than convey the inexpressible experiences of his youth. It created them.

All the thirty-two-year-old Hofmann wanted to do in 1938 was synthesize a chemical compound that would stimulate the human respiratory and circulatory systems. He had gone to work for Sandoz, a Swiss chemical company, in 1929, after graduation from the University of Zurich. Sandoz, founded in 1886, had started out manufacturing dyes and, later, saccharin. There wasn't even a formal pharmaceutical department until 1917, when Professor Arthur Stoll isolated an active substance called ergotamine from ergot, a fungus found in tainted rye that had been used as a folk medicine for generations.

In its natural form and in quantity, ergot was a deadly poison and a scourge responsible for the deaths of hundreds of thousands of people over many centuries. In the year 857 in what is now Germany, a contemporary accounting of the events of the year recorded that "a great plague of swollen blisters consumed the people by a loathsome rot, so that their limbs were loosened and fell off before death."

Historians now attribute this and similar events throughout early history to long-term exposure to infected grains, a condition known as St. Anthony's fire, after the French monastic order that devoted itself to caring for the plague's victims. Ergot was not suspected as the cause until the late seventeenth century. Eventually, ergotism's toxic effects were classified into two categories: gangrenous ergotism and convulsive ergotism. The description of the symptoms on a University of Hawaii botany website is enough to permanently put you off rye bread:

> *Convulsive ergotism is characterized by nervous dysfunction, where the victim is twisting and contorting their body in pain, trembling*

and shaking, and wryneck, a more or less fixed twisting of the neck,
which seems to simulate convulsions or fits. In some cases, this is
accompanied by muscle spasms, confusions, delusions and halluci-
nations. . . .

In gangrenous ergotism, the victim may lose parts of their ex-
tremities, such as toes, fingers, ear lobes or in more serious cases, arms
and legs may be lost.

Some believe that the advent of these gruesome symptoms without a
known cause, especially the convulsive symptoms—which, along with
hallucinations, sometimes included mania and psychosis—led to accusations of witchcraft, followed by witch-hunting hysterias such as the
famous Salem witch trials in 1692 and 1693. Studies have even correlated years of rye scarcity—suggesting an increased willingness to
consume tainted rye—with years of abundant witchcraft accusations.

But in small doses, the muscle- and blood vessel–constricting properties of ergot could be useful to hasten childbirth and staunch bleeding after delivery, capabilities that had somehow been divined by
alchemists and midwives and made use of for generations.

Arthur Stoll's accomplishment was to isolate the compounds in ergot
that caused the constrictions: ergotamine and ergobasine. In its refined
form, the compound could be precisely dosed to avoid a host of side
effects from other unhelpful compounds in ergot—properties that
made Sandoz a lot of money and launched the pharmaceutical research
and development department that hired Hofmann twelve years later.

Within a few years researchers had determined the chemical structure of the various biologically active compounds in ergot, all of which
shared a common nucleus. This chemical starting point was called
lysergic acid, or, in German, *Lysergsäure*.

Hofmann developed a synthetic process to build the ergot compounds from their component chemicals. Using this method, he re-created ergot's active ingredients as well as novel but similar compounds that, based on the potency of the ergot compounds, could reasonably be expected to have medical uses.

In a sense Hofmann was playing God, combining lysergic acid with various other organic molecules just to see what happened. He created twenty-four of these lysergic acid combinations. Then he created the twenty-fifth, reacting lysergic acid with diethylamine, a derivative of ammonia. The compound was abbreviated as LSD-25 for the purposes of laboratory testing.

He had hoped for something that could stimulate circulation and respiration. But his hopes were dashed. LSD-25 did show an effect on the uterus. As Hofmann explains in his book on the discovery, *LSD: My Problem Child*, the uterine-contracting effect only amounted to 70 percent of that of ergobasine. The research report also noted in passing that the experimental animals became highly excited during testing. "The new substance, however, aroused no special interest in our pharmacologists and physicians; testing was therefore discontinued."

Hofmann went on with his ergot research and produced some very successful compounds, including a drug called Hydergine, which improved peripheral circulation and cerebral function in the elderly, and became one of Sandoz's most important products. Hydergine is still used in the treatment of dementia and Alzheimer's disease.

But for some reason, even as the years passed, Hofmann couldn't stop thinking about the apparently useless LSD-25. Maybe it was the memory of all those oddly excited animals in the test pens. Hofmann never said, beyond calling it "a peculiar presentiment—the feeling that this substance could possess properties other than those established in the first investigations."

So, five years after lysergic acid diethylamide was tossed on the ash heap of pharmaceutical history, based on nothing but his odd presentiment, Hofmann decided to synthesize it again. He would later tell intimates, "I did not discover LSD; LSD found and called me."

It was a Friday in the middle of a world war, April 16, 1943. Hofmann was in the final stage of the synthesis of just a few centigrams of the material, the part where the LSD crystallized into a salt, when he suddenly felt very strange to the point that he had to leave work and go home. When he returned to the lab the following Monday, he wrote a memo to his boss, Stoll, explaining what had happened:

> *I was forced to interrupt my work in the laboratory in the middle of the afternoon and proceed home, being affected by a remarkable restlessness, combined with a slight dizziness. At home I lay down and sank into a not unpleasant intoxicated-like condition, characterized by an extremely stimulated imagination. In a dreamlike state, with eyes closed (I found the daylight to be unpleasantly glaring), I perceived an uninterrupted stream of fantastic pictures, extraordinary shapes with intense, kaleidoscopic play of colors.*

When he recovered, Hofmann set about trying to figure out what had so strongly affected him. In a 2006 *New York Times* interview, Hofmann said that he first suspected the fumes of a chloroform-like solvent he had been using. Now he intentionally breathed in its fumes, to no effect. It was only then that he was forced to the conclusion that he must have somehow ingested a trace of the LSD, an idea he discounted at first because he had been very careful to avoid contamination, knowing the potential toxicity of any ergot-related compounds. The only point of access would have been through the skin of his fingertips, and the amount involved would have been so tiny that he could not imagine it could produce such a significant reaction.

Now that his intuition about LSD was showing tantalizing signs of proving justified, Hofmann decided there was only one course of action. Self-experimentation.

At 4:20 in the afternoon of April 19, without informing anyone at Sandoz except his lab assistant, Hofmann dissolved 250 millionths of a gram of lysergic acid diethylamide tartrate—the crystallized salt form of the compound—in a glass of water and drank it. He expected it to do absolutely nothing.

Hofmann was dealing with the LSD as if it might be deadly poison. That's why he had begun his tests with such an infinitesimal dose, a thousand times less than the active dose of any other psychically active compound he knew of. He had planned to increase the dosage by tiny increments until he got the first inkling of a reaction, expecting it to take many dose increases before that happened.

But just forty minutes after that initial dose, he wrote the one and only entry in his lab journal:

17:00: Beginning dizziness, feeling of anxiety, visual distortions, symptoms of paralysis, desire to laugh.

"I was able to write the last words only with great effort," he wrote in *My Problem Child.* "I had to struggle to speak intelligibly."

Hofmann asked his lab assistant to escort him home, which wasn't as easy as it might have been. Because of wartime restriction on automobile use, both men were on bicycles. On what must have been an extraordinarily adventurous bike ride, Hofmann felt his condition take a threatening turn.

"Everything in my field of vision wavered and was distorted as if seen in a curved mirror. I also had the sensation of being unable to move from the spot. Nevertheless, my assistant later told me that we had traveled very rapidly. Finally, we arrived at home safe and sound, and I was just barely capable of asking my companion to summon our family doctor and request milk from the neighbors."

The powerful effects were as frightening as they had been unexpected. Hofmann had no idea how the experience might play out in the next few hours, and beyond. For all he knew, the drug might permanently damage his psyche. Perhaps it might even physically injure or kill him. These fears were what prompted him to request the milk, a nonspecific palliative for a range of toxic substances. The hubris of what he had done in testing this potent drug on himself filled him with anxiety and regret. He would only realize later how important that fearful mind-set would be in shaping the nature of his experience, which he described compellingly in his book:

> *The dizziness and sensation of fainting became so strong at times that I could no longer hold myself erect, and had to lie down on a sofa. . . . Everything in the room spun around, and the familiar objects and pieces of furniture assumed grotesque, threatening forms. They were in continuous motion, animated, as if driven by an inner restlessness. The lady next door, whom I scarcely recognized, brought me milk—in the course of the evening I drank more than two liters. She was no longer Mrs. R., but rather a malevolent, insidious witch with a colored mask. . . . Every exertion of my will, every attempt to put an end to the disintegration of the outer world and the dissolution of my ego, seemed to be wasted effort. A demon had invaded me, had taken possession of my body, mind, and soul. . . . I was seized by the dreadful fear of going insane. I was taken to another world, another place, another time. My body seemed to be without sensation, lifeless, strange. Was I dying? . . . Another reflection took shape, an idea full of bitter irony: if I was now forced to leave this world prematurely, it was because of this*

lysergic acid diethylamide that I myself had brought forth into the world.

Hofmann wasn't dying. In fact, when the doctor arrived, he detected nothing more alarming than dilated pupils. Blood pressure, respiration, pulse were all completely normal. The doctor left his bag shut: no medications were required. He simply put Hofmann to bed and waited by his side. Hofmann began to come to himself.

His account continued:

The horror softened and gave way to a feeling of good fortune and gratitude, the more normal perceptions and thoughts returned, and I became more confident that the danger of insanity was conclusively past.

Now, little by little, I could begin to enjoy the unprecedented colors and plays of shapes that persisted behind my closed eyes. Kaleidoscopic, fantastic images surged in on me. . . .

By the time his wife arrived home, Hofmann was able to speak coherently about what had happened to him. The next morning he wrote:

Everything glistened and sparkled in a fresh light. The world was as if newly created. All my senses vibrated in a condition of highest sensitivity, which persisted for the entire day.

As remarkable as his experience had been, in the aftermath it struck Hofmann that perhaps the most remarkable thing of all was that, despite the extreme intoxication he had experienced, he could remember every detail of it with, one might say, acid-etched clarity.

Hofmann sent his report to Stoll the following day and copied

Ernst Rothlin, head of the Sandoz pharmacological department. Both men were skeptical that such a small quantity of the drug could have produced the outlandish result Hofmann claimed.

"Are you certain you made no mistake in the weighing? Is the stated dose really correct?" Stoll asked.

Rothlin's skepticism exceeded even Stoll's.

In a 1976 interview with *High Times*, Hofmann said Rothlin insisted that he had exaggerated the drug's effect. "[Rothlin] claimed he had a strong will and could suppress the effects of drugs. But after he took 60 micrograms—one quarter of the dose I had taken earlier—he was convinced. I had to laugh as he described his fantastic visions."

Now it was clear that a remarkable discovery had been made. However, Hofmann did not yet see a clear connection between his frightening experience on what would become known as "Bicycle Day" and his transcendent moments as a child. That would come later.

First the drug had to be tested extensively on animals to determine any acutely toxic effects that Hofmann had merely been lucky to survive. Animal tests would eventually provide some curious results. Mice given LSD moved erratically and showed "alterations in licking behavior." Cats' hair stood on end and they salivated, indications they were having hallucinations that were threatening or enticing. When researchers introduced mice into the cats' cages, instead of attacking, the felines would ignore the rodents' intrusion or sometimes even appear frightened by them. Dosed chimpanzees did not show any obvious signs of being affected, but the normal chimps around them tended to become extremely upset, which Hofmann attributed to the test animals' failure to maintain social norms perceptible only to the chimps.

Aquarium fish swam oddly, and spiders altered web-building patterns. At low doses, Hofmann noted, "the webs were even better proportioned and more exactly built than normally: however, with higher doses, the webs were badly and rudimentarily made."

The salient fact was this: none of the animals in the tests seemed to suffer acute harm at the active dose, and the lethal dose was a hundred times higher than what was necessary for psychic effect, leaving a wide safety margin.

Now that he was reassured that LSD wouldn't kill him or destroy his brain, Hofmann's curiosity about his own experience only intensified. He decided to continue his LSD research informally, "in the friendly and private company of two good friends of mine.

"I did this," he later wrote, "in order to investigate the influence of the surroundings, of the outer and inner conditions on the LSD experience. These experiments showed me the enormous impact of—to use modern terms—set and setting on the content and character of the experience."

With a mind-set free of fear, in aesthetically pleasing surroundings, and supported by friends, the LSD experiences did not mirror insanity, as did his initial "bum trip," as much as they re-created those luminous, visionary moments of his past.

"In some of my psychedelic experiences I had a feeling of ecstatic love and unity with all creatures in the universe," Hofmann said in the *High Times* interview. "To have had such an experience of absolute beatitude means an enrichment of our life."

But he also learned something else: controlling for set and setting had its limits. "In spite of a good mood at the beginning of a session—positive expectations, beautiful surroundings and sympathetic company—I once fell into a terrible depression. This unpredictability of effects is the major danger of LSD."

Both those particular lessons—the possible transcendence of the LSD experience and its potential to threaten—would reverberate through the next half century.

2.

NICHOLAS

(A SIGN)

Nicholas Blackston was only seventeen when he divined his future. The omen that would seal his fate appeared as he sat, crying, on a creek bank in the woods behind his parents' home in semi-rural Paducah, Kentucky. He'd come there, as he so often did, to pray for God's guidance. Nick had always felt he had an open communication with God, a closeness that was the negative image of the separation he felt from other kids, and even his parents, who loved him but couldn't fully understand him. His problem had a primal cause: he saw things others did not. As a child going to sleep in the tiny room he shared with his sister, Jessica, in the family's trailer, he watched as small, fuzzy dots appeared above his Lego table, then flowed toward him like water, undulating closer until they engulfed his face with an animate presence that made him tingle and fall into morning. By day a stuffed animal might flip across his bed of its own accord, or the hands on his alarm clock would start spinning. He often had the eerie feeling something shadowy followed behind him. Sometimes the sense was so strong he'd whip around, hoping to catch full sight of whatever it was, but he never moved fast enough.

When he was four or five, sleeping on the couch with his mother, his head to her feet, Nick woke in the middle of the night to discover a demonic figure looming over his face, staring. Suffocated with terror, it slowly dawned on him that his Teenage Mutant Ninja Turtles toy had somehow morphed into this malevolent, breathing thing. He screamed. "I actually heard myself scream, so I know that I was awake," Nick says. "And as my mom shot up, I saw it go back to its original shape, and I tried to explain to her—and I told her, and of course, she just comforted me and told me, 'You were having a nightmare.'"

But Nick thought he knew the difference between a dream experience and a real one. "That's what frightened me about some things sometimes. You can tell when something's just the wind, you can tell when it's something else. The fear that comes from it is just from seeing something that's not supposed to be there."

Nick's dad, Charles Blackston, a handyman and volunteer fireman, was a loving man, but he focused most of his affection on his wife, Jean, a lunch lady at the local school. Nick had a vague sense that his father had experienced troubling things in his emergency work over the years, but he never talked about any of it. He always brought his radio with him when the family went out, and Nick got embarrassed when it went off in Applebee's and his father ran off. The rest of the family would have to grab whatever they could from their plates and catch up.

When Nick had his own emergencies concerning things that weren't supposed to be, it was his mother he told. She responded with loving sympathy . . . and incomprehension. If it was a stage, Nick never completely grew out of it, which complicated his childhood and adolescence. His sister could be sympathetic; once, when he saw a self-propelled stuffed animal, she said she saw it too. But when Nick made the mistake of mentioning any of his puzzling perceptions to his peers, he paid the price of instant and total ridicule. In a fourth-grade world culture class, the teacher decided to acquaint the children with the concept of meditation. She invited them to sit on the floor, close their eyes, and see what they might see. Nicholas found himself looking at the world from the void of space. He felt the nothingness surrounding him and saw the lovely living presence of the distant globe so vividly that, in his excitement, he forgot his caution and blurted out his vision. The classroom broke into a gauntlet of ridicule, and even the teacher chuckled derisively. Nick resolved to shut up from then on and concentrate on fitting in.

It didn't work. Always uncertain of the right thing to say, he couldn't join in convincingly. At recess in elementary school, while the other kids ran around playing, he'd lie on his back watching clouds float by. Sometimes he'd zone out and find himself staring fixedly at the leaves on a low branch, thinking how human the veins looked. And then the bell would be ringing and all the others would be disappearing into the school as he ran to catch up. He always seemed to be trying to catch up.

He felt slightly embarrassed that he lived in a trailer and didn't have things other kids had, like store-bought Halloween costumes. One year his mother sent him to school with a green sweatshirt, green sweatpants, and a gorilla mask for the Halloween parade. He stood in the back of the line, holding the mask instead of wearing it. This was a parade all right. A parade of shame.

His discomfort and seclusion drew mockery and taunts at school, where his mother was the beloved lunchroom lady and he was nothing. It left him depressed and angry, which made him even more reclusive for fear of what his repressed rage might lead him to do. When he got home, he would build elaborate Lego villages, alternative universes where he placed himself, imagining all kinds of scenarios that had in common a central fact: he wasn't an outcast. He wasn't powerless.

In sixth grade Nick got assigned to a bus with the high school kids. His vulnerability blinked in neon. A big redheaded kid made Nick a project. As the redheaded kid walked past down the center aisle, he'd grab Nick's head with his two meaty hands and bounce it off the window. Nick choked down the tears but said nothing, rage boiling inside. When he got home he'd tell his mom he'd had a good day. The only thing worse than knowing he had to face the redheaded kid again the next morning was the thought of his parents getting involved.

That same year, 1997, his dad got a good-paying job as a fireman at the plutonium enrichment plant outside of town, and finally could afford to build a house. Nick got his own room, but somehow even that turned out wrong. Being physically separated from Jessica, who had been not just a sister but his closest friend, only increased his isolation. After a day of getting picked on or bullied, he'd come home and blow up on her, for which he hated himself.

One afternoon when Nick was twelve, he stood on his elevated back porch, overlooking a fourteen-foot drop. As he peered over, his thoughts raced in an unbreakable loop. He could see no escape—no escape from seeing things, no escape from ridicule, no way he was ever going to fit in. He was defective, and the only way to solve the problem was to turn off the lights. He walked to the edge and looked down, trying to work it out. He imagined diving headfirst, hands at his sides. As soon as his head hit the hard ground, he was pretty sure his neck would snap. Lights out.

So now he had it figured, but still he stood there. He began to sing "Silent Night," his voice barely above a hum, but rising as he reached the chorus, which he repeated, over and over, until he was almost shouting:

> *"Sleep in heavenly peace*
> *Sleep in HEAVENLY peace. . . ."*

And then he did it, launched himself over the ledge.

But even in midair, something in him refused to cooperate. He landed on his feet, uninjured, but scared now at what he'd almost done.

When he told his mother, her face went white as marble. He could see the hurt in her eyes. He'd never wanted to hurt her.

He agreed to see a Christian counselor. The man seemed nice enough, but Nick was too ashamed to tell him the prime cause, all those things he saw that couldn't be there. So he told the counselor the result but not the cause. What he said was that he felt another person inside of him, filled with anger and set to explode. He'd built up so much anger, he'd desensitized himself to even gruesome thoughts. He'd imagine falling on the bullies who tormented him and savagely beating their faces until they came apart in pulpy masses of blood and bone. In his imagination he felt no remorse. He felt nothing at all. It scared him, and was the real reason he took the abuse and never stood up for himself. Once he started to fight back, he feared that he wouldn't be able to stop himself, that he might end up hurting someone—badly.

He had a few more counseling sessions, which his parents attended. He still kept his secret, but he got a punching bag out of it, "to blow off steam." When the counselor asked if there was anything that made him feel calmer, Nick said yes: going out into the woods. So the counselor said, "Go out in the woods when you have those feelings and just yell at the top of your lungs. Let these feelings out and this anger out in a constructive way, without hurting yourself or anyone else."

Nick did as the counselor suggested and found he could really bellow when he knew nobody could hear him. He yelled until his voice bounced off the trees. That helped. He felt connected to nature in the woods, as connected as he felt disconnected to the world of boys and men. So he yelled, and when he was calmer, he prayed.

Things got a little easier in high school. The weird events he'd witnessed as a child faded away, leaving only a feeling that he remained somehow different. Nick joined the marching band, found friends, even had a girlfriend. He discovered a passion: paintball. He loved the thrill of the hunt, the stealth, the teamwork it required to outflank and outmaneuver his adversaries. He loved the guns. Paintball became his obsession. He persuaded his grandfather to let him build a paintball field down in the wooded bottoms of his 240-acre farm. Nick wrestled old tractor tires, shipping flats, and pieces of this and that into position on a football field–size stretch alongside a creek, and his friends swarmed around the obstacles, trying to hunt one another down.

As his senior year approached, other kids were thinking about college. Nick had assumed he would go to college, too, possibly study to be a meteorologist. He loved watching the clouds blow past and the wind swirl the trees and the thunderheads rise up above the river. Maybe he could turn weather watching into a career.

But recently another thought had come into his mind and wouldn't leave: joining the military. He'd been fifteen when the jets smashed into the Twin Towers, the Pentagon, and a field in Pennsylvania, and he was well aware there had been fighting and dying ever since.

But he felt drawn to the idea. It wasn't just his boyish love of playing war with his paintball weapons—the one social activity he participated in with passion. He sensed, without quite being able to articulate it, that the military offered a built-in place to belong, to bond with a band of brothers as they all struggled to adapt in a completely foreign environment. He could reset the game and begin again. Still, he hesitated. Would he be giving up too much, all those things young people were supposed to want? He just didn't know.

So Nick told all this to God; he said, "You know what, if You have something better planned for me, let me know. But if You want me to go to the Marine Corps, then give me a sign."

He waited. The stream slithered beneath his feet, licking at the root-riddled banks. To his left, a narrow path cut through the undergrowth where deer would step down and drink from the water. He

could always tell the paths that the animals used, worn from feet following one after another, year after year. It was a nice, clean path. To
his right, the creek was a different story. It swerved sharply, cutting
steeply into the bank, exposing tree roots and large rocks that had in
turn been covered with vines and brambles. He said, "Okay, this nice,
clean path, is the path of going to college and becoming a meteorologist. And that over there with the brambles is the Marine Corps."

And he waited some more. The sky yawned, still and void above the
trees. There wasn't so much as a ripple on the water or a puff of wind.
Nothing happened. Nick felt sucker punched. God had always been so
responsive to him. Now, in what felt like a critical moment, he had
been abandoned. The one connection he'd felt so certain of had failed.
He broke down and began to cry.

As the world shrank to the frustration pouring from his chest, an
odd feeling broke through. He stopped in mid-sob and looked up.
Despite the complete absence of any breeze, a dead leaf had detached
itself from one of the still-green midsummer trees and fluttered down.
It passed over the deer path and danced down to the rough, vine-
tangled part of the creek. He stood up, instantly certain that his choice
had been made. He gave a little shout, like a battle cry, and plunged
down through the cold creek and up into the scrambling vines, as if to
confirm his decision to take the rough route. Then he ran home and,
still panting, told his mother, "I'm gonna join the Marine Corps."

One day he would wonder why it hadn't occurred to him that a
dead leaf might have been not a beacon but a warning.

Nicholas took the Armed Services Vocational Aptitude Battery and
scored high enough to have a lot of choices about how he would serve,
but when the recruiter briefed him on all the specialties he could
request—occupations that might have a future in the civilian

world—Nick shook his head. "I just want to be infantry," he said. He wanted a gun in his hand, not a welding torch. No matter what the recruiter said, Nicholas wouldn't yield. When the day came for Nick's papers to be signed by his parents, the recruiter appeared at his front door with the sheaf in his hand. Nick's mother invited him in, offering him the good chair by the fireplace. When she reached for the stack of paper, the recruiter pulled it back. Maybe he was making one last attempt at getting this bright young boy to change his mind and take the sane option. Maybe he just couldn't stand knowing what he knew—and what Nicholas would learn only too soon.

"You know what your son wants to do, right?" the recruiter said.

"Yeah," she said, "he wants to be in the infantry."

The recruiter stared at her for a moment. "Do you know what that means?"

"Yes," she said, her voice breaking, her full, still-youthful face quivering. "He's gonna be on the front lines."

"No," the recruiter said. "Your son's gonna be a bullet sponge."

3.

WERNER AND STAN

(THE MAELSTROM OF POE)

Not long after Albert Hofmann became the first human to ingest LSD, Sandoz delivered a cache of the drug they would trademark as Delysid to a Swiss psychiatrist, Werner Stoll, the son of Hofmann's boss, for human testing. The younger Stoll's test subjects would include both healthy volunteers and mental patients. Stoll even took it himself and reported a staggering experience that sounded something like riding a roller coaster through bursting fireworks. He went from euphoria to depression and back several times. At one point, he said, "I felt myself one with all romanticists and dreamers, saw the maelstrom of Poe. . . . Often I seemed to stand at the pinnacle of artistic experience; I luxuriated in the colors of the altar of Isenham, and knew the euphoria and exultation of an artistic vision."

At another, he reported, "I was depressed and thought with interest of the possibility of suicide. With some terror I apprehended that such thoughts were remarkably familiar to me. It seemed singularly self-evident that a depressed person commits suicide. . . ."

Here, in spades, was the LSD duality that Hofmann had discovered. In fact, Stoll reportedly told other researchers in personal communications that one of the subjects of his study, given the drug without her knowledge, committed suicide shortly thereafter. "The devastating effects of a completely inexplicable psychic disruption were too much for her," one researcher says Stoll told him.

If true, no mention of it was made in his formal report on the trial results, which noted primarily the ways in which LSD prompted something like a temporary insanity in the healthy subjects given the drug. He concluded that the new drug might be useful in the study of psychosis, which had proven so resistant to treatment and difficult to understand. As an aside—interesting, considering the potency of his own experience—he suggested that mental health professionals might find it useful to spend a few hours inside the world of the psychotic by taking the drug themselves.

The bizarre effects and awesome power of LSD provoked a sensation in the scientific world when Stoll's study was published in 1947. Sandoz sent samples of LSD to psychiatric research institutes, university departments, and individual therapists, asking them if they would be interested in experimenting with the new substance.

One of these packages arrived at the school of medicine of Charles University in Prague, where a twenty-three-year-old medical student named Stanislav Grof was assigned to babysit the study subjects for the six to eight hours during which they would be under the influence.

"I was fascinated by what I saw and heard and was eager to volunteer for a session myself," Grof wrote of the experience. "Unfortunately, to my great dismay, the faculty board decided that students should not be used as experimental subjects."

The moment Grof was no longer a student, immediately after graduation, he volunteered for an LSD study. He wasn't disappointed. One thing became immediately apparent: this was no mere temporary insanity. As he recalled in a 1990 *Yoga Journal* interview, "I couldn't believe how much I learned about my psyche in those few hours. . . . The sheer intensity of the array of emotions I felt simply amazed me. . . . I was hit by a radiance that seemed comparable to the epicenter of a nuclear explosion, or perhaps the light of supernatural brilliance said in Oriental scriptures to appear to us at the moment of death. This thunderbolt catapulted me out of my body. First I lost my awareness of my immediate surroundings, then the psychiatric clinic, then Prague, and finally the planet. At an inconceivable speed my consciousness expanded to cosmic dimensions. I experienced the Big Bang, passed through black holes and white holes in the universe, identified with exploding supernovas, and witnessed many other strange phenomena that seemed to be pulsars, quasars, and other amazing cosmic events." Later, he wrote, "I was able to see the irony and paradox of the situation. The divine manifested itself and took me over in a modern scientific laboratory in the middle of a scientific experiment conducted in a communist country with a substance produced in the test tube of a 20th-century chemist."

He would later write that although the LSD effects "lasted only a few hours—and its most significant part only about ten minutes—it resulted in a profound personal transformation and spiritual awakening and sent me professionally on a radically different course than the one for which I had been trained and prepared."

Grof's particular trajectory—a singular focus on the transformation he had experienced in his initial exposure to a radically different kind of consciousness—would first shape the therapeutic movement Hofmann's discovery spawned, then sustain it through dormant decades, long after scientific research into psychedelics crashed and burned.

But that's getting ahead of the story.

4.

NICHOLAS

(WHAT MAKES GRASS GROW)

As the bus to boot camp passed through the semitropical marshes surrounding Parris Island, the uniformed drill instructors ordered all the teenagers in their jeans and T-shirts to put their heads between their knees NOW. Nick did as he was told, and as he stared at the vinyl seat cover, he felt the bus lurch to a stop with a squeal of brakes. Nick, excited, nervous, about to start a new life, heard the doors open, then the unmistakable sound of boots stomping down the aisle. "PUT YOUR HEAD BACK DOWN, MAGGOT!" boomed a voice like a nightstick. "Your ass is MINE now. When I tell you something you will respond with 'Yessir' or 'Nosir' after everything I say. I JUST SAID SOMETHING!"

Soon Nick stood on the yellow footprints in front of the processing center—the same yellow footprints, he was told, in which thousands of Marines had stood before him. "You are now aboard Marine Corps Recruit Depot, Parris Island, South Carolina, and you have just taken the first step toward becoming a member of the world's finest fighting force, the United States Marine Corps."

It was surreal, giddy, scary. In short order his head was shaved and his feet inspected for flatness—they still did that! They stripped him to his underwear, poked him with needles, pumped him full of serums. He was tested and equipped and assigned to a barracks.

As Nick lay on his barely cushioned rack, he could sight above the new boots stiff on his feet and see the bridge leading off the island on which he was, for all practical purposes, a prisoner of the U.S. government. Behind him was the parade deck where he'd graduate, if he was lucky, in thirteen weeks.

He thrived. Sure, the physical stuff was tough. But even though he hadn't had enough social confidence to play organized sports, he'd always excelled at the physical fitness tests in gym, and that put him ahead of the game at boot camp. They ran *everywhere*, climbed, crawled, did push-ups until they puked. But he learned that you could puke, wipe your mouth, and keep on going—that when his muscles failed, he could do push-ups with his heart. This is what he now understood the drill instructors were trying to impart: his built-in limits were a myth. He had the capacity to endure and accomplish far more than he had ever imagined.

His favorite form of PT torture was the obstacle course. They bellied through mud pits, vaulted walls, crawled under rolls of barbed wire, hauled themselves up ropes, all while the drill instructors screamed in their faces. At least on Parris Island, unlike in high school, all the obstacles were visible, and he and his fellow boots all faced them equally, together.

Nicholas was smart enough to comprehend immediately what he needed to do to survive: no more and no less than exactly what he was told. He discovered the relief of no longer thinking for himself and giving over entirely to the higher power of the drill instructor, no matter how difficult or debilitating the demands. Besides, quitting was simply not possible. You could die but you could not quit.

He was annoyed by the few in his platoon who didn't get that, watching them step into shit again and again, blundering into snares he mostly avoided. Nick could count on one hand the times he had been called on the quarterdeck for punishment. Sometimes they made you do push-ups, but sometimes they just messed with your head, screaming nonsensical orders rapid-fire—*"Take off your left shoe. Unlace it. Put the laces in your pocket. Put the left shoe on your right foot, your left hand in your right pocket"*—until you followed the orders without even thinking about whether they made sense or not, without thinking at all. He only screwed up seriously one time, when his platoon got called to formation, which meant everyone had to have their footlockers stowed and be standing at attention before the drill instructor counted down. In his haste he fumbled his junk and couldn't get the lock snapped shut in time. He twisted it into the closed position and lurched into line.

That's when he heard, or thought he heard—could *swear* he had heard—the drill sergeant say, "If your shit's not fixed, go fix it now."

Nick turned back to snap the lock shut. Nobody else moved. In the shocked silence, he realized he'd just committed a high crime. He'd broken formation. Before he could even gasp he felt powerful hands grip his uniform, lifting him off the floor. His head bounced off the racks; spit flew in his face. As soon as the storm had passed, his rack mate was whispering, "You okay?"

"That was awesome," Nick responded, surprised to discover he'd found it more thrilling than terrifying.

The Marine Corps was shaping up to be all that he had hoped.

Nick bonded with his fellow Marines. He became the Catholic lay reader in Sunday services, which earned him the nickname Reverend. Time and again the men in his platoon learned that they had to depend on one another, work as a team. If one of them failed, all paid the price. When someone collapsed doing push-ups, the rest did them for him. If someone missed formation, they all were punished. They slept together, sweated together, chanted together, learned to kill together. The martial arts instruction was basic and brutal. No elegant moves, no grace points: it was about ending the fight quickly and permanently. A part of him he'd always feared, the part perpetually on the brink of explosion, stirred. It blew when one of the guys who didn't get the program, a kid they called Ford, refused to wake up five minutes early with the rest of the platoon. Their DI had granted them leave to get up early before he came through yelling, "LIGHTS! LIGHTS! LIGHTS!"—which meant they could be first in line for chow, which meant they'd actually have time to eat. But Ford just rolled over in his bunk, and even when the guy standing fire watch got in his face, Ford only kicked out of bed grudgingly, dragging his feet and bitching and whining instead of getting his shit together.

Nick felt a flare of rage and found himself on the ground, on top of Ford, his hands on the boy's throat as Ford sputtered, "You're fucking crazy!" and Nick's buddy, Winter, was pulling him off. "Whoa, Rev," Winter was saying. "You just choked someone out!"

Just a scuffle no drill instructors noticed, and then they were all on the drill field as usual.

"What makes grass grow?" the DI bellowed. They all knew the answer, and barked it in unison: "Blood, sir, blood!"

5.

HUMPHRY AND ALDOUS

(TO FALL IN HELL OR SOAR ANGELIC)

The immediate enthusiasm among psychiatric researchers for LSD sparked by Werner Stoll's study might be seen as puzzling in at least one respect. As even Hofmann noted, "The picture of the activity of LSD obtained from these first investigations was not new to science."

In fact, LSD intoxication was virtually identical to the effects of mescaline, a natural compound produced by a number of plants in the western hemisphere, most prominently the relatively rare and slow-growing peyote cactus in the American Southwest and Mexico. Mescaline-containing plants had been used by Native Americans in religious ceremonies for thousands of years. The powers of peyote were known to Europeans at least as early as 1560 when a Franciscan missionary named Bernardino de Sahagún noted, "Those who eat or drink it see visions either frightful or laughable. . . . [It] stimulates them and gives them sufficient spirit to fight and have neither fear, thirst, nor hunger. . . . It causes those devouring it to foresee and predict; such, for instance, as whether the weather will continue; or to discern who has stolen from them."

The importance of peyote in the Indians' spiritual lives made the

Catholic Church view it as a threat to conversion. The Spanish Inquisition outlawed peyote rituals in 1620. Anyone caught ignoring the
command was tortured and killed. Nonetheless, clandestine use survived through the centuries.

Europeans, however, pretty much forgot about peyote until it
turned up again north of the Rio Grande following the Civil War.
Native groups throughout the western United States, facing cultural
eradication after decades of war, racist government policies, and the
destruction of the great bison herds, formed revivalist religions mixing
elements of traditional beliefs with Christianity. Peyote, concentrated
in the button-like blossoms of the cactus, formed the backbone of the
new faith. Its ritualistic use created a psychic space that rationalist
Western culture could not penetrate, a direct communication with God
that bypassed white institutions. As one of the leaders of the movement, Comanche chief Quanah Parker put it, "The white man goes
into his church house and talks about Jesus. The Indian goes into his
teepee and talks *to* Jesus."

Naturalists began to collect and study the peyote cactus. Mescaline was identified as the active ingredient in 1896 and synthesized in
1919. A flurry of physicians, scientists, artists, and intellectuals self-
experimented with the drug. Their accounts for some reason focused
primarily on the closed-eye visions it invoked.

The mini-vogue continued into the 1920s, but synthesizing mescaline in sufficient quantity proved difficult and expensive, and the
experience was deemed too varied and unpredictable to have practical
purpose. By 1936, one writer could lament that "this extraordinary substance remains in almost complete obscurity."

LSD would change the situation dramatically as shipments of Sandoz's
newest product went out around the world. The fact that it was effective
at a thousandth of the dose required for mescaline made it economical to

produce for wide study, but it also hit Western science at a moment when the discovery of an array of psychoactive drugs was about to transform psychiatry. Within a few years the synthesis of chlorpromazine—also known as Thorazine, the first antipsychotic medication—would offer an effective alternative to destructive lobotomies, shock treatments, and permanent institutionalization of the mentally ill.

Humphry Osmond, an English researcher who had been a ship's psychiatrist in the British Navy during the war, was one of those who found the new interest in the chemistry of mental states compelling. He'd become fascinated by the similarity of earlier reports of mescaline intoxication to psychotic states. He'd also noted the structural similarity of the mescaline molecule to that of adrenaline, naturally produced by the human adrenal gland.

Stoll's report on LSD's ability to create a "model psychosis" that was virtually identical to the mescaline state gave a tantalizing boost to Osmond's theory that some substance produced in the body like adrenaline might be responsible for psychoses, and also meant it would be possible to work extensively with a readily available substitute for the costly mescaline.

Unfortunately, his employer, St. George's Hospital in London, did not share his enthusiasm. Facing a brick wall blocking his research aspirations, Osmond answered an employment ad in the *Lancet* and fled halfway around the globe to take the most unlikely of positions: clinical director of the mental hospital in Weyburn, Saskatchewan, Canada.

Weyburn was a bleak railroad town forty-five miles from the U.S. border, due north of the state line between North Dakota and Montana. Winter lows mired in the negative numbers and summers started late and ended early. The town's population barely exceeded the five thousand inmates of the hospital. Abram Hoffer, the director of research

there when Osmond arrived, described the hospital population this
way: "Admission was for them a life sentence, and conditions were
appalling."

But Osmond had been promised ample funding to pursue his passion, and this unlikely outpost soon found itself on the leading edge of
psychiatric science. As Stoll had suggested in the first study of LSD,
Osmond initially looked at the drug as a way to understand psychosis
from the inside, and as a possible link to the as-yet-unknown biochemical process that brought about the disease in the first place. If those
processes could be pinpointed and understood, perhaps it would be
possible to chemically reverse them and, ultimately, cure psychosis with
a drug as surely as you could cure a bacterial infection with penicillin.

Osmond's own first experiment with mescaline reinforced his idea
that the drug allowed him to experience mental illness. In an essay on
the experience he titled "On Being Mad," he emphasized the paranoia,
frightening delusions, and disassociation characteristic of the psychotic:

> *Every so often the walls of the room would shiver, and I knew that*
> *behind those perilously unsolid walls something was waiting to*
> *burst through. I believed that would be disastrous. . . . I asked for*
> *some water. I drank the glass which [my friend] brought, and found*
> *that it tasted strange. I wondered if there might be something wrong*
> *with it: poison crossed my mind. . . .*

Osmond continued studying how people reacted to LSD, purely to
better understand the bewildering variety of experiences it produced.
Then he went a step further.

As recounted in Erika Dyck's book *Psychedelic Psychiatry: LSD from
Clinic to Campus,* on the eve of a professional conference in Ottawa in
1953, Osmond and Hoffer both had difficulty sleeping in the uncomfortable accommodations of the hotel. They gave up on their tossing

and turning and stayed up all night talking. At about four a.m., Hoffer later related, one of them remarked that the LSD experience bore a lot in common with delirium tremens, the agitation, delusions, and hallucinations that accompany severe alcohol withdrawal. It struck them both as a hilarious comparison—it *was* four a.m.—but when they stopped laughing, they began to take the idea seriously. Delirium tremens could be fatal, but medical literature of the time noted that, of those who survived, some emerged with a transformed personality and achieved lasting sobriety. Osmond and Hoffer assumed that the reason for the transformation did not directly relate to the physiological crisis but instead owed to the extremity of the subjective experience. Which made them wonder: Could LSD—which they could personally attest provided an extreme experience—be a safe way to induce a delirium tremens–type event that might have a similar transformative effect? It seemed like a long shot.

Back in Weyburn, they were astounded when, in their first minitrial, one of two hard-core recidivist alcoholics quit drinking on the spot after a single therapy session with LSD and remained sober throughout the six-month follow-up. Over numerous trials that followed, Osmond reported that the success rate stayed remarkably stable at nearly 50 percent, about twice that of traditional alcoholism treatments. Similar results came in scores of trials treating hundreds of subjects over the next fifteen years.

The idea that a drug-induced, experience-motivated change in awareness could push back a notoriously tough condition like alcoholism clearly implied that the same might be useful in dealing with a wide range of psychological afflictions. That conclusion occurred to others around the world who had also received those packages from Sandoz and witnessed in their trial subjects and themselves remarkable experiences that in the course of hours could effect seemingly lasting transformations.

By the mid-1950s, researchers had experimented with LSD during therapy for various neuroses, depression, addiction, psychosomatic illness, and emotional and physical trauma. Scores of trials including hundreds of subjects were conducted, and most reported positive results. In 1954, psychiatrists at an English hospital set aside an entire ward for conducting LSD therapy with patients who had severe, chronic, treatment-resistant mental illness. They concluded that sixty-one out of ninety-four patients recovered or improved after six months. LSD appeared to be "of utmost value in psychotherapy," the lead investigators concluded, "both in cases otherwise resistant to therapy and as a method for avoiding the prolonged time necessary for a full psychological analysis."

In study after study, researchers got similar results and made similar conclusions. A 1958 analysis of all published research concluded that the large success rates came about because "1, LSD-25 lessens defensiveness; 2, there is a heightened capacity to relive early experiences with an accompanying release of feelings; 3, therapist-patient relationships are enhanced; and 4, there is an increased appearance of unconscious material."

These successes were often ignored or discounted for methodological reasons. Some studies had too few subjects, or lacked a control and double-blind design—a mode of research in which neither the subject nor the researcher would know if the drug ingested was the test drug or a placebo, in order to ensure wishful thinking or presuppositions by subjects or investigators would not influence the result.

An even more basic criticism was that the use of LSD in conjunction with therapy introduced too many variables. As many early investigators noted with bemusement, the LSD experience was extraordinarily suggestible. One wrote: "Researchers variously reported that psychedelics mimicked mental illness (when given in a setting that provoked it), illuminated Freudian theory (when administered by a competent

Freudian), evoked Jungian archetypes (when administered by a sensitive Jungian). . . ."

Ironically, it was exactly the property of extreme suggestibility that made testing LSD in a variable-controlled, sterile laboratory setting so problematic. This was just what Osmond and a growing group of other researchers had learned *not* to do. Such harsh clinical environments were apt to provoke fear and anxiety in people who had taken LSD, and then magnify that fear to possibly disastrous levels by isolating the subject from any empathy in the form of a sympathetic and reassuring therapist.

What had been clear to Hofmann almost immediately had by this time been observed independently by Osmond and a host of others: for LSD to have the greatest positive effect, subjects needed to take it in a safe, supportive, and aesthetically pleasing environment with a clear idea of what to expect. When difficult issues arose—as they often did—the safe setting and supportive presence of a therapist would allow the subject to process this emotional dynamite, defuse it, and transcend it.

In the fifteen years after Stan Grof, the Czech med student turned research psychiatrist, first had his stunning experience with LSD in 1954, he conducted more LSD therapy sessions than anyone in the world, involving hundreds of patients and thousands of doses. In the remarkable variability of subjects' experiences after taking the drug, Grof observed a pattern: it seemed that precisely the psychological and emotional issues most relevant to each particular subject would, without special prompting, find a way to emerge in the therapy sessions. And in each subsequent session, the subject would explore the issue at ever deeper levels until the root of the problem was reached, and often resolved.

In his book *LSD: Doorway to the Numinous*, Grof concluded, "This unique property . . . makes it possible to study psychological undercurrents that govern our experiences and behaviors to a depth that cannot be matched by any other method or tool available in mainstream psychiatry and psychology. In addition, it offers unique opportunities for healing of emotional and psychosomatic disorders, for positive personality transformation, and for consciousness evolution."

Grof was not going out on a limb in the context of the time. The cumulative experience of an ever-growing number of therapists working with LSD and mescaline powerfully endorsed his conclusions and in some cases went even further. Another global review of studies in 1963 concluded: "Some spectacular, and almost unbelievable, results have been achieved by using one dose of the drug."

Osmond, too, believed that the transcendent experience that could occur with LSD was precisely what made it effective—a radical departure from the usual way of understanding how drugs worked to benefit patients. Most effective drugs had a direct biochemical impact on the illness or the affected area of the body. Although LSD clearly affected the brain, the curative changes seemed only indirectly related to the physiological changes it provoked.

Osmond's research director, Hoffer, made the point directly: "As a general rule," he wrote, "those who have not had the transcendental experience are not changed; they continue to drink. However, the large proportion of those who have had it are changed."

The "transcendental experiences" Hoffer referred to made no tidy category. They were a hydra-headed phantasm covering territory from lurid to sublime. One subject from an early alcoholism trial described his transforming vision of, in essence, meeting himself in hell: "How can I explain the face, vile, repulsive and scaly, that I took by the hand into the depth of hell from whence it came and then gently removed that scaly thing from the face and took it by the hand up, up into the light and saw the face in all its God given beauty."

Osmond's treatments proved successful enough that the Canadian government would eventually issue a report saying LSD was no longer an experimental treatment for alcoholism but one that had proven effective.

Osmond, who had begun from the premise that the drug experience was merely a window into a devastating mental illness, had come around to a far different idea. "For myself," he wrote, "my experiences with these substances have been the most strange, most awesome, and among the most beautiful things in a varied and fortunate life. These are not escapes from but enlargements, burgeonings of reality."

But Osmond was still a relatively obscure scientist in the frozen wastes of the Canadian outback. What he had to say would ultimately have far less impact on the larger culture than the thoughts of a world-famous English novelist and intellectual living in California. Of course, Aldous Huxley would sniff out the back-room gambling going on way up in Weyburn. How could he not? He was the man who, two decades before Osmond took his first dose of mescaline, had imagined a drug eerily similar to LSD, a drug he named "soma," and made it a key plot element of his classic novel *Brave New World*:

> *"There is always* soma, *delicious* soma, *half a gramme for a half-holiday, a gramme for a week-end, two grammes for a trip to the gorgeous East, three for a dark eternity on the moon. . . ."*

No sooner had Osmond (with Canadian colleague John Smythies) published a paper on his work than he received an interested and encouraging letter from the great writer, suggesting that Osmond visit him in LA. The stars almost instantly aligned, as Osmond recalled:

> *The opportunity came, strangely enough, in a matter of weeks, when I went to Southern California for a psychiatric meeting. I took with me a few capsules of the cactus alkaloid mescaline, for*

Smythies and I had decided that our efforts in exploring drug-induced changes in one's perceptual world would benefit greatly from cooperation by those most able to describe experiences and whose perceptions were already well sharpened by many years of thought and inquiry. Aldous Huxley obviously filled our bill of particulars perfectly.

So, in the late spring of 1953, Osmond traveled the 1,673 miles from Weyburn to Los Angeles, arriving at Aldous and Maria Huxley's home in the Hollywood hills on the evening of May 4. Osmond wasn't sure what to expect from the visionary author. Perhaps he'd find a wild-eyed mystic, credulous to a fault. But in fact Huxley appeared to be every bit as hardheaded as Osmond could have hoped. He "found him shrewd, matter-of-fact, and to the point." All of which, when he thought of it, wasn't surprising: contrary to popular conception, he noted, "the history of mysticism has always concerned the practical, hard-headed, socially effective people."

Osmond had arrived in time for dinner and received a warm welcome and fine food. Huxley could barely contain his excitement about what was to come, proudly displaying the Dictaphone he'd obtained to record notes during the following day's experiment.

It was only then that Osmond began to worry about the consequences of his actions. He barely slept that night:

Next morning, as I stirred the water and watched the silvery white mescaline crystals swirling down and dissolving with a slightly oily slick, I wondered whether it would be enough or too much. Aldous . . . would be sad if it did not work. But what if it worked too well? Should I cut the dose in half? The setting could hardly have been better. It was a delicious May morning in Hollywood, no hint of smog to make the eyes smart, not too hot. Moreover, Aldous seemed an ideal subject . . . and we had taken to each other, which was very important for a good experience. But I did not relish the possibility—however remote—of being "the man who drove Aldous Huxley mad."

Too late for second thoughts: Osmond handed Huxley the glass with a solution containing the 0.4 grams of lab-synthesized mescaline and Huxley eagerly drank it down. An hour passed, an hour and a half. *Two hours.* Huxley said he felt little if anything, and impatiently began to suggest the dosage had been too small. But Osmond urged patience, and soon both men were rewarded.

Huxley found himself staring at a flower arrangement in a vase in his study, an arrangement he had remarked upon just that morning for its "lively dissonance of colors."

That somewhat prissy assessment suddenly belonged to a different world. As he would write in *The Doors of Perception*:

> *That was no longer the point. I was not looking now at an unusual flower arrangement. I was seeing what Adam had seen on the morning of his creation—the miracle, moment by moment, of naked existence.*
>
> *What rose and iris and carnation so intensely signified was nothing more, and nothing less, than what they were—a transience that was yet eternal life, a perpetual perishing that was at the same time pure Being, a bundle of minute, unique particulars in which, by some unspeakable and yet self-evident paradox, was to be seen the divine source of all existence.*

Being Huxley, he didn't stop there. He not only described his moment of satori, he developed a theory to explain it, one that has only become more intriguing with the passage of half a century. Reality, he wrote, "has to be funneled through the reducing valve of the brain and nervous system. What comes out at the other end is a measly trickle of the kind of consciousness which will help us to stay alive on the surface of this particular planet." Mescaline and LSD, he theorized, inhibited the systems in the brain designed to shut out impractical stimulation, so humans could keep coloring within the lines and go about the business of survival without being distracted by the astounding awesomeness of the universe—or as Huxley put it, "the glory, the infinite value and meaningfulness of naked existence, of the given, unconceptualized event."

Huxley went on to predict that access to these drugs would become a turning point in the history of Western culture, fomenting a spiritual revival "as the result of biochemical discoveries that will make it possible for large numbers of men and women to achieve a radical self-transcendence and a deeper understanding of the nature of things."

Huxley's large vision and powerful expression would echo throughout the century and become ground zero for those who saw in these powerful, problematic drugs something of lasting value, something whose attendant difficulties were worth struggling with. *The Doors of Perception* would become fixed in the cultural memory, while Osmond, if remembered at all, remained a footnote.

But in one aspect at least, Osmond would have the last laugh. In an exchange of letters following their eventful meeting, he and Huxley engaged in a friendly competition to come up with a generic name for a class of drugs that included mescaline and LSD. They considered various candidate nomenclature over several years—including "hallucinogens"—that they both agreed were inadequate or misleading (i.e., the visions invoked were rarely actual hallucinations). Then, in 1957, Huxley thought he had a winner: phanerothyme, derived from Greek words for manifest and spirit, or soul. It had a nice ring to it: soul, manifest.

He even put it in a catchy rhyme:

To make this mundane world sublime,
Take half a gram of phanerothyme

Entering into a writing contest with Aldous Huxley would, under most circumstances, be a fool's errand. But Osmond took him on, countering with something less fanciful and more precise: a term meaning "mind manifested," which neatly got around the enormous variability of experiences prompted by ingesting these compounds. The one constant, Osmond felt, was that the effects were almost entirely in the subjective reality of the taker.

It was the more practical, less poetic, term. Nonetheless, Huxley had inspired him to make it rhyme:

To fathom Hell or soar angelic,
Just take a pinch of psychedelic

6.

RICK

(BRAVE NEW WORLD)

The funny kid in his high school Russian class had to be crazy; that was a given. Rick Doblin appreciated the comic relief the kid provided by cutting up in class, and—truth be told—he *liked* the kid. But he'd heard the rumors. The kid had tripped on LSD, and Rick knew what that meant: at least part of him had been damaged. Rick kept looking for signs of derangement, but just because he couldn't see them didn't mean they weren't there. One day, when they were supposed to be learning Russian declension, Rick noticed him reading a novel with an odd title: *One Flew Over the Cuckoo's Nest*.

The kid caught him looking. "You should read this," he said.

Rick did. He'd never read anything like it before. From the first sinewy, roiling sentences, Rick found himself seeing the world from inside the head of a mute Native American, Broom Bromden, judged to be crazy, but whose perception knifed through reality like a spinning blade. By the end, the idea of "sanity" lay smashed into shards on the asylum floor, and the inmates seemed sounder—and certainly less cruel—than their keepers.

Insanity and the inside of asylums were completely alien to him: Rick's world consisted of a stable and loving family in an architecturally distinctive home in a well-off neighborhood in the upscale town of Winnetka, Illinois. His father was a doctor, and both his grandfathers had built successful businesses. Despite his place of privilege, he powerfully identified with the book's theme. His family had lost relatives in the Holocaust, and even as a little boy Rick obsessed about the idea that an entire continent could descend into a self-immolating genocidal rage, claiming the lives of millions of innocents. From a very early age he felt the possibility of that kind of cultural insanity as a personal threat.

Now he could see that Hitler and Big Nurse had a lot in common.

When Rick finished the book, he told the kid from his Russian class how riveted he'd been.

"Ken Kesey wrote that book on acid," the kid said.

Which was not entirely true. Kesey, who had first taken LSD as a guinea pig in CIA-funded studies at the Menlo Park, California, Veterans Administration hospital in 1959, later said the general mood and voice of the book and the protagonist had been inspired by his psychedelic-fueled visions. As far as actually writing under the influence, he admitted only to the first few pages.

But what a first few pages they were, including the appearance of the archetypal Big Nurse, one of the great entrances in American literature:

Then . . . she sights those black boys. They're still down there together, mumbling to one another. They didn't hear her come on the ward. They sense she's glaring down at them now, but it's too late. They should of knew better'n to group up and mumble together when she was due on the ward. Their faces bob apart, confused. She goes into a crouch and advances on where they're trapped in a huddle at the end of the corridor. She knows what they been saying, and I can see she's furious clean out of control. She's going to tear the black bastards limb from limb, she's so furious. She's swelling up,

*swells till her back's splitting out the white uniform and she's let her
arms section out long enough to wrap around the three of them five,
six times. She looks around her with a swivel of her huge head.
Nobody up to see, just old Broom Bromden the half-breed Indian
back there hiding behind his mop and can't talk to call for help. So
she really lets herself go and her painted smile twists, stretches to an
open snarl, and she blows up bigger and bigger, big as a tractor, so
big I can smell the machinery inside the way you smell a motor
pulling too big a load. I hold my breath and figure, My God this
time they're gonna do it! This time they let the hate build up too
high and overloaded and they're gonna tear one another to pieces
before they realize what they're doing!*

Rick didn't know the subtleties of Kesey's relation to acid, but now he
had to deal with this disturbing fact: that such a carefully crafted,
visionary work of art, a paradigm-shifting kind of art, could possibly
come from a mind grasped in LSD's tentacles—it was no less than a
blow to his worldview. His parents didn't even drink, and neither did
he. Not even caffeine. And psychedelics were in another universe of
evil, a blow-your-mind, make-you-jump-out-windows, eat-your-brain,
mutate-your-babies kind of evil.

This was 1970, and the early wave of excitement over the positive
results from the use of LSD and mescaline in psychotherapy had crashed.
The dark side of psychedelics had surfaced even before Albert Hofmann
discovered that his derivative of ergot compounds made the world seem
a fundamentally different place. When World War II ended and the
American military raked through the ashes of the Nazi Reich for any
useful technology the enemy had been developing, they discovered studies testing the use of mescaline on inmates in the Dachau concentration
camp as a truth drug. When they weren't blasting out prisoners' lungs in
high-pressure chambers, or tossing them naked into vats of ice water,

making notes on their clipboards as their victims screamed in agony and froze to death, they were forcing mescaline down unwilling throats, then conducting harsh interrogations. Though one report said interrogators had found it "impossible to impose one's will on another person even when the strongest dose of mescaline has been given," another concluded that mescaline-aided interrogation could consistently elicit "even the most intimate secrets . . . when questions were cleverly put."

These crude reports were enough to spur the American military, and soon the newly inaugurated Central Intelligence Agency, to embark on a decades-long program to develop psychedelic drugs for any number of imagined national security uses—as a truth serum, as a serum that would make captured CIA agents *incapable* of telling the truth to enemy interrogators, as a chemical weapon that could incapacitate enemy troops en masse, as a diplomatic sleight of hand that would embarrass unfriendly foreign leaders, or as an aid in coercive interrogation, i.e., a way to intensify torture. The Agency even created a brothel in San Francisco to lure unwitting subjects, who were then slipped LSD in their drinks and observed through a one-way mirror.

In the mostly useless campaign to make this powerful mind-bending drug a weapon of some sort, the U.S. intelligence authorities dosed hundreds of their own agents, military officers, and enlisted men, and unsuspecting civilians and foreigners, sometimes combining the unpredictable mental effects with physical and psychological stress designed to instill maximum fear and anxiety. This crude and brutalizing approach produced its share of casualties, including lasting psychotic breaks and suicide.

But the CIA's obsession with psychedelics, part of a secret program called MK-ULTRA, had another unintended consequence: by more or less indiscriminately introducing hundreds to the psychedelic experience directly—and hundreds more indirectly through the mushrooming civilian clinical studies funded by clandestine CIA dollars—the

Agency helped create a demand and inevitably a black market in psychedelic drugs.

One of the many who got his hands on a hit of the Sandoz-manufactured LSD, floating free from all the loosely audited experimental trials, was a thirty-year-old eccentric named Owsley Stanley, the grandson of a U.S. senator. His acid experience impressed him as the key to a new, more profound and caring cosmos and launched Stanley on an historic quest. He hooked up with a Berkeley chem major named Melissa Cargill, and in three weeks at the university library in Berkeley they taught themselves how to manufacture fantastically pure LSD, which he loosed upon the streets of a growing bohemian enclave in San Francisco's Haight-Ashbury. Those 3,600 colored capsules passed hand to hand in the spring of 1965 were the first of millions of acid trips he would be directly responsible for.

"I never set out to 'turn on the world,' as has been claimed by many," Owsley told *Rolling Stone* magazine in a 2007 profile, four years before he died in a car crash. "I just wanted to know the dose and purity of what I took into my own body. Almost before I realized what was happening, the whole affair had gotten completely out of hand. I was riding a magic stallion. A Pegasus."

One of Owsley's earliest and most consequential clients was Ken Kesey, who needed a new source of inspiration now that he was no longer picking up spare change and free acid as a guinea pig in the CIA-funded trials in Menlo Park. Unlike the first wave of acid acolytes, Kesey wasn't an academy-educated intellectual or professional behaviorist. He was the salt of the earth, and he didn't want to study LSD, he wanted to ride it like a wave. He just happened to bring the rest of the culture with him. Fueled by Owsley's product, Kesey and a growing group of rabble-rousing fellow travelers began staging outrageous bacchanals called acid tests—a play on the confluence of the drug's new street name with a process in which strong acid is used to distinguish gold from base metals. The term was meant to imply that the use of LSD in these circumstances could reveal some ultimate truth. Actually, Kesey's parties mostly revealed what happened when large numbers of random strangers consumed immoderate amounts of psychedelic in wildly uncontrolled circumstances as a tsunami of sound rolled over them from the tolling guitars of the Grateful Dead.

Just as the Kesey-Owsley confederation was electrifying the West Coast, a Harvard professor named Timothy Leary was doing his best to light up the East. Leary, who had begun as just one of the scores of academics studying the fascinating effects of the new drug in clinical trials, became his own best (or worst, depending on perspective) subject. Harvard grew impatient with Leary and his partner in the psychedelic experimentation, another Harvard professor named Richard Alpert, when it got around that the pair had been handing out informal homework to students in the form of psychoactive chemicals. When both men were eventually dismissed—Alpert for defying an order to surrender his entire psychedelic stash to the university for safekeeping, and Leary for going AWOL from his teaching assignments—a front-page editorial in the student-run *Harvard Crimson* applauded: "Harvard has disassociated itself not only from flagrant dishonesty but also from behavior that is spreading infection throughout the academic community."

Fine with Leary. He'd concluded from his acid trips that the rules and limitations of conventional society were false fronts, head games designed to control and manipulate. He began to advocate a juiced-up liberation theology based on the psychedelic experience, and he learned to enjoy getting under the skin of the unenlightened. For an academic, he had a surprising knack for attracting attention.

In a 1966 *Playboy* interview he delivered this gem:

"An enormous amount of energy from every fiber of your body is released under LSD, most especially including sexual energy. There is no question that LSD is the most powerful aphrodisiac ever discovered by man. Compared with sex under LSD, the way you've been making love, no matter how ecstatic the pleasure you think you get from it, is like making love to a department-store-window dummy."

Between Leary's hype, Kesey's beat charm, and Owsley's prowess in the laboratory, psychedelics went viral, creating a drug subculture in which millions of unscreened Americans experimented with drugs of uncertain purity produced by less talented chemists than Owsley.

Young people began showing up in emergency rooms during and after acute panic reactions to LSD trips—or to whatever drugs had been sold as LSD. Nobody could be sure how many or what percentage of all LSD users ended up in the emergency room, but a survey of medical practitioners in Los Angeles at the time concluded that during an eighteen-month period from 1966 to 1968, at least 4,100 patients had sought medical help for some kind of mental or emotional crisis brought on by taking LSD.

Though not insignificant, the sometimes tragic outcomes of bad drug reactions represented only a small percentage of the hundreds of thousands of LSD trips undertaken in that time frame. An analysis of adverse reactions to uncontrolled use, carried out by doctors at Bellevue Hospital in New York, put the incidence of LSD-provoked psychotic breakdowns at seven per one thousand illicit LSD trips, most often occurring among those with prior history of mental disturbance. Less serious and quickly dissipating adverse reactions, mostly anxiety or transitory depression, occurred about 2 percent of the time.

But having once touted the potential of a psychiatric miracle drug, the media had little interest in such moderating details. An explosion of lurid, sketchy stories of spectacular psychotic breaks, suicides, and crimes motivated by drug-induced insanity began to pop up in the headlines.

Given the nature of LSD, many of the scary stories had a mythic feel that lodged firmly in the public mind. They were often anecdotal, lacking names or confirmation, but indelibly vivid, such as the *Pageant* magazine article reporting that "one patient tried to kill himself when he thought his body was melting, and he remained suicidal for more than two weeks after only one dose of LSD."

One of the Harvard students Leary dosed with LSD was said to have been nearly killed when he walked into rush-hour traffic on Boston's Huntington Avenue "believing he was God and nothing could touch him." *Plain Truth* magazine put together a litany of horror stories of the type that could be found in dozens of other publications:

"One LSD tripper took the drug and believed that he could fly. He jumped out of a 10-story window and fell to his death. . . . Another, driving his car while under the influence of LSD, looked on all the red lights as something beautiful, beckoning him onward. He crashed and killed the occupants of another car. One young fellow took LSD once. It didn't turn him on so he quit. *Two years later* he suffered a severe mental breakdown! A 17-year-old, high on LSD, thought he was losing his sight because of the drug and tried to tear out his eyeballs. . . . Another youth took the drug and was impelled on a compulsive search for someone to rape!"

The drug in the news seemed to bear little resemblance to the drug on which so many research dollars had been spent over the previous two decades. As one meta-survey of scientific literature measured it, "between 1950 and the mid-1960s there were more than a thousand clinical papers discussing 40,000 patients, several dozen books, and six international conferences on psychedelic drug therapy. It aroused the interest of many psychiatrists who were in no sense cultural rebels or especially radical in their attitudes. It was recommended for a wide variety of problems including alcoholism, obsessional neurosis, and childhood autism."

In 1960 a physician named Sidney Cohen surveyed the results of forty-four physicians who had conducted drug trials using 25,000 doses of LSD or mescaline with 5,000 subjects under widely varying conditions. Cohen found "no instance of serious or prolonged physical side effects" or any evidence of addictive potential in either those 25,000 sessions or in the wider literature on psychedelic drug studies. He did find adverse psychological reactions, but they were rare, and mostly related to preexisting mental illnesses.

"Considering the enormous scope of the psychic responses it induces," Cohen concluded, "LSD is an astonishingly safe drug."

As recreational use exploded, accompanied by the barrage of increasingly frequent headlines, almost twenty years of promising clinical experience all but vanished from view. In the spring of 1966, conservative Democratic senator Thomas Dodd, chairman of the Senate subcommittee on juvenile delinquency, convened emergency hearings on the acid threat. In a clear reference to Leary and his followers, Dodd dismissed "the pseudo-intellectuals who advocate the use of drugs in search for some imaginary freedoms of the mind and in search for higher psychic experiences." He urged sweeping laws to prevent the spread of the LSD scourge, which he claimed was literally driving America's youth mad and turning them into violent criminals.

Even the prospect of raving rapists and instant maniacs couldn't completely account for the fear that drove the anti-psychedelic tide. Behind the frightening and memorable specifics of bad trips loomed a more profound unease. The release of LSD into the public consciousness coincided suggestively with widening fault lines of a culture that would soon be at war with itself. Feminism, environmentalism, anti-militarism, anticorporatism, secularism, and the civil rights movement all underlined a growing discontent with the status quo, a status quo most notably guarded by a white, male elite. It was paranoid to imagine that the spread of LSD had actually caused any of the above. But the powers that be were in a paranoid mood. Besides, it was hard to avoid seeing a connection. The LSD experience intrinsically challenged the rationalist, materialist underpinnings of Western culture. Images of orgiastic dancing, flamboyant clothing, and pulsing light shows at the acid test parties all presented a highly visible challenge to bedrock values and mores. It didn't help that Tim Leary, now acid's most visible acolyte, was talking about a new LSD-based religion and urging millions of young people to turn on and drop out of traditional society.

Even Cohen, after concluding that LSD was "astonishingly safe" in clinical use, grew alarmed by its proliferation among young people. Called to testify before Congress, he said, "We have seen something which is more alarming than death in a way, and that is the loss of all cultural values, the loss of feeling of right and wrong, of good and bad. These people lead a valueless life, without motivation, without any ambition. . . . They are deculturated, lost to society, lost to themselves."

A lonely voice questioning Dodd's crusade came from a surprising source, a former U.S. attorney general and first-term senator from New York, Robert Kennedy. Many published accounts have claimed, always vaguely sourced, that Kennedy's wife, Ethel, had experienced LSD therapy, with positive results. True or not, Kennedy grew testy when he discovered that LSD research programs were all being shut down.

"I think we have given too much emphasis and so much attention to the fact that it can be dangerous and that it can hurt an individual who uses it . . . that perhaps to some extent we have lost sight of the fact that it can be very, very helpful in our society if used properly," he said, adding that he feared "FDA interference with the scientific investigation of so promising a drug as LSD."

But Kennedy's marquee value could not begin to stem the anti-LSD tide.

Not wanting any part of the white-hot controversy, Sandoz ceased distribution of LSD. (A half century later, the listing of achievements on a web page dedicated to Sandoz history includes the discovery of penicillin that could be taken orally but makes no mention of Albert Hofmann's invention.) The FDA and the National Institute of Mental Health completed the shutdown of the sixty-some ongoing clinical studies of psychedelics. In the fall of 1968, Congress made possession of LSD a criminal offense, and in 1970 psychedelic drugs were placed in the most restrictive legal category, Schedule I of the new Controlled Substances Act, reserved for drugs of abuse that had no accepted medical purpose.

The new laws made any further medical research with LSD or any other known psychedelic all but impossible. The stigma attached to any researcher expressing an interest in doing psychedelic research finished the job, and what had been the most active area of psychiatric research ceased to exist. As one prominent researcher put it, "It was as if psychedelic drugs had become undiscovered."

Of course, seventeen-year-old high school senior Rick Doblin, whose discovery of the shocking truth behind *One Flew Over the Cuckoo's Nest* happened at precisely the moment that LSD was placed on Schedule I, knew nothing of all this. What he knew was that "acid kills" and turned normal people into violent, raging lunatics. He'd been exposed to all the same cultural clues as Jeffrey MacDonald, who, on February 17, 1970, bludgeoned and stabbed his pregnant wife and two young children to death with a board and an ice pick. To deflect guilt from himself, MacDonald came up with what he thought would be a convincing myth: He said that a group of stoned hippies had invaded his home and murdered his family while holding candles and chanting, *"Acid is groovy. Kill the pigs."*

Rick had undoubtedly seen the "Killers Chanted Acid Is Groovy" headlines at the time of the crime, before MacDonald's story fell apart. He would have had no reason to disbelieve them. But now a revealed literary truth began working on him. A great work of art, and the story of its inspiration, had planted a seed inside him that would soon sprout and change the course of not only his life but the history of psychedelic drugs.

7.

NICHOLAS

(TIRES, GRILLE, KILL)

I t occurred to Nick, after the intensity of boot camp and the brief elation of graduation were behind him, that becoming a Marine might not have been such a great idea after all. More or less randomly assigned a role, he found himself at the School of Infantry at Camp Geiger, in Jacksonville, North Carolina, trying to qualify as a machine gunner. He did love the firepower. The M240G spewed bullets at intoxicating speed, and the .50-cal bullets could blast through concrete walls.

But it wasn't so much fun sitting cross-legged in the snow in stinging 7°F windchill, trying to absorb the powerful kick of the 26-pound machine gun in his 150-pound frame. As he held down his frozen finger on the trigger, repeating the mantra they taught him to time the proper number of rounds to fire at any threat, *"Die, motherfucker, die,"* his teeth chattered so hard he was afraid they might break. He couldn't help but wonder what the kids he knew from high school were doing. While he struggled to contain the rocking gun, making fine adjustments in aim with his frozen hands, they were in college, dating, and partying.

When the guns had run through all their ammunition, Nick unfolded himself with difficulty and began to walk off the firing line.

"I *said* GET OFF THE LINE!" the instructor screamed behind

him. Nick looked back and saw one of the trainees literally frozen at his gun. He and another Marine hurried back, grabbed the frozen man under his armpits, and lifted. He came up off the frigid ground, his legs still locked in the pretzel shape. As they carried him off, his legs slowly unbent and his body began to shake. Nick looked around: no shelter, not even a windbreak. Nick and the other Marine let the shivering man down, then pressed their bodies against his, one in front and one at his back, as Nick had seen penguins doing in some nature documentary, hoping to provide the warmth that would keep him from hypothermic shock. A miserable situation all around, but just the beginning of many more miserable ones, he was realizing.

It was hard not to think these thoughts, as all around him his fellow infantry trainees spoke a language consisting almost exclusively of gripes. In that dyspeptic fog, it was easy for Nick to come to the conclusion that his reward for fighting for others' freedoms would be that his own had been completely stripped away. He felt like he was in lockup, a weapon-firing machine with no room for humanity.

Nick kept struggling. On one of their many "humps"—a forced night march of three, five, or ten miles with full packs and gear—when it came time for Nick to carry his heavy machine gun up those hills, at some point he realized he wasn't going to make it. He was carrying the gun above his shoulders, one hand on each end, and his arms felt as if they were about to break off. He said nothing, but the Marine next to him, a guy named Brian Floyd, noticed.

"Here, let me get that off of you," Floyd said.

"I just need a little rest," Nick said. "I'll take it back when we get to the road."

Dizzy with gratitude and relief, Nick studied Floyd's face as they continued. His dark skin almost disappeared into the night, but his smile flashed white when Nick thanked him over and over. Or was that a grimace?

In boot camp, Floyd, who had wanted to be a Marine since he was twelve years old, had been on the deck below Nick's in the barracks—that's what Marines called floors: the second floor to Nick's third. Nick didn't think they'd ever talked. It was only by chance they were both assigned to become machine gunners and wound up in the same infantry school class.

Floyd wasn't only risking fatigue by helping Nick out. You were only supposed to trade off on the M240G when the instructors told you to change. But it was dark enough that Nick could hand off the big gun in exchange for Floyd's rifle without the instructors noticing. By the time they got out to the road, they'd been forced to spread out, so Nick couldn't keep his promise to take it back.

Nick half expected Floyd to resent him for that, so he was almost shocked when, with a weekend leave coming up, Floyd approached him and said he was going home to Fayetteville and asked if Nick wanted to come with him.

From the moment they set out for North Carolina, the two of them clicked, as if they'd known each other all their lives. It was a lucky coincidence that when infantry school ended, they happened to both be assigned to the 1st Battalion, 6th Marines, a storied infantry unit with a history of heavy combat.

In World War I, the 1/6 fought in the biggest battles in France, one of only two American units to earn the French Croix de Guerre three times. It also took part in some of the deadliest battles of World War II, island-hopping in the Pacific. In separate incidents, two 1/6 Marines saved comrades by throwing themselves on live grenades, earning post-humous Medals of Honor.

Nick and Floyd were attached to a mobilized assault platoon of up-armored Humvees. They would be the guys riding exposed in the turret, the vehicle's first defense and its major firepower. When they joined the 1/6 at Camp Lejeune, North Carolina, in the winter of

2005, the unit had recently returned from a tour in Afghanistan. Nick, just eighteen, encountered a weary group of battle-hardened men, and the first thing they told him was to forget everything he'd learned in the battle simulations. Real combat, they told the new men, made the simulations look like Ultimate Frisbee. Then they told them to clean the barracks.

Nick didn't mind being hazed. He saw it as mental preparation for going to war, which they would do in short order. Within a month of his arrival, the unit got orders to Iraq, to the city of Fallujah, scene of what had been to that point the largest battle of the war. He'd seen some of the hottest action on TV during infantry school, in no small measure featuring machine gunners blasting away from their Humvee turrets in narrow urban alleys. *Oh, man,* Nick thought, *that's the stuff we're getting into!* He was nervous and excited at the same time. Soon he'd be kicking ass and taking names, just what he'd always imagined.

But before he shipped overseas for the real thing, Nick's unit flew to California, where they engaged in combat simulations. One simulated mission took place in an area of abandoned base housing. The houses were falling apart, their windows boarded or broken out. The mission was to simulate a "strong point" position in which Nick and his comrades were supposed to secure an area and protect a perimeter.

Nick and a guy named Pool were standing in the back of a truck, a high-back Humvee, steadying their elbows on the roof as they covered the ground in front of them with their rifles, loaded with blanks for this pretend war. A corporal had gotten down off the truck and was on foot in front of the Humvee. They were all watching a car a few hundred feet down the road. It backed up, came forward, turned left, turned right— suspicious, to say the least. "If that thing comes at us, be ready," the staff sergeant told them. "Tires, grille, kill." If an unidentified car came at your position and didn't heed commands to stop, you shot out the tires first, then fired at the grille to kill the engine. Only then, if it still kept coming, did you raise your sights to the windshield and blow away the driver before he could conceivably drive a car bomb right into you.

Even though it was only a simulation, Nick felt an adrenaline surge, at once excited and anxious not to blow his assignment. He thumbed off his safety and allowed his finger to rest on the trigger, already breaking two key weapons rules right there. The car came around again, the faint chug of its engine the only sound above their breathing. Nick heard a gun bark. *His gun.* He watched in horror as a shell ejected from the breach of his rifle, arced lazily through the air, then landed on the canvas roof, skidding, stopping, rolling back toward the depressions made by Nick's elbows.

"Who the fuck was that?" the staff sergeant screamed. Pool sheepishly pointed in Nick's direction. Nick raised his hand.

"We'll deal with that later," the sergeant hissed acidly.

Later turned out to be Nick in the push-up position, the sergeant kneeling beside him, bending his trigger finger back until Nick felt sure it would break. As he ripped off reps through the pain, the sergeant screamed, "Do you know how serious this is? You do that in combat and a real bullet hits someone, your ass is grass! You could have killed your own man!"

When the physical punishment ended, they made him write a mock letter to the parents of the corporal who had been assigned to stop the car at the checkpoint, apologizing for accidentally blowing their son away.

Nick thought he'd been let off easy with the push-ups and the twisted finger. When he saw his deployment orders, he knew instantly they were his real punishment: he had been separated from Floyd and the rest of his platoon and assigned to the guard force, a kind of deployment-long KP consisting of manning the guard towers on base while his bud Floyd and the rest of the guys rode out into Fallujah and did what Marines were supposed to do.

8.

RICK

(HIDDEN REALMS)

One day in 1959, six-year-old Rick Doblin's parents explained to him that the world at large did not mimic the heavily Jewish enclave of Skokie, Illinois, he had been born into. As far as Rick knew, Judaism was a universal religion. The revelation that out of one hundred people in America only one or two would be Jewish horrified him. His concern was not so much the obvious—discovering he belonged to a tiny minority. It was the broader philosophical implication: What if everyone else had it right and the only path to salvation was Jesus?

You didn't run into a lot of kids like Rick Doblin in the 1950s American Midwest. Or anywhere.

A smallish, well-proportioned boy, he had tight brown curls and the concerns of a forty-year-old. Part of his precocious nature could be explained by the recent history of his family. His mother's grandfather had emigrated from Chicago to Palestine in 1923 and become a leader in the fight for a Jewish state, often at odds with the governing British Protectorate. His father's father had come to America from Poland in his teens to avoid being forced into the Polish army. The relatives who stayed behind died in concentration camps during World War II. His father, a pediatrician and a voracious reader, approached life with the cool rationality of a scientist or a scholar. Both his parents were liberal, politically active intellectuals who blamed irrational hatreds for the manifest evils of the world.

So, from the beginning, Rick was predisposed to be serious. When all his peers jumped up and down for the mop-headed quartet from Liverpool, Rick rolled his eyes. Even the group's name was stupid. Why should anyone want to listen to a bunch of insects? And the lyrics—just silly love songs. Nor could he share his classmates' passion for cars, which to him were merely a way to get from one place to another; or football—overgrown morons running around, slamming into one another. Trivialities, a distraction from the momentous events transpiring in the world.

Even in 1964, still just ten, Rick felt the weighty issues of the day personally. He became enchanted with an amazing new technology: you could call a phone number and automatically get connected to a recorded message. The message changed every couple of weeks, but it was always serious stuff of a political nature, which appealed to Rick. The automated message was called Let Freedom Ring, sponsored by the ultraconservative John Birch Society, but Rick didn't know that, or how his intensely liberal parents would feel about it. He called every couple of weeks and listened to the new messages, which were stridently anticommunist and remarkably paranoid, but the speakers seemed so sure of themselves. One of the messages promoted a book called *A Choice Not an Echo* by a John Bircher named Phyllis Schlafly, who would soon become famous for opposing the feminist movement. Rick read the book, which was basically a political tract for Barry Goldwater's 1964 presidential campaign. Schlafly had a lot of unpleasant things to say about Lyndon Johnson and made much of allegations that migrant workers were being exploited on Johnson's Texas ranch. Johnson sounded awful, and Rick was against exploiting migrant workers. He taped a Goldwater poster in the front window of their house, embarrassing his parents profoundly. The fact that they let the poster stay in the window, at least for a little while, said a lot about their parenting style. Rick's embrace of ultraconservatism would be short-lived, but he would find other ways to test his parents' tolerance in the years to come.

Rick was eager to grow up—not so he could drink, date, or drive, but in order to get about the business of changing the world. He was bitterly disappointed after his bar mitzvah when he discovered that the rabbi's declaration that he had become a man failed to actually make him one. He woke the morning after the ceremony the same serious, constricted, overintellectualized kid he'd always been and feared he always would be.

But he had changed, politically at least. By 1968 he'd swung from the far right to the far left. He volunteered to work for Eugene Mc-Carthy, a leftist Democrat campaigning on an antiwar platform in his hawkish, heavily Republican neighborhood. But Rick once again threw himself into it. All of fourteen, he became McCarthy's precinct captain. When the campaign crashed and burned, Rick wasn't ready to go home. He flipped to the other side and wangled an appointment as a messenger for Chicago mayor Richard Daley at the Democratic National Convention. He put on his red, white, and blue page's uniform, ready to run around handing messages to delegates. As he arrived at the International Amphitheater on Chicago's south side, he had to present his credentials in order to pass through a perimeter strung with barbed wire. He didn't think much about it until the third day of the convention. That evening he passed by the media room. Inside, television screens were tuned to live footage of riot-gear–clad police plunging into crowds and beating screaming demonstrators with batons. As he turned from the nightmarish images on the screen—the police pumping their batons, the demonstrators chanting *"The whole world is watching"*—he saw that the men inside the convention hall, wearing suits with flag lapel pins, were chatting and laughing as if nothing at all were transpiring beyond the flesh-tearing wire. Suddenly Rick saw the seeds of the same cultural insanity that had convulsed Europe.

By now, of course, Rick's precocious political passions had become fashionable. The war, continuously escalating and demanding ever more American soldiers, concerned *anyone* soon to turn eighteen in an intensely personal way.

But despite this ideological convergence, Rick remained apart from his peers. His shyness around girls bordered on pathological; he could barely bring himself to speak in their presence. He had no patience for the team sports that could have made him part of the herd. But he found himself obsessed with the solo sport of handball. Its limits were its virtues: no screaming, no spitting coaches, no teammates, no fans.

It also happened to be the sport that all the football players and other big jocks played to keep in shape in the off-season. Rick, though smaller and less physically gifted than his opponents, discovered talents he hadn't realized he possessed: single-minded focus and a fierce drive. He became the school handball champion, grew lean and muscled. Still, his separation persisted.

Which was just as well. Rick had a vision of the past and future, and his place in it, that few peers could match or even relate to. It began with his grandfather, with whom Rick had always been close. Nathan Perlman had inherited a small company from his father and turned it into a big company that employed as many as five hundred people. The prosaic product, metal stampings used in the assembly of furniture, created a sizable fortune. When Rick turned twenty-one, he, like the other nine grandkids, would inherit a nice chunk of it. Rick saw it as a kind of destiny: he felt at the end point of a multigenerational process. His grandparents and great-grandparents had been immigrants whose sole preoccupation was survival. The next generation flourished in America, assimilated, established themselves. His parents, secure and anchored, gave him the sense they could and would support him in whatever he chose to do. The preceding generations' hard work had put him in a position to think grandly and aim at finding ways to fight the next level of threats: cultural insanity, hatred of Jews, murderous instincts in general, nuclear destruction. In dedicating his life to that goal, he could become worthy of his advantages.

In high school, Rick assigned himself a course of readings on an individual's moral obligation to oppose unjust authority. He pondered Tolstoy, Thoreau, and Gandhi, which led him to confront what he would do about Vietnam.

He couldn't claim to be a conscientious objector. He wasn't opposed to all wars—certainly not the war against the Nazis or the Israeli struggle to survive amidst hostile neighbors. Which meant that, to resist *this* war, he would have to put his own freedom on the line by refusing to register for the draft, which was a crime. He figured the system would catch up with him eventually and he'd wind up in jail. But that would take some time, time he intended to use.

Rick enrolled in a tiny, nontraditional private liberal arts college in the beach resort town of Sarasota, on Florida's Gulf Coast. A brochure had arrived at his home, sent to students who'd achieved high scores on standardized tests. True to its name, New College was less than a decade old, conceived by a group of progressive educators, artists, and professionals at striking odds with the overall conservative nature of Sarasota County. Built on 110 spectacular acres along Sarasota Bay, the college stretched from the bay across US 41 to the perimeter of the Sarasota airport. The land had been part of the former estate of circus magnate Charles Ringling, and some of the school's buildings had originally been 1920s mansions. The palms and the sparkling water might appeal to anyone, but the avant-garde academic philosophy had a special lure for Rick. The founders believed the students' own curiosity should be the driving force in their education, without the encumbrance of formal requirements, standard courses, or concern about grade point average. Just the thing for a young man on an idiosyncratic, grandiose, and as yet undefined mission.

When Rick arrived at the campus of only a few hundred students, it didn't take him long to recognize that the wild experimentation went far beyond the classroom. The campus, designed by I. M. Pei, centered on the Palm Court, a plaza studded with a grove of stately royal palms, the smooth gray trunks rising straight as power poles, elevating heavy emerald fronds that rustled in the breeze overhead. A twenty-five-meter swimming pool tucked into a far corner of the grounds beckoned, the center of a kind of student lifestyle Rick could never have invented in his most fervid adolescent imaginings.

It only took a day or two for Rick to follow the gleeful shouts and splashing to the pool, where he beheld an acre of shining wet flesh, bouncing breasts, bulging buttocks, dark triangles of pubic hair, and pink nipples. A kid who couldn't summon the nerve to talk to girls back home had been plopped down in the middle of a year-round sun-kissed, carefree nudist colony populated by nubile twenty-year-olds romping like sleek-skinned seals.

Rick had most definitely not seen this in the brochure.

There was more.

After the sun set, spectacularly, in an explosion of roseate light over the Gulf of Mexico, the frolic continued in dance parties that stretched until dawn. A not-inconsequential percentage of the dancers were tripping on LSD.

Despite his eye-opening encounter with *One Flew Over the Cuckoo's Nest*, Rick had not quite relinquished the fear that taking LSD could eat away his brain. But these dancing waifs by the pool in Sarasota were fearless, not only unafraid of the drug itself but of the consequences of doing it openly. The campus police force did not concern them. In fact, the college cops were regarded as protectors, totally on their side. It seemed to the students that the whole purpose of campus institutions was to insulate them from real-world consequences, to allow them to experiment freely not only academically but socially, psychologically, and chemically.

So Rick gave it a try. He took the acid with a friend on a Saturday afternoon a few weeks into his freshman year. As the drug took effect, waves of something powerful swept him away. Trees breathed and furniture had an attitude. The sky throbbed. A thriving, heaving universe seethed around him. It was scary but also fascinating; all the markers of normality had jumbled into calamitous confusion, but paradoxically some things gained remarkable clarity. Looking at his companion, Rick believed he saw not just the physical attributes of the outer person but the inner qualities as well. Not deduced them. *Saw* them. His friend, relaxed, open to experience and emotion, comfortable in his skin, approached life with a light heart.

All of which contrasted with the vision LSD gave Rick of himself. He couldn't grasp exactly how, but the drug effects, while confusing, seemed to lift him out of the ruts of his normal mind-set, allowing him to see himself as if from a distance. What he saw was a boy still trying to become a man, cut off from his emotions and other people, overdeveloped intellectually and underdeveloped emotionally, fearful of losing control. As disquieting as this vision was, it told him something transformational: he had made himself who he was, and with the assistance of the LSD experience he could change—the change he'd been searching for ever since the day of his bar mitzvah.

After a few hours, when the peak of the experience passed, Rick remembered that it was Saturday evening, steak night at the Hamilton Center, the student dining hall. Even in his still-altered condition, the concept of steak night exerted a powerful lure. He set out from his dorm room and began the short walk. He became acutely aware of the complex mechanics of the human stride, the right heel striking down, the left leg driving forward, the balance tipping to the right toe, which lifted as the left heel struck earth and the process was repeated. And repeated. And repeated. And repeated. Time disappeared, or it got stuck. The act of walking engulfed him in an eternity of motion.

Then he found himself entering Hamilton Center. The familiar surroundings—the tables, the chairs, the buffet counter, the tray he held in his hand—had become an alien landscape, the usually lifeless objects squirming with animation. Perhaps he wasn't as far past the peak as he had imagined. It took focus and concentration just to stand in line, the conventions of a lifetime suddenly a complex code he could only guess at. A slab of steak appeared on his tray, a seared, bloody hunk of mammalian muscle tissue.

What am I doing here?

He managed to find a seat and even sawed off a piece of muscle and put it in his mouth. As his tongue touched the meat he thought, *What do I do now?* Chewing and swallowing was clearly beyond him. He spit the steak into a napkin and fled the hall.

When he calmed down, he realized that his body had known he wasn't hungry even if his mind hadn't, a reminder of all the things we do mindlessly, by rote, in our normal consciousness. The realization calmed him, and now the LSD-induced effects really were waning. The riot all about him began to dissipate. Normalcy reappeared on the horizon, a spot that grew larger as it got nearer, until it absorbed him once more.

Except things didn't go back quite the way they had been. They couldn't, not now that Rick knew this overwhelming experience of another kind of reality was just a swallow away. His acid trip hadn't been totally easy or pleasant. Some of it still troubled him. But in retrospect, he decided, the bad moments had all come when he had resisted the dissolution of the world as he knew it, when he'd desperately tried to keep control, in the usual sense of steering in the familiar ruts. He felt if he could just relax next time, go where the winds from that other world were trying to blow him, something important would happen. In the vibrant, animated universe he'd inhabited for just a few timeless hours, he believed he'd glimpsed a richness and range of emotion he'd been missing his entire life.

His experience humbled him. He'd been swept up in that late-sixties idea of a new generation rising, so certain of its superiority, calling bullshit on the corporate manipulators, the profiteers, the war makers. Now, late in 1971, the revolution, such as it was, had been beaten back. Richard Nixon had embarked on a campaign of clandestine abuses of power to keep it that way, declaring Timothy Leary "the most dangerous man in America" even as he unleashed an invasion of Cambodia and prepared an indiscriminate bombing campaign against North Vietnam. The youth movement had risen in protest, not just against the war, but, as Rick saw it, against all the exploitative and predatory tendencies of a culture overly concerned with material comforts and bent on domination of its environment and its rivals. But the larger culture had swallowed this rebellion whole, perverting principles into mere fashion and action into catchwords. Much of the blame for that failure, Rick felt, belonged to the movement's young leaders, who believed their outrage and a few acid trips qualified them to run the world. Their arrogance had sown the seeds of the movement's own destruction.

If Rick or anyone else intended to change the world, they would have to change themselves first, to find the tendrils of their culture's self-destructiveness deep inside and root them out. Or as he thought of it: "You can't create paradise with all these conflicts inside of you."

That Rick saw himself as one of these would-be paradise creators, even though he was just a random freshman at a virtually unknown college, is an indication of how seriously he took his self-assigned mission of saving the world from future Holocausts. And because he took it seriously, he took his LSD experience seriously. LSD had shown him his profound imperfections and offered a tool he believed could potentially help him work them out. But he bumped into a paradox. The very tool he felt certain could help defuse his faults actually triggered them.

On his second LSD trip, once again he thrilled to the vividness of the colors, the animation of objects normally perceived as inanimate, the unfamiliar intensity of sensations and emotions. And once again, just as he connected with this riotous, roiling reality and the border between Him and It began to disappear, he realized that with expansion came dissolution. If even the few steps from one side of his dorm room to the other had become an almost unbridgeable chasm, how could he hope to find his way back to his familiar self, the Rick he was *supposed* to be, the bright boy who carried his parents' dreams? He panicked, seized up, fell into a defensive crouch, then held on miserably, afraid the drug's grip would never loosen, hating himself for being a coward.

"So then I decided, *Okay, I need to do that again.* But what kept happening was that I would get stuck at earlier points in the trip; it would be like the same theme," Rick says, the memory of the frustration still vivid forty years later. He could see the path ahead— diminished ego, more openness, and increased empathy, the ability to see eternity in the now and lose his fear of death. He could visualize what he needed and what he felt the world needed. He just couldn't get there. Time and again the fear would win out and Rick would swirl into a sink of self-loathing: "I was bad. I was weak. I was unable to do the work that needed to be done."

Instead of getting easier, with each trip he hit the wall sooner and harder. "It went from, like, six hours to five hours, from five hours to four hours to two hours, and then I would just have to be holding on because the LSD was still going but I couldn't let go and I would just feel a total failure.

"One time I hit this block really early on and there was so much stress and tension that I kind of felt like my brain was heating up. And then I started feeling like it was dissolving my brain. I had this image of how my brain was sort of seeping out. And it turned out I had a slight cold, so I had like this nasal drip, but I convinced myself that it was melted brain. And part of me didn't believe it, but part of me was scared of it, that that was really happening."

His worst fear from high school Russian class was manifesting itself: acid dissolves your brain. Still, he kept at it, convinced that the fault was in him, not the experience.

In the anomalous bubble in time and space called New College in 1971, finding the drugs to continue his pursuit presented no difficulties. They seemed to flow in with the tide of Sarasota Bay, enough to fuel the all-night dance parties and nude lounging at the pool and all the self-exploration Rick could handle. Some guy he barely knew came by with half a pound of synthetic mescaline, enough for 400 to 500 doses. Rick bought it all. He left the capsules in the sock and underwear drawer in his dorm room. When people approached him on campus to ask if they could buy some, Rick would say, "I'm on my way to class, but just go into my dorm room, take as many as you want." They'd rummage through Rick's unmentionables, take the mescaline, leave the money, and it all felt natural, even virtuous. Not once did anyone so much as shortchange him.

Less than halfway through his freshman year, Rick had discovered the exhilaration of merging with others at the all-night parties. Reaching a dreamlike exhaustion as the sun rose, the revelers would dive in the pool, fracturing the dawn reflected in its mirrored surface, then eat breakfast as the breeze rose from the bay to rustle the fronds of the Palm Court.

After the LSD wore down, Rick quickly recovered physically, but the emotional turmoil persisted. He lost interest in his studies. A psychology class caught his interest, but beyond his vague notion of saving civilization from itself, he still had no idea how he would direct his energies or what he wanted to do. He felt muddled and confused, as if he urgently needed to be somewhere else and do something else. But what?

Rick went to the guidance office. The counselor was a guy Rick judged to be in his thirties, conservatively dressed but with a calm, accepting demeanor.

"I'm on the verge of dropping out," Rick told him. "I'm not sure really how to handle these LSD experiences I've been having, but I think that they're important."

The counselor didn't try to dispute him. In fact, he seemed to agree. First he gave Rick a piece of string and told him to tie it around his finger. All this psychic exploration is a worthy pursuit, he told him. But you still have to live in the mundane world, take care of business, put one foot in front of another. Every time you look at this string or feel it, it will remind you to stay grounded.

Then he handed Rick a thick manuscript, a book not yet published, called *Realms of the Human Unconscious: Observations from LSD Research*, by a Czech psychiatrist named Stanislav Grof.

9.

NICHOLAS

(DREAMLAND)

Prior to the war, Camp Baharia, just outside Fallujah and about forty miles west of Baghdad, had been operated as a Baath Party resort, an opulent oasis fortress where Saddam's cruel and corrupt sons, Qusay Hussein and Uday Hussein, would often stay. By the time Nick landed there, not much remained of the opulence. A handful of palms and some nondescript shrubs dotted the shoreline of a lake where the Baathists once pedaled paddleboats. The blue water shocked an otherwise colorless world of dun walls, gray canvas, rusting metal, and pale desert. Scattered hulks of amusement park rides rusted into the sand alongside the broken-down kennels Nick suspected of having had other uses beyond housing dogs. You don't need guard towers for dogs, and the camp was surrounded by towers. These were where Nick had been condemned to spend much of his tour, at least eight hours a day. When he finally got relieved from guard duty, Camp Baharia was a creepy place to lay your head, thinking of what went on there when the Hussein boys had free rein, and what was going on now, in the off-limits quadrant of the base that always seemed to be emitting a stream of black helicopters and blacker SUVs. The Marines nicknamed the base "Dreamland."

Dreamland was a flat, dusty, hot patch of sand behind eleven-foot-high concrete walls, surrounded by a hot and even dustier desert. A huge junkyard of burned-out cars and ruined military equipment was the only point of visual interest beyond the walls. From up in the bullet-pocked tower, furnished with a white molded plastic chair and a metal desk that grew hot to the touch on 120°F afternoons, he oversaw an apocalyptic landscape as the sun beat him senseless and raging swarms of biting flies they called "filth flies" for good reason appeared determined to pick every last ounce of meat off his bones.

At first Nick survived by using his talent for floating away in his mind, staring into the desert until it all disappeared. He lost even that refuge one morning in tower two. As the sun rose, Nick was doing his normal staring into the desert when he and his watch partner heard the battered metal stairs creaking. Their relief, a Hispanic guy named Roland, appeared at the top. Nick glanced down the two flights of spiral stairs behind Roland. Empty.

"Are they only going to put one guy in here?" he asked, surprised.

Apparently they were. Nick shook his head. "Good luck to you, then," he said. Sarcastic. He headed back to the barracks, grabbed a shower. When he came out, everyone was running to the vehicles. Nick sprinted to catch up with one of his friends and tug his arm.

"What happened?"

As the friend turned, Nick saw the shocked look. "Oh, man," his friend said, "someone got sniped in tower two. I thought it was you."

Nick would discover that his replacement, Roland, had barely had time to do his inspection of the gun and was writing in the logbook when a sniper opened fire and hit him in the arm. Nick was relieved to learn Roland would recover but felt guilty about his sarcastic comment, as if somehow that had brought on the attack. He also realized that the sniper must have had him in his sights all along, just waiting for the sun to rise higher before taking a shot.

After that, Nick couldn't let his mind wander while up in the tower, at least not in daylight. He just had to sit there, sweating in his suffocating flak jacket, his only comfort sips from plastic bottles of water that were at best lukewarm and at worst like something out of a microwave. One time a private on guard duty snapped from the stress and slapped a lieutenant. Nick endured sixteen hours straight in the tower after that. The extra shift wasn't a punishment, he was told. Just necessary because of the staffing disruption.

When he finally climbed down from the tower, he was too exhausted to do anything but dread going back up. His off time wasted away until he had to ascend those spiral steps again. Inside his head, he kicked and screamed the whole way, but still he climbed.

Initially, Nick loved hearing the haunting, undulating call to prayer from the nearby mosques as the sun rose, but one morning as he was listening he thought, *Now they're going to pray to God to kill me, and I'm praying to God to kill them*. It started a chain reaction in his mind, a dead-end journey of theological futility. Standing in his guard tower, miserable, uncomfortable, bored, and aware that he could find himself at the end of a sniper's bullet at any second, his childhood faith came unmoored—began to seem, in fact, childish.

One of the towers overlooked a Marine checkpoint where locals came to seek compensation if their property got blown up. Iraqi police often hung out there, and they loved to fire their weapons. They'd shoot into the air, at stray dogs, at abandoned cars, whatever. The policemen were loud, undisciplined, obnoxious. Even Nick had to admit that these cops, his allies, made a tempting target. When, inevitably, one day they drew fire from snipers, they responded with what Nick and his mates called "the Iraqi death blossom," emptying their weapons at whatever was moving, in all directions, in an explosion of automatic-weapons fire. Nick had been out patrolling the perimeter of the base when his truck rolled up in the aftermath. A kid who had been playing in the street had dropped to the ground like a sack of mud. A man ran to the child, his scream telling Nick more than he wanted to know about loss. As the man plucked the now-still boy from the dirt and held him to his chest, blood flowed from the child's head, soaking the man's shirt. Nick had to catch himself: he was watching the tragedy unfold when he needed to be watching his sector. He forced his eyes away but he couldn't do the same with his thoughts.

He couldn't stop thinking about that kid, any kid, forced to live in that type of world.

Here he was near the supposed location of Eden, and instead of paradise he found himself in hell. And as part of the camp guard, he didn't even feel like a Marine, not as he'd imagined a Marine to be.

He could only stand at the gate as his old unit rolled up from a mission in the city, shadows of beards showing through the white dust that covered their faces and everything else, laughing and cursing and hollering about the firefights they'd been in. One day they rolled up more subdued than usual.

"Hey," Nick said, craning his head to find his machine gunner friend. "I haven't seen Floyd."

"He got hit," one of them said. Floyd's Humvee had been chasing an insurgent's vehicle into parts unknown, they told him, something you weren't supposed to do, and it led them into an ambush. A bomb blew up right in front of the Humvee, and Floyd, the most exposed, up in the turret where Nick was supposed to be, caught a piece of shrapnel in his helmet. His forehead shattered open like a cracked egg.

As Nick listened wordlessly, a searing heat rose from his gut and engulfed him in a wave of shame and grief mixed together.

"Is he alive?"

"They medevaced him out, but we don't think he made it."

Nick wandered off, hardly aware of where he was going or what he intended to do. One thought occupied his entire attention. He should have been with Floyd. He should have had Floyd's back when it counted, just as Floyd had always had his back. He was *supposed* to have been with him. He plucked whisks from a broom and lit them on fire, watched them burn down to points of glowing coal. Then one by one he plunged them into the soft underside of his arm, barely distinguishing the searing pain on his skin from that within him. He didn't stop until he'd burned an angry scar the shape of the omega symbol. The end of Floyd and the beginning of the end for him.

Actually, it looked more like a horseshoe than an omega, but he wouldn't know that until people began asking him if he was a Colts fan.

Nick mourned his friend for weeks until one day, waiting in line at the PX, he heard some guys mention Floyd. One of them said, "He's doing pretty good."

Say what?

It turned out that Floyd had flatlined for two minutes on the flight back to Bethesda. Medics brought him back to life in midair, but he stayed in a coma from the moment of the explosion until he woke up weeks later in the Walter Reed Army Medical Center intensive care facility. In multiple surgeries, doctors managed to put his cranium back together as handily as if they'd been working a jigsaw puzzle, filling in some missing pieces with titanium plate. Floyd not only woke up but regained all his faculties, physical and mental. It was something of a medical miracle, written up in the journals. President Bush stopped by to pose for pictures. The official Marines website did a story on the nineteen-year-old's recovery in which he said, "I'm hoping to do twenty years in the Corps, and maybe even more, because there's nothing else for me to do in this world."

Floyd was waiting when Nick got off the bus at Camp Lejeune in October 2005, nearly seven months after he'd left for Fallujah. Nick couldn't even see a scar until he got close: a line where they'd cut him open from ear to ear over the top of his head, and a dark burn mark on his forehead where shrapnel had cracked open his skull. Otherwise, you would never know he'd been so severely injured. Nick and Floyd went off to the nearest tattoo parlor to celebrate. Floyd got a new tat of an immortal dragon and Nick had his omega scar turned into a more proper tattoo, though the unfortunate resemblance to the Colts logo remained. And so did the depression, lingering around him in a black fog that refused to lift.

10.

RICK

(PERILOUS TERRAIN)

S tan Grof's book changed everything for Rick. It did more than change things: it connected them. Ever since God failed to show up for his bar mitzvah, Rick had had an aversion to religion. He'd actually believed in that transformation stuff, and when it didn't happen, it wounded him deeply. Now he didn't want to take anything on faith. He wanted to be able to see it, touch it, test it. If he had faith in anything, it was science—which didn't ask you to believe anything without hard evidence.

His LSD trips had rattled him in part because they had given him a brief flash of a world that appeared more spiritual than material, a conglomeration of weird energies and dream logic. The acid world made quick work of the rationality he'd prided himself on, and yet it seemed more real in some ways than familiar reality. Was he crazy? Whenever he pursued an answer to that puzzle, he became frightened and disturbed that he was headed down a path that led ever further into the thickets. How could he know, or trust, where it would ultimately take him?

Grof had an answer for both his questions. In administering LSD to himself and others on thousands of occasions, he'd recorded experiences that were crazier than anything Rick had encountered. He and his patients had reexperienced their own births, or traveled into space and witnessed the big bang, or relived human evolution. Telepathy, out-of-body experiences, precognition—all sorts of wildly unlikely phenomena. What Grof had concluded after fifteen years of research was that, real or surreal, ecstatic or terrifying, exhilarating or agonizing, the experiences were not created by LSD but uncovered by it—a preexisting territory of human awareness normally deeply hidden from conscious view, as essential or more essential to psychic healing than the childhood memories and traumas prized by Freudian psychotherapy. These fantastic acid visions, whatever their origin, appeared to be the key to a process by which human psyches explored their inner terrains, worked through their traumas, gained insight, and—with the reassuring, encouraging, gently guiding presence of a therapist—healed themselves.

Grof's insight wasn't just philosophy: it wasn't abstract; it had a built-in reality test, the string around the finger. Did an obsession release its grip? Did a depression resolve itself? Did a cancer patient find peace in the shadow of death? Ultimately, if the goal was healing, it didn't matter whether somebody really imagined or remembered life in the uterus or a flight to the stars. If those inner experiences helped people become happier, healthier, more alive, then they had provable worth.

For Rick, that reality testing was the saving grace.

But the revelations for Rick in Grof's work didn't end there.

The psychedelic experience, Grof concluded, not only produced healing but often led people to a certain view of the universe and their place in it, a set of values based on a direct perception that they were more than their identity as male or female, white or colored, Jewish, Muslim, Christian, Hindu, or Buddhist. If the mystical experience afforded by psychedelics allowed people to identify themselves not by ego or tribe or nation but as part of a universal life force shared by all, then it would follow that they would become less threatened by diversity, more tolerant, and better able to live together without trying to kill one another.

Imagine Rick as he turned the pages of the manuscript, seeing all his obsessions knit together as if by an unseen hand: his conviction that these arduous, devastating LSD trips were nonetheless important; that they could promote healing and self-improvement; that the self-improvement would lead to qualities and values that could change the world; that none of these claims had to be taken on faith. They could be tested through experimentation, observation, and, ultimately, hard clinical facts, in research labs and clinics.

It seemed too good to be true.

And it was, in a sense. There was a very big catch, which Rick realized with a devastating sense of loss: *I'm learning about it just as it's all being ended and all legal research is being shut down.*

Grof's studies seemed so compelling, Rick found it impossible to believe that complete abandonment of such promising research could actually happen. He imagined that thousands of people would be devoting themselves to bringing psychedelics back into the lab and the clinic. He knew then and there that he wanted to be one of those people.

He wrote Grof a letter asking about opportunities. In early 1972, Grof wrote back. There *were* no opportunities, he said. Psychedelic research was over. One or two ongoing projects would linger for a few years, but by 1976 the shutdown would be total.

It came to Rick that it all fit together like masonry stones in a giant wall blocking his path. LSD—the one thing he'd come to believe had the potential to heal himself and possibly even the world—had been criminalized, just as he had been by his refusal to participate in the military draft. Even his parents, who supported his antiwar views, had begged him to register, if only to avoid the criminal record that would mean he couldn't ever be a doctor or lawyer or work in some other high-status career, as they had always wanted for him.

Another wall circumscribing his future, shutting down his options.

But Rick was a handball player. He knew walls were obstacles but could also be opportunities if you played the angles, used caroms to your advantage.

The system had criminalized both LSD and Rick's draft resistance. So be it. Maybe the universe was acting with a purpose: the way he saw it, since he was already outside the law, he had nothing to lose by becoming an underground psychedelic therapist.

But before he could help heal anyone else, he decided, he needed to heal himself. He needed his own psychedelic therapy. Classes would only get in the way. He would do as Leary had suggested almost a decade earlier and drop out.

Fortunately for Rick, this was New College and it was 1972. The guidance counselor, the same one who had given him Grof's manuscript, recommended that, instead of dropping out, he take a leave of absence for the third term of the year. He even asked the college administration to grant permission for Rick to live on campus as a nonstudent so he would continue to be surrounded by supportive peers. Astoundingly, the request was granted.

Rick succinctly summarizes the situation this way: "I didn't have to go to classes but I could hang out with my friends and trip and explore."

As it turned out, despite the ease and the freedom, just tripping with his friends couldn't get him past his block. As before, the trips kept taking him to that dark place of self-loathing and despair. His persistent failure only made things worse. As the term ended, he decided to drop out for real, hitchhike to California, and learn more about psychedelic therapy from Stan Grof himself, who was offering a weeklong seminar in practicing LSD therapy. Rick would study with the master as he searched for a path around the roadblocks in his own psyche.

First he went home to Illinois and actually said some version of the following to his parents: *Mom, Dad, I want to drop out of college and go to California to study LSD, and I want you to pay for it.*

His parents, in the parlance of the time, freaked out. Here was the eldest of their four children, an exceptionally bright, motivated boy who they had dreamed would become a doctor or lawyer or scientist and do big things in the world. Now he hadn't even gotten through his first year of college, was doing lots of drugs that all the newspapers said would make him insane, and, as if to underline that fear, had come up with some crazy plan to make a career out of an illegal substance. And he wanted them to support him in this deluded effort.

So of course they were upset. An emotional confrontation ensued. They came as close to a breach between them as they ever had. They begged him to reconsider, but Rick insisted. He was going with or without their support. That's when his parents' surreal emotional calm, their cool rationality, and ultimately their apparently unconditional faith in their son turned things around.

Or, as Rick saw it: "That's where I got this lesson in what love can be from my parents. What my dad said is that he thought it was a mistake, but he thought that if they didn't help me I would stick with it longer just to prove that I was right and they were wrong."

11.

NICHOLAS

(AMERICAN DREAMS)

Beverlee Joann Appleby, eighteen, of Summerville, South Carolina, was as sweet and innocent as her name. She'd grown up an only child, adored by her mother and father, an imposing former naval master chief petty officer. Beverlee, a pretty, petite brunette with long, soft hair and a dazzling smile, had never lived away from home or even had a boyfriend.

But she wanted one.

She'd been a fan of the NBC series *American Dreams*, a family drama set in the Vietnam War era. More precisely, she was a fan of the character played by Will Estes, the teenage son JJ, a high school football hero who defies his father's wish for him to accept a college scholarship and joins the Marines. More precisely, she was a fan of the way Will Estes looked in a Marine uniform. The uniform shots were so beguiling that Beverlee managed to overlook the negatives: during the course of the series, JJ would go to Vietnam, get wounded, be captured by the enemy, then, when he finally made it back home, suffer from post-traumatic stress disorder.

"I got it in my head that I was gonna go for the perfect Marine because I wanted to be with a Marine. My dad was, like, 'Oh, brother, here we go.'"

Despite, or because of, her own marriage to a naval man, Beverlee's mom wasn't thrilled with the obsession either. "She always told me, 'Don't go for anyone in the military because it's only gonna be really difficult and a really hard relationship, and you don't want that.' And I said, 'Yes I do.' So I just got on Myspace and started looking for the perfect Marine."

In no time she was in deep Myspace conversation with a Marine named Andrew. They started chatting, became friends. Then a photo of one of Andrew's Marine buddies popped up on his Myspace page. Nicholas Blackston.

"I saw his picture, and I said, 'Oh, wow. This guy's really attractive,'" Beverlee says.

"And I read his Myspace page, and it made me laugh—I forgot what exactly he wrote but it was really funny. So I just decided to write him an email."

Nick was on leave back home in Paducah when Beverlee's message popped up. Nick had been self-medicating his lingering postdeployment depression by running around to as many parties as possible, drinking with old high school acquaintances, playing paintball. None of it made him feel much better. He just couldn't connect with his old life and his old friends. Then, out of nowhere, here was this young beauty—he checked out her photo on Myspace—reaching out to him through cyberspace. Not only that, she loved paintball! It had long been a fantasy for Nick—find a girl who'd enjoy playing paintball with him. She even joked about it. "I'd probably shoot you in the foot," she said. He loved that.

By the time Beverlee confessed that she didn't know a thing about paintball, or even given it a passing thought before she saw it on Nick's Myspace interests page, they were already fast cyber friends.

"You lied," Nick said.

"I didn't lie," Beverlee said. "I said that I find paintball very interesting and that I'd like to play sometime." Which, after she read that Nick "love, love, loved" paintball, was true. In any case, Nick leapt at the bait—a beautiful girl who expressed interest in paintball: What's not to like?—and that launched them into a long and voluminous email correspondence.

Nick had always found it easier to communicate with girls than boys, and the same held true now that they were women and men.

"We talked through emails for the longest time," Nick says. "Never in my life was I ever so open with somebody, and actually myself. We built a really good relationship through those emails. I was just trying my hardest to get her on the phone."

But that wasn't happening.

Beverlee thought her new Marine was perfection. She wanted nothing to ruin that. And she knew one thing that would ruin it instantly, a thing she had reason to fear, given that Nick's hometown was a place called Paducah.

"I can't stand country accents. I was afraid he'd have one."

Nick's leave ended and he returned to Camp Lejeune, just four and a half hours up the coastal highway from Summerville. When Beverlee finally relented and picked up the phone, she was relieved, ecstatic, to hear Nick had a standard vanilla accent, just like the TV newspeople. Now that they were actually speaking to each other, their connection grew even stronger.

Then another land mine: in one of their phone conversations, Beverlee casually mentioned Andrew, the Marine she'd originally contacted on Myspace. "Do you know him?" she asked.

Nick did. He told her Andrew was in his company.

"Oh, well, I'm friends with him," Beverlee said.

Nick's Marine alarm went off. He knew how Marines were,

especially after coming back from Iraq. He found Andrew and asked him if he "knew a Beverlee." Andrew enthusiastically said he did.

Oh, man, Nick thought. Obviously, Andrew had planted the flag first, and the Marine code in such matters, if unwritten, was clear. Nick had to back off. Instantly.

But the more Andrew talked about Beverlee, the more uneasy Nick felt. Andrew's interest in her . . . well, Nick concluded he had other things in mind besides building an actual relationship.

Still, the code. Nick had to relent.

Only he couldn't, not completely. He continued to send Beverlee texts and emails, although he didn't go as far as asking her out. Andrew did. As Nick puts it, "He jumped on the gun before I did. I think he realized what was going on."

Beverlee accepted Andrew's invitation. Nick thought she was trying to make him mad, or jealous, but Beverlee had a simpler reason.

"I was eighteen and had never had a boyfriend, and when Andrew asked me out, I said yes."

Now Nick seriously had to back off. So the first thing he did was call her. "If you're gonna be dating him—I work with this guy, and I'm gonna be going on another deployment with this guy, and we don't need that kind of drama going on," he said. They talked for the longest time.

But Nick wanted to mean what he said about backing off. So when Andrew approached him and said, "I'm going down to Summerville this weekend. Do you want to go down there with me and go surfing?" Nick knew he probably should say no. But he longed to meet Beverlee in person. So he went along. When they drove up to her house and got out together, Beverlee came running out the door and ran right past Andrew into Nick's arms.

Andrew gave him a look, like, "What's up here?"

They all went out to Outback Steakhouse together, and Beverlee brought along a friend, theoretically for Nick. But the friend intuited what was going on between Beverlee and Nick; it wasn't difficult to see. When Andrew went to the bathroom, she said, "I'm gonna leave you two alone," and left the table.

That gave them the chance to admit their feelings to each other and agree that they'd gotten themselves into an awkward situation.

Then Andrew and Bev's friend returned to the table and the charade continued.

After a long, mostly silent drive back to the base with Andrew, Nick called Beverlee.

"Look, we can't do this. If you're gonna be with him, you're gonna be with him, and that's that."

As soon as he hung up, Beverlee called Andrew and told him she couldn't go out with him again.

"The next weekend, I ended up going down to visit her," Nick says. "This was in December. I'm always fast about things, and I had an idea in my head that I was going to ask her what she wanted for Christmas, and she was going to be, like, 'I don't know, what do you want?' And I'd be, like, 'I want you.' And I had it all planned out, so I asked her, 'What do you want for Christmas?' She goes, 'I want you.' It just ruined my plans. But it was really awesome."

They were a couple from that moment on.

12.

RICK

(PEAK EXPERIENCES)

As Rick hitchhiked across America on the way to Stan Grof's workshop, he saw a sign for something called a "Rainbow Gathering" to be held in Granby, Colorado. He had no idea what it was, but it was a moment in time when the nature of the script and images on a hand-lettered poster could communicate a great deal. And what the trippy lettering and radiating colors communicated to Rick was a sense of a psychedelic consciousness rising from the Great Plains. As he made his way toward Colorado one ride at a time—from pickup truck to aging sedan to broken-down VW bus—he sensed the seemingly flat highways gaining elevation with every mile.

When the last ride let him off in Granby, Rick hiked to the gathering spot in the surrounding mountains and found himself in a ragtag tent city with thousands of mostly young people talking about peace and brotherhood and enlightenment. Mostly, though, it was a bunch of longhairs running around naked, garnished by the conspicuous presence of some Native Americans and free food, and punctuated by an ominous minor chord. As the throng gloried in imagined innocence, dancing bare-skinned in the wilderness, the improvised music collapsed beneath the THUMPATHUMPA of martial helicopters lowering like locusts, followed by the pounding hooves of a posse of mounted police parting them like bulls charging through a wheat field.

When the gathering was over, Rick kept hiking through the mountains alone, craving solitude after so much hyper-togetherness. In a few days he hit a road and stuck out his thumb again, continuing west.

The Mann Ranch in Ukiah, California—the site of the Grof seminar— was 115 miles northeast of San Francisco; a sprawling hacienda on a bald hilltop attained after a 1,500-foot climb up a winding country road. All two dozen of the seminar attendees, of whom Rick was easily the youngest, stayed together in the A-frame ranch house with the ruggedly handsome Grof, recently turned forty-one, and his new bride, a lovely and accomplished thirty-year-old named Joan Halifax. Halifax, a medical anthropologist who studied indigenous peoples in Mali and Mexico and had a strong personal interest in Buddhism, had married Grof just weeks earlier in an outdoor wedding in Iceland. Grof wore a knit sweater over a turtleneck and Halifax a brocaded traditional gown with a white headdress that rose in a plume. They exchanged vows as the best man and maid of honor held branches above their heads. After the ceremony, the assembled raised their arms in a blessing, the mountains looming behind them.

The marriage would be short-lived. On a Flickr posting of wedding photographs Joan would later write, "It was an amazing event, though we hardly knew each other. Somehow the wedding was for everyone else. Hard to see that looking at the photos but I remember the feeling, as though I was in someone else's story."

But in the summer of 1972, they seemed very much in love.

Grof, possessed of thick, dark hair, a square jawline, a broad forehead, and penetrating dark eyes, had grown up with a keen interest in making animated films, until a friend handed him a copy of Freud's

Introductory Lectures on Psychoanalysis. He literally couldn't put the dense tome down, reading through the night. Within days he'd decided to alter his life's course, enter medical school, and become a psychiatrist and a psychoanalyst. But as his goal neared, he became increasingly disenchanted, not so much with Freud's theory, but with the paltry results analysis achieved. A course of treatment could take years, decades, and even then the underlying psychological problems could persist.

He was considering abandoning psychiatry and going back to animation when the first package from Sandoz arrived.

After watching hundreds of LSD sessions and experiencing the drug many times himself, Grof had reached the conclusions he laid out in the book that had so impressed Rick: the fantastical and often fantastically difficult experiences that arose during psychedelic intoxication were not artifacts of the drug but emerged from deep recesses of the human psyche, which LSD somehow brought into consciousness. These profound aspects of the subject's inner world didn't just pop up at random but appeared to be chosen by an innate intelligence, activated or freed up by the LSD, that had the ability to select precisely the material most urgently required for processing in order to clear the psychic roadblocks that had been preventing emotional healing or growth.

While some of these experiences could be frightening and painful to the point that some subjects believed they were physically dying, the LSD state was also powerfully suggestible. A reassuring, sympathetic therapist could almost always help the patient through, until mythic monsters turned into insignificant ants and death morphed into rebirth. Time and again Grof found that breakthroughs in the drug sessions translated into dramatic and lasting relief of symptoms and often complete cures of conditions that had been severe and persistent.

It was a marker of how prestigious early LSD research had become in the mid-1960s, and how quickly the tide had turned, that Grof was invited to leave Czechoslovakia to become chief of research at the

Maryland Psychiatric Research Center of the University of Maryland School of Medicine, an invitation he accepted. It took him until 1967 to actually arrive at the medical school campus in Catonsville, completely unaware that the future prospects for LSD research in the United States had become bleak in the interim.

As Grof wrote in *LSD: Doorway to the Numinous*, one of his many books:

> *At the time of my departure in March 1967, LSD was legally manufactured in Czechoslovakia . . . listed in the official medical pharmacopoeia as a therapeutic agent with . . . such reputable drugs as penicillin, tetracycline antibiotics, insulin, and digitalis. LSD was freely available to qualified professionals. . . . The general public knew very little about psychedelic drugs, since the reports concerning research with such substances were published almost exclusively in scientific journals. . . . There was no black market traffic in psychedelics and no non-medical use of them. Anyone interested in self-experimentation could have an LSD session provided it was conducted by an approved professional and in a medical facility.*
>
> *The situation I found in the United States contrasted sharply. . . . Black-market LSD seemed to be readily available in all parts of the country and for all age groups. Self-experimentation with psychedelics flourished on university campuses, and many large cities had their hippie districts with distinct drug subcultures. The casualties from the psychedelic scene were making newspaper headlines. Almost every day one could read sensationalist reports about psychotic breakdowns, self-mutilations, suicides, and murders attributed to the use of LSD.*

With an anxious eye on the deteriorating research environment, Grof and his new colleagues continued multiple studies of LSD-assisted psychotherapy. Grof also traveled periodically to California to work with Abraham Maslow, one of the founding theorists of humanistic psychology, a reaction to Freudian and behaviorist schools of psychology. Freud and the behaviorists had focused on mental illness and pathology. Maslow believed the proper study of psychology needed to include the higher potentials of the mind, the ways it could transcend troubles as well as fall into them. He called this capacity self-actualization and studied what he termed "peak experiences" as the means by which people fulfilled their potential. These concepts gained popular currency and made Maslow one of the few psychologists other than Freud most American college graduates knew by name.

Now Maslow believed humanistic psychology hadn't gone far enough. He found Grof's work on LSD states revelatory, especially its emphasis on direct spiritual experience, the highest peak experience of all. He and Grof wanted to chart a new understanding of the human psyche, finding space for the strange material that emerged at times spontaneously without any drug stimulus, and more commonly in psychedelic therapy sessions. At Grof's suggestion, they called it transpersonal psychology. Grof defined his territory this way: "Experiences involving an expansion or extension of consciousness beyond the usual ego boundaries and beyond the limitations of time and/or space."

This perilous terrain included experiences that traditional psychology might label psychotic, but Grof and Maslow believed were actually openings that, if recognized and worked with, could and often did lead to beneficial personality change. Phenomena experienced as memories from the womb or even of the moment of conception; apparent clairvoyance; out-of-body travel; identification with plants or animals; recall of previous lives; encounters with nonhuman intelligences; complete loss of ego and merging with a universal awareness—Grof had found all to occur, repeatedly, in LSD sessions.

At first Grof struggled with what to make of these experiences. He'd been an atheist and a scientist in a Marxist regime, so accepting them as anything other than hallucinations or fantasies ran against his grain. It wasn't necessary to believe that these experiences were "real" in a material sense to recognize that they had great therapeutic importance. They could be elaborate metaphors that the subconscious forms as a way to work through its most profound issues.

Except, to those who experienced them, they often felt *more* real than ordinary reality. And besides, some of the content of the experiences seemed to pan out in everyday life, such as a woman who, during the course of four LSD sessions Grof conducted, experienced a vivid identification with a Czech nobleman in the process of being beheaded, as if reliving his life—up to and including traumatically re-dying his death. Her richly detailed vision clearly placed the experience at the time of a pivotal real-life battle and subsequent executions that had occurred in 1621. Despite having no background in Czech history, she recounted many obscure details that, upon Grof's later research, he judged to be historically accurate, including a complex accounting of the baroque relationships between the royal family of that period and its vassals. Two years after these sessions, Grof wrote, the woman met the estranged father she knew little about and hadn't seen since she had been a small child. Trying to impress his long-lost daughter, the father produced an extensive genealogy of their family, all descending from a noble who had been decapitated in 1621.

This is just one of many such hard-to-categorize experiences, including some of his own, that forced Grof to consider that something besides psychically charged fantasy might be at work, as he explained in a 2010 interview: "In one of my sessions, I became a carnivorous plant digesting a fly with experiences that I couldn't conjure up in my everyday consciousness."

So where was it coming from? Grof didn't think he had physically transformed into a Venus flytrap, or had ever *been* a Venus flytrap, but he wondered if his consciousness had somehow accessed the internal experience of a plant from a larger ocean of consciousness that contained all living awareness.

This radical thought, one that many or even most of Grof's colleagues might have found nutty, actually had a pedigree among some of psychology's greatest minds. Freud contemporary and rival Carl Jung believed that human consciousness was shaped not only by individual experiences but by a collective unconscious containing mythical archetypes and cultural "memories" that encompassed all of humanity, and in fact all of life. Jung often told how he began to think along these lines. He said he was in the psychiatric hospital in Zurich when a schizophrenic grabbed him by the lapel and pointed out the window at the sun, urging Jung to move his head from side to side so he could see the sun's penis. The penis, the patient informed him, made the wind blow.

Jung thought this was merely an amusing delusion until four years later when he was reading a paper on new research into Mithraism, an ancient Persian religion based on sun worship. The paper said the cult believed that the wind was generated by a tube hanging from the sun, and the tube could be observed by looking from east to west—by "moving your head from side to side." Jung concluded that there was no possible way the schizophrenic could have known this esoteric fact of a long-vanished religion, especially since the research that brought it to light only happened in the years after Jung encountered him. This was only the first of many similar incidents that Jung said had led him to the collective unconscious.

Long before Jung, William James, often called the father of American psychology, pointed to the importance of the alien realms experienced in altered states of consciousness. In *The Varieties of Religious Experience*, a series of talks published in 1902, he reflected on some experiences he had had while intoxicated by nitrous oxide—laughing gas.

One conclusion was forced upon my mind at that time, and my impression of its truth has ever since remained unshaken. It is that our normal waking consciousness, rational consciousness as we call it, is but one special type of consciousness, whilst all about it, parted from it by the filmiest of screens, there lie potential forms of consciousness entirely different. We may go through life without suspecting their existence; but apply the requisite stimulus, and at a touch they are there in all their completeness, definite types of mentality which probably somewhere have their field of application and adaptation. No account of the universe in its totality can be final which leaves these other forms of consciousness quite disregarded. How to regard them is the question—for they are so discontinuous with ordinary consciousness. Yet they may determine attitudes though they cannot furnish formulas, and open a region though they fail to give a map. . . . Looking back on my own experiences, they all converge towards a kind of insight to which I cannot help ascribing some metaphysical significance. The keynote of it is invariably a reconciliation. It is as if the opposites of the world, whose contradictoriness and conflict make all our difficulties and troubles, were melted into unity.

It was precisely the mapping of this unmappable region of experiences—experiences that may or may not be real from a rational perspective but seemed to have a substance and reality of their own nonetheless—that Grof and Maslow had in mind. Grof pursued it directly, continuing his work with psychedelic therapy in Maryland. But as the sixties turned into the seventies, the path he so avidly pursued hit an unpleasant end. Maslow died of a massive heart attack while jogging in 1970. Then in 1971 Grof's LSD research got shut down in the cascade of antidrug regulation.

A year later, when Rick landed at the Mann Ranch seminar, all

Grof could do was attempt to pass on what he'd thought he'd learned in nearly twenty years of psychedelic research. Proscribed from doing the research itself, he could only hope that perhaps one of the assembled students might conjure a way to carry the work further.

Of the group, by far the least likely to succeed at that task had to have been the newly arrived college dropout and psychedelic invalid. But Rick found himself buoyed by Grof's talks, which reassured him that his acid breakdowns would ultimately lead to a breakthrough if he stayed with it. He now felt certain that, somehow, he would become a psychedelic therapist and work to bring back the research that had been shut down all over the world.

To Rick, Grof was an inspirational figure but an elusive one. Though they were all sharing the same ranch house twenty-four hours a day, outside of the formal talks the participants didn't see much of Grof or his new bride.

"The rumor was they were in their room practicing tantric sex," Doblin recalls. "At least, that's what my eighteen-year-old mind wanted to believe."

The seminar ended too soon for Rick. He felt like he was just getting started. He had heard of another growth opportunity in the vicinity, a monthlong encounter group, another sort of Intense Togetherness, radical honesty experience in which the group shut out the outside world. They stayed in cabins in a park setting, focusing only on one another, up to and including expressing themselves through naked body painting.

In the encounter sessions, a fellow seeker, a decade older than Rick, told him about primal therapy, which was enjoying a moment following the 1970 publication of *The Primal Scream* by Arthur Janov. The idea was that we were all, to one degree or another, held hostage by repressed pains or suffering inflicted on us early in life. Conventional talk therapy, which activated only the verbal centers of our brain in the cerebral cortex, couldn't undo the damage of the early trauma, which was centered in the emotion-controlling limbic system of the brain. The therapy supposedly worked by revisiting the early traumas, peeling them back to the root until the patients reexperienced the claustrophobic calamity of birth itself and, while feeling the pain, fully expressed their suffering—thrashing, screaming, whatever it took—for the first time, thus ending the repression and removing the blockages.

Rick figured maybe it would be another way to attack whatever it was that had been holding him back in his LSD explorations.

When the group session ended, he moved, alone, to a rented room in a nearby house and put himself in the hands of the older fellow. The young man had no credentials, but he had read *The Primal Scream* and knew how to hyperventilate; to Rick he seemed "adept at sort of letting himself go, whereas I was holding myself back in all these different ways."

At his young "therapist's" direction, Rick remained in isolation in the room for three weeks. He left the room for no more than the hour each day during which the primal scream sessions were conducted in another room, this one soundproof and padded.

Rick loved it, except they weren't permitted to have any books, which to him constituted a huge sacrifice. But he was allowed a journal, in which he was supposed to write down his dreams. He woke three or four times a night, groped for the notebook, and dutifully scribbled down the pulsing amoebas of image and emotion conjured by his subconscious, trying to capture their evanescent forms before they popped like soap bubbles. He began to find them fascinating. Forty years later, it still pains him that the notebook dematerialized as irretrievably as the dreams had, and is lost to history.

The other downside: during the therapy he couldn't communicate with anyone, including his parents. "I mean, just imagine, your son is, like, going through this brainwashing, as they might think of it," says Rick, a parent of three now himself. But they bore it all. It was too late to do otherwise.

At the end of the three weeks, he returned the favor to his therapist by sitting for him as he did a daylong LSD session, during which, Rick recalls, the fellow's ability to lose himself got a little out of hand: "He totally lost the distinction between inner and outer and took off his clothes and wanted to run around outside naked. I had to wrestle with him to keep him from doing that. He later said he thought the fight we had was inside his head and not real."

Rick left the experience feeling deflated. He had thrown everything he could think of at his blockage—his many LSD experiences, the workshop with Grof, the encounter group, and the three-week stint screaming in a padded room, and "they didn't enlighten me enough the way I had naively hoped."

Perhaps the most obvious possibility—that Rick had compounded the confusion of late adolescence through unwise and excessive exposure to unpredictable mind-altering drugs and unproven therapies—was not the explanation he settled on. Once again he was convinced that the fault was his own inability to break free of his stunted, ego-dominated patterns. He couldn't get free of himself, and that made him feel like a failure if not a fool. Once more the cranial pressure redlined. He found himself back in that emotional/intellectual vise that had once made him ready to believe his brain might actually be melting.

And now he had nothing to do, and nowhere to go.

13.

MICHAEL

(THE PIT)

O ne day in 1967, twenty-year-old Michael Mithoefer was riding his motorcycle on the sidewalk near Trinity College in Hartford, Connecticut, going three miles per hour, when he had what felt like a powerful insight.

He didn't need to go any faster. He didn't need *anything*.

"It was like that Zen saying," Michael says. "When you're searching for something, it's like looking for the bull when you're riding on it. It's, like, what you were looking for is already here. You just need to be aware of it."

He was a couple of hours into an LSD trip at the time.

His insight, like so many insights people have on psychedelic drugs, proved nearly impossible to put convincingly into words. But it had impact and staying power. He believed he'd felt, for a timeless instant, what it meant to be ecstatically present in the moment, made complete by the simple—or not-so-simple—fact of existence.

His whole life, Michael had been a superior student and an independent spirit. He'd been accepted to Columbia University but felt going straight from high achievement in secondary school to high achievement in an Ivy League college amounted to mindlessly striving for something he wasn't sure he wanted. He needed to "get off the treadmill" for a time, so he moved out of his parents' home and lived in Boston with some friends.

"I took a couple courses—typing and speed-reading. So I had kind of a story about getting ready for college that I could present. But that was 1965, so it was a bit of a miscalculation, because suddenly Vietnam was heating up."

No college deferment? The draft board was happy to hear it.

Michael went in for his physical but failed it. His arm had been broken badly the year before when a horse threw him, and he still had a metal plate securing his shattered bone. He'd been in Mexico with his father—a pulmonologist and academic physician—accompanying one of his dad's many fascinating acquaintances, a Swiss anthropologist who was studying the Lacandon Indians, considered the last Stone Age people in North America. The anthropologist, Gertrude Blom, had arranged a mule train into the remote area in southern Mexico where the Lacandones lived. While they waited for the plodding mules to arrive, they practiced their riding skills with some horses.

"But they didn't have any bridles. And they weren't very well trained."

Michael's horse bolted the first day, stumbling on a little footbridge and tossing Michael to the other bank, shattering his arm, the same one he'd broken the year before, pole-vaulting in a high school track meet.

But eventually the arm would heal, the metal plate would come out, and the draft board would be waiting.

He needed to get into college in a hurry.

Michael had some friends at Trinity, and he liked the campus, with its ivy-draped Gothic buildings and expansive commons. He had assumed he would follow his father's path and go to med school. But he soon discovered the only chemistry that interested him came dissolved in sugar cubes.

Unlike many of his fellow students availing themselves of the latest campus rage, LSD had no appeal to Michael as a party drug. In fact, he couldn't even grasp why some people would submit to such a challenging experience over and over again, muddling it up with drinking and other drugs for fun. He and his group of close friends agreed on that. They took LSD only rarely, with more serious intent. For them it was an inner exploration, something important.

"I would say I was looking for some spiritual experience or connection," Michael says.

It would be years before he learned about the concept of "set and setting" developed by LSD psychotherapists, but he more or less had the serious mind-set part down. The secure setting? Not so much. There was the motorcycle. And the sidewalk.

"We had a notion that we were there to support each other through the experience, but as far as assuring we would remain in a safe environment, uh, that didn't occur to us."

He got lucky. Instead of encountering a tree on his motorcycle that night, he bumped into an enlarged sense of consciousness. He had a few other interesting trips in the same vein before he had a different kind of experience.

This time after he took the acid, nothing happened for what seemed like an unusually long time. That of course was one of the problems with buying drugs on the street: you never really knew for sure the content or the dosage. After some more time passed with no reaction, he decided that whatever he had swallowed must have been too weak, or defective. So he took another dose.

Five minutes later the first dose kicked in. Hard.

Now it was clear he'd just ingested by far the largest amount of LSD he'd ever taken, and he felt more than a little nervous about it. He went up to his friend's room, where the conversation took an unfortunate if understandable turn: they started discussing a guy named John who had done acid, had a psychotic break of some kind, and ended up in the hospital getting electro shock treatment.

As Michael began to feel the full effects of the double dose, he didn't just hear the story about John, he began to inhabit it. He saw John in the bottom of a deep pit. Someone had pulled up the ladder so John was trapped. Then Michael felt himself being drawn into the pit himself. Just as he was about to disappear into it, he yanked himself back and realized he was still in a dorm room, albeit one with a pit of despair yawning at his feet.

"I have to get out of here," he said, more to himself than to his friends, who might as well have been on another continent.

He managed to stand and walk out the door. The problem was it was winter in Connecticut. That became apparent when he stepped out the front door to see the snowdrifts from a recent dumping. Inside the snowdrifts, ferocious purple lizards thrashed about, devouring one another in a cannibalistic frenzy. So that didn't help.

He went back inside to find some warmth in his own room. The refrigerator loomed before him—or what he believed had once been a refrigerator in some other dimension. He pulled open the door to reveal mostly empty shelves and, glowing in an eerie light, a carton of orange juice. Mustering superhuman concentration, he managed to pull out the carton of juice and pour it into a glass, not because he was thirsty, but because he hoped the routine process of drinking, and the sweetness on his tongue, might ground him. So far, so good. Then he picked up the glass. The simple cylinder began to warp and waver in his hand as if made of rubber.

A jolt of nausea hit his gut. Now he noticed the light itself, the sickly artificial light, had taken on a malevolent cast. The very space around him throbbed in menacing syncopation. A hostile world closed in on him, and he could muster no sense that it would ever change back to the genial, nourishing one he had left behind. Time had simply stopped, and he was trapped now, just as John had been trapped in the pit. It wasn't as if he were afraid it wouldn't end; it was simply impossible to conceive it ever *would* end.

This is what insanity is like. Somehow he managed to navigate to another friend's place, one he knew hadn't taken any LSD. Michael had to pound on the door. The friend took years to appear, bleary-eyed, his girlfriend stirring unhappily in the bed behind him. He let Michael inside and led him to a mattress on the floor, where Michael sat, forever. He couldn't feel his body. His disembodied mind floated around the room in a futile loop. The darkness dragged on infinitely. What had he done to himself?

At some point he became aware of a faint glow leaking through the curtains. *He'd made it to morning.* He let his mind tentatively explore its connection to his body. He was back, if still somewhat tenuously. Shakily he stood and let himself out. The morning air hit with a frigid slap, and he realized he was barefoot. A patch of grass had melted through the snowdrift. He took an icy step, then another, and he was standing on the cold, cold grass, once again connected to the familiar, sustaining earth.

14.

NICHOLAS

(TAKING THE LEAD)

N ot much went on for Nick between deployments. He woke up at 5:30, did an hour or two of PT, played video games, and worked hard at avoiding work details. Just stuff he had to endure to get to the weekend, pull off those boots, strip out of that uniform, and head up the road five hours to see Bev for a couple of days, then drive five hours back, and repeat. As he fell for her, Nick's depression began to fade. It helped a great deal that he could tell Beverlee anything, including the weird stuff from childhood. She listened without judging him, even when he told her he no longer believed in God. That was difficult, because Beverlee was very spiritual, very much a believer; but she wasn't forceful about it, she didn't argue. In the end her presence, and the simple existence of love, was enough to start turning Nick around.

Nick began to see his existential crisis in Iraq as wrongheaded. The Muslims he'd heard from his watchtower weren't praying to kill him—or kill anyone. The realization that every religion had its extremists, and any doctrine could be misused, opened him back up to the positives of faith. He felt the old feeling of connection with something larger flowing back to him, but in a new, more open-ended way. He was nineteen now, still a teenager, but he felt he was growing up fast.

By early 2006, preparation for his next deployment accelerated. Nick got sent up to Virginia and out to California for some training exercises. War games training in the Mojave Desert charged him up. The A-10 close-air-support gunships split open the sky above his head and he could smell the diesel exhaust in the crisp dawn and see muzzle flashes as the guns spoke and the choppers thumped past. This might as well have been all-out war, albeit one fought with blanks and flash powder. Nick couldn't deny its horrible beauty, and found himself nervous but excited about his impending return to Iraq. They'd dismantled his camp guard unit at the end of the Fallujah deployment, so this time Nick knew he wouldn't just be standing watch in a tower.

Then during a training exercise Nick stepped in it again. A lieutenant named Moran chose Nick to demonstrate a fireman's carry. The lieutenant lay on the ground, as if wounded, and Nick had to pick him up, drape him around his shoulders, and run. He'd gone barely a few steps with his heavy burden before his foot slipped in mud and pitched him forward, body-slamming the lieutenant into the ground.

"Just get up and keep going," the lieutenant said between clenched teeth. Nick did, but with a sick feeling in his gut.

Later his worst fears seemed to be confirmed when he was handed a new assignment: removed from the 1st Platoon and reassigned to the 3rd. *Oh, man,* he thought. *It's because I dropped my lieutenant.*

It wasn't. As Nick trained with his new platoon, the new lieutenant, an all-American–looking blond in his mid-twenties named Brooks Boehlert, approached him.

"You're a machine gunner, right?"

Nick admitted he was.

"I want you to be my machine gunner and I want to be in the lead and in the shit. Can you handle that?"

So Nick hadn't been branded again. He felt relieved and honored but nervous—not so much about the danger of war, but the danger that he'd screw up again, this time in a real fight. He knew that he'd have to be on his A game, but he desperately wanted to get into action to make up for Fallujah.

He'd get his chance.

15.

RICK

(CONCRETE REALITY)

When Morton and Arline Doblin made the move north along the shores of Lake Michigan from Skokie to Winnetka in 1965, it was a short seven-mile trip into a different world. Morton's success as a pediatrician and Arline's substantial inheritance made it possible to buy a plot in the exclusive North Shore neighborhood, but they were still Jewish, and in 1965, Jews still couldn't buy land on the North Shore. So a gentile willing to buy a plot large enough for four homes was found who would resell the subdivided property to them and three other Jewish families.

Rick was eleven at the time and in retrospect notes how even in America, two decades after World War II, he was growing up rubbing against the same strain of cultural insanity that, in a far more virulent form, had resulted in the Holocaust. The arbitrary demonization of the Other wasn't an abstraction in the history books for him. It was as real as the house he lived in.

But so was the soaring potential of the human spirit. Rick had to look no further than the interior of this new home, a one-of-a-kind architectural masterpiece by one of Frank Lloyd Wright's apprentices, Don Erickson. Two Chinese pagoda–style roofs soared twenty-two feet above the living space, creating twin domes, each with an eight-foot-square skylight in the center, towering above a space filled with living plants. Eventually, a tree would grow to the ceiling. Everywhere, the design invited the outside inside and projected the inside out, blending opposites and opening to nature. Rick could see from his bed up through the skylights. On clear nights he fell asleep pondering the stars.

Asked by *Chicago* magazine to articulate the intent of this unusual design, the architect's widow, Pat Erickson, said, "A liberation. Allowing you to expand and be free, to explore. Nothing is restricting or confining."

It only made sense that, lost and adrift, craving the liberation that had proven more elusive than he had ever imagined, this was where Rick returned as the summer of '72 sputtered to a close.

Rick retreated to his old bedroom, shared with his brother, to try to figure things out. He asked his father to make an appointment for him with a psychiatrist, who immediately wanted to take a battery of psychological tests. Rick loved that idea, couldn't wait to see the results. But the shrink told him it didn't work that way.

He told Rick, "These are like X-rays. I will use them to help treat you, but you can't see them. You couldn't handle it."

Rick said, "Isn't it your job to help me heal myself?"

"You just wouldn't understand," the shrink said.

"In that case," Rick said, "I'm not going to take the tests."

After Rick left, the psychiatrist called his father. "Your son is argumentative and oppositional," he said.

"When I heard that," Rick says, "I told my dad I was never going back."

He was going to have to figure it out himself.

Each morning his brothers and sister went off to school and Rick lay on his bed, staring through the skylight. Weeks passed. The presence of the house soothed him, took him out of himself. He started thinking about how someone had conceived and built a physical expression of such inner freedom and fearlessness. It was hard to miss that the house felt like a psychedelic experience made into stone and timber.

And that was the test, he decided. What good were alleged insights from the psychedelic experience if they couldn't prove useful in the world of ordinary consciousness made concrete?

"I realized I couldn't get where I wanted to go through tripping alone," Rick says. "I needed to get grounded. My mental world was so fluid and confused, but I thought if I could just get into the physical world I could move out of this confusion. So what came to me was that I needed to try to build something."

Having never built so much as a set of shelves, starting off at the Don Erickson level was out of the question. But there was something Rick connected with physically, the only physical thing he excelled at: handball. He knew handball courts intimately. Four walls and a floor. Literally concrete. A court would be impressive, but not necessarily beyond the abilities of a first-time do-it-yourselfer. Not if he was willing to work as slow as he had to and keep at it as long as it took.

But where would he build it?

Instantly New College came to mind. New College had no handball court; it was one of the few complaints he had about the place. Plus he owed a debt. New College had shown him a rare degree of empathy, kindness, and generosity. Here was a way he could return something for all he'd received—give something of himself, something lasting and intimate, and at the same time finally begin to integrate his acid visions into the real world.

Once again Rick turned to his father.

"I said, 'I want go back to college but I don't want to be a student. I would like to donate this handball court, and I'd like to build it.'"

He just needed his father to donate money to the college for the materials.

Only one father in a thousand, or ten thousand, would have responded with something other than "You want me to do *what*?"

Morton Doblin was that one. And New College was New College.
When the Doblins, father and son, approached college administrators
with the idea, they were willing to entertain it but expressed a concern:
allowing a complete novice to build a large structure could only result
in a lot of concrete blocks lying around campus and an unfinished eye-
sore in the middle of it.

And Rick said, "Look, if I don't finish it, people can just take it all
apart for bookshelves. People use these blocks all over the place. But I
will finish it."

The liability issues alone were enough to give the college's lawyers
heartburn, but as luck would have it—and Rick's luck was almost
supernatural—the college's director of development was an avid handball player. He invited Rick to play with him at the University Club in
downtown Sarasota. Rick won, going on to become the city champion. But even in defeat, the director of development must have been
charmed, because he approved the handball court project.

So it was settled. Rick would leave his childhood home for Sarasota
again, to build a handball court directly across from the nude swimming pool. But first he had something to prove to himself.

On the way to Sarasota, Rick detoured to New Orleans, where a
New College tripping buddy was working as a legal aide. After living
off his father for so long, Rick wanted to try a little experiment to see
if he could live on only the money he could make on his own. He got
a hot dog stand in Lafayette Square, sold his blood, and lived on beans
and rice for two months.

The austerity program ended when he arrived at New College to
discover that Ellen Caples, a wealthy railroad heiress, had died, leaving
her mansion—among the first built on Sarasota Bay—and its fifteen
bay-front acres to the college. Now that Rick was not only handball

buddies with the director of development, but a *donor*, the natural next step—in a novel by Kafka—was for the director to ask Rick if he would mind terribly living in the mansion as a caretaker while New College made plans for its use.

Rick graciously accepted and moved his meager housewares into his new early-twentieth-century Mediterranean Revival digs. The stucco-and-tile two-story main house wrapped around three sides of a patio that opened to the bay. Inside, Rick found two living rooms, a sunporch, four bedrooms, and four baths. The grand dining room rose the full two stories and overlooked the grounds, lushly landscaped with towering palms and Spanish moss–draped live oak.

He slept soundly there, a slumber troubled only by an odd, and oddly transparent, dream. Mrs. Caples's apparition materialized beside him and led him to an elevator, in which they descended to hell. They found themselves in a reception area where blood-red signs on the wall prohibited human contact of any kind. Horrified, Rick fled through an exit only to see a wall slam down in his path. He burst through the wall with a splintering crash. Before he could exhale in relief, he looked down. Beneath his feet, the floor was wired for electrocution.

The next morning the mist of despair the dream had imparted evaporated in the glorious Sarasota sun. As Rick puttered around the kitchen, a little intimidated by the scale of his surroundings, he came upon an old-fashioned can opener stashed in a kitchen drawer, a simple metal triangular punch about six inches long. Embossed on its base was the name of the manufacturer, the Handy Button Machine Company. Rick read it twice and felt a thrill. It was the company Rick's great-grandfather had founded. Instantly he felt he belonged here in this mansion.

Rick made himself at home. He had an understanding with the college: no parties, no guests. He made an exception for his new girl-friend, a beautiful young student named Sharon, the nude lifeguard at the nude swimming pool, the niece of New College's first chairman of the board. He snuck her in at night, and in the morning, before he snuck her out again, they would breakfast at tables set out between the neighboring mansions of the Ringling Brothers, Charles and John, as if John and Mable Ringling's fifty-six-room Venetian Gothic palace, Cà d'Zan, which housed a museum's worth of fine art, was their private treasure.

And that was just the beginning of a day that played out like a psychedelic fantasy. After breakfast, Rick pedaled his bike to the far side of campus and set to work on his handball court, right across from the campus pool. He'd work, very carefully and *very* slowly, in the hot sun, sometimes laying only four perfectly leveled blocks per hour as perspiration poured from the brown curls coiled around his head, streaming into his eyes and blurring his vision. He kept at it steadily until late afternoon, when—dirt-caked, cement-spattered, and sweat-soaked— he'd toss down his trowel and sprint the short distance to the pool, strip down, dive in, and pretend to drown until Sharon dove in and pretended to save him.

Refreshed physically and spiritually, he'd ride his bike back to the mansion to meet up with his Boy Scout troop. Early in his residence in the mansion, he'd noticed a group of twelve-year-old boys playing outside the houses across the street. Sometimes they'd follow him on their own bikes. Turned out, they needed a Scout leader. Rick volunteered, and now most afternoons he led them in a series of educational activities—such as tracking in the woods, guest-taught by an otherwise bitter Vietnam veteran whom Rick had befriended—then led them back home in the bike cavalcade like a mother goose followed by her goslings.

When night fell, Rick played Indian chief. He'd been impressed by the heavily romanticized Native Americans he'd met at the Rainbow Gathering, enough so that he'd bought a bow and set of arrows and set targets up around the mansion grounds to hone his aim. After all, he was charged with being an unofficial security guard for the mansion. Maybe his prowess with a bow would scare off would-be intruders.

But he never released a bowstring in anger. He waited for the sultry Florida summer night, then—with no intruders in sight—put a feather in his hair, slipped naked across the courtyard toward the open space, and sent hissing, sparkler-tipped arrows arcing into the bay, to his girl-friend's delight.

He settled into what felt then like an eternal rhythm, living his idyll in the mansion, working in the medium of concrete block, plumb lines, mortar, and sparklers. Of course, he became a local attraction, the campus eccentric, a nonstudent with some kind of semiofficial impossible-to-conceive position as handball court architect/contractor/live-in mansion security guard. And everyone knew of his long-term commitment to an outlaw profession. Psychedelic therapist? It sounded more like a clever name for a rock band than a career path.

But for Rick it all made sense. As he worked to fulfill his fantasy of building the court, his mind focused on solving the endless puzzles presented by even the most humble attempt to transform imagination into concrete reality, from keeping the cement mix a consistent density in the pounding sun to getting all four sides of the wall to meet on the square, perfectly plumb, each wall an unblemished plane. He came to see the pure concept of the court as equivalent to the pure vision of the altered state, and the translation of the idea into mortared block as equivalent to the integration of the psychedelic vision into normal waking consciousness. As he worked through a balmy winter into the swoon-inducing sauna of a Florida summer, what Thomas Edison said about genius proved equally true of the work of elevating conscious-ness: 1 percent inspiration and 99 percent just plain sweat.

Although the task stretched on endlessly, he did have moments of completion. Each time he finished a section of wall, exhausting the range of his three-story scaffolding, he felt a satisfaction he'd never experienced. He came to look forward to the intermezzos, the days he spent adjusting the scaffold to begin a new section. The scaffolding was a complex structure in its own right, and it took a lot of climbing and balancing to move it. Those were the days Rick took a dose of LSD before going to work. He calculated the dose carefully. He wanted to better appreciate the new heights attained by his dual projects—the construction of the court and the reconstruction of Rick—not fall off the scaffolding and break his neck.

16.

MICHAEL

(FERTILE SOIL)

After college, Michael moved to what could loosely be called a commune outside Cooperstown, in upstate New York. He had grown up in Cooperstown—a village, really—among 2,500 full-time residents and throngs of summer tourists. It was a real-world version of Disney's idea of Main Street, with the National Baseball Hall of Fame and Museum tacked on. The "commune" didn't have much of a structure. As Michael remembers it, "It was pretty much the idea of living together, cooperating, and playing music and cutting firewood and making cider. Doing odd jobs."

He worked on motorcycles, painted houses, chipped ice off of people's roofs in the winter. Basically "working as little as possible to buy big bags of brown rice and potatoes and onions."

It was there that Michael met a Cooperstown girl he'd vaguely been aware of, a friend of his younger brother, named Annie. She'd come up from school in Boston to hang out and caught Michael's eye. She stayed for ever longer stretches, and soon they were a couple, and after a year of commune life they decided to move out and get a place together.

Michael says: "We got sick of having to ask like twelve people if we could use the one pickup truck or figure out where someone had left our tools."

Annie: "I don't remember how we made the decision to take off and go to Hartford together. Do you?"

Michael: "I don't either. We didn't do a whole lot of strategic planning at that time."

Annie: "But I don't remember—did I pack a suitcase? I guess we must've."

Michael: "I don't know if we *had* a suitcase."

They went to the used-car place, asked for the cheapest junk heap on the lot, and drove out in a $50 Plymouth Valiant, which miraculously made it all the way to Hartford, where Michael had parlayed his experience trying to keep the communal pickup truck running into a job as a mechanic fixing Jaguars. The garage belonged to "an eccentric Jaguar guy who raced Jaguars and fixed Jaguars and appreciated cheap labor more than he did skill. We worked for very little, but he taught us a lot of stuff."

"You certainly got greasy," Annie observes.

Annie couldn't really complain, though. She got a job painting apartments with Michael's brother's girlfriend and came home splattered with paint. Both jobs lasted about six months, until Michael learned he'd inherited some stock from his grandmother. They sold the stock and bought a sailboat, a forty-foot catamaran that they fixed up for $12,000. They lived on the boat and sailed it out of Fort Lauderdale. They boat-bummed around the Bahamas, then sailed down to Jamaica.

"It was a great experience," Michael says, "but I began to think; I'd be in these places and I'd realize, 'Well, this is really great, and people are being very nice to us,' but it felt like we were taking a lot and not giving anything back. I realized, 'If we get sick, all we'd have to do is find a phone and we could be in Miami in the hospital very quickly. If these people get sick, there's no place to go.'"

For the first time since Chem 111 at Trinity, Michael began to think once more about going to medical school.

He'd ended up majoring in English and dreamed about writing novels. Since college, he'd squeezed out some poetry, thinking the novels would follow if he just had more free time to write. Now he had oceans of free time and he sailed them instead of shutting himself in a room somewhere and writing his novel. So he wasn't going to be an author. He had to come up with another plan.

During hurricane season they docked the boat, secured it as best they could, and went back up north, this time to Vermont, where Michael found work in another garage and Annie got a job in a hamburger place "for about two hours, before she got pissed off and quit."

"Well," says Annie, "they served breakfast, and somebody complained about their breakfast. And I just was not a waitress."

Michael was working in the garage across the street. Mid-morning, Annie came in, still in her waitress uniform.

"You got a coffee break?" Michael asked.

"No," Annie said. "I quit."

"I kind of liked it," Michael says. "It showed spirit. We said, 'Oh, yeah, cool. You shouldn't take shit from those people.'"

All along, they'd been planning on going back to Florida in the fall, to sail again. But something had shifted back in Jamaica, and somehow just sailing no longer seemed like enough. Michael had noticed some locals farming with draft horses—big, beautiful animals cutting unforgettable profiles as they stamped across the fields making furrows in front of deep-red peak-roofed barns. Despite his unhappy equine history, Michael felt captivated.

The notion of getting back to the earth had a lot of currency in the first years of the 1970s, so it wasn't a big step for him to think about selling the boat and buying a farm. It would have been hard to get more back to the earth than organic farming with draft horses.

He and Annie went out to look at a farm for sale. He knew he ought to ask about the soil, which they said was "sandy loam," but he had no idea if that was good or bad. So he called up Mr. Eldridge, the ag teacher he hadn't seen since high school, and said, "Hey, Mr. Eldridge, is sandy loam good?"

"Yeah, sandy loam is good," Mr. Eldridge said.

"Okay, thanks!" Michael said, and drove off to the federal land bank office. He'd moved up in the world automotively and now had a $100 Chevy wagon in which Annie and his sister waited for him while he went in to speak to the loan officer.

"I'd like to borrow some money to buy this farm," Michael said, pointing to the real estate listing.

The loan officer gave Michael a long look, lingering on the hair spilling down his shoulders.

"What you gonna do with it," he asked finally.

"Organic farming. With draft horses."

"Do you have any farming experience?"

"No, but we had a big garden."

"Do you have any experience with draft horses?"

"No, but I've been reading about them. And I took riding lessons when I was growing up."

"What happened?" Annie asked when Michael reappeared at the Chevy.

"I didn't get the loan," Michael said as he opened the door. "Fuck it. I'm gonna go to medical school."

17.

NICHOLAS

("MAN, YOU'RE SCARED")

After coalition forces first took Fallujah in 2004, Ramadi, sixty-eight miles west of Baghdad, became the hotbed of the Iraqi insurgency and the headquarters of Al Qaeda in Iraq, which had free run of the city of half a million, save for two Marine outposts on the perimeter, which existed in a perpetual state of siege.

On June 18 of that year, hundreds of troops from American and Iraqi security forces began a major push to oust the insurgents. After early success the mission soon bogged down and the coalition forces found themselves engaged in heavy street fighting with the numerous well-armed insurgents practicing hit-and-run tactics and harassing them with suicide bombings, snipers, and roadside IEDs. Nick saw letters and emails coming back from Marines already in the middle of it, and the scary mess they described curdled his enthusiasm.

One theme in particular caught his attention: the letters described a tactic in which insurgents would start a firefight with a convoy just to get the machine gunner to pop up, exposing himself in the turret, which was a big round basketball hoop for grenades and a bull's-eye for snipers. In other words, Nick would be riding in a coffin on wheels with a giant target on the side that said HIT ME. On the flight into

Kuwait, he kept imagining riding in the turret of his Humvee as a sniper's bullet bore down on his neck where it peeked out from his body armor. He'd heard that when you got shot it felt like getting whacked with a two-by-four. He could picture it all too clearly. Now he was just waiting for the day, the moment, when his premonition would be fulfilled.

When he landed on September 9, he wrote in his journal:

I'm in Camp Virginia Kuwait, I just got all my packs and bags all settled in. I put a cross and my St. Christ. Medal around my neck and I gave a cross to my friend Hernandez. He saw my religious stuff and he said, Man, you're scared, aren't you? I am. I have this scared alone feeling in my chest. I already want to go home. My nose keeps bleeding, just like it did all last year. I miss Beverlee so much. I wish I would have given her a better kiss before I left. . . . We leave here today to go to Ramadi. In Jesus name I pray that I live through this deployment. I can't wait to hold her in my arms again, touch her soft skin, kiss those lips. I just don't feel like I'm ready. I feel like I'm going to get hurt. God Give me the strength and courage to do this.

Nick's unit left Kuwait for Ramadi, on the banks of the Euphrates River. Marines were bivouacked at Camp Hurricane Point, a spearpoint of land thrusting into the river and cut off from the city below by a cement wall. Two larger bases, Camp Ramadi and Blue Diamond, were on either side of the Marine encampment, and it was another case of contrasting lifestyles. Those other bases had elaborate chow halls with Indian or Somali civilians serving food from a sumptuous buffet. They had modern gyms with the latest in exercise machines, and satellite TV. But, just like in Fallujah, the Marines at Hurricane Point made do with thrift-store weight sets, a tent with food served in aluminum foil vats on folding tables instead of a chow hall, and only cruddy bootleg DVDs for their tiny portable DVD players. The generally accepted theory? Marines always got the crap to keep them good and pissed off so that when the time came they could just fling open the kennel doors and out they'd spill, spoiling for a fight.

Nick had been in Fallujah as part of the mop-up phase, after the main battle had been fought. Ramadi was still very much unconquered territory. The thunderclap of random explosions provided the nighttime sound track, punctuated by the staccato beat of small-arms fire unleashed in short bursts at weddings or funerals, or building into a steady roar in gun battles between Sunni and Shiite factions intense enough to spray stray bullets onto the base.

Sometimes bullets tore through the tin roofs of the hooches. One morning, all the sergeants gathered in a circle, off to the side, making their plans for the day. A firefight roared out in the city. Seconds later, a hail of bullets began cracking all around them.

"Holy Jesus!" one of the sergeants yelled. He was grabbing at his pants leg: a bullet hole burned right through the fabric.

One unit ventured out to learn the city and came back with a live rocket-propelled grenade embedded in their truck's shattered windshield: the assailant had forgotten to take the pin out, making for a harmless wake-up call instead of another "face of the fallen" photo in the newspaper back home.

In his new barracks, Nick spent a long first night. When he couldn't sleep, he wrote again in his journal:

Sept 15: It's a little past midnight on hurricane pt ramadi. I've heard so many war stories that I don't think I will sleep well. This is going to be so rough. I don't know how I'll make it, but I will. . . . It's like Vietnam here, in some ways worse. There's no front line, and they get the first shot.

He lay back in his rack and stared at the bottom of the bunk above him. Beverlee's face, so beautiful, looked down at him from the pages of the calendar she'd had made at Walgreens so he could count off the days until they'd be together again. He lay there feeling like he was at the bottom of a deep pit with no ladder out, only a tiny pinch of light, unreachable, far above him. He lay there unsleeping, waiting for Day One and his first trip outside the wall.

18.

RICK

(WHO WOULD BE BORN)

As the walls of his handball court began to come together, so did Rick's life. Building something wasn't just therapy, it was challenging, absorbing, and fun. Getting it done forced him to learn the basics of construction, but Rick wanted to know more. As it happened—and this was the kind of synchronicity people engaged in psychedelic exploration often remarked on—Sharon's father, Harry Boothe, was a successful Sarasota contractor who taught a course for people trying to pass their contractor licensing exam. As it also happened, Harry didn't think much of Rick. Or, more precisely, when he did think of Rick, the thoughts were not entirely pleasant.

So Rick decided he could kill three birds with one well-aimed arrow. He'd ask to take the course for free. Harry would be irritated, of course, but he would accept, wanting to prove Rick couldn't hack it. Rick had no doubt he could pass the course and prove that, despite what Harry thought, he was worthy of his daughter.

His confidence flagged when he came up against the actual course material—dense, voluminous, and technically difficult. Rick struggled to keep up. When the time came to take the test, it was hard to say who was more shocked, Harry or Rick, when he passed it. Barely.

So began Rick's self-described career as "Sarasota's youngest and dumbest contractor."

He was also the slowest. It took him more than a full year to complete the handball court, possibly the longest continuously constructed handball court in world history. But it was a beauty, all plumb and square, shining like a cut jewel at night beneath lights donated by his grandmother.

He had never really intended to *use* the contractor's license, but the more he'd learned about building, the more he began to believe that the handball court wouldn't be his last project. Suddenly it came to him what he wanted to do next.

After all, it was the house in Winnetka that had brought him here to begin with. The design of that house, the rendering of visionary ideas into stone-and-lumber reality, had had an outsized impact on his life and pulled him out of the self-created divot he'd been stuck in.

Now he not only had the knowledge to attempt to build the house, he had the money. Or he would—about $80,000, which seemed a fortune in 1974—on November 30, his twenty-first birthday, the day he came into the first half of his inheritance from his grandfather.

About that. While Rick was putting the finishing touches on the court—a grand structure: four walls twenty feet high by forty feet long, a partial ceiling, and, eventually, a deck and lights for twenty-four-hour play—he made a visit home. As soon as he arrived, his father handed him a piece of paper. It said that Rick was voluntarily postponing the payout of his inheritance, with a line on the bottom for Rick to sign. Rick refused.

His father was upset—clearly in Rick he saw someone who needed to mature before he could responsibly spend that money—until Rick told him he wanted to use his inheritance to build his own house. Participating in the design and construction of the house in Winnetka had been one of the highlights of Morton Doblin's life. Spending the family inheritance to carry that forward into the next generation didn't seem so rash an idea. Nobody could say that the ability to design and build a home wasn't a worthwhile skill, and the Florida real estate market was booming, so perhaps it wasn't a bad investment either.

Rick bought a plot among the cabbage palms and Florida pines on the eastern fringe of Sarasota, where cattle ranches and orange groves were closer neighbors than bay and beach. He designed a cedar, teak, and granite structure, vaguely pyramidal, with a sloping two-story wall of beams and glass opening to the woods and sky, topped by a skylit octagonal turret and a teak sundeck. It was like somebody's acid-induced vision of a cabin in the woods, and indeed, Rick's guiding principle in its design had been to make it a comfortable, reassuring place in which to trip. Nothing was hidden, all the bones were visible, all the materials were natural. He made the floors of river gravel, just like in his parents' home in Winnetka. Since the interior woodwork was all unfinished, no paint or plaster could cover over any flaws in the quality of the work. He installed solar panels and natural gas, and gave young artisan friends commissions. One artist created a quasi-biblical stained-glass vision of a white-bearded man releasing a bird to fly over the rainbow and installed it in a twenty-panel mural that took up most of one side of the house. A relatively inexperienced carpenter built an intricate mosaic of tinted wood that covered an entire wall. When he took weeks longer than planned to finish, Rick didn't push.

Often working bare-chested and barefoot, wearing only baggy corduroys held up by a braided hemp belt, Rick loosely supervised a crew of longhairs, not all of them professionals, selected from friends and friends of friends. They ate communal meals prepared by girlfriends and wives and talked about forming an intentional community while a full-blooded timber wolf named Phaedrus barked enthusiastically at the end of his chain in the yard. Now and then Rick would stop work to play with the wolf, who he had adopted as a two-month-old pup after the Humane Society confiscated its pregnant mother from an irresponsible owner. Rick roughhoused with him, bounding around like a pack mate, even sticking his chin deep in the vise of the wolf's jaws. Phaedrus, capable of ripping his master's throat open, put up with it good-naturedly.

The house was beautiful enough, and perhaps the story of the magnetic young man behind it curious enough, to attract the attention of the local newspaper and a feature magazine. Tourists started showing up to gawk, and carpenters working at conventional job sites came in the evening, after work, to admire what could be accomplished if time and money were secondary considerations.

Another thing that happens under those conditions: the house took too long to build and cost too much. Rick went through his entire inheritance and had to borrow an additional $20,000 from his father but still ran out of cash before he could quite finish it. Between that and the fact that he'd built by far the most expensive house in that semirural neighborhood, it became clear that he wouldn't be able to sell it for a profit, as he had hoped, in order to buy a custom-built yacht and sail around the world.

He could, however, learn how to make more than a hobby out of building: he now knew to build the right project for the right location and bring it in on time and budget. He formed a construction company and named it Braxas, his own spin on Abraxas, a mystic deity appearing in Gnostic texts who just happened to embody the difficult dualities Rick had been struggling to reconcile by becoming a builder. He'd read Hermann Hesse's *Demian* and been captured by this quote: "The bird fights its way out of the egg. The egg is the world. Who would be born must first destroy a world. The bird flies to God. That God's name is Abraxas."

He painted the quote on the side of his pickup truck, which cut a swath through the local construction trade, amusing some, baffling others. A few may have even been impressed.

Rick's building business accelerated over the latter half of the seventies into the first years of the eighties. He built eight custom houses for individual customers and did well enough to persuade the bank to loan him money to build three big spec houses, the sale of which would firmly establish Rick as a successful contractor. But for once his luck deserted him. Interest on the commercial loans he'd floated reached a historic high point of 18 percent just as the local housing market began to collapse.

In his years as a contractor, Rick had a lot of vivid dreams, but one in particular stuck with him. He found himself in a gleaming white hospital room with a desperately ill old man. Rick somehow knew that the old man had survived a Nazi massacre, falling into a mass grave and emerging only after being buried under dirt and corpses for three days. The survivor had gone on to live a long life, a life that was about to end in this hospital room with Rick. In the dream, the man turned to him and said, "I couldn't die until this moment because I've had a mission for the last forty years, and I didn't know what it was. And now I know what it is and I can die."

"Well, what is it?" Rick asked him.

The man looked at him with fading eyes and said, "It's to tell you to be a psychedelic psychotherapist."

In the years since he'd become a builder, Rick had had occasional psychedelic experiences, and he felt the old roadblocks had diminished. He'd learned how to let go of his compulsion to try to control the uncontrollable world with his intellect alone, and as a result he felt freer, less fearful, clear enough to help others, and ready to move forward. He'd never lost sight of his goal of becoming a psychedelic therapist, but the dream served as a vivid reminder. If that wasn't enough, the collapse of the Sarasota real estate market took him the rest of the way. He didn't like leaving the housing business on a down note, but "I had to sort of accept the fact," Rick says.

He reapplied to New College. When he was accepted, he designed an independent study program leading to a degree in transpersonal psychology. He'd had fun writing it up: "Happily, no understanding of the physical side of being human is complete without a study of sexuality. Therefore, a class in Psychology of Women is included as well as one in Human Sexuality"—"Bravo!" his supervising professor wrote in the margin—"as well as field work of an independent nature." ("Provocative!" the professor added.)

It was early summer. He'd be starting back at school in September.

To cover his debts, Rick sold the one asset he still had—his house—to his parents.

19.

MICHAEL

(SAILING AWAY)

Within hours of getting turned down for the organic-farming-with-draft-horses loan, Michael called the University of Vermont. If he was going to go to medical school, he'd need to take the chemistry and biology courses he'd avoided at Trinity. Though classes had already begun, he found a loophole: he could still enroll as a nondegree student, since he already had a college degree.

The next day he and Annie loaded up the Chevy wagon and drove to Burlington, rented a trailer, and bought textbooks. Michael had to read the first page of the organic chemistry text twelve times before he could go on to page two. But once he crossed the threshold, an odd thing happened: the subject matter fascinated him. A year later he had As in both courses and an acceptance to the Medical University of South Carolina in Charleston.

After med school, Michael did an internal medicine residency at the University of Virginia, where—harking back to his feeling in Jamaica of wanting to be able to intervene in crisis situations—he decided to specialize in emergency medicine.

His first year of practicing emergency medicine was an anxious time, "never knowing what's going to come in, am I going to be able to handle it. But once I got used to it, then I enjoyed it quite a bit."

He'd even see an occasional victim of a bad acid trip. Diagnosis: acute anxiety, mostly.

"I did have the perspective that you didn't need to shoot them up with a whole lot of drugs. You could put them in a quiet room, talk to them, have someone be with them, and wait for it to wear off. But most of it was pretty routine emergency medicine: accidents, heart attacks, overdoses, illnesses of all kinds."

The work was demanding and exhausting. Michael would often get home thinking he wanted nothing more than to go to sleep. But as soon as his head touched the pillow, his day would start replaying in his mind and he'd find himself second-guessing decisions he'd made.

Oh, my God, maybe that person did have an ectopic pregnancy and I sent her home and she's dying right now.

Although he hadn't ever made a clearly wrong call, he was sometimes haunted by the thought that he could have done more, or been more vigilant in making sure his instructions were followed to the letter, and maybe that could have saved someone who hadn't made it.

"It was really sad sometimes, but I thought I was dealing with it adequately by basically feeling sad and then moving on to the next thing. Sometimes I'd talk to Annie about it, but I didn't talk a lot about it."

He counted himself as someone who was good at getting through the emotional pain.

After a busy shift in the ER, however, he sometimes felt an aching pain in his hip. He attributed it to standing for hours on the cement floors of the ER.

Hard floors and hard realities aside, Michael liked the immediacy of emergency work, the plunging in to stop the bleeding, defuse a crisis, save a life.

He also liked the hours.

Michael volunteered to work virtually nonstop during the summer—hurricane season for him, but vacation time for the other docs. They were glad to oblige, and in exchange he would get the winter months, sailing season in the Caribbean, to wander from port to port.

Perfect. For Michael, at least.

Annie had gotten a nursing degree while Michael was becoming a doctor, but she'd also had two babies—Emily and Heather, three years apart—and had been staying home with them while Michael established his medical career. By the time he had been working in the ER for a few years and proposed selling the house to buy a live-aboard sailboat, Emily was eight and Heather five.

"Michael's always been the adventurous one," Annie says. "He's always had lots of ideas of different things to do. He's the explorer, the adventurer. I'm the one that kind of checks it out—'Are you sure it's okay to go?' I worry about all the things ahead of time. I've got the garden and the cats, that kind of stuff."

But Michael was persuasive. "This is our window," he told her. "When the kids get old enough, they aren't going to want to be on a boat with their parents. Let's just do it now. Otherwise we'll never do it."

So they did.

The first winter on the boat, they sailed around the Virgin Islands, 1,200 nautical miles from Charleston. On the return, they hit a gale in the Turks and Caicos at night. The sea turned to foam and waves pounded the boat for eighteen hours. Annie was terrified.

"But it was absolutely perfect that we got to do that, because I realized that we *could* do it," she says. "The kids slept through it. The boat was just great. I could trust the boat."

Trusting the boat was a metaphor that would resonate in years to come.

They kept sailing, homeschooling the girls. As they were making their way home the third spring, Michael says, he was already planning for the fourth year's sail, when "the kids had a little powwow, and Emily was like the spokesperson for the two of them. She said, 'We want to go to real school next year. You guys aren't real teachers. How do we know if we're learning enough?' We said, 'Lighten up. You're only eleven.' But we thought, 'Okay, basically, in this situation, any one person should have veto power. No one should be forced to stay on a boat another year.'"

20.

NICHOLAS

(GOING CYCLIC)

Every day in Ramadi started off the same: behind that concrete wall, climbing on top of the truck, putting on a flak jacket, saying a prayer, dusting off the sand that settled everywhere, even on his teeth, getting his gun ready. The second they rolled into the city, it was game on. Sometimes they had a mission to search a house or detain certain people. Other times they just sat somewhere and waited for someone to shoot at them so they could shoot back.

One day Nick's lieutenant, who rode in one of the two rear dismount seats, went into a house with Sergeant Mack, the nominal vehicle commander, who sat in the front passenger seat. That left their driver, a friendly, open-faced Southerner named Myles Sebastien, who everyone called Seabass, and the radio guy, a little guy, named Boznack, who sat beside Lieutenant Boehlert in the back. "He was about the size of Beverlee," Nick says of Boznack. "And someone like that, as a Marine—you have all these kind of alpha male (at least they think they're alpha male) guys, you know—they always pick on those little guys and stuff like that. But he—he had a little Napoleon, I guess, syndrome. He was—I guess we would say he was a badass little package. We used to call him Bone Crusher. Uh. He was just, uh . . . he was a great dude, actually."

Normally anytime the lieutenant got out, Boznack had to go with him, so if the lieutenant needed to talk to higher-ups the radio was right there. But for some reason, this time they didn't take Boznack.

Boehlert was in his late twenties, a professional Marine from an upper-middle-class family. He could be friendly with his men, trading stories about his childhood and college experiences with the younger guys in those long, tedious hours when they were sitting on a location and nothing much was happening. Still, he took care to stop short of revealing something that might come back to haunt him. But the guys and the platoon would always find something to say behind his back even as they admired his cool in tight spots. They called him the Terminator for his stiff military bearing and the way he moved almost as if his upper body were welded into a single unit, machinelike.

Mack was halfway between Nick and the lieutenant in age, a man comfortable with his authority as a sergeant, invoking it without hesitation when necessary but never caring about it for its own sake. He'd talk to Nick and the rest of them without pretension. They could even skip calling him sergeant and just call him Mack in casual moments. He didn't give a shit about that as long as you were being respectful. He had enough to worry about just keeping up with the lieutenant, who was notably fearless and was always hopping down to go investigate something, as he had just done.

"Uh, Mack," Nick said. "The lieutenant just got out of the truck."

"What?" Mack said. "Jesus." And he hustled out to catch up, leaving Nick, Boznack, and Seabass behind.

As they waited, Nick kept his head down inside the truck. He'd learned how to do this and still keep his hand on the gun and his eye on the road by reaching up into the turret with his right arm and ducking his left shoulder down so he could watch through the dusty, fly-splattered windshield. As he was doing this, he noticed a couple of kids, maybe twelve and fourteen, staring at them from the window of a house adjoining the house that was being searched. Nick stared back. There was something strange about the older kid, and Nick tried to make out what. His gaze was intense, and he had unusually large, bulging eyes—kind of like bug eyes, Nick thought. The kid gave him a thumbs-up. Then the kid waved and hopped up and down, giving him the upraised thumb again and waving some more, obviously trying to get Nick to respond.

Well, I'm not gonna stick my head up out of the turret, Nick thought. *For all I know, that kid's trying to get me to stick my head out of the turret so I can get sniped.*

But he didn't want to be unfriendly; it was just a kid, and kids were who he was trying to make Iraq safe for, after all. So Nick stuck his thumb up and raised it high above the turret. The kid stopped hopping and looked at Nick coldly. Then he extended his middle finger.

"That kid just shot me the bird," Nick told Seabass and Boznack. But when he looked back at the window to point them out, both kids had vanished.

"That was some strange shit," Nick said, and then they started chatting, still waiting for Mack and the lieutenant to come out of the search house. Nick wasn't sure how long later, but at some point he looked down the street "and I just saw this little silhouette of a kid with a gun, AK-47, just right at his hip. Not at his shoulder, firing like a professional—hip firing, like in some movie. And I just remember seeing the crack from the muzzle break, and I was, like, 'What the hell? Is he shooting at us?'"

"Yeah," Seabass said. "He's shooting at us." Just as he said that, Nick heard a bullet crack inches away; it sounded like the windshield or the front hood. "At that moment—just in an instant—I realized . . . you know, I *had* to. I got up on the gun, shot in his direction, and, um . . . it kicks up so much dust and dirt and debris, especially when you hit the buildings, because they're like brick—kinda mudlike brick—and things turn to powder. I just remember the kids standing there, and another kid had come out by the time I was already on the gun, and I just remember shooting in their direction, and they just turned to dust and smoke in that area. You know, I never saw me hit them or anything."

When the kids disappeared, he remembered what the Marines he replaced in Ramadi kept warning him to watch out for after he'd been fired on. *A guy will come outta here, someone's gonna come outta there, and then you're gonna get ambushed.* They'd also told him to forget about timing his burst to *Die, motherfucker, die. Go cyclic,* they told him. *Just hold down that trigger.*

He was into his fifth or sixth *Die, motherfucker* when he figured he'd almost certainly fired enough bullets to take out the threat in front of him. He swayed the gun around at the rooftops . . . *Die, motherfucker* . . . the alleyways . . . *Die, motherfucker* . . . the street behind them . . . *Die, motherfucker.* He kept firing and firing, going cyclic as they had told him to do, gripping that trigger as if his life depended on it, which it damn well might.

"It took me over," he says. "I just wanted to make sure that no one was gonna pop out and get me. So I was just shooting like crazy and, um, trying to prevent anything from coming out. It was more just reaction—which, um, I shouldn't have been reacting to the enemy like that."

In the middle of his frenzy, a white vehicle emerged from an alleyway, "and the first thing I thought in my head was that, you know, this firefight's kinda already been going on for a while, you know, I've been shootin', it's loud," Nick says. "You can see rounds kickin' up off the dirt, so you know if you're gonna pull into this alleyway and you see all that stuff, you . . . unless you're, you know, not paying attention, you shouldn't just pull up into something like that. You should be able to see it and back off. But he pulled outta that alleyway just a little bit, and the first thing I thought was that this was a vehicle that was gonna come ramming at us and blow me up—and blow us all up. And so I turned to the vehicle, and it's, you know, it's supposed to be 'tires, grille, kill,' but when you have a machine gun . . . And, uh, I just remember pointing it at the tires just to stop it, and I just remember seeing the tires blow out and the hood pop up, and, um . . . the guy inside it, seeing him trying to hold on to the steering wheel while I was shooting up the vehicle. And . . ." He trails off, then continues.

"I had ran out of ammo at that moment and yelled out, 'Reload!' Boznack already had a can of ammo ready for me, and they were stoked—it was the first firefight we had been in as a truck and as a platoon. And I got my ammo, and when I picked it up to put it up there, I just looked at what I'd done—pieces of building, like, falling off, smoke and dust still kicked up, and then there's a . . . there's a vehicle up there, shot up. And I didn't see the guy in there at that time, and I remember seeing him whenever I was shootin' him, just shaking as he was holding the wheel and stuff. Shaking as if he'd been taking bullets."

Adrenaline still rioting through his body, Nick regained enough sense of his position to feel a sudden nauseating swirl of guilt and regret.

"I think at that moment I realized what I did was a little, in my opinion, overkill. But, you know, from a military point of view they would say, 'You know, you did what you had to do to take care of us, to help us get out,' because those guys in the building still needed to get out and get back in."

In fact, Mack and the lieutenant had sprinted the few meters from the search house to the Humvee while Nick was reloading.

"What happened?" the lieutenant, out of breath, asked when Nick stopped shooting.

"We told him about the kids, um, engaging us and everything, and then, uh, Boznack said, um, 'Yeah, and then that white vehicle came out.'"

The lieutenant looked up into the turret, right into Nick's eyes, and said, "Well, what about that white vehicle?"

"And then I got scared," Nick says, "because, you know, you're supposed to do tires, and if it doesn't stop, then you shoot the grille. If it still doesn't stop, then you shoot the person. But it was kind of all in one moment, you know, it's a machine gun, and I kinda got, um, I couldn't, I kinda froze, and Seabass spoke up for me and told my lieutenant exactly what happened. And I'm just, like, 'Oh, man, I'm gonna get in trouble.' And, you know, he didn't really say much afterwards. He just . . . he had to call it in on the radio. But we don't . . . we don't . . . we never went and checked out what we had killed or shot. We—you didn't go pick those things up. Unless it was real close by. If it was, like, in a building and those situations happen, they'll cordon off the building and we'll take out the bodies and all that other stuff. But the street stuff, we don't go and mess with them because you go over there to mess with the bodies, then you're gonna get ambushed by someone else because that's . . . you know . . .

"And, uh, I always remembered that Seabass, how he helped me out in that situation. You know, he explained it to the lieutenant for me. I mean, he told him that a vehicle came out and that we thought he was coming at us, 'so Nick took him out.' The lieutenant asked, you know, 'Did you follow the rules of engagement, your ROEs?' and everything, and I said, 'Yes, sir,' and Seabass vouched for me. Because technically I did, but it was just in such a small amount of time that it was just 'tiresgrillekill,' just one thing."

So Nick was in the clear, officially. But the rush of the firefight and the thrill of survival gave way to lingering doubt. Nick couldn't know for sure if the man in the white car really had a trunk full of explosives and a willingness to kill himself for the privilege of killing Nick, or if he was just trying to get home. That uncertainty hung around like a low-grade fever. It was always there in the background: the image of the man still gripping the wheel, his body reverberating with the impact of bullets.

He may have killed those kids too. He'd never know for sure. It was as if they'd simply vaporized. They'd been firing the AKs and then he'd blown the world apart and they'd vanished in the maelstrom of pulverized dirt and brick. Maybe they'd only been injured and limped away. But either way, they were just kids. That's not what he'd signed up for or trained for.

Nick had imagined he'd be battling hardened insurgents with black masks and RPGs and AK-47s, not boys. "It could've been set up to where those kids were to shoot at us and get us distracted while that vehicle came and slammed into us and blew up. But you just never know."

At least, Nick never would.

Now he couldn't afford to dwell on it.

"I just . . . you come to this realization that worrying about it, complaining about it, is not gonna get you anywhere. You're not getting home any faster—unless you die, and then you'll get to go home a lot faster than anyone else. . . . I dunno, you tell yourself to suck it up a little. Someone else will say, 'Suck it up, Marine. Suck it up.' That's what you do. Yeah, I was nervous, I was scared, but you just . . . that's the thing, you just . . . I mean, that's part of being human; anyone would be. But from our training as Marines, you know how to keep going even though you're scared. You know how to get past that situation. And . . . throughout the rest of the situations, I just slowly became more and more numb, and more and more disconnected from where I was in reality."

But that night, at least, Nick and Boznack and Seabass still buzzed with the excitement of their first taste of combat, and Nick didn't think about the rest of it. "Guess we're all gonna get our combat action ribbon now, 'cause Blackston managed to get us into a firefight," Seabass said, and they all laughed.

21.

RICK

(BREATHING LESSONS)

L ife had stripped Rick bare. He'd run through his inheritance, spent ten years building a business only for it to smack into a dead end, and at the age of twenty-eight he was starting college all over again, living in the house his parents now owned on a $650-a-month allowance.

But he wasn't cowering. Weeks before he was to start New College, he was back in California, this time at the already venerable institute for the exploration of all things alternative, Esalen, a retreat built on a Big Sur mountain ridge overlooking the Pacific, featuring a clothing-optional pool fed by hot springs gushing from a hole atop a fifty-foot cliff.

Rick had come for another weeklong workshop with Stan Grof, who had been invited to be scholar-in-residence there by Esalen cofounder Dick Price in 1973.

Price, just a year older than Grof, equaled him in dashing good looks and dynamism. He'd founded Esalen with a figure from the emerging beat generation and a fellow 1952 Stanford graduate, Michael Murphy, whose grandmother had owned this unique real estate when it was little more than a spectacular piece of wilderness with a small motel and a family retreat. Murphy had spent a year in India and become enamored of Eastern thought, and Price had been inspired by attending a lecture by Aldous Huxley in which Huxley contended that Western man had a vast untapped potential and called for the development of novel methods to bring it to the fore. Both Price and Murphy believed that one of those methods would be the judicious use of psychedelic drugs. For Price it was about bringing the deep forces underlying personality out of hiding and working through them in an active, positive way. His penchant for conducting Gestalt therapy sessions while hiking through the wilderness area surrounding Esalen would become a trademark. (In fact, Price died hiking in 1985, at fifty-five years of age. His body was found by a stream in the valley where he liked to hike and often meditated. An investigation concluded that he had been killed by a falling rock loosened by recent rains.)

In 1956, as Grof was deciding that the bizarre experiences and states induced by LSD were not pharmaceutically induced psychoses but a genuine window into the depths of a human psyche trying to heal itself, Price, then twenty-six, had what was diagnosed as a manic schizophrenic breakdown. Price didn't see it that way. He called it his "state."

"In some categories it would be called mystical," he said in a 1985 interview. "Really a re-owning and discovery of parts of myself where I set myself in relation to a larger cosmos. But don't try to talk to a psychiatrist in these terms; to them, this is simply a symptom of 'very deep-lying illness.'"

Hospitalized against his will for eighteen months, Price emerged wanting to find a way to improve care for people going through similar crises rather than relying on the tranquilizers, electroshock treatment, insulin shock, and other therapies that he'd found so brutalizing.

As Price explained in the interview: "Rather than seeing someone through a particular type of experience, it was an effort to suppress and negate in every possible way what I was going through. There was a fundamental mistake being made and that mistake was supposing that the healing process was the disease, rather than the process whereby the disease is healed."

In working with people in psychological distress, Price stressed the equality between what would traditionally be called patient and therapist. His words for them were *initiator* and *reflector*, partners in a collaboration that centered on a nonjudgmental experiencing of difficult psychic material, aiming, as Price said, "to live through experience rather than having it blotted out."

Change, Price believed, came from acceptance, not resistance. The role of the "reflector," what Grof would come to call the "sitter," was to create a safe environment, reassuring and gently encouraging the initiator—or client, or patient—not to shrink from difficult feelings but to explore them.

Grof had come to very similar ideas on how to navigate the volatile psychic states that emerged with LSD. He'd also independently concluded that some dramatic spontaneous states of apparent distress were misdiagnosed as psychotic when in fact they were the emergence of material from the deep unconscious, almost indistinguishable from what happens with LSD. He noted that throughout history and in almost all cultures these experiences had been considered the key to spiritual growth and positive transformation.

"The process I was witnessing in others and experiencing in myself also had a deep similarity [to spontaneous religious experiences and] shamanic initiations. [Although] Western scientists had ridiculed and rejected these sophisticated procedures . . . my observations convinced me that such modern fields of psychoanalysis and behaviorism could bear no comparison to the depth and scope of such ancient knowledge."

Such spontaneous experiences had become much more than a professional concern for Grof.

In 1975 a woman named Christina had been referred to him by the famous mythologist and comparative religions scholar Joseph Campbell. Christina had had what may well have been diagnosed as a psychotic breakdown. A middle-class American woman living a reserved and unfulfilling life in Hawaii, she suddenly experienced inexplicable sensations while in labor with her first child:

"I started to shake uncontrollably. Enormous electrical tremors coursed from my toes up my legs and spine in the top of my head. Brilliant mosaics of white light exploded in my head, and instead of continuing Lamaze panting, I felt strange, involuntary breathing rhythms taking over. It was as though I had just been hit by some miraculous but frightening force, and I was both excited and terrified. . . ."

That excitement disappeared after Christina was given two shots of morphine by her concerned doctor. The opiates succeeded in deleting the excitement, leaving only the terror, a devastating fear that she might be losing her mind, followed by a desperate attempt to "pull myself together."

When the same thing happened during the birth of her second child, doctors injected Christina with tranquilizers. That ended the visions, but the way the doctors had reacted only confirmed her fear that she was losing her mind. Still, for a number of years she managed to live the life expected of a wife and mother. She taught art and took yoga classes. It was one of her fellow yoga students who suggested she attend an event with an Indian guru known for seeing through people's facades to their true nature. The guru looked Christina over, then slapped her forehead. With that one jolt, as Christina recounted it, all the forces she'd been trying to suppress broke loose. "I started to shake uncontrollably. . . . [A] multitude of visions flooded my consciousness.

I wept as I felt myself being born; I experienced death. . . . I was on an experiential roller coaster and I knew I could no longer contain it."

As the surreal experiences continued, her carefully constructed life fell apart. Her marriage dissolved and her husband gained custody of the children. She became paralyzed by fear and anxiety. That's when she connected with her old college professor Joseph Campbell.

From the moment she read Grof's book *Realms of the Human Unconscious*—the same book that had captivated Rick Doblin— Christina recognized her condition immediately. Grof's confidence that what had beset her was not illness but a spiritual crisis that provided an opening to growth and healing infused her with hope. Soon their relationship became more than doctor-client. Both recently divorced, they fell in love and married, becoming not only husband and wife but professional collaborators. Christina coauthored *The Stormy Search for the Self,* including a full account of her "spiritual emergency," which she continued to work through even as she led workshops with her husband at Esalen. The term *spiritual emergency* had been chosen carefully to emphasize that although it often presented as a crisis, something positive, a spiritual awakening, could "emerge."

Grof also noted that although a multitude of ancient traditions recorded spiritual crises occurring spontaneously, as with Christina, these experiences had been found too valuable to simply wait for them to show up on their own. Almost all non-Western cultures had some method to produce altered states on demand, whether it be by using peyote, magic mushrooms, sweat lodges, self-torture, or drumming and chanting.

Now that he could no longer legally use LSD or other psychedelics, Grof had thought to look at some of the ancient systems for methods that did not involve drugs of any kind. One array of practices in particular kept coming up in an astonishingly wide range of cultures, all involving the most basic fact of life: breath.

Grof discovered that a wide range of cultures, including early Christians, had developed techniques of breathing designed to alter consciousness. "The original form of baptism practiced by the Essenes involved forced submersion of the initiate under water for an extended period of time," he wrote. "This resulted in a powerful experience of death and rebirth. In some other groups, the neophytes were half-choked by smoke, by strangulation, or by compression of the carotid arteries."

But in the end he didn't have to resort to anything so extreme. He had to look no further than his new wife's experience in childbirth, in which a full-fledged altered state had been precipitated by energetic, rapid, prolonged hyperventilation. Over time, Stan and Christina refined their technique to add loud rhythmic music to the breathing. They found that, when executed properly, the breathing plus music could bring on a psychedelic-level altered state within an hour.

One theory of how it worked goes like this: the panting hyperventilation in breathwork sets in motion an in-body chemical chain reaction. It depletes the carbon dioxide in the blood, which raises blood alkalinity, which forces the hemoglobin in the blood to retain oxygen. It also causes some arteries to constrict. Together, these reactions reduce the oxygen available to brain tissue, but not uniformly. Oxygen in the parts of the brain that normally direct and structure thought declines more quickly than in the parts of the brain that directly sense and feel. The result is an alteration in consciousness, giving temporary primacy to unstructured sensory information and emotions. This mimics Huxley's idea that psychedelics work by inhibiting the brain's "reducing valve," allowing in more of the raw data streaming in from the world without corralling it into the conventional categories, narrowed for pragmatic purposes.

Stan found that with breathwork, as with LSD therapy, the altered state tended to activate an innate healing intelligence that brought to the surface precisely those images, memories, and experiences an

individual needed in order to work through psychic trauma and dysfunction. The Grofs named the technique Holotropic Breathwork,
derived from Greek words meaning moving toward wholeness.

The breathing thing was new to Rick, and he attacked it with a
vengeance, breathing *really* hard and *really* long, until Grof came up to
him and said, "I don't often see people breathe so hard and so long
without any kind of reaction."

Rick said, "I'm just so grateful to be here. I don't need to experience
anything else but that."

Eventually, Rick did have experiences with breathwork that were
more typically dramatic. At one point he had a vision that he was being
tortured by the Inquisition. "That felt the closest to what you would
say was a past life, but I don't see it that way. I just remember having
these wood boards put on either side of my leg and then they would
smash my legs."

The pain seemed vivid enough, although all the while Rick knew
he was at Esalen, voluntarily continuing to breathe in rhythm to the
music. But in his vision he knew he might be killed at any moment.
Trapped, with escape impossible, he saw that he might still triumph
simply by being aware, alive in the moment.

Another time he saw himself as a fetus about to be born. "I felt all
these contractions. And then I remember feeling like maybe I could
work with them. So instead of this thing being all done to me, I start
feeling that I can sort of harmonize my breathing, that I could be part
of wanting to be born instead of just being forced to be born. So there
is this transition from the fighting to the opening and going with it."

The breathwork was done in groups, with each participant acting as both breather and sitter. Despite Rick's own experiences, he
was skeptical of some of the dramatic acting out of his fellow work-
shoppers.

"I was very dubious of the way in which breathwork seemed to give people permission to let themselves go. Stan, I think, sometimes kind of gives the sense that these visions that you have are always coming from some true place rather than your imagination. So I felt that there was a lot of manufacturing of stories. So I had to be dubious about myself. Was I manufacturing these stories? It didn't feel like this convincing sense of a past life or sense of actually being born."

As for the Inquisition torture scenario, "I could have been reliving my fear of being busted—'Here's my mobility going away.'"

And it made more sense to Rick to think of the difficult birth experience as related to his struggles with learning how to let himself go while tripping rather than an actual memory of birth.

Although the experiences produced insights Rick considered worthwhile, the effort and distraction of the breathing seemed to put a lid on where the experience could lead him.

"Some people like the control of that because if you slow down the breathing, you can diminish the intensity. But I have a harder time generating those kinds of experiences. I think my defenses are so rigid and strong that for me the psychedelics are more reliable than having to do that hard work myself with the breathwork."

The workshop lasted five days, during which Rick learned that Stan and Christina were planning a monthlong version in September. He badly wanted to attend, but he was supposed to be starting classes. It was his first month of school in ten years. He couldn't just blow it off.

And then he thought, *Wait a minute, this is New College.*

22.

NICHOLAS

(OF MAN AND SUPERMAN)

Ramadi in the fall of 2006 was unlike anything the U.S. military had experienced in Iraq—or anywhere since the fall of Vietnam three decades earlier.

"The whole area was enemy controlled," Marine lieutenant Jonathan Welch told American journalist and war blogger Michael J. Totten in early 2007. "If we went out for even a half-hour we were shot at, and we were shot at accurately. Sometimes we took casualties and were not able to *inflict* casualties. We didn't know where they were shooting from."

Another officer, Army captain Jay McGee, told Totten, "There were areas where our odds of being attacked were 100 percent.

Sitting in Hurricane Point, Nick never knew the big picture. Nobody discussed why they did what they did. He only knew that every time he went outside the wire, they seemed to get into some deep shit.

Literally.

In the insurgent-controlled city, raw sewage ran in the streets but no water in the taps and no juice in the electrical grid. Trash sat uncollected until it covered almost every surface, which made the detection of

IEDs—which were disguised to look like just one among billions of pieces of trash—even more difficult. And it was like that with the Iraqis themselves. Any one of them—the men giving them hearty smiles and big, sweeping thumbs-up; the kids racing around, kicking rags instead of soccer balls—could be secretly plotting their doom. Once, a suicide bomber blew himself up in the middle of the street right before they rolled through. His intestines were still scattered all over and nobody seemed to care except the dogs racing up stealthily to feast on the carnage. Nick's Humvee stopped there right beside the whole gory spectacle. Someone pulled out a bag of Goldfish crackers and they all started snacking—no problem—as if in celebration of the fact that here was at least one Iraqi who was no longer a threat.

Each day when they rolled out beyond their barricaded walls, Nick's eyes darted around, from the trash piles and sewage seeps—any one of which might hide a bomb—to the shrapnel and bullet-pocked rooftops and the vacant, glassless windows in which lurked who knew what hidden peril, like eye sockets in a skull.

Sometimes the dangers weren't even disguised or hidden but naked for all to see and coming right at you. Just short of two weeks after Nick first fired his gun in anger, he found himself in that same location, near a street code-named Firecracker. From the very same alley where the boys had emerged hip-firing their AKs, a man walked calmly toward them as if he were out for an afternoon stroll, only he had an RPG on his shoulder. Nick could see the distinctive silhouette of the firing tube joggling up and down with his gait. Thinking that the man's preternatural calm meant he was either hopped up on drugs or a serious professional, Nick jumped up on his gun as the man took a knee. When Nick sighted on the man, he found himself staring straight down the barrel of the launch tube sighted on *him*. He pulled the trigger.

Nick learned later that an observation drone circling the area caught the heat signature of rocket fire going up in the direction of the

Humvee, but on a trajectory that took it too high. Nick figured that meant he'd probably shot the man in the chest, knocking him backward just as he got off his round, which otherwise would have come straight at him. Nick couldn't know for sure, because after he went cyclic on the trigger, the entire area disappeared into a cloud of dust.

When the dust cleared, the guy wasn't there anymore. Boznack got a call on the radio for the lieutenant: eyes in the sky saw two men drag the injured or dead shooter away and put him into a maroon Buick Opel, which took off. Nick's platoon sped off in pursuit. Just as they'd been warned, the Opel headed straight for the souk—a heavily mined and completely enemy-controlled and -saturated area.

But the lieutenant wasn't backing down. Nick knew he couldn't say anything, but in his mind he was screaming, *Are you serious?*

As they rolled into the ramshackle marketplace, the men standing around with guns stared at Nick in surprise. Nick stared back, close enough to see the bloodshot eyes boring into him. It felt as if this were a freeze-frame in a movie, a wave suspended in midair. Then the wave crashed. The men started shooting. Nick swung his gun wildly around but he could barely get a bead on any one target because the Humvee kept moving and the insurgents were all scrambling for cover, with new ones coming out of nowhere. Everyone in the vehicle was yelling at once: *"We got a guy over here with an RPG! Oh, there's a guy over here to my right!"* And Nick could swivel only so fast.

As they lurched down the narrow alleyways, Nick had to duck and push aside the snarled tangles of electrical wire stretching from power poles into open windows. But the wires came too quickly and one looped around his gun and caught it.

"Oh, shit." The wire yanked the gun and spun his turret 180 degrees. The lieutenant, who saw the turret spin and Nick stumble and fall, thought the worst. He grabbed Nick, "You okay? You okay?"

"Yeah, that effin' wire caught my gun," Nick said.

"Well, I thought you just got shot." The lieutenant ordered a halt, Nick got back up on the gun and disentangled it. Then Seabass stepped on the gas again. They were approaching a corner when a kid jumped right in front of them. The kid, maybe thirteen, had an AK in his hands. He'd just rolled around the corner—no idea what was coming the other way—and would have been flattened if Seabass hadn't slammed on the brakes. The kid froze in the middle of the street, not ten feet from Nick, and Nick put the gunsight right on him, not thinking about his target being just a kid, only that there were so many targets and any one could end it for him if he wasn't fast enough.

The kid unfroze and dashed back around the corner. Nick fired, too late. All he did was gouge new divots in the wall.

Now every single vehicle in the convoy was engaged with somebody shooting from somewhere. Small-arms fire pinged off their armor like hail, and the roar of the big guns made it impossible to think.

Not that Nick needed to. His body, pumped full of whatever his brain was dumping into his system, was all in. He was Superman for the duration. His head spun on a swivel and he reacted and fired directly from his brain stem.

Inside the Humvee, Boznack and the lieutenant huddled above the radio, trying to hear over the firefight, as base intel officers tracked the maroon Opel on the drone feed. As they snaked through the maze of alleys, the lieutenant screamed "Turn here! Turn here!" at Seabass, who fishtailed crazily around corners as fire rained down from every rooftop. Back at the base, everyone had heard by now that 3rd Platoon had gone into the souk—the big no-no—and everyone was racing around, armoring up for a rescue. But for the time being, the platoon was on its own. At one point Seabass zigged when he should have zagged and Nick found himself staring at a stone wall, a dead end.

They were stuck. Nick waited for the swarm to come over the rooftops and fire directly down on him, waited for that blow he'd been imagining since he landed in Ramadi, the feeling of a stiff board slamming into him and then . . . what? *Oh, man, we're dead, we're dead,* he was thinking as Seabass surged forward, then backed into the first leg of a three-point turnaround. The Humvee slammed into a house with a shuddering crash that almost knocked Nick out of his perch. "I thought we had gotten blown up," Nick says. "And when I realized that we had hit the building behind us, you know, we're all yelling at him, we're, like, 'Get us the eff outta here!'"

When he pulled away, bricks toppled from the wall.

They finally managed to get back on the main drag, heading toward the closest forward operating base and safety, when Nick saw something sticking out of the rubble of a collapsed building. As it came closer, Nick realized it was a pipe, a big wad of what looked like C-4 explosive stuck to the end. He screamed at Seabass to stop. "There's a b . . . a b . . ." He couldn't get the words to come out. But Seabass slammed on the brakes. "They all looked at me like 'What?'" Finally he got it out: "'There's a *bomb* right there,' and they're, like, 'Where?' and I was just, like, 'Just back up the vehicle, we're too close!' And they're, like, 'Well, where is it?' And I'm, like, *'Just back up the vehicle.'*"

Finally Seabass backed up and they all saw the massive booby-trapped bomb. They thought for a minute about trying to shoot at it and blow it up but decided they were too close to risk it.

"We'll just have to go around," the lieutenant said.

Nick looked at the path they would have to take: it went straight through a huge puddle from all the broken water mains. It looked deep. They had all been warned about driving through water, a favorite place to hide waterproofed IEDs. But they would have to risk the bombs they couldn't see to get around the one that was in plain sight. "We just kind of had to, like they say, 'pucker your asshole' and wait for it to blow up."

They surged into the water, leaving a wake, and once again Nick waited to die, wondering what he'd feel as the bomb's shock wave tore through him.

He held his breath and tried to pray, but the prayer came out as the repetition of a single word. "No, no, no, no, *please*, no."

The water parted for them, and nothing blew up. Just as Nick began to breathe again, halfway between the souk and the forward base, the riled-up insurgents launched an all-out attack on the base. And the base responded. It sounded like a fireworks factory blowing off all at once.

"It was going on, like, right in front of us. From the base, firing into the city, back and forth. We had to park in this horrible spot—they call it the Gauntlet—and just sat there and let them engage and just watched our sectors and made sure nobody was gonna come and get us. I looked back at the souk and saw one or two Black Hawk helicopters, and they were flying over the top of the city, engaging enemies, and I'm, like, 'Wow, we really pissed off the hornet's nest.' But it felt really cool to see how all that stuff came together just for us. We were the only ones out there on one little mission, and it turned into this situation, and before we knew it, we had all our guys out there. And that felt really good to know you had that backup.

"We drove back and we came through the gate; you know, the word gets spread, what's been going on. And you can also hear it going on out in the city. And they're, like, 'Oh, that's Light Horse getting into a huge firefight.' I just remember when we got off those vehicles, I had links, ammo—you know, whenever you get done shooting, it shoots links outta the side, and brass down below, so there's, like, links and brass all over it. And all the other vehicles had rounds where they'd cracked on the vehicle and stuff, and we just looked like we'd went through hell. And just seeing the look on the guys' faces when we got back—I just remember they were looking at us like 'Oh, my gosh.'

"You get a big rush. While it was going on, I was, like, 'Oh, I'm gonna die, I just wanna hurry up and get it over with.' It's just that waiting—'When's it gonna be? When's it gonna hit me?' But whenever you get back and realize nothing did happen, then you kinda get that ego thing, and you're, like, 'Oh, man, I'm invincible.'"

23.

RICK

(ECSTASY AND AGONY)

T he workshop Stan and Christina Grof taught at Esalen in September 1982 focused on the search for spiritual growth in non-Western cultures. They called it the Mystical Quest. Rick, who had correctly guessed that he could persuade his New College advisor to approve the workshop as "off-campus study," thought he already knew his life's quest. For a decade he'd been reading everything he could get his hands on about psychedelics. The authors awed him: "I felt that all these people that wrote the books were so much smarter than I was and were living in another world, and I was just the struggling and bumbling student."

But Rick's single-minded persistence had gotten him to Esalen on his Mystical Quest, and it turned out just being there landed him in some rare company. Between the participants and the guest lecturers, Rick rubbed auras with many of the people who'd written those books.

"So I felt like finally the books were becoming alive as people. I moved beyond the books to the people, to the authors. And I learned that there was this incredible underground community of psychedelic therapists who had continued to work with LSD, this whole community that I assumed had been squashed, that all the research was dead, that everything only existed in books, and that I was going to try to bring this back. But it then turned out that, no, this community had survived."

One morning Rick overheard a woman talking about a novel psychoactive drug. "I felt like, at first, the way that she was describing it, it didn't seem very interesting to me. It was just [that] it helps you get in touch with your feelings and it helps you talk to people more, and it helps you listen better and it makes you feel warm and loving. I'm, like, 'Well, I already feel warm and loving, and I already can talk to people.'"

From the description, Rick sensed the drug lacked the mystical drama of LSD and had none of the fantastic perceptual changes and cosmic connections.

Rick ended up buying some anyway, just out of curiosity. He brought it back to Florida to try with his girlfriend. He didn't expect much. He certainly didn't expect it to change his life.

"It was phenomenal. It was just so deep and there was so much that we were able to express in terms of love for each other. And it felt genuine. This wasn't the drug speaking: this was *us* speaking. It was clearer and didn't affect the perceptions the way psychedelics did. We had this sense of astonishment at how little difference there was between the MDMA experience and our normal way of being together."

And yet, that ineffably subtle difference seemed infinitely important. "It was this flow of self-acceptance and listening that helped with the rough edges of this process that I was still engaged in of trying to take the difficult psychedelic experiences that I'd had and smooth them out, integrate them, and eventually take what I had been trying to suppress and let it out. I could see incredible potential."

Rick wasn't the first to feel that way.

In 1976, on the advice of an acquaintance, a brilliant but eccentric chemist who lived in the rural rolling hills east of Berkeley synthesized

3,4-methylenedioxy-N-methylamphetamine in his ramshackle back-yard lab. This mouthful formulation of a drug had been discovered in 1912 by the German company Merck. It was patented two years later as a potential precursor chemical for the manufacture of a drug that stopped bleeding after surgery, then was quickly forgotten. The chemical structure was similar to that of amphetamine and mescaline, so in the 1950s it provoked a passing second look as a possible stimulant and also was briefly considered, then discarded, by the same secret American military program that eventually focused on LSD.

But somehow word got out that the drug had some interesting psychoactive properties. By the time the chemist's friend got curious about this new drug and recommended he take a look, it was being used by a tiny handful of counterculture cognoscenti with a taste for the exotic and firsthand access to someone with experience in chemistry labs.

Nobody had more experience with this very particular kind of chemistry than the eccentric chemist, Alexander "Sasha" Shulgin. A leading researcher for Dow Chemical in the late 1950s and early 1960s, Shulgin had a professional interest in psychoactive chemicals that had turned personal. About the time that Aldous Huxley had his first psychedelic trip, Shulgin began studying mescaline's chemical structure. Then, on a spring day in 1960, he tested the psychic effects on himself. The experience transformed the world around him, and within him, in miraculous ways that nonetheless seemed to him far more "real" than the everyday world he'd known his entire life. The most telling of his many insights that day was that this experience had all "been brought about by a fraction of a gram of a white solid, but that in no way whatsoever could it be argued that these [perceptions] had been contained within the white solid. . . . I understood that our entire universe is contained in the mind and the spirit. We may choose not to find access to it, we may even deny its existence, but it is indeed there inside us, and there are chemicals that can catalyze its availability."

From that day on, Shulgin wanted to devote himself exclusively to the exploration of these remarkable substances. He got his chance the following year after he developed the first biodegradable pesticide, which made Dow a fortune. Dow gave him the customary dollar bill for the patent, then added something far more valuable to Shulgin than mere money: the freedom to work on whatever he chose. He chose to work on synthesizing and evaluating compounds whose chemical structure led him to believe they might be psychoactive. Like Hofmann, he tested these on himself, beginning with what he guessed to be many times less than an effective dose and gradually working his way up. Since he was usually investigating drugs that hadn't existed until he developed them—and because he became valuable to the Drug Enforcement Administration by helping them identify and classify potential drugs of abuse—he was able to continue his work openly even after known psychedelics had been placed on Schedule I. At first, Dow dutifully patented some of Shulgin's psychedelic discoveries. As the anti-psychedelic feelings began to heighten in the mid-sixties, his superiors made their discomfort clear, and Shulgin cut his ties with the company and continued his research freelance.

By the time MDMA was brought to his attention, he'd tested scores of compounds on himself, generating everything from states of paralyzing fear to mildly amusing visual distortions to ecstatic visions. He decided to test the new drug on a train trip to Reno with his wife and two friends. They packed a dinner to eat in a dining car decorated with white tablecloths and candelabras. While his companions mixed martinis, Shulgin asked if they'd mind him taking the MDMA instead.

He started with 25 milligrams but felt nothing. Still nothing at 40 milligrams, and nothing at 60.

At 81 milligrams he got something. From his lab notebook, which he'd packed along with the picnic foods: "53 mins, smooth shift into light intoxicaton. Blended very well into cocktail hour."

Pleasant if not earthshaking. By the time it had worn off a couple of hours later, he thought of MDMA as "a possible no-calorie martini."

But back home in his hillside compound, Shulgin decided he wasn't quite done with MDMA. He upped the dosage to 120 milligrams. This time it was no cocktail hour.

From his lab notes:

> As the material came on I felt that I was being enveloped, and my attention had to be directed to it. I became quite fearful, and my face felt cold and ashen. I felt that I wanted to go back, but I knew there was no turning back. Then the fear started to leave me, and I could try taking little baby steps, like taking first steps after being reborn. The woodpile is so beautiful, about all the joy and beauty that I can stand. I am afraid to turn around and face the mountains, for fear they will overpower me. But I did look, and I am astounded. Everyone must get to experience a profound state like this. I feel totally peaceful. I have lived all my life to get here, and I feel I have come home. I am complete. . . . I feel absolutely clean inside, and there is nothing but pure euphoria. I have never felt so great, or believed this to be possible.

Shulgin knew that some psychologists and psychiatrists had been having great success for years using LSD, psilocybin, and the other psychedelics as a tool in psychotherapy. He also knew better than most that the unpredictable and sometimes frightening effects of those drugs could make them difficult to work with, even potentially dangerous if situations were mishandled.

In MDMA he had found a drug that seemed to simply dissolve problems. He hadn't gone through a rocky process; he was just suddenly *there*. He had had a moment of fear at first, but that simply fell away. There was nothing like the bizarre perception shifts of LSD—no demons emerging from the wall or serpents coiling in snowdrifts. In retrospect, it was hard to know exactly why he'd felt any anxiety at all on MDMA, but he thought it was probably because he had sensed something powerful coming, and he didn't know which way it would turn. In the end, there'd only been a profound peace, total acceptance, awe for the beauty of the world, a transcendent *normality* that lingered long after the drug wore off. Wasn't that the wished-for endpoint of all therapy?

Shulgin felt he had to share this, and he knew just who to share it with: a Jungian psychotherapist, a friend of his named Leo Zeff. Since 1961, Zeff, considered the leader of the underground psychedelic psychotherapy movement, had been conducting therapy sessions with a range of psychedelic drugs, quietly continuing even after they'd been made illegal. He hadn't done any studies of the results, but he'd built a reputation by word of mouth, and the reputation was that people felt they accomplished more in one session with Zeff than they had in years of traditional therapy. Now, after more than fifteen years, Zeff was retiring.

When Shulgin went to visit Zeff in his small apartment, the short, white-haired therapist was looking over some of the mementos of his extraordinary career. He asked Shulgin if there was something he might want to take. Instead Shulgin had something to give: a vial of freshly cooked MDMA. A few days later Zeff called Shulgin to say he wasn't going to retire after all.

Zeff continued his practice, focusing on MDMA, until his death in 1988 at the age of seventy-five.

By 1982, when Rick discovered MDMA for himself, the use of the not-yet-illegal drug in therapy had been quietly but steadily growing for five years. From the start, Zeff had spread the word about MDMA's therapeutic impact evangelistically among other therapists. He even coined a catchy nickname for the drug, a scramble of the initials in the chemical shorthand that evoked the presumed state of purity and innocence it brought about: Adam. His efforts, by all accounts, were phenomenally successful. The online Urban Dictionary lists Zeff as "the Johnny Appleseed of MDMA." Estimates of the number of therapists he persuaded to use MDMA in their practices range up to 4,000, and the clients they treated number as many as 200,000. But as Zeff would have been the first to point out, Adam sold itself.

Rick, still just a therapist wannabe, had the same reaction that so many before him had had:

"I just thought, 'This potential is amazing.' It helped you to trust in the process of opening up and to see that, even with difficult things, feeling them and integrating them was the better thing, the better choice."

24.

MICHAEL

(HEAL THYSELF)

Back in Charleston after his sailing voyage, Michael reluctantly sold the boat and he and Annie bought a house on Sullivan's Island, a sleepy beach town half an hour from downtown. But things had shifted for Michael.

"Once I was back and working in the ER, not working so I could go sailing later, it began to be just not that engaging. After ten years, what had been exciting and stimulating began to be more of a hassle: a constant radio going off, doing twenty things at once. I guess you just don't enjoy that multitasking as much as you get older.

"And I was feeling drawn towards something—a different relationship with patients. I was always doing things to people, which was actually very good sometimes. That's what it called for. Putting a tube in and making somebody breathe, that kind of thing. But I was kind of developing a longing for more of a collaborative way of working with people . . . and also kind of feeling that I was catching the tail end of psychiatric problems. I was seeing people who were having heart attacks because they hadn't been taking care of themselves, who were stabbing each other, who were taking overdoses. A lot of what happens in the ER is a result of psychological problems coming to an end result.

So it also felt like it would be more satisfying to intervene at a different point."

As he began to look around for a new career path, he came across an article in a magazine about a psychiatrist named Stan Grof.

"I thought, '*Wow,*'" Michael says.

He went to the medical school library and found a book by Grof. He looked on the back page: nobody had ever checked it out. What he read in it confirmed the *Wow*. Here was someone who seemed to have discovered the principles underlying the powerful psychedelic experiences he'd had in college, both the good and the bad, and how to put them to use in a healing collaboration between therapist and patient. In other words, without knowing Michael existed, Grof had taken the loose ends of Michael's career aspirations and knit them neatly together.

"I didn't even know if the guy was still alive, and then I found out that not only was he alive but he had a breathwork training program."

Michael signed up for the training program and applied for a residency in psychiatry at the same time.

For three years Michael worked in the ER on the weekends while he trained to be a psychiatrist during the week, then periodically flew out to California for a series of weeklong breathwork training sessions.

Learning to do breathwork therapy—which was basically psychedelic therapy without the psychedelics—while also learning traditional late-twentieth-century psychiatry provided an enlightening contrast.

"When people were in the hospital and they became upset, the idea was to give them some drugs to calm them down. There was the idea of processing things in therapy, but if people were really having an intense process, most psychiatrists and nurses and psychologists were not comfortable with that. So at one point I came back from a Grof training session to the psychological trauma unit, which was a lot of people with PTSD, and I said to my attending, 'How about if we take some people and, instead of giving them Ativan and Haldol, what if we just sit with them and help them process it?' And he said, 'Well, that's a good idea. Are you going to be here twenty-four hours a day? Because there's no one else here who'd be able to tolerate that.' So I said, 'Okay, I see your point. I guess we can't implement it here.'"

Michael saw people arrive at breathwork sessions who probably would have been drugged and institutionalized by traditional psychiatrists; in fact, some had been for months at a time. They'd been hearing voices or thought they'd been abducted by aliens, and Grof would take them in.

"I thought, 'I hope to hell this guy knows what he's doing.'"

In breathwork, they'd still appear to be clearly disturbed, but as Grof kept them engaged in the process and urged them to work through their experiences, "the improvement was remarkable. If they had been truly psychotic, that would not have been possible," Michael says. "Stan saw a distinction between a psychotic and someone who was in the midst of a spiritual or emotional crisis, a distinction mainstream psychiatry often missed or dismissed."

Though Michael had been intrigued by the idea of breathwork, he had also been skeptical. Remembering his LSD experiences, he found it hard to believe that simply hyperventilating in time to pounding music could provide the intense altered state that theoretically could lead to deep exploration of the psyche.

"I was afraid that it wouldn't be powerful enough. In another way, I was afraid it *would* be powerful enough and that I'd have that same terrifying experience I'd had on LSD."

In general, the participants made quite a racket, and Michael had to laugh at himself: he'd left the ER partly to get away from all that intensity and noise and chaos. Now he'd changed career paths and flown across a continent to plop down in the middle of this noisy, chaotic, and intense breathwork session.

But after half an hour or forty-five minutes of breathing to the music, Michael found himself oblivious, in three-miles-an-hour-on-the-sidewalk territory. "I thought, 'This is an amazingly powerful technique. These states of consciousness are not as far away as I thought they were.'"

As his perception of reality shifted in the indescribable yet oddly familiar way, he braced against the possibility of getting stuck in that pit again, but it didn't happen. He felt safe and protected, and the fact that he was entering an altered state without any fear allowed the tangle of anxiety that had lingered in his psyche for forty years to finally relax.

"I felt relief, but it felt like something deeper than that. It wasn't anything I could put into words. It felt like a shift."

In later sessions, some of the fear reemerged. He felt himself "getting stuck and not feeling good, wondering if this was ever going to end," but never so intensely or so hopelessly as in his LSD experience. For one thing, unlike having a potent molecule in his bloodstream, with breathwork he knew he could simply stop hyperventilating and he'd come out of it. But that never proved necessary: the techniques he was learning—staying with the feeling, not fleeing it, moving through it—"had a cumulative effect of not only resolving that experience but resolving that gestalt we all carry.

"Everybody, or most people, can have periods of feeling depressed or stuck or hopeless. So it was kind of just working with that universal set of feelings. That doesn't mean that I never have any of those feelings, but I think the breathwork experiences largely cleared a lot of that energy from my psyche and my body."

"Staying with the feeling" is what Grof called "process," and it is the kind of thing that is easily mocked because it's so vague and self-dramatizing.

"It's very difficult to define but a really valid concept," Michael says. "The first step is having the perspective that 'this is something I can work with' rather than 'this is reality.' That's a necessary step, but I think there's something beyond that, in which you can stay with it, really be able to feel it, and really be present with all of those feelings and how they are in your body, and see what comes with it. Things happen that sometimes involve images, sometimes involve realizations about your life, and sometimes just seem to be some energy shift. The more you find you've moved through whatever it is that's eating at you, the easier it is to remember and be curious about it instead of trying to push it away, even in the moment. It just frees up a lot of energy that was maybe being used to try and control that or keep it in the background."

One thing eating at Michael had been so entirely suppressed, he hadn't even known it was bothering him. A year into the training, after one typically intense session that had already lasted a few hours, he thought he was done.

"I had this sitter, a guy from Norway, I think. He said, 'How are you doing?' I said, 'I'm doing well, but I've got this pain in my hip. It feels like if you could just pull on my foot and stretch that leg a little bit, it would be helpful.'"

The man obliged and pulled on Michael's foot. It was as if he had pulled a trigger setting off a cascade of images, a movie reel of all the people who had died in the ER over Michael's ten-year tenure.

"It was really like a movie: I was seeing them all, and I was just overcome by grief, guilt, shame."

It was only then that he realized the hip pain he'd felt after all those long days in the ER hadn't simply been about walking the hard floors. His mind had associated that pain with all the feelings he'd been repressing, feelings that now flooded him in an overwhelming wave, carrying with it a sense that he was doomed to suffer the lacerating shame and guilt for the rest of his life.

"Just then I heard a man on the other side of the room crying, and

I was really jealous because I felt like I couldn't cry, like I couldn't access that."

Facilitators began to hover, but Stan Grof must have sensed that something significant had occurred, because he came over to where Michael lay on his mat and lay down beside him.

"How are you doing?" he asked.

"Well, this has nothing to do with breathwork," Michael said. "This is just life."

Grof said, "What's happening in your body?"

Michael told him about his hip, and Grof began to work on it, "and finally the dam just burst and I sobbed. I wailed and cried for forty-five minutes, an hour, an hour and a half. A long time.

"That really changed things. It's not like it was all resolved, but it felt like it was an incredible opening to just be aware that I was carrying all that and to be able to cry about it and to have people there who could hear that and still be there with me. I just felt so ashamed that I had let these people die and all the stuff that comes with that kind of thing. And apparently I was carrying that in my hip. It was very queer. That's where I was carrying it. I don't know how that works, but it convinced me that bringing attention to what's happening in the body can be very helpful."

Michael had come to the workshops intending to learn to use breathwork to treat patients in his psychiatric practice. It surprised him how much of the training turned out to be dealing with his own issues, but it seemed clear now that only by going through it himself would he be of any use to anyone else.

25.

NICHOLAS

("GOT A LIGHT?")

The Superman feeling didn't last long. Eleven days after Nick's platoon survived the ambush, they got called on a recovery mission for some Marines in Charlie Company who'd gotten lost and done the same thing they'd done: wandered alone into the souk. Trying to find their way out, Charlie Company's truck hit an IED, which blew them across the road into another IED. By the time Nick's platoon arrived at the burned-out hulk of the Humvee, all the weapons had been taken by the locals and one of the bodies was missing. This was not something they could ignore. Everyone but Nick and Seabass dismounted and searched the area until someone noticed a hand sticking out of a garbage heap. They dug out the dead man and put him in a body bag.

"They made my radio guy get out, and they were gonna put this dead Marine in the seat," Nick says. "So, like, I was having to help them pull the guy in there, and I'm just kinda, you know, feeling him through the . . . and because of my stuff, paranormal stuff, when I touched him, I felt like I could see his mutilation. Because they had told me about him and stuff, and I felt like I could feel it—his presence—and it was just kinda bothering me. And I had to help set up a dead guy in the seat—you know, it's in a body bag—and then it was just sitting beside me the whole time, and here I am, kinda sitting in the turret with this, you know, dead Marine sitting beside me."

They returned to base and delivered the body for processing, which meant that the mortuary affairs unit would sort through and catalog all the personal effects found on the body: the rules-of-engagement pamphlet every Marine carried in his left breast pocket, uneaten MRE packages, notes to or from people at home, lists of things they most missed from "the world," photos of sweethearts, wives, children—sometimes even sonograms of fetuses. Then the body would be put back in the bag, the bag zipped back up, and placed in a metal box. The metal box would be slid into a locker in cold storage, awaiting placement on a flight to Dover Air Force Base in Delaware, where whoever loved the man in the bag would be presented with concrete proof that they'd lost him forever.

The fact that there was a mortuary affairs team—people who did the work nobody else wanted to know about or think about—meant that as soon as he'd turned the body over, it shouldn't have been Nick's problem anymore.

Only it was.

A few days later he was walking down the center of his hooch, in the aisle between the racks, when out of the corner of his eye he glimpsed a dark shape propped up against the wall. A body bag. An icy hand gripped his heart. He forced himself to turn and look at the wall. No body bag. But Nick couldn't brush it off. He remembered all the weird stuff from his childhood, the stuff that popped up unbidden and made his life hell. *Not here,* he thought. *I don't want that stuff here.*

The more he tried to will it away, the more he obsessed about it. Every hour he got through without another spooky incident only underscored how many hours there were in a day, a week, a deployment. And however many hours he got through, it wasn't long enough.

Nick, who'd taken up smoking, was having a cigarette sometime later. Suddenly he sensed a dead, mutilated Marine next to him saying, "Hey, got a light?"

Maybe he was imagining it, but he couldn't deny that he believed in such things as ghosts and spirits, or at least troubled energy, and so, being in a combat zone where people were dying constantly, "I knew that there just had to be a lot of negativity floating around there. I thought about it one time when I was smoking, looking at the ground, about how much blood had been spilled on this sand since the beginning of time. This place was just . . . a hell. You know? And there I was in the middle of it, trying to somehow still push forward while people are dropping left and right."

26.

RICK

(FORCES OF NATURE)

Rick returned to Esalen yet again in the spring of 1984 for another Grof workshop, this one directly focused on using breathwork to help people undergoing serious psychic trauma. This amounted to a training course in psychedelic therapy without the psychedelics. Rick soaked up what he could in the sessions, then aimed to add the one element the workshops were missing.

When the weekend came, he and a few others slipped off the Esalen campus to a private beach south of Big Sur. A waterfall poured down a cliff face at the edge of the sand and carved a channel of freshwater until it bubbled up against the surf. Here they'd stage their own workshop, this one using psychedelics instead of breathing. They ran the sessions themselves, taking turns sitting for one another late into the night, then slept under the stars. After one of these tripping weekends, Rick was walking back toward Esalen, when a car came around a curve and passed by. Stan Grof.

Rick knew that Grof didn't want to be responsible for any illegal activities, "but he didn't really want to be the police to stop it either. As he drove by he was just looking at me. And I kind of felt like he was saying, 'Do you know what you're doing?' And I just looked back at him and I felt, like, 'Yeah I do know.'"

Within days of his return to Florida, Rick would have a chance to try to prove that, in the highest-stakes way imaginable. He'd been home less than a week when he got a desperate call from one of his closest college friends. The friend and his girlfriend had taken some MDMA Rick had given him. During the experience, the woman, who had a long history of severe depression, suddenly recalled the roots of her problem: a repressed memory of having been brutally raped and almost killed. Rick's friend had no idea how to help her work through the emotions that surfaced with the recovered memory. It was a classic demonstration of the dangers of unscreened and inexpertly supervised use of psychedelics: the feelings overwhelmed her to the point where she checked into a hospital to stop herself from committing suicide.

After a week in the hospital, the woman was discharged with a prescription for the same antidepressants that she had always been given, which had never helped. It only convinced her that nothing *could* help, and she once again began to talk about suicide.

"Can you help her?" Rick's friend asked.

"I was just, like, '*Oh, my God.*' I had just been through this training but it doesn't mean that I'm trained or I'm ready or I know what to do. But then I felt like this is one of the crucial turning points in my life—that it was this sort of call to action—and if I turned away, my life would be completely different."

Rick rallied some friends who had experience with MDMA and agreed to take shifts to provide twenty-four-hour coverage. Then he called the woman and said, "As long as you promise not to commit suicide while you're with me, then I'll take the chance of working with you."

She agreed, and Rick moved her into his house with the round-the-clock care. They did an initial MDMA session, during which she recalled even more traumatic events in her life, including an earlier experience as the victim of a kidnapping.

"It was like layer upon layer upon layer," Rick says.

Rick knew from sitting with people in Grof's workshops that he couldn't attempt to "fix" the traumas that were emerging under MDMA's influence, but that by encouraging the woman to face them with curiosity and courage instead of fleeing or denying them, which the drug theoretically gave her the strength to do, she would gain power over the memories rather than continue to let fear of them shut down her life.

Recalling the therapy in a 1985 collection of oral histories called *Through the Gateway of the Heart: Accounts of Experiences with MDMA and Other Empathogenic Substances*, the woman, speaking anonymously, said of her trauma:

> By talking about it I was able to face the fear of the experience and to understand what it had done to my life. It was frightening to think that I had tried to ignore that day to the point where I didn't know where the pain had come from, nor could I remember what had happened. I had gone through life having nightmares and feeling guilty, telling myself that it was not normal to be affected by something that occurred such a long time ago. The most destructive feeling that resulted from the rape was a feeling of inner emptiness: I didn't feel love or hate for the people who had hurt me; I didn't feel anything toward myself and even less for life itself.

The session seemed to help. She no longer felt acutely suicidal, but in the days that followed, the waves of repressed memories kept coming and she cried nonstop.

Rick had a feeling that she needed something more. "She and I just talked about it and we agreed she would try taking LSD. The metaphor for me was that MDMA is the diamond polisher and LSD is the diamond cutter, and that there is a way that maybe we can go to the heart of the trauma."

Two weeks after the first session, Rick gave the woman a dose of LSD. After about two hours she had a vision of being on an alien planet with two blazing suns beating down on her, baking her to death.

She began to panic. Rick reassured her, but he felt the session had gotten stuck in a fearful place. He asked her if she'd be willing to take a half dose of MDMA, hoping the drug's ability to create a sense of protection would allow her to process the terrifying material that the LSD had brought to the surface.

"At this point I would have tried anything," the woman recalled in her oral history. "I thought the MDMA would help me cope with this pain, so I said yes. It didn't ease the pain but it helped to open up the emotions that were bottled up inside."

The alien planet with two burning suns resolved into a recovered memory. After she'd been raped and beaten, the rapist had thrown her on the ground and left her in the blazing sun to die. For the first time, she was able to talk about the circumstances that had led to the rape. She had been a virgin, and the man had been someone she knew, someone she was on a date with. He made a pass, and when she said no, he forced himself on her, then started beating her. Beneath the trauma of the attack, a deeper injury emerged: she'd lost all faith in herself, blamed herself for getting into the situation.

In *Through the Gateway*, she recalled the breakthrough moment, referring to Rick as "my friend":

> *The room seemed to fill up with people from my past who had hurt me, and with people who had tried to help me. My friend's eyes seemed to be calling out to me, but then all of a sudden he changed and became transformed into the rapist. His toes and legs were those*

of the rapist but I knew that the figure was my friend. It was hor-
rifying to see him as the man who had caused me so much pain. The
only reason I could deal with it was because my friend was so strong
in being himself that even though his body seemed to be that of the
rapist, the rapist could not take over his mind, and I could turn to
him for support.

I started to feel the horror of that day and I started vomiting.
Getting sick was more than just a physical illness. I was vomiting
from my soul, getting rid of pain, of an evil that had been destroy-
ing me. I felt that I was becoming stronger with my friend's help.
The rapist was grabbing me inside and wouldn't let go. I wanted to
vomit so badly, feeling that if I did I could be rid of the rapist—at
least he would be outside and no longer a part of me.

Later I felt I had got rid of so much, but I still felt nauseous,
there was still a burning lump in my stomach. But no matter how
hard I tried I couldn't get it out. It seemed to be the only part of the
rapist that remained. Maybe it will always be there and I will have
to learn to live with it. But it doesn't have to dominate my life.

Thirty years later the woman, a successful professional, says she still
finds the experience too disturbing to want to discuss at length. "But the
most important part," she says, "is that, yes, I had chronic PTSD and I
tried lots of different things and my life was really difficult and MDMA
really turned it around and saved my life. That's what is important."

With the dramatic success of his first attempt at practicing psychedelic
therapy, Rick was more convinced than ever: MDMA was a second
chance at history. By the time Rick became convinced of LSD's potential for healing, it had been criminalized. MDMA, possibly an even
superior drug for psychotherapy, was still legal.

But not for long. Even as Rick was rejoicing in this success, MDMA was poised to burst out of its therapeutic niche, paralleling the LSD explosion twenty years earlier. Into the early 1980s, the producers of MDMA had been a relatively small group of chemists centered in the Northeast who distributed mainly to therapists and those interested in using the drug therapeutically. But as the number of people who'd had positive experiences with MDMA expanded, it was only a matter of time before someone decided its charms could generate some serious cash in the mass market. It happened first in Texas, where some marketing genius decided the "Adam" label was too stodgy and came up with one of the most enticing drug nicknames of all time: Ecstasy.

In 1984 the new recreational drug craze would seize national attention at an instantly hot Dallas nightclub called Starck. Sold there at $12 a hit, Ecstasy made dancing feel great and staying up all night easy. But even in the party context, the drug's powerful impact on perception was inescapable. Here's an account of first-time Ecstasy use from that period, recalled in the *Austin Chronicle* in 2000:

> *The street lights got brighter, I could see the stars, car lights, even the shadows in this alley were, you know, more so. And I felt this tingle that began in my fingers and spread all over my body, coming in waves, just this indescribable feeling of aliveness. It was as if the nerves in my skin had been dormant all these years and were just now waking up and stretching. . . . After this initial rush of pleasure came an overwhelming—and I mean over-fucking-whelming— feeling of total and complete positivity. Any and all fears I had harbored about doing my first drug were waylaid instantly. It was pure bliss, but it didn't knock me off my feet, or feel scary in any way.*
>
> *My girlfriend . . . and I . . . lay in the wet grass and watched the stars and cuddled. And we talked. We talked for hours. We talked*

about everything. Everything. It was probably the best, most open and honest conversation I've ever had with anyone in my entire life.

Word-of-mouth reviews such as this fueled an explosion. From 1984 to 2001 the graph line for the number of first-time users of MDMA in the National Survey on Drug Use and Health would shoot straight up, reaching a peak of nearly 2 million new users in 2001 alone. Right from the start, emergency room doctors noticed a spike in would-be Ecstasy partiers coming in with something resembling what they called "amphetamine psychosis": anxiety, paranoia, and panic attacks. Many of them had taken as much as five times and in some cases fifteen times the therapeutic dose, consumed other drugs simultaneously, then danced all night in hot, crowded, and poorly ventilated dance clubs, with little to drink but dehydrating alcoholic beverages—dance clubs often restricted access to water in order to drive up the sales of liquor and overpriced soft drinks. Given MDMA's tendency to increase heart rate and blood pressure, this volatile mix spawned more serious emergency room visits from Ecstasy users who'd become dangerously hyperthermic as well as some fatalities that got enormous media attention. Increasingly, what was sold as Ecstasy contained a rogue's gallery of other drugs, some of them acutely dangerous. By the end of the 1990s, the DEA estimated that only 40 percent of what was sold on the street as Ecstasy actually contained MDMA.

Ecstasy began to provoke the same fearful reaction LSD had prompted twenty years earlier. Everyone knew that federal drug enforcement officials, who had taken half a decade to ban LSD, wouldn't delay on Ecstasy.

Even Rick knew that. But that didn't dim his excitement.

"Now we had this chance, this incredible opportunity when it was still legal, to introduce various people to it who would be in positions of authority and power, so that when the crackdown came we would be gathering our forces."

We?

Oddly, this tapped-out contractor and twenty-eight-year-old undergraduate believed he would be a player in the legal future of psychedelic therapy. To Rick, it seemed a reasonable progression. So he began to play the part.

Around that time he was reading a book by an assistant secretary-general of the United Nations, Robert Muller, called *New Genesis: Shaping a Global Spirituality.*

Muller was a visionary statesman. Although he had suffered under Nazi occupation, as a member of the French underground he attempted to stop the killing of captured German soldiers. He'd been devoted to the United Nations mission from its founding and was considered the organization's conscience. Two years earlier he had been instrumental in the founding of the UN's University for Peace in Costa Rica. The book Rick read made the case that underlying disputes between nations were conflicts between religions, and that the path to true world peace required the recognition of the universal spirituality upon which all religions were based.

Rick thought he'd glimpsed that universal truth—and others might, too, he believed, if they were just willing to swallow a pill with sincere intention.

So Rick wrote Muller a long letter, expressing his views. He can sum it up succinctly: "I just said, 'I really respected your book and I agreed with your thesis, but I noticed that you didn't say a single thing about psychedelics in your whole book. . . . Even if they're not real mystical experiences, they resemble mystical experiences.' And I said, 'Since every new way of killing gets virtually unlimited money from the Defense Department, we have the technology of death galore. This is the opposite. This is a technology of spirituality, of mysticism, of life. Would you help us try to bring back psychedelic research?'"

In the letter, Rick told Muller about the potential of MDMA and noted it was still legal.

Even Rick expected that to be the end of it. "But to my utter shock he wrote me back and he said, 'You understood my book. And there's a bunch of people in the spiritual community that would be interested in your ideas.' And he gave me a list of four or five people. And I read between the lines and I thought, 'He's telling me to send these people MDMA.' And I did, and in fact I'm still in touch with a bunch of those people."

Rick continued his MDMA outreach to respected spiritual leaders around the world, including a contemplative Benedictine monk, Brother David Steindl-Rast, internationally known for his efforts to forge reconciliation among the world's religions; Rabbi Zalman Schachter-Shalomi, a founder of the Jewish Renewal Movement, which aimed at deepening the direct spiritual experience of Jews; and Wayne Teasdale, a Catholic monk, professor, and author. With their cooperation, Rick launched a test project he called MDMA Assisted Meditation. "So I was shipping these caps of MDMA and they would take it in half doses in meditative settings. And they would report back to Robert Muller."

One of them, Brother David, was quoted in *Newsweek* saying that people spent twenty years meditating in order to feel the way MDMA made you feel in an afternoon.

Rick showed his correspondence with Muller to the woman who'd turned him on to MDMA in the first place, who showed it to several other people, one of whom showed it to Laura Huxley.

Laura Huxley, an Italian-born concert violinist and filmmaker, married Aldous Huxley in 1956, after the death of his first wife. She had been deeply involved in the human potential movement her husband had launched, and had given Price and Murphy her support, actively participating in Esalen's founding.

If there were such a thing as "psychedelic royalty," Laura Huxley was it, carrying on her husband's belief that drugs like psilocybin, mescaline, and LSD could lead to spiritual liberation if used with serious intent. Huxley's last work, a utopian novel called *Island*, featured a fictional psychedelic-type drug called moksha that was administered during life crises, as part of psychotherapy, and to help the dying let go of this life and make the transition to another existence.

When Huxley himself was dying of cancer in his home in the Hollywood Hills on the fateful day of November 22, 1963, just as John F. Kennedy expired from an assassin's bullet, he scrawled a message on a piece of paper and handed it to Laura. It was barely legible except for the first words, in large letters, which said, "LSD—Try it." She interpreted the scribble below as "100 micrograms, intramuscular."

He was asking for moksha.

After consulting with his doctor, who decided that at this point it could do no harm, she gave him one injection and later another. He had been horribly uncomfortable and agitated all morning. After the LSD injections, Laura later said, he became quiet and peaceful, then "like a music that becomes less and less audible, he faded away."

Huxley had died one week before Rick Doblin's tenth birthday. Now, two decades later, Laura knew everyone who was anyone in the psychedelic community. Of course, she had never heard of Rick until a friend showed her the correspondence with Muller. She was impressed enough to contact Rick through an intermediary to inform him that Dick Price had organized a meeting at Esalen of some of the most significant figures in the psychedelic movement to plan for the defense of MDMA against the inevitable crackdown. She invited Rick to attend. The fantasy had become a reality. Now Rick really was part of "we."

The people who Rick had idolized—Grof, Shulgin, Price, Zeff, and another psychedelic luminary, Terence McKenna—were now not just his inspiration but his colleagues. McKenna, thirty-nine in 1984, had written a number of books about psychedelic plants and their implications for human consciousness and had become a leading figure in those circles. At the meeting in Esalen, Rick found himself having a lively debate with McKenna about MDMA. McKenna believed the fact that the drug did not exist in nature made it potentially dangerous. Rick, far from intimidated, demanded proof. And then he went further: "I said, 'We should arrange for a study of MDMA, and we should do it now while it's still legal. I'll put up a thousand dollars.'"

Dick Price, who had been listening, immediately offered a thousand dollars of his own money.

The result was a study of the effect of MDMA on twenty-one subjects, all of whom took a single dose in a California beach house under the supervision of Leo Zeff as doctors checked blood pressure and monitored body temperature and psychologists performed neurocognitive evaluations. The elevated pulse and blood pressure readings all fell in tolerable ranges and quickly subsided after the drug wore off. All participants felt the experience was a positive one. Mental functioning continued to test high even during the peak of MDMA's subjective effects. Rick, who served as a monitor in the experiment, called it "a beautiful experience."

He decided to try to keep the positive results quiet for the time being. He didn't want to tip off the Drug Enforcement Administration that they were preparing a defense, afraid to provoke the agency into banning the drug sooner than it otherwise might.

Rick knew for sure he was in the mix when Zeff offered to give Rick psychedelic therapy sessions to improve his political abilities. Rick did MDMA himself, intending to focus specifically on his attitude toward the DEA, so "I didn't completely project my shadow and [act like] the DEA is all evil and I'm always angry at them. I was trying to play on their humanity rather than demonize them."

This was the big insight that began Rick's mainstream career. He had been a draft resister, a drug resister, resigned to living and working underground. But now he felt it didn't have to be that way. President Jimmy Carter had pardoned the draft resisters his first day in office in 1977. Now Rick had an opportunity to work within the system, by the system's rules, to find, or force, common ground around what he believed to be an incontrovertible truth: psychedelics, used with care and expertise, could do people and the world a lot of good. The force of that truth, he realized—not his anger, not his disdain for authorities— would have to be his most powerful weapon.

On the eve of engaging the most powerful government on the planet in a nearly hopeless rearguard action, Rick camped alone at Esalen on the beach.

Despite his audacious self-confidence, despite being accepted into the ranks of the psychedelic elite—or maybe because of it—Rick felt small, unequal to what lay ahead, more alone than ever. He took some MDMA and watched the sun sink beneath the Pacific. The darkness deepened as the drug took hold. He found himself tiptoeing at the edge of an unspeakable void, gaping into a bottomless maw of ocean and stars. The vacuum sucked at him, pulling him apart piece by piece. The "Rick" who had always loomed so large in his conception, who had tried to dominate the world with intellect and reason, peeled off into the void, layer by layer. He watched himself disappear with something between awe and terror. Just as the reduction was about to become absolute, as he floated to the edge of oblivion, he felt a gentle tug. Somehow he recognized the force as gravity—not merely the gravity he'd learned about in physics, but something intimate, personal, nurturing, caressing him like a lover. And for the first time he believed and trusted that when you let go, you weren't gone. This loving force would hold on.

27.

MICHAEL

(GETTING TO THE ROOT)

As intense as the breathwork training had been for Michael, it may have been tougher on Annie, who was staying at home with the girls, wondering what weird, scary thing Michael was up to on the other side of the continent.

"She thought I'd been kidnapped by a cult in California, basically," Michael says.

"The stories were pretty strange," Annie says. Although she had had her own psychedelic experiences in college, the idea of tripping without any drugs seemed a little crazy to her.

"I guess the difference for me would be, when you're taking LSD and you say, 'I saw an animal come out of the woods, and it was all green,' I'd say, 'Okay, well that's the drug experience.' But Michael goes off to a group and hyperventilates, and then he comes back and starts talking about this past life he might have had, it's also, like, *good God*. Is that really possible with hyperventilation? And who are these people? And are they gonna take my husband away?"

Annie once again came up against the insecurity of being the one who always seemed to hold back in the relationship. Michael was out there, doing his adventurer/explorer thing alone, and Annie couldn't entirely suppress her fear of being left behind.

"I worried maybe I would lose him to somebody else out there. Or he might change and not want to be with me. There are all kinds of things that would come up around when one person starts to do something different and change."

It took Michael three years to get certified in both breathwork and psychiatry. During that time Annie began having panic attacks. The first one came during an adult ed night class in French at the College of Charleston. She'd been enjoying the class, making good progress, when her heart started racing out of control. She couldn't catch her breath and nearly passed out, convinced she was about to die. A classmate took her to the emergency room, where she got an EKG showing her heart was in perfect condition.

But the attacks kept coming. She couldn't find a cause, or even a trigger. A prescription for Xanax didn't help, and she became seriously depressed. With Michael's encouragement, and despite her doubts, Annie went to a breathwork session out in the sticks in Pennsylvania. She drove through a snowstorm to get there, afraid the entire time that she'd have a panic attack in the middle of the session. It didn't happen, but a woman in the room, in the throes of an altered state, started screaming, which terrified Annie. She managed to keep on with her breathing through it all, taking the facilitators at their word that she should use everything that happened during the session as part of her process. The screaming made her scared, and fear was her problem, so, yeah, she could use that.

Ultimately, in doing the breathwork, she uncovered a complex origin of her panic. Underlying the fear was anger and a feeling of constriction and loss of control beginning with a domineering father and including frightening experiences as an adolescent with menstrual cramps so bad that they made her faint. As instructed, she tried to allow those memories to come up and let the feelings move through her without rejecting or resisting them. Over time, the scary stuff became less scary, and the panic attacks less frequent, until they vanished entirely. She realized the attacks had only been a bleeping alarm warning of a serious imbalance in her life rooted in her insecurities. The breathwork allowed her to explore the areas that had always been too painful and to untangle the psychic knots that she'd been trying to ignore, with potentially catastrophic consequences.

"I feel like it saved my life and our marriage—just so many things have been made better by it," she says.

Annie went on to train with Grof, as Michael had, until both were certified to do breathwork therapy; and as Michael continued his outpatient psychiatric practice, they began to offer sessions together about once a month.

Of course, Michael didn't need to be a psychiatrist, or even an MD, to do breathwork therapy. Back when he'd been planning his transition from the ER, he'd asked to speak with the dean of the medical school.

"He said, 'Well, you could certainly do this other ways, but especially if you're gonna do something that's different, having the paper makes a big difference,'" Michael remembers. "It's just like shorthand. 'Okay, he's board-certified in psychiatry.' That probably means more than it should in some ways, but that sort of calms people down. And I think it is true: the more you're doing something different, the more it helps to have very solid, mainstream kind of credentials."

During his psychiatric residency, Michael saw up close how psychiatry had more or less been taken over by the use of psychoactive medications—antipsychotics, antianxiety drugs, antidepressants—all of which were designed to treat symptoms rather than address the underlying causes of the disease. And all of which were prescription medicines—except of course, for psychedelics, the one class of psychoactive drugs that *did* purport to get at underlying causes.

Michael found himself spending most of his time in the hospital unit treating eating disorders and psychological trauma. The patients, almost all women, had suffered sexual abuse or rape, the kinds of things that resulted in PTSD. When he began his own practice, that was the focus.

"It was the one area of psychiatry remaining in which psychotherapy was clearly the treatment. Antidepressants were the treatment for depression, and antipsychotics were the treatment for psychosis, and antianxiety drugs were the treatment for panic and generalized anxiety and stuff. But nobody thought that, though they could help with the symptoms, there were any medications for the treatment of PTSD. I think that was what was appealing: it really required psychotherapy, which I was much more interested in than just giving people medicines. So, in my practice, I used medicines a lot, but I never did it without therapy too. If people just said, 'I have a chemical imbalance and I want to take medicines. I'm not interested in therapy,' I'd say, 'There are lots of good psychopharmacologists in town. I'll refer you, but that's not how I work.'"

In private practice he often recommended breathwork as a course of treatment. "Not everyone was open to that," but if they were, they'd go to the monthly sessions and then sometimes continue to process what came up in individual appointments. Michael found he was getting good results with people struggling with PTSD, depressions, and eating disorders, all without using the usual medications.

"After a while, we began to get referrals from psychiatrists who had patients that were kind of stuck."

To add to his arsenal of nondrug therapies, Michael trained with a psychologist named Francine Shapiro who had developed a mouthful of a technique called eye movement desensitization and reprocessing, referred to by its acronym, EMDR. Shapiro had come across the idea by happenstance. One day she was having unusually vivid and painful memories when she noticed that her eyes began moving back and forth spontaneously, and as she focused on the eye movements, she found herself rapidly resolving thoughts and feelings that had long haunted her.

Curious about the connection between the eye movement and the emotional breakthrough, Shapiro searched the psychological literature and discovered a few case reports from a psychiatrist who had observed the same phenomenon occurring spontaneously with several of his patients decades earlier. But he never studied it further. Shapiro did, theorizing that the eye movements were connected directly to brain activity that might be involved in reprocessing painful memories, disentangling the remembered events from the fearful emotions they evoked. She eventually developed a complex treatment in which talk therapy is combined with eye movements prompted by an intense light moving along a horizontal track. As their eyes follow the moving light, patients were encouraged to hold certain relevant images or thoughts in their minds and then discuss the insights and implications that come up.

"When I first did the training with her, most of my colleagues thought I was crazy," Michael says. That was more than twenty years ago, and only recently, after massive research, EMDR has become one of the few treatments recommended in the American Psychiatric Association guidelines for PTSD. Now some of the same colleagues who thought he was crazy send him referrals.

The first time Michael did EMDR himself was in a training session in a large hall. "We're divided into pairs, and it's kind of noisy. They say, 'Don't start with something really, really difficult in this setting. Just start with something that has a moderate charge for you.' So I just thought, 'Okay, what's something not that important?' And I came up with when I was in fifth or sixth grade, playing baseball after school— just like a pickup game—and I felt really dissed and left out because Michael Green—a guy who kind of seemed to take charge—told me I couldn't bat because I hadn't been in the field the inning before. And I realized . . . it was almost laughable, but I was still carrying some of that feeling of being unfairly treated. So I start doing the EMDR, and I'm really right back there in fifth grade, feeling how it felt. And then suddenly it just pops into my head: 'Oh. That's actually the *rule*.' He was just playing by the rules. And it felt like a tremendous relief. I really could feel it. *It wasn't personal*. So in some way I'd taken it personally for thirty or forty years by then. It's pretty hilarious. And that's what happens. People think, 'Oh!' and suddenly these insights pop into their head."

All of this reinforced for Michael the value of working with nonordinary states. But he knew that breathwork and EMDR didn't work for everybody.

"Some people seemed to need another tool. And so I became increasingly aware that it didn't seem right that we couldn't explore psychedelics as possible treatments. You read about these doctors that are in managed-care contracts, and they're not allowed to mention expensive chemotherapy to people. It felt a little bit like that, you know? People are coming to me, saying, 'What can I do? Nothing else is working,' and I'm not allowed to say, 'Well, there's this class of compounds that have been shown to be effective in the research that was done before, but we can't talk about that.' It seemed unacceptable from an ethical point of view."

Michael decided that there had to be a way, despite what was by now a three-decade-long prohibition, to investigate the healing potential of psychedelic drugs. He kept circling around to the irony that psychedelics had been used for spiritual and healing purposes for hundreds, even thousands, of years, a positive force in countless cultures.

In fact, they still were.

Which got him thinking. . . .

28.

NICHOLAS

("KEEP THE GLOVE ON")

Less than two weeks after the Charlie Company ambush, on October 21, Nick's Light Horse platoon combined with Bronco platoon for a patrol in the city. They were a mirror image of vehicles and armament traveling in parallel along facing alleys. Bronco was led by Lieutenant Daniel Moran, the lieutenant Nick had accidentally body-slammed back in training, and Lieutenant Boehlert's close friend.

Now the two lieutenants shared a joint mission: escorting the explosive ordnance disposal unit. The very nature of the EOD was to *look* for trouble, to roll into the most heavily booby-trapped territory with their thickly armored vehicles, their robots, and their bomb suits searching out IEDs to mess with. At night.

Night missions were spooky, but at least Nick could stand up in his turret without feeling like a neon bull's-eye. The enemy didn't have night vision gear, or at least that's what they'd been told. Nick savored the unaccustomed luxury of a breeze puffing through his body armor as they rolled into the maze of alleyways. Nick's Humvee, with Lieutenant Boehlert aboard, was in the lead going down one alley, and Moran's Humvee led down the other, when the sky ripped apart.

"I remember seeing this huge fireball go in the air," Nick says. "And my lieutenant said, 'What was that?' and I said, 'There's a huge fireball in the sky,' and then the only thing I remember coming out of his mouth was '*Bronco*.'"

Boehlert issued sharp, urgent orders and Seabass whipped the Humvee around the corner and into the parallel alley, approaching from the front.

Bending down and looking through the front window, Nick saw Lieutenant Moran lying on the ground, smoke rising from his body. Another Marine, a guy named Blanco, stumbled toward their Humvee, looking wobbly, as if he'd just been woken from a deep sleep. When Seabass opened the door, they were looking at Bronco's Humvee immersed in flames. Even from a few car lengths away, he felt the intense heat from the fire on the exposed skin of his face. The EOD guys were throwing a flame-retardant blanket on the still-smoking Lieutenant Moran, and Blanco stood there, looking at them, tottering.

Where were the others? Were they still in there?

Blanco was talking; he was confused, rambling. Then he said, "Take off my glove, bro. It's hot."

Blanco held his hand out toward them and Nick and Seabass both looked at it. His glove and his hand were the same thing, a charred, smoking clump; you couldn't tell where glove ended and flesh began.

"It was just—it looked really bad. And Seabass was real calm, and he said, 'Man, you need to keep your glove on. Don't take it off.' And that's one of the things they taught us in the training when it comes to burns: Don't remove anything because you'll take the flesh with it."

The corpsman came by and took Blanco and Lieutenant Moran off, leaving Nick and Seabass to watch the vehicle burn and slowly come to the realization that Blanco and Moran were the lucky ones. Three more guys—the driver, Collinsworth; the radio guy, Manny; and the machine gunner, Elrod—were missing and presumably still in there, in that fire.

As they watched it burn, they could see silhouettes through the flames. Nick desperately looked for some way to approach the vehicle to fight the fire and attempt a rescue, but the vehicle started cooking off: all the ammo and explosives began to ignite. *Boom. Boom. Boom.* The open spot in Nick's turret faced the fire. He turned it sideways and ducked down just in time as the rounds from the exploding munitions pinged into the armor surrounding him. Seabass had jumped back in the Humvee and was backing them off to a safer distance.

"Every time there was a moment where we'd think we could go in there and maybe put it out or do something, more rounds would start cooking off, and then the grenades would go off, and then . . . We ended up having to back our vehicles out and get away from it because that vehicle was a liability. We had to sit there and let our guys burn and just watch it because we couldn't do anything about it."

Nick felt bad for his lieutenant, who had to give the order to back off. That had been his best friend lying smoking on the ground, his best friend's crew burning alive in there, so Nick was impressed with how Boehlert "held his stuff together. He was a pretty good officer. He didn't show—he stayed very professional, and that had to be hard for him."

It was hard for all of them.

Nick knew the men only slightly, but he'd gone through training with them, lived in the same barracks with them, gone through the same hell, faced the same dangers. As they waited for an opportunity to approach the vehicle, images raced through Nick's mind of the men inside. Collinsworth had been one of those guys always on the offensive. He'd picked on Nick constantly, always giving him a hard time. Nick didn't like it, but he didn't take it personally. "That's just the kind of person he was."

But that day, when they were getting ready for the mission, out of nowhere Collinsworth had given Nick a big smile and said, "What's up, faggot?" but in a good-humored way that made Nick smile back.

"I realized that that was his way of actually being nice, seeing that smile. And I remember, in that moment, kind of forgiving him for all the stupid stuff that, you know, just picking on me before. And I had no idea that he'd be leaving.

"The other guy, Manny—his name was Nicholas as well. His full name was Nicholas Manoukian, but we called him Manny. He was a radio guy. He didn't even know me; he wasn't even in my platoon. But whenever I'd be back in the barracks back in the States, training or whatever, anytime guys were joking around with me, just picking on me for the smallest things, he always took up for me. And it always surprised me, because I was just, like, 'I don't know you.' He was new to our unit, too, and I didn't go to Fallujah with him or anything, and I was just, like, 'I don't know this guy, but he's nice enough to back me up.' He was just a nice guy. Had a wife and everything, Manny did."

By then there was no doubt that that woman had lost a husband. Manny and Collinsworth had to be dead.

What Nick felt, more than anything, was rage. "We were furious," he said. "You know, anytime that they ever got us, it's just, it's something that feels like a low blow, you know?"

When the fire and explosions had finally died down—hours had passed—they crept back toward the still-smoking wreckage. As they moved in, a brick wall burst open, a secondary explosion timed by the insurgents to inflict casualties on whoever responded to the first one. Nick was knocked back by the impact but unhurt. When the dust settled, they couldn't see Lieutenant Boehlert, who had been on foot near where the explosion went off. They tried raising him on the radio, but the answering static mocked them. Then the static broke into violent coughing, followed by Boehlert's voice, shaky but cogent. "It just kinda rattled his noggin a little bit."

Ignoring the threat of a tertiary strike, they moved in on what was left of the wall, trying to trace the wires on the secondary explosion to find out where the insurgent who had triggered it had been holed up. That led them to a nearby house, but the bomber was long gone. While that was going on, another platoon rogered up on the radio to alert them: there was movement behind the vehicle.

That's where they found Nathan Elrod, twenty, just a year older than Nick. Elrod was a gunner, too, and, like Nick, he'd decided in high school that he wanted to be a Marine. "A good, nice, and caring person," the sixteen-year-old Elrod had written in an essay on the kind of man he wanted to be. "A U.S. Marine, and a hero." The impact of the IED blew Elrod out of his turret. He'd been lying in the dirt, minus both legs and part of one arm, for hours. When they got to him, his blood seeping away into the filth of the street, he was conscious and talking. They carried him into the vehicle. He had no idea what had happened to him.

"I can't . . . I can't breathe," he told them.

And then he died.

Lieutenant Moran and Blanco both survived. Moran suffered third-degree burns over 50 percent of his body, multiple fractures in his back, damage to his lung, a concussion, and a crushed spleen. Blanco's hands and legs and face were all badly burned. Moran would require thirty surgeries and spend three years recovering from his wounds. Both men would be dealing with their injuries, in one way or another, the rest of their lives.

But they would have lives.

That night Nick's platoon sat there waiting for the fire to burn out and guarding the wreckage, which had become a tomb. At one point Nick noticed an Iraqi grilling meat for dinner in his little yard just on the other side of the wall as if nothing had happened, and he seethed with helpless rage. It wasn't until after sunrise that they were able to tow the charred hulk away, the Marines' remains inseparable from the chassis. As they went, pieces of the wreck fell away.

After that, Nick couldn't even look at fire. Which was a problem, because they had to burn their mail. He just couldn't do it for days. But he knew he couldn't go through the rest of his life avoiding the sight of flames, so he took his accumulated letters out to the fire pit and forced himself to watch as the papers curled, then blackened. He just stood there crying until he felt a hand patting him on his shoulder.

"Everyone understood," he said.

29.

RICK

(DRUG WARRIORS)

The group meeting and making plans at Esalen called itself the Association for the Responsible Use of Psychedelic Agents. The acronym, ARUPA, a Sanskrit word meaning formless, was an appropriate description of a group with no charter, a shifting membership, and no designated leaders. It occurred to Rick that ARUPA was not the most solid platform for going toe-to-toe with an organization as formidable as the DEA.

He was thinking this over back in Florida when he sought out a friend who had studied with the architect, futurist, and systems analyst R. Buckminster Fuller. The well-heeled friend happened to have chartered a Fuller-associated nonprofit organization to promote conservation and energy efficiency he'd named Earth Metabolic Design Laboratories. But the organization had fallen into inactivity. The friend suggested that Rick take it over.

"I looked at the mission statement and I said, 'Okay, I can reinterpret this to include conservation of mental energy as well as physical energy.'"

Rick filed the necessary paperwork and brought it to the Esalen group, who enthusiastically embraced the idea. Soon Rick, along with two key members of ARUPA, sat on the board of a nonprofit. Henceforth, the mission of the Earth Metabolic Design Laboratories would be to secure and advance the future of MDMA as a psychotherapeutic drug.

The sudden materialization of a certified nonprofit organization devoted to the cause made Rick a leader in the coming confrontation with the DEA.

His next move was even bolder. He understood better than most the value of a sizable stash of a highly marketable drug. Knowing he wouldn't be able to rely on the government for a supply for any future research, he raised $4,000 through donations to commission a DEA-licensed chemist to synthesize one kilo of MDMA, which was about one-thirtieth the cost of what the same amount would have cost at the Starck rave club. That single kilo of white powder, ultimately synthesized and kept under lock and key at Purdue University, would supply research material for decades to come.

One more thing: he made an arrangement with New College. For suing the DEA, he would get full college credit.

On July 27, 1984, the DEA formally announced that it intended to place MDMA on Schedule I of the Controlled Substances Act.

Schedule I might well be symbolized by a skull and crossbones. Possession of any drug on the list comes with tough criminal penalties. No prescriptions can be written for Schedule I drugs, and doing research with them requires an arduous, expensive, time-consuming, and by no means certain application process involving multiple federal agencies. In order to be remanded to this most restrictive category, the Controlled Substances Act requires that the drug have: (1) a high potential for abuse, (2) no currently accepted medical use in the United States, and (3) a lack of accepted safety for use under medical supervision. A drug found to have this trifecta of demerits is in rare, bad company. Even cocaine and methamphetamine, drugs that have wreaked untold damage in society, are listed as Schedule II drugs only because they are considered to have some medical use—cocaine as a local anesthetic for eye and nose surgery, and methamphetamine in the treatment of hyperactive children.

Now that the DEA had spoken, the pro-MDMA group, which had kept its strategic silence, sprang into action. Rick had been quietly working on collecting petitions from the prominent and respectable, all urging that MDMA research be allowed to continue under Schedule III, a much less constricting category of control for drugs with an accepted medical use and only moderate potential for abuse and physical dependency. Schedule III would still outlaw street use but permit clinical research and prescription by a physician. Rick flew to Washington, where he met with an attorney named Richard Cotton in the DC office of the venerable New York–based firm Dewey, Ballantine, Bushby, Palmer & Wood. Cotton, a contact of Sasha Shulgin's, agreed to take the case pro bono and quickly drew up papers requesting a hearing and naming as lead plaintiff in the suit a highly respected professor at Harvard Medical School, psychiatrist Lester Grinspoon. Rick hand-delivered the hearing request and the testimonials to the DEA office. He still has a photo of himself reflected in the window of the office door, wearing jeans and a dress shirt, his hair still long and untamed.

"That was a sweet moment," Rick says.

Also an impactful moment. A DEA chemist at the time, Frank Sapienza, told the *Los Angeles Times*, "After the announcement, all hell broke loose."

According to Sapienza, the DEA hadn't even been aware that MDMA was being used for therapeutic reasons until the documents Rick delivered hit the office.

From the *Times* story: "The DEA was deluged with letters from angry psychiatrists and therapists who challenged the DEA's research and classification procedures. They were outraged that the DEA plan would virtually eliminate all research and clinical use of the drug, and they demanded a public hearing."

The government had no choice but to accede. Hearings were scheduled to be held in Los Angeles, Kansas City, and Washington.

People in newsrooms all over the country began to drool. A government clampdown on an exotic party drug made a fine story. Add an uproar from respected professionals claiming a drug called Ecstasy could be *good* for you, and you had something of a media superstorm.

This suited Rick perfectly. He saw the moment in the national spotlight as a chance to completely change the public perception of MDMA in particular and psychedelics in general. Not all his allies felt as he did. As he would later tell a reporter, "When the publicity wave started coming to MDMA, the attitude of a lot of the people was 'We've been thinking of ourselves as an underground counterculture and now there's this publicity wave coming and what we should do is dive down and hold our breath and we'll be safe down there on the ocean floor.' And my attitude was 'Let's see if we can surf on this.'"

Now that the long history of therapeutic use of psychedelics had been largely forgotten, Rick saw an opportunity to focus attention on psychiatrists and researchers with impeccable credentials speaking up about the drugs' potential, not to mention the cadre of distinguished spiritual leaders he had connected with. Rabbi Zalman Schachter-Shalomi publicly compared psychedelics to a sacrament. Of MDMA he would later say for publication, "I felt the great delight of loving the universe and being loved by the universe."

Brother David Steindl-Rast told the *Los Angeles Times* the MDMA experience was "like climbing all day in the fog and then suddenly, briefly seeing the mountain peak for the first time. There are no short-cuts to the awakened attitude, and it takes daily work and effort. But the drug gives you a vision, a glimpse of what you are seeking."

All of this amounted to extremely unwelcome noise to the ears of those directing America's then decade-old "War on Drugs," a term that dated to the very creation of the Drug Enforcement Administration in 1973, when President Nixon declared "an all-out global war on the drug menace." The language of all-out war did not permit ambivalence, a fact reflected in the DEA's conduct in seeking to place MDMA in Schedule I. They had clearly decided that no drugs related to psychedelics could be said to have any value whatsoever and that arguing the contrary would only encourage massive abuse by the public. (But that horse had already bolted out of the barn: the DEA estimated that MDMA use had increased from 10,000 doses in all of 1976 to 30,000 doses *per month* in 1985. In fact, Rick was told by his sources in the Ecstasy trade that the real number was more like *2 million* a month.)

Articles appeared in *The Washington Post*, *Time*, and *Newsweek*, all responsive to the claim that MDMA therapy had been safe and helpful to thousands of people when used in clinical settings. The *Time* piece began, "This is the drug that LSD was supposed to be, coming twenty years too late to change the world. . . . Users say it has the incredible power to make people trust one another, to banish jealousy and to break down barriers that separate lover from lover, parent from child, therapist from patient. Yet, unlike LSD, it does not break down one's ability to tell reality from fantasy, so it appears free of many of that drug's unfortunate side effects."

But the articles weren't unremittingly positive. Harvard psychiatry professor Dr. Norman Zinberg told *The Washington Post*, "I think the therapists giving it are fools. People [who take it] get sentimental and lugubrious and think they've discovered the truth."

The initial burst of publicity culminated in an episode of the Phil Donahue show, which at the time was the most popular talk show on television. Donahue devoted the entire program to the MDMA scheduling controversy with a well-stocked panel of people from both sides of the debate. A drug abuse expert spoke about how MDMA could get a kid "completely messed up" after just one dose. Impressively erudite therapists countered by saying how helpful MDMA therapy had been in their practice, and grateful patients told their own stories from the audience with telegenic emotion. As the ARUPA group had envisioned, millions of Americans got their first inkling that this psychedelic drug might do more good than harm.

But a nasty surprise awaited MDMA advocates. Rick had suggested that the show invite Dr. Charles Schuster, a brain researcher at the University of Chicago who had been working with the World Health Organization on drug abuse issues. Rick had met Schuster when he flew to Geneva in a futile effort to prevent the inclusion of MDMA on the international version of Schedule I. The two had a promising conversation in which Schuster said he supported placement of MDMA on the far less restrictive Schedule III, which would make it available to doctors for treating patients.

When the cameras rolled, Schuster repeated his belief that MDMA belonged on Schedule III, then dropped a bomb. He announced that research with MDA, a psychoactive drug chemically related to MDMA, indicated that very large, repeated doses caused brain damage in rats. He went on to say that he believed there was "a 99 percent chance that we'll get exactly the same results with MDMA as we got with MDA."

The DEA representative on the show, Deputy Assistant Administrator Gene Haislip, pricked up his ears. It was the first time anyone in the organization had heard that MDMA might be neurotoxic.

Within weeks the DEA announced that, owing to the increasingly widespread use of a drug that potentially caused brain damage, it was using emergency powers to place MDMA on Schedule I immediately. Any hope that the suit would keep MDMA legal during the hearing process—allowing more patients to complete their treatments and more allies to be won over by experiencing the drug themselves—was destroyed.

Some blamed Rick for the miscalculation. Tension within the pro-MDMA alliance had been growing already. Rick, with the platform of his nonprofit and his unstoppable energy, had become the most quoted advocate for therapeutic use of the drug. But his refusal to condemn nontherapeutic use irked his more conservative colleagues.

It was no accident that in the brief opposing the emergency scheduling of MDMA, the named plaintiffs in the suit against the DEA, two psychiatrists and two professors, began the second paragraph, "We emphasize that we support the DEA's efforts to make street use and recreational use of MDMA illegal."

As Rick recalls it: "I was making a bunch of people nervous that were on our stationery. They personally didn't believe that criminalization was a good thing but they didn't want to be identified as supporting recreational use. Because of my positive experiences at the all-night dances at New College and my appreciation for recreational use, which can be life-affirming and therapeutic in its own right, I felt morally bound to say that we are fighting to protect therapeutic use of MDMA, but the whole enterprise of criminalization is a bad idea."

Rick acknowledges that this made it sound like "I was promoting drug use and people should take these drugs for fun."

A cover story in *Tropic*, the Sunday magazine of the *Miami Herald*, featured a close-up of Doblin's face and the headline "The Selling of Ecstasy: How a Sarasota College Student Became the Timothy Leary of the '80s."

This connection with the Leary disaster of twenty years earlier was exactly what many of the supporters of MDMA therapy wanted to avoid. These were accomplished, foundation-, university-, and government-funded researchers, therapists, and psychiatrists for whom being mentioned in the same sentence as Leary could be tantamount to career suicide, not to mention sink any hopes of continuing MDMA research.

Under pressure to moderate his views, Rick, who had been the principal contact for the Donahue show, backed himself off the guest list, commenting from the audience instead of the stage. And then he went further. He resigned from his Earth Metabolic Design Laboratories foundation, handing it over to the others. His only conditions: he wanted to retain control of the research MDMA stash, and to hold on to the portfolio of animal MDMA safety studies he'd set in motion.

He had no specific plans for that data. He only sensed that, at some point in the future, it might come in handy.

The hearings began in the spring of 1985 and took the form of a series of testimonies and rebuttals from various expert witnesses. The plaintiffs produced evidence from years of clinical use that MDMA psychotherapy had proven safe when used under controlled conditions and remarkably effective in treating a range of psychological conditions, as well as beneficial in healthy people looking to improve their overall life satisfaction. The DEA countered with witnesses bearing long scientific résumés who called those informal studies of MDMA psychotherapy "heavily biased" and "almost entirely anecdotal and subjective in nature."

"Although these reports make interesting reading, their lack of scientific design, methodology and controls makes them scientifically unsound," one expert witness testified.

The biggest dispute came over the meaning of the phrase *no currently accepted medical use.*

One of the government's most impressive witnesses, Ronald Siegel, a UCLA psychopharmacologist with an international reputation, summed up the DEA case on this issue succinctly:

"MDMA has no currently proven medical use in treatment in the

United States. Thus far, case reports and clinical observations, though suggestive, are insufficient for demonstrating treatment effectiveness."

This turns out to be a moderate version of Siegel's actual opinion, which he voiced to writer Joe Klein for an article in *New York* magazine as the hearings were getting under way:

> *"My reaction is 'Here we go again.' Every few years you get one of these miracle drugs that's going to save the world and make everyone feel good. My favorite was PCP. Remember what they used to call that? The* Peace Pill. *At low doses, people were reporting serene, tranquil, peaceful experiences. Then it hit the street . . . dosages increased, and it was cut with God knows what, and you began to get all the reports of bizarre, violent behavior. So now we have Ecstasy. If you take it, you might become a self-actualized, empathetic, caring person, or you might become a nauseated person, or you might have a severe psychotic reaction. Among street users, we're seeing all the above."*

But the DEA legal team didn't want to get lost in the weeds of pro and con reports about therapeutic usage. They contended the question of accepted medical use was black-and-white in its simplicity: any drug that hadn't been extensively researched, tested, and approved by the FDA for a specific purpose could *not* be said to have an "accepted medical use."

The MDMA supporters argued that FDA approval was far too narrow a definition and that medical professionals alone could determine what was acceptable medical use. In the case of MDMA, they contended, the clinical experiences of scores of therapists and thousands of patients was proof enough of an "accepted medical use."

The parties also clashed over whether MDMA had a "high potential for abuse" and whether it was "safe for use under medical supervision."

The plaintiffs argued that MDMA had only low to moderate potential for abuse for an array of reasons: the desirable effects of the drug disappeared or drastically diminished both at higher doses and if doses were frequently repeated; it didn't cause physical addiction or cravings in users; and it didn't cause pathological behavior in the way that alcohol, opiates, and even other psychedelics could.

To the DEA, the rapid spread of recreational use of the drug was evidence enough of a high potential for abuse. The plaintiffs countered that, given the amount of uncontrolled use of MDMA, the resulting negative medical and social consequences were infinitesimal, a sign of the benign character of the drug. Use of a drug did not represent abuse in the absence of significant negative consequences, they contended.

The agency introduced evidence that baboons, set up in cages with a device by which they could inject themselves with various substances, would choose to self-administer MDMA as they would cocaine. The plaintiffs countered that (1) the study consisted of only three baboons, (2) one of the baboons chose *not* to self-administer the MDMA, and (3) the two that did self-administer did so at levels far below that of cocaine and not that much higher than that of the control, a simple saline solution.

They also clashed on the issue of whether MDMA could be safely administered under medical supervision. The DEA introduced a gruesome exhibit detailing experiments with dogs showing that injected MDMA was six times as lethal as mescaline, which meant that the dose level of MDMA required to kill 50 percent of the test subjects was one-sixth that of mescaline. When it did prove fatal, it wasn't pretty. Before dying, the lethally dosed dogs exhibited "salivation, gagging, emesis and defecation. . . . [C]onvulsive episodes are preceded and followed by barking, yelping and apparent hallucinations. The dog . . . runs wildly about the room, bumping into walls and furniture."

The plaintiffs pointed out that innumerable medicines considered quite safe for medical use were lethal in animal studies at doses less than that of MDMA.

The DEA submitted documentation, including a study by a neurology researcher named George Ricaurte, showing that large doses of MDA injected into rats caused damage to neurons in the brain. MDA, a popular drug in the 1960s and early 1970s, sometimes called "the love drug," had psychoactive effects similar to MDMA except that it caused a more pronounced, more "psychedelic" shift in perception and the psychic effects lasted much longer. The plaintiffs pointed out that few animal studies had been done with MDMA, and although it was structurally similar to MDA on a molecular level, it reacted very differently in the body. For one thing, MDA was lethal at a third as high a dose as MDMA.

After months of documents flying back and forth and hearings in California, Missouri, and Washington, DC, final arguments were presented before the administrative law judge, Francis Young, on February 14, 1986. Young considered the case for three months before issuing his ruling on May 22.

Rick had been attending the hearings, following them around the country for the better part of two years, living out of suitcases. Despite his falling-out with the core group of plaintiffs, he continued to research DEA contentions, gather information and potential witnesses, and supply suggestions on a strategy to Cotton. "They were glad for my work, they just didn't want to be associated with me" is how Rick remembers it.

Now the thick seventy-one-page judge's decision was in his hands. As he read through the document, his body reacted as if he had swallowed 120 milligrams of MDMA. His heart raced, his blood pressure spiked, and he could hear his pulse pounding his eardrums as if they were timpani. The first seven pages contained the dense boilerplate common to legal documents, and then he got to this:

"DEA [contends that it] need only ask the FDA whether the drug or substance in question has received FDA approval in order to ascertain the existence, *vel non*, of 'accepted medical use.'

"There is no denying that such a situation would greatly simplify the scheduling task of the DEA staff. It provides a quick solution to the problem for DEA. It provides a certain answer. But it is wrong."

But . . . it . . . is . . . wrong. Those four simple words arced from the page like an electric shock. The clarity, the energy, the judge's thinly veiled contempt for the self-serving reductionism of the DEA's position, all made itself stunningly apparent.

Young continued to buttress his point by examining in great detail the legislative and regulatory history of the FDA's authority in medical regulation. He quoted a 1975 directive from the FDA itself that said, "Good medical practice and patient interest thus require that physicians be free to use drugs according to their best knowledge and judgment."

Having settled the question of who determines "accepted medical use" in favor of the medical community over the FDA, Young then turned to the question of whether MDMA specifically could be considered to have an accepted medical use within that community. For that, he analyzed a raft of court decisions that, taken together, established a minimum standard hinging on the idea of "a respectable minority of physicians." If a respectable minority of physicians believed something to be acceptable medical use, it *was* acceptable medical use.

For Young, this was a slam dunk. He quoted extensively from the testimony of a dozen highly respected psychiatrists, all of whom believed MDMA psychotherapy was responsible and useful medical practice, then added, "No testimony to the contrary by any witness is brought to the attention of the administrative law judge by the Agency or any other participant."

Young moved on to another crucial question: Could MDMA be safely administered under medical supervision?

Young tipped his hand early when he had this to say about the drug's toxicity: "The doses of MDMA administered therapeutically by psychiatrists to patients have been less than one percent of the [lethal dose]." The judge compared this to drugs used for general anesthesia, whose minimum effective dose can be as much as 50 percent of the lethal dose. Use just twice as much as the minimum amount that works, and you kill someone.

The comparison, he noted, "indicates a very high margin of safety with MDMA when it is used in treatment."

It wasn't just that MDMA didn't kill people, he wrote, but that there was little evidence that it was even slightly damaging when used therapeutically under a doctor's care. He cited the more than 120 patients who had been treated by the plaintiffs over five years, noting that "none of them suffered apparent harm."

Of the DEA's contention that MDMA use caused damage to neurons in the brain, Young said, "There is very little evidence to support this suspicion."

And even if there was such evidence, Young said, that wouldn't necessarily merit placement on Schedule I. Young pointed to another drug, fenfluramine, known to damage the same neurons MDMA was suspected of damaging. In fact, there are many other drugs that cause changes in the brain very similar to the changes MDMA was alleged to cause that were nonetheless considered therapeutic rather than toxic.

Fenfluramine, a diet pill, would be removed from the market in 1997 when it appeared that frequent, long-term use could damage the heart. But in 1986, as Young pointed out, the FDA had "approved the daily use of fenfluramine in humans on a chronic basis. Fenfluramine is a controlled substance, but this proven neurotoxic substance is only in Schedule IV."

He punctuated that last sentence with a period, but you can feel the exclamation point lurking. So his final conclusion was not a surprise:

"Because MDMA cannot be patented, no pharmaceutical company has had the financial incentive to carry out the extensive animal and clinical tests required by the FDA. . . . Nevertheless, the overwhelming weight of medical opinion evidence received in this proceeding concurred that sufficient information on MDMA existed to support a judgment by reputable physicians that MDMA was safe to use under medical supervision."

That left the final requirement for placement in either Schedule I *or* Schedule II: that MDMA had a "high potential for abuse."

Spending twenty-three pages discussing one hundred findings of fact from the hearing involving highly technical research trying to establish comparative measures of abuse potential, Young ultimately concluded, "Before it can be said that, in the context of [the relevant law], MDMA has a 'high' potential for abuse, the known facts as to MDMA must be compared to the known facts as to human abuse of other substances. When these comparisons are made, it cannot be concluded that the facts show that MDMA has a 'high' potential for abuse."

Judge Young had shredded the DEA's case point by point, so emphatically that Rick might have found his final ruling anticlimactic if it hadn't been such a resounding vindication: "The administrative law judge finds that the evidence of record requires MDMA to be placed in Schedule III."

Three weeks later Charlotte Johnson, the attorney for the DEA, responded. She dismissed Judge Young's decision as based on "faulty reasoning, failure to understand the materials presented, and bias."

She concluded: "Counsel for the agency urges the Administrator to reject the opinion of the Administrative Law Judge and find, based on the substantial evidence in the record, that the substance MDMA is most properly placed in Schedule I of the Controlled Substances Act. . . ."

Johnson had lost the game, but it was her ball, and she was taking it with her when she left.

The DEA would repudiate Johnson's characterization of Judge Young as biased, but it accepted her recommendation. After two years of hearings, the ruling was rejected. MDMA was placed, permanently now, on Schedule I.

The pro-MDMA group appealed to the U.S. Court of Appeals. After months of more hearings, filings, and heated argument before the bench, once again the court ruled that the DEA had based its decision on an incorrect interpretation of the legal meaning of *accepted medical use* and *accepted safety under medical supervision*. The court order temporarily lifted MDMA from Schedule I and ordered the DEA to once again reconsider its scheduling decision.

The DEA took less than a month to reconsider. Most likely it took less than five minutes. It rewrote the definition of *accepted medical use* by coming up with eight benchmarks that just happened to exactly mirror the requirements for FDA approval. After three years and two judicial repudiations, it came to the identical conclusion it had at the start: MDMA was too dangerous, too readily abused, and of no accepted medical use. It would stay on Schedule I, along with heroin.

30.

MICHAEL

(CATNIP)

Considering that Annie had been nervous about Michael going off to California alone to do breathwork, her equanimity would be seriously tested by his latest project: trekking down to a remote Peruvian jungle to take an exotic psychedelic concoction with witch doctors.

In the spring of 1998, Michael accepted the invitation of a friend who had established what she considered reliable contact with reputable shamans in the Peruvian jungle. The friend made the arrangements for Michael to join a group flying down to Peru to experience a weeklong ritual healing involving the use of ayahuasca, a complex brew of Peruvian plants. Ayahuasca is a Quechuan word meaning "vine of souls." Its primary psychedelic component is DMT, dimethyltryptamine. Although it is believed that the human brain naturally produces trace quantities of DMT, it is listed as a Schedule I drug. However, it was legal for traditional indigenous use in Peru as well as in some modern state-sanctioned religions that blended elements of Catholicism with the traditional practices.

Unknown to Michael, five years earlier a UCLA psychiatrist named Charles Grob spent a month in Brazil studying fifteen randomly selected members of one of the sanctioned churches who said they had been using ayahuasca as a religious sacrament at least twice a month for a minimum of ten years. He found that the fifteen were in excellent physical and psychological health—so it appeared that frequent use of ayahuasca was not damaging. Beyond that, their case histories indicated that many of the group had had severe and chronic problems with alcohol abuse, drug addiction, and violent or irresponsible behavior.

Those problems, Grob concluded, had "completely disappeared. They went from being quite dysfunctional to pillars of local society."

How the Quechua Indians ever discovered ayahuasca's psychedelic properties is somewhat mysterious. The DMT comes from a variety of plants, but most commonly *Psychotria viridis*, a berry-producing rain forest shrub with waxy oblong leaves. But you could chew the DMT-containing leaves all day and nothing would happen. A stomach enzyme called monoamine oxidase breaks down DMT immediately.

The other main ingredient in ayahuasca is a common jungle vine, *Banisteriopsis caapi*, which contains precisely the substances that inhibit the stomach enzyme, allowing the DMT to flow unadulterated in the blood to the brain. Combining the two plants into a bitter concentrated tea is in itself a twelve-hour process.

That shamans in a preliterate culture without the slightest inkling that such things as stomach enzymes even existed nonetheless knew how to inhibit them has puzzled botanists for years. The shamans claim the spirits of the plants came to them in dreams and told them how to make the ayahuasca brew. A possibly more rational theory is that the antienzyme vine, *B. caapi*, had its own appeal, as one of the plant's monoamine oxidase inhibitors, harmaline, was also a mild psychedelic. Even jaguars recognize the benefits of chewing *B. caapi* leaves, which they eat like catnip, then roll around playfully on the jungle floor and stare as if fascinated at the tree canopy. This would have particularly impressed the shamans, who considered jaguars to be their spirit companions. If the shamans frequently then began to use *B. caapi* alone for its mildly psychedelic properties, it makes sense that they might also try it in combination with other medicinal plants. At some point, over many generations, they may have stumbled on the combination that produced ayahuasca. And if they did that, they sure weren't going to forget it.

Michael wasn't going to forget it either.

Michael and the rest of the group traveled to a small village where they met the shaman and his party: some women to do the cooking, a couple of men to catch the fish, and a few kids, just because. The combined group then bounced for three hours on dirt roads in the back of a truck, which brought them to a big river. There they boarded large dugout canoes with outboard motors, which took them to a smaller river where they climbed into small dugouts to continue in the shallower current. Very shallow. They had to keep jumping out to drag the canoes over mudflats. After a couple hours they came to an even smaller river, more of a creek, where they left the canoes and had to walk.

Michael had been warned that there would be some jungle walking involved.

"When we were still in the town we said to the guide, 'Should we get some of these rubber boots in case of snakes?' He was barefoot, and he said, 'Well, you could, but the main problem is the snakes up in the trees, and they'll bite you in the neck, so you'll be dead in minutes. So boots aren't that important.'"

As they gingerly pushed ahead down minimal trails covered with a thick canopy, every hanging vine looked exactly like a viper ready to strike.

"That was good for focusing your attention," Michael says. "We'd take turns walking first, and your job was to be very mindful of what was ahead of you."

The camp at the end of their journey injected new meaning into the phrase *middle of nowhere*. The only proper structure was a little grass hut with no sides and a thatch roof. Their sleeping quarters consisted of crude platforms on which they placed thin mats in mosquito net tents, which mostly kept out the critters. Except if you had to get up in the middle of the night to pee. One night Michael decided he didn't want to risk going into the jungle and unwisely took care of business standing right under the edge of the thatched roof.

"I felt something on my head. It was probably a tarantula. It was a very large, fuzzy thing. Thank God I didn't have time to think or I probably would have frozen, but my arm took care of it for me."

When someone asked why they'd had to come so far away from civilization to take the ayahuasca cure, the shaman told them, "The spirits are better out here."

"Away from all the *stuff*," Michael says. "I think it was that kind of thing."

Accommodations, such as they were, plus a week of ayahuasca rituals cost about $100 a day, with food thrown in.

"Very, very bland food. We'd eat these little fish from the river. On the third day we were having this little fish, and one person said, 'These fish are *great*. I'm gonna make this when I get home, and I know how I can do it. I'm gonna buy seven fish, take the bones out of six of them, put 'em all in the first one, and then eat that one.'

"So the food was terrible, and you weren't allowed to have any salt. There's this whole diet to prepare for the experience that involves not having any flavor."

They sat around all day in the heat, swatting mosquitoes, waiting for evening and the ayahuasca ceremony to begin.

At dusk they walked down to the river to wash. The women brought water in big pots in which leaves had been steeping and poured it over them. They said the leaves gave the water a scent that would attract beneficial spirits.

After they'd been cleansed and scented, they gathered around the shaman, each of them picking a spot on the bare ground. The friend who had done this before had warned them that they would be lying on the ground for hours at a time and advised them to bring two sheets, gathered at the edge like a bedroll, to try to keep bugs from crawling in. The shaman put the tea, which had boiled down to a thick sludge, in cups, a different amount for each participant. Only he knew why the dosage varied, which it did from person to person and night to night. He apparently didn't feel much obligation to explain his methods.

After the bitter stew had been drained, Michael lay back in the sheets Annie had stitched together for him, noticing the heart she had embroidered above the seam. He tried to empty his mind of expectations and wait for whatever would come. The shaman began a hypnotic chanting in Shipibo. From time to time he came over to Michael and put his hands on his head and then blew on him. They had been told that he would take their soul and send it to a glass house in the sky for repair, then blow it back in through the top of the head.

Michael had no idea what that meant, but it did kind of feel like something significant was happening. As the ayahuasca took control, he felt his body dissolving, as if the part of him that was "Michael" had no place to be. The more he tried to hold on, the more he disappeared into an alien world of fantastic colors and images. When he tried to see beyond the small clearing where he lay, the jungle looked back with a million eyes, then dissolved into radiating energy patterns that made his stomach lurch. He tried to concentrate on his breath. As he focused on that most basic rhythm, the rise and fall of his chest, the passage of air in and out of his lungs, he became aware of an almost unbearably beautiful singing. It was the shaman, and somehow his song seemed to be guiding the energy patterns. He felt moments of ecstasy, and others of sheer terror.

"One problem was you couldn't really think or put together any coherence—not entirely. So when I could think at all, I'd be thinking, 'Why did I do this, again?'

"You definitely get that this is not a recreational drug. You don't have to worry about people abusing this drug. This is an intense thing. It's not necessarily fun a lot of the time."

At one point, feeling lost, he found himself searching for Annie's heart, unable to find it. He tried not to panic, tracing the seam with his fingers from end to end, over and over. He must have hunted from top to bottom six times before he finally felt her heart, "and then it was, like, 'Okay, I'm connected to her, and she's out there.'"

And with that, his experience just flipped, from terror to bliss. The world outside his embroidered cocoon transformed. The twisting shapes and threatening shadows gave way to a crystalline clarity pierced only by the beauty of the shaman's songs.

Soon Michael felt the familiar world returning as if out of a lifting fog. Hints of dawn outlined the trees with a faint glow. He and the others crept back to their platforms and slept for a few hours, until the heat of another steamy day woke them. They sat in the shade as the previous night's experience worked through them. Then they napped, ate their meal of bony fish, and started all over again with the washing in the river and the anointing with water scented by leaves.

Over the course of the week in Peru, Michael says, the ayahuasca became a teacher—a stern one. One night, deep in ayahuasca's tendrils, Michael's internal journey was interrupted by a voice, a disembodied voice, addressing him. Somehow, he says, he knew it was the voice of the vine.

"Okay," he said to the voice, "just come out in front and show me how can this be real, how can the spirit of a vine be talking to me? Just settle this once and for all and show up."

The voice in his head, as clear as ever, said, "This is not about a show for you. This is about you learning to listen. I'm communicating

to you through your own mind, and you've got to listen. And I will
show you, but I'm not going to do it for you."

Then, he says, he had a vision of a pit filled with snakes. Suddenly
he was in the pit, serpents slithering and hissing all around him. He
found himself in that dark, eternal place where he'd been trapped in
that early LSD trip.

"I was so in it, it was like this was my *life*." Once again, time seemed
to stop, leaving him stuck in the pit. Only this time "I finally had this
realization: 'Wait a minute. This is not how I actually experience life
from day to day most of the time.'"

With that thought, the pit vanished, replaced by another vision. He
was peeling back the cover of a gigantic sardine can, revealing dark,
squirming, awful things inside. This can, he suddenly understood, was
his subconscious, and the squirming awfulness inside it were his fears
and doubts. He almost laughed. *It was all just crap in a can*—it didn't
control him. He thought, *How much better to see it than to have it
hidden.*

He felt calm, almost normal. Something caught his eye at the edge
of the clearing, a sinewy, muscular form prowling closer. Michael recognized it as a jaguar. As he watched, he says, he realized it was not
made of flesh but radiating energy. The spectral creature bounded
once on its powerful legs, then leapt into Michael's body.

The last evening, Michael was back inside his sewn sheet, lost in the
psychic underbrush and struggling once again. As he hacked through
the jungle in his mind, he came upon a sign hanging in the brush.

Trust, it said.

"Once I saw that, it just went through my whole being, and I let go."

31.

NICHOLAS

(ALL GUMMED UP)

By December of 2006, the Americans had come out of their defensive crouch and begun to push deeper into Ramadi, targeting strategic points where they could establish garrisons for joint use of coalition forces and Iraqi police. They hoped that from these strong points they could slowly push outward until they controlled the entire city. In the five months since the beginning of the battle, the leaders of local tribes had become fed up with the Al Qaeda–driven insurgency and had begun to throw their support to the American-supported government, a movement dubbed the Anbar Awakening. The tide was beginning to turn against the insurgents, but Ramadi remained deadly. On December 11, *Time* printed an article on Ramadi titled "The Most Dangerous Place in Iraq." In it they noted that the holds on the new garrisons were tenuous. "The blocks around the compounds are flush with insurgents who watch the movements of Iraqi security forces and U.S. troops, waiting to attack at unpredictable moments."

There were dozens of attacks every day, and easily as many IED explosions. Each time Nick headed out on a mission, he was waiting to die, waiting for the thud of that two-by-four or the flash of a bomb. One time two mortar shells dropped to either side of his Humvee, one after the other. And one after the other, instead of exploding, they just cracked open as if someone had dropped a clay pot. They *always* exploded. Just not this time. "It was kinda cool," Nick says. "Like, 'DENIED!'"

Nick was pretty good about keeping his stuff together. While he was awake.

It was a different story when he tried to sleep. One night he dreamed that he was in his parents' old trailer, in the living room, watching his mom watch a TV showing old war footage from Vietnam. There were choppers and bombs bursting, and as he watched, a red-hot rage built inside of him.

"I just felt evil, I guess. And my mom was yelling at me and crying, asking me why am I like this, why am I like this? And I just remember yelling at her. There was so much anger and fear going on at the moment. And then I felt this presence behind me, and I saw in my mom's eyes this scared look, kinda like, *There's something behind you.*"

He had no time to react before the thing grabbed him by the elbows, pulling them behind his back until they touched. He couldn't see what had him, only the terror in his mother's eyes.

He woke up in Iraq, sitting up, his elbows bent behind his back. He couldn't move. His legs were rigid, extended. He rolled on his butt like he was a teeter-totter. Even conscious, he still felt something behind him, gripping his elbows and pushing against his back with hard feet. Nick wanted to scream but he couldn't. Then whatever had gripped him released its hold. Despite his fear, he fell back into sleep, right back into the same dream. His mom was crying and shaking and Nick tried telling her it was all a dream, that there was nothing wrong. His mother couldn't be comforted. She told him she was worried about him. Behind her the TV was flashing all kinds of war scenes, and the thing, whatever it was, gripped him all over again, squeezing his buttocks with a piercing pain that felt like nails in his flesh. He woke again, still feeling the pain. He climbed out of his rack and walked off by himself so nobody would hear him cry.

His dreams weren't always bad. Sometimes they were the only thing that got him through the day. Throughout his deployment, Nicholas's gift for lucid dreaming delivered knee-weakeningly vivid images of being back home with Beverlee. "They were more real than you and me standing in front of each other now," he says. "I would be embracing her, and giving her a kiss, and telling her that I know that I'm dreaming right now and that I didn't want to wake up. And I would wake up and lie there for a little bit, missing her so bad, then I'd suck it up, put my boots on, and go."

On December 17, Nick got a chance to call Beverlee. It was the anniversary of the day they had first gotten together in South Carolina. Nick tried to keep it light. He told her how much he missed her but skipped the bad dreams and the mortar fire dropping all around his Humvee. He knew that, in one sense, his deployment was harder for her than it was for him. He at least could see what was coming at him. She had to wake up every morning and not know if that was the day she would get word that he was dead or injured.

Beverlee's voice over the phone, with its sweet, almost childlike timbre, riveted him, almost lifted him from this bleak and barren outpost, and tugged him halfway around the world. He wanted to give in to her presence, but he couldn't afford to. When the phone clicked, she would be gone, and he would still be in Ramadi.

As they were saying good-bye, Beverlee surprised him.

The next morning she wrote a post on her Facebook account: "Yesterday was my first year anniversary with my amazing boyfriend Nick. He is currently over in Iraq right now and was getting ready to go on a mission for three days. So, when he called me I proposed to him! Of course, he said yes and now I am officially engaged! I am one step closer to being Mrs. Beverlee Blackston!!"

At dawn on December 20, two days later, Nick's platoon mustered. As he mounted his Humvee, he popped a stick of Juicy Fruit gum into his mouth, and as he chewed he prayed. He did this every mission, tried to pray quietly, but he felt he had to voice the words and he knew Seabass heard him. He appreciated that Seabass had never made a joke of it or interrupted him. But this morning was different.

"Are you praying?" Seabass asked.

"Yeah."

Seabass was silent for a moment, as if deciding. Then he said, "Would you say a prayer for me? Because me and my wife's anniversary is coming up."

Nick prayed for them both. He chewed his gum and said the words: "Please God, bless Seabass and let him survive to see his wife again. Let me survive to see Beverlee again." He repeated the prayer as he chewed the gum, the chewing and praying merging into a kind of sacrament. As they convoyed out into a still-hostile part of the city where they would form a perimeter around the site of a possible new garrison, the rhythmic working of his jaws worrying the gum continued the prayer without him having to think about it. He knew it was silly, but in some unexamined backwater of his brain he felt that as long as he was chewing the gum, he'd be safe.

Nick's platoon had been ordered to head out into hostile territory, get the target building cordoned off and cleaned out, and set it up as a base of operations. They knew it was a hot area: several weeks earlier they'd seen a news clip on Al Jazeera of Al Qaeda militants parading around those same streets with AK-47s, making the point that this was their territory, and Americans better not enter. When Nick's truck arrived at the targeted site, they took up their positions and sat there. Hours passed as morning faded into blazing afternoon. Several enemy mortar shells landed off to Nick's right, and bits of rock and dirt pelted down around them, making the explosions seem closer than they were. The tension and the heat were unbearable. At some point even chewing seemed to add to the sweat streaming from under his helmet. Nick picked the gum out of his mouth and stuck it to his Kevlar vest. At around two in the afternoon, as they waited for their relief, which was scheduled to arrive at any minute, their spirits began to rise. Seabass and Nick bantered back and forth, another ritual. "Look at Seabass," Nick said. "He's so fat, his stomach is touching the steering wheel. No wonder he hits so many potholes: he can barely turn the thing."

"And you've got a fat neck!" Seabass fired back. "Your neck's so fat, you can't spin around fast enough to see the incoming rockets." They all laughed.

And then: a big, black void.

"I was just in another place. It's like you're swimming above water and something just pulls you under. There was an explosion, but it was so big, so intense, I don't remember hearing it or seeing anything. I just remember being somewhere else. And I was in that place for such a small time, but it was . . . for me, it was comparable to when I wake up in a lucid dream and realize that I'm dreaming. It's that moment where you're, like, 'Ah, this is a dream,' starting to understand where I was at, and I was, like, 'Aha, wait a minute,' and then I'm back in this slow-motion world of flames just slowly curling around in front of me, just confused, no idea what was going on."

At first the world was soundless, except for the pneumatic pulse of air moving into and out of his lungs. But then, he heard somebody screaming horrifically. "It was kind of disturbing. I found out later that that was my radio guy: he saw the fire right next to him, and then his door wasn't opening, so all he saw was fire and not being able to get to the door, so it scared the crap out of him. He thought he was about to burn alive. So he said later that was him screaming."

"Smoke started to fill up the vehicle, and I didn't want to get out. We've just been attacked: they're waiting for us to get outta the vehicle so they can start picking us off like target practice. So I didn't wanna poke my head up. So I kept my head down and I could feel a little bit of a warm glow and I could see some of the flames, but there was just so much white smoke; the only way it can get out is through this turret, so it's almost like a chimney. So all this white smoke is coming up past my face, but I'm trying to keep my head down enough, and I'm debating in my head, 'Do I wanna burn alive, or do I wanna get sniped in the head?' Which way is the—how do I wanna do this, you know? And my lieutenant popped me on the leg just after I'd had that thought, and he said, 'Everybody dismount!'"

Nick looked out the top of the turret and saw the light, thinking to himself, *Here it goes: time to get shot.* He popped out and stood, shocked when nothing happened. As he reached for his rifle, an astonishing amount of small-arms fire opened on him.

"Then somehow my mind was racing at the speed of light. I was able to comprehend everything. I felt supersmart. But everything was going slow motion. I couldn't hear anything; I was almost outside of myself, in a way.

"I remember watching a tracer bounce over to my left foot and just kinda bounce off the shoe, and I remember thinking, *Oh, man, there goes my foot.* But nothing ever really did happen with my foot; there was hardly even a mark on my boot from where the tracer had hit and burnt it, so I was kinda confused by that.

"And then all the stuff moving around me in slow motion starts to get a little bit faster, and sounds start to come back. I realized that we had been hit, that we had been blown up."

Now the bullets came cracking past his face, so loud it felt like someone clapping hands on his ears. Nick froze, waiting for a bullet's wallop, knowing it was coming, wondering if it would be in the back or the neck or the head. He yearned for a door to hide behind, but he was a long way off the ground: you never wanted to fall off the turret or you'd break a leg. But now he leapt, his legs unreasonably strong beneath him. He didn't choose to jump; his body propelled him. He felt shoved into thin air. His knee hit the ground first and bounced hard and high, as if it were made of rubber. He felt no pain.

He scrambled over to some rubble, feeling an impulse to hide, then realized he was too far from the vehicle.

"I was trying to think. 'Do I wanna stay over here by the rocks?' and then, like, 'No, I don't have a weapon. This is not a place to be.' So I ran across and I got up against the vehicle."

By then all the smoke had cleared out of the Humvee. Nick could see there was no fire. Boznack's door was open, his seat empty. But Seabass sat immobile in the driver's seat.

"Seabass, get the fuck outta the vehicle," Nick said.

"I can't move," Seabass said.

"What do you mean you can't? Get the fuck out!" Nick wondered if the driver's door was stuck. He stifled the impulse to rush around to help Seabass. They were still under fire. The drill instructors had pounded it into him: his first responsibility was to eliminate the threat. But his rifle was still on the roof. His secondary weapon, an M79 grenade launcher, a breech-loading weapon that looked like a shotgun and fired grenades that you popped up like a mortar, was lodged back behind his ammo cans, which he now saw had been hit by shrapnel, then damaged when some of the rounds had cooked off. He reached for the launcher and it almost came apart in his hands. The stock had been knocked loose, and Nick couldn't be sure it would fire without blowing up in his face. But he grabbed the weapon and a grenade from the back and ran, crouching, to the front.

The lieutenant knelt behind the door, returning fire, and Mack pumped out rounds from his rifle by the front right fender. Nick couldn't see what they were shooting at. "Where's the target?" he shouted, but they were too busy shooting and trying to work the radio to answer.

Then Nick noticed Boznack's door was open, and his seat empty. Where was he?

"I was looking around, and I said, 'Boznack!' And he comes walking around the back of the vehicle, just kinda out of it—just kinda dragging his rifle behind him like a little boy dragging a stuffed animal, bullets hitting all around him."

Nick ran over to grab him and saw only vacancy in his eyes. He pulled him to the Humvee, yelling at him to come out of it, but Boznack showed no sign of hearing. "He had his, like, ears blown out. And I remember grabbing him and leaning him up against the vehicle next to me, and just kinda trying to yell at him. And he just kept going, 'What? What?' and I was, like, 'You need to watch this back area over here!'"

Nick stuck his head back inside the Humvee. Seabass was still in his seat, only now his head slumped forward, moaning as he exhaled, drooling and bubbling spit from his mouth with each breath.

"Seabass, get out!" Nick shouted.

Seabass began to make sounds—awful sounds. Nick had heard those sounds before on his grandfather's farm when they would slaughter the cows. "They make this noise like a moan, but garbled—in the back of their throat." Seabass sounded like those dying, terrified animals. And then he started to shake, and slobber dripped from his mouth.

Nick yelled to Mack, who came in through the front door where he'd been taking cover.

Mack looked at Seabass and said, "We gotta get him the fuck outta here."

It was only then, for the first time, that Nick fully grasped the situation: one of them had been hit; they were alone, pinned down, under fire.

"I just remember wanting so bad for someone to show up and help us out."

Then someone did. Another Humvee, Bravo 1, pulled up between them and the enemy and started pounding away with their M240G and everything else they had. A corpsman ran up, took one look at

Seabass, and started yelling "Fuck! Fuck!" so loud Nick could hear him over the firefight going on just feet away. "Fuck! We need an immediate medevac! Immediate medevac! Immediate medevac!"

Nick kept catching himself paying too much attention to the flurry of activity around Seabass. He had to focus on returning fire. He felt a razor slash of guilt. He was the machine gunner, responsible for avoiding or eliminating all threats before it got to this. He had failed. He tore his eyes away from Seabass and worked his weapon. But he could see out of the side of his eye when they dragged Seabass away. And then the lieutenant was asking him if anyone else was hurt. Mack said, "No." Nick was about to say no, but something stopped him.

"I started thinking about myself, and I felt burning on my butt, so I said, 'I think I got burned from the fire, sir.' And he's, like, 'Where at?' And I'm, like, 'On my butt.' And I'm holding my little M79, looking in the other direction, and he's, like, 'Here, just turn around.' So I turned around like that, and I remember he just grabbed my pants and goes, 'You're bleeding.' And that's when I felt it, whenever he said it was bleeding. I felt all of the burning, like, 'Aaaagghhh.' And he said, 'You're a machine gunner. You do a lot better on your gun than you do out here. You get up on your gun.' And so I got back in the vehicle and got back up on the gun. When I got back up on the gun, the first thing I did was try to find somebody to shoot. I wanted to find somebody and get some payback, you know? But of course the vehicle had pulled in front of us, so there was no way that I could really engage anybody, but I still needed to man the gun."

It was then as he was sitting, hands gripping the machine gun, that his eyes were drawn to the emptiness of Seabass's driver's seat. As he looked down into the vacant seat, he found himself staring at his own face. But that was impossible. For an instant he felt as if he were slipping away again. And then he knew what he was looking at: his own image rippling in a deep, still pool of blood.

32.

RICK

(FULL FLOWER OF DEPRESSION)

Many in the ARUPA-Esalen-psychedelic research axis saw the DEA's defiant dismissal of the judge's recommendations as a final judgment on MDMA psychotherapy, leaving them with just two options: go underground or give up.

But Rick saw the defeat at the hands of the regulatory system as more of a speed bump than a brick wall. If they couldn't win in the courts, they could win in the lab.

Those who didn't share Rick's optimism could be forgiven. As Judge Young himself pointed out in his ruling, *"Because MDMA cannot be patented, no pharmaceutical company has had the financial incentive to carry out the extensive animal and clinical tests required by the FDA."*

Bringing even a plain vanilla drug through the multiple phases of clinical trials took years or even decades and cost millions of dollars. It was a process even pharmaceutical conglomerates hesitated to embark upon without a near-certain promise of fabulous profits once the drug won approval. The idea that a thirty-three-year-old college student with no corporate affiliation, no infrastructure, no scientific credentials, and no capital could usher an unpatentable, severely stigmatized Schedule I drug through the FDA maze was, plainly, ludicrous.

But not to Rick. He ginned up another nonprofit organization and got to work.

He gave his new organization a mouthful of a name to make it sound as serious and boring as a name containing the word *psychedelic* could possibly sound. The Multidisciplinary Association for Psychedelic Studies, chartered in 1986, had no illustrious board of directors, as had the Earth Metabolic Design Laboratories. Instead, Rick elected himself, an acquaintance with whom he used to trip at Grateful Dead concerts, and an ex-girlfriend he'd had a "beautiful" breakup with one night under the influence of MDA.

Rick's new co–board members would be unlikely to force him into exile, as the last group had done. As Rick put it, "These were people that agreed with whatever I wanted and would let me do it."

What he wanted was codified in the MAPS vision statement: "a world where psychedelics and marijuana are safely and legally available for beneficial uses, and where research is governed by rigorous scientific evaluation of their risks and benefits."

Rick hadn't forgotten that the quick studies the ARUPA group had done of MDMA's clinical safety and effectiveness had been picked apart in the hearings as sloppy science. He also knew that even the huge volume of research done on LSD and other psychedelics in the fifties and sixties didn't meet the exacting methodological standards required to persuade the FDA of anything.

But he wasn't starting from nothing. He had the animal studies he'd paid for through his original nonprofit, and he had no doubt those studies would meet with FDA approval; some had been conducted by the National Center for Toxicological Research, the FDA's own research wing. They involved administering large amounts of

MDMA to rats and dogs daily for twenty-eight days, then killing the animals and conducting exhaustive autopsies to assess the effect of the heavy dosing.

Rick had insisted on being present in the autopsy room as four or five dogs at a time were dissected on metal tables. He stood in the middle of the gore, telling the researchers about his hopes for the therapeutic use of MDMA as they cut, measured, and weighed various organs. It was his way of reassuring himself the animals had not been sacrificed in vain. The testing revealed that none of the dogs had suffered any acute harm from the drug—no liver damage, no damage to the heart or brain cells. Although the testing was not sophisticated enough to measure serotonin levels, it fulfilled the basic FDA requirement for any drug before human trials could be embarked upon, and it formed the basis for MAPS to open a "drug master file" with the FDA, the initial step for anyone attempting to get a new medicine approved.

"All we really had," Rick says of the nascent MAPS, "was an organization with no money, with a drug master file for MDMA, with a source of supply of MDMA and these animal studies that permitted us to go into human studies."

Before he could even begin that process, Rick found an urgent personal use for the exculpatory animal testing in the master file. Rick's grandmother had suffered from depression at various times in her life. Now in physical decline, she was having a severe relapse. She had undergone multiple courses of treatment with electroconvulsive shock, lithium, and every other medication in the FDA-approved pantheon. Nothing had helped.

Rick believed that MDMA psychotherapy might at least alleviate her psychic pain for a time. His grandmother's psychiatrist and his parents agreed to attempt the therapy, but only with legal permission. Rick applied to the FDA for emergency approval—a one-off human trial. Both his grandmother and his parents signed a statement that they were aware of the hypothesized neurotoxic effects of MDMA. The FDA refused, saying that his grandmother needed to be protected from brain damage even if she was dying. In a matter of months, his grandmother's condition worsened to the point that she became so depressed she refused to eat, and had to be force-fed, futilely. She died, Rick says, never having emerged from the "full flower of her depression."

33.

NICHOLAS

(HEAVY DUTY)

After the shooting stopped, Nick saw that the blast had blown out the truck's front tires. The vehicle was disabled, but sound-looking enough that they tried to start it. It cranked but wouldn't catch.

As they sat there, waiting for a tow, a family of Iraqis—parents and kids—walked across the road in front of them holding a white flag. They never even glanced at Nick or the bloody scene around them. Nick felt fury building at their apparent lack of concern. He imagined turning his gun on them and mowing them down.

When the tow vehicle came, the crew hitched up the Humvee with the survivors still sitting in it, then dragged them backward through the city. Nick sat impotently in his turret, angry and humiliated, as the destroyed front wheels carved furrows in the road. Another parade of shame.

Back at base, they were told to clear out their weapons and report to the battalion aid station, which was designed for minor injuries; it was not a full-scale field hospital, like the one over in Camp Ramadi where Seabass had been taken. As Nick was cleaning off his Kevlar, he stopped cold. There, still stuck on the side, was the wad of Juicy Fruit.

His unanswered prayer. He'd just gotten tired of chewing and stuck it there. Nick cried.

It took him a while to pull his shit together and head to the aid station. Sergeant Mack was headed there too.

"Seabass didn't make it," Mack told Nick.

"I don't know, I don't think I could really believe it," Nick says. "I mean, I knew he wasn't lying to me, it's just—you're just, like, 'No.'"

Nick was still reeling when they told him to drop trou and lie facedown on the table. Even after all he'd been through, the embarrassment of lying on his stomach with his pants pulled down around his ankles stung him.

His buttocks and thighs were covered with red dots from fragments of his own ammunition, set off by the same single piece of metal that had severed Seabass's artery. The medics told him he just had contusions. When his wounds healed up, it would be apparent that the dots were actually small pieces of metal embedded in his fatty tissue.

But the medics didn't look that closely. They just bandaged up his butt and thighs and gave him a brace for his knee, which had now started to hurt like hell and could barely support any weight. Then they handed him 800 milligrams of ibuprofen.

Nick was talking and walking, or at least limping. He could answer questions appropriately and find the way to his hooch. But none of it felt solid. The world seemed hollowed out, a facade standing inadequately for the reality he'd known as recently as that morning.

Before he left the aid station, the medics had to fill in a sheet with the silhouette of a human form on it, making a mark everywhere they'd found an injury. Nick's looked like some kid had scribbled all over it. They offered to put him on the light-duty roster for a week, which meant he wouldn't have to leave the base on any missions. He refused.

"I mean, Seabass had died. I could still move, he had died; it wasn't right for me to take a week off, you know? And apparently everyone else had made that same decision without us kind of collaborating on it. Whenever we walked outta there, we'd all refused the light duty."

He went back to the hooch and got out of his stinking, singed, and bloody clothes and fell into the showers. It was eight p.m., and for the first time since the attack he was alone. As the hot water coursed over him, he felt Seabass, dead now for almost six hours, come into the room.

"I'm sorry, Seabass! I'm so sorry!" Nick cried, the tears washed away by the torrent from the showerhead. "I'm sorry I took out the gum. I'm sorry I didn't stop it, didn't see it coming."

Nick couldn't say how long he stood under the shower spray, but at some point he pulled himself together enough to towel off, get dressed, and head back out. First he had to go to the motor pool and face the charred Humvee to pull out the rest of his equipment. It shocked him to see how little damage the truck had sustained. It stank of smoke, but he could see now that the truck itself hadn't caught fire, just a box with food and supplies stored inside. There was little visible damage other than a long gash in the truck's hood made by a single piece of shrapnel. Nick traced its path. From the point of impact, it carved a furrow along the truck's hood, then tunneled beneath the driver's-side window. Its path picked up again in the driver's seat—Seabass's seat—where that jagged grenade fragment had sliced across it, but not before it pierced Seabass's thigh, plowing through it, top to bottom, severing the femoral artery along the way. He'd bled out into the cushion, leaving the thick, sickly brownish stain.

Numb, Nick pulled out the rest of his stuff and went right to his new truck—one of the spares they always had hanging around the motor pool. There he met his new driver, a refugee from another platoon that no longer existed due to all the losses it had suffered.

Nick, the new driver, and the other survivors of the attack climbed into the new truck and went back out that very night. Nick couldn't sit on his left side, which still felt as if it were on fire, and he couldn't bend the knee that had smashed into the ground and was now hot to the touch and the size of a soccer ball. By shifting around uncomfortably, he discovered he could balance on his right buttock with the foot on the leg with the bad knee elevated on the radio mount. And that was fine with Nick. Rather than sit around weeping for Seabass's ghost, at least this way he had a chance to get some payback.

"I was just full of anger, and my pains that I felt—anytime a complaint would come into my head, like, 'Agh, this hurts,' I'd think about Seabass, and it'd go away. You know, because he suffered a lot more than I was [suffering]. And so that kind of helped me push it down."

34.

RICK

(HIPPIE OF THE YEAR)

f Rick was going to run an organization dedicated to providing "rigorous scientific evaluation of the risks and benefits" of MDMA, he was going to have to learn how to do rigorous science. He set out to teach himself, beginning with his senior thesis at New College. It was an evaluation, twenty-five years after the fact, of what many considered to be one of the most rigorous early studies on the effects of a psychedelic. On Good Friday, 1962, in Boston University's Marsh Chapel, Walter Pahnke, a physician, psychiatrist, ordained minister, and Harvard PhD candidate, administered capsules of white powder to twenty Protestant divinity students just prior to the holiday service.

Ten of the capsules contained nicotinic acid, a stimulant. The other ten contained psilocybin. The thesis was that spiritually inclined individuals engaged in a sacred ritual might react to the psychedelic drug by having a full-blown religious experience. It was an attempt to re-create in a contemporary Western context the religious visions obtained in the peyote rituals of Native Americans and to assess their impact on individuals' lives. The stimulant administered to half the group was meant to serve as an "active" placebo, because clearly a sugar pill wasn't going to make anyone think he had been given a psychedelic drug.

True, the effects of nicotinic acid—a warm flush sensation created by dilation of the blood vessels and a systemic feeling of relaxation—bore little resemblance to a psychedelic trip, but what did? Pahnke had chosen subjects who had never taken psychedelics, hoping that they would be more easily fooled by the stimulant. This was important, because in trying to assess purely subjective effects—and little was more purely subjective than a mystical experience—the expectation in the minds of both subject and observer could easily create a false positive. This lack of a double-blind aspect—which left both the researchers and subjects uncertain of who got the good stuff—was a flaw common to the early psychedelic studies, and a key reason why they were so often dismissed.

As it turned out, Pahnke's double-blind attempt failed. After brief confusion among those given the nicotinic acid when its effects began to be felt, the overwhelming perceptual changes brought on by the psilocybin were so obvious to all that the study participants, who were in the church together, might as well have worn labels.

The crumbling of the double-blind procedure would have been "quite damaging" to the credibility of the results, Rick wrote, if the experiment had been purely intended to measure psilocybin's ability to produce mystical experience in isolation, regardless of set and setting. But in this case the religious context of the Good Friday service and the spiritual bent of divinity students were all part of the exercise. Pahnke had chosen the participants and location precisely because he wanted to observe the effect of the drug administered in a spiritual set and setting.

However, Rick wrote, "restraint should be used in attributing the experiences of the experimental group entirely to psilocybin."

In Rick's critique it is possible to see the beginning of a transformation: a "Tim Leary for the '80s" attempting to remake himself into someone who could research psychedelic medicine with the sober caution that would be required if it had any chance of ever winning FDA approval.

Pahnke's paper on his experiment stressed the positive results. Nobody suffered any apparent physical harm or long-term psychological harm, and an overwhelming majority of those who took the psilocybin felt the experience had been profound and had made a positive impact on their lives, even six months after the fact. One subject said that he had vividly experienced the passion of Christ, identifying with it completely. Another said that after first going through a period of paranoia and feeling imprisoned in the church (which had bars on the windows and a guard at the door to keep the subjects from going outside during the experiment), he began to experience "the dropping away of the external world," followed by "the sudden sense of singleness, oneness" that made "the rest of normal waking consciousness" seem like a mere illusion.

Pahnke died in a scuba diving accident in 1971. Fifteen years later, Rick reinterviewed most of the participants of the study, who still believed taking psilocybin that day had fortified their spirit and improved their lives. But he found flaws in the experiment. His thesis assessment, which was ultimately accepted for publication, indicates the distance he had come:

> Pahnke failed to report the administration of the tranquilizer thorazine to one of the subjects who received psilocybin [and had an acute anxiety reaction]. There is no justification for this omission. . . . In addition, Pahnke underemphasized the difficult psychological struggles experienced by most of the psilocybin subjects. These very serious omissions point to an important incompleteness in Pahnke's interpretation of the effects of psilocybin.
>
> Some of the backlash that swept the psychedelics out of the research labs and out of the hands of physicians and therapists can

*be traced in part to the thousands of cases of people who took psyche-
delics in non-research settings, were unprepared for the frightening
aspects of their psychedelic experiences and ended up in hospital
emergency rooms. These unfortunate instances of panic reaction
have many causes, yet some of them stem from the way in which the
cautionary elements of the Good Friday experiment were inadequately discussed in Pahnke's thesis, in subsequent scholarly reports
and in the popular media.*

*[The] optimism regarding the inherent safety of the psychedelic
experience did not fully acknowledge the complexity and profundity
of the psychological issues associated with psychedelic experiences.
With some proponents of psychedelics exaggerating the benefits and
minimizing the risks, a back-lash against these substances was
predictable.*

Rick graduated from New College in 1987, sixteen years after he
had begun as a freshman. He aced his Graduate Record Exams, putting him in the top one-tenth of 1 percent—enough to get him interviews at some of the highly competitive clinical psychology programs.
In each case, Rick says, "I had these great talks and usually most of
them would be clearly superexcited about what I was doing."

But at the end of each interview, Rick would say, "I want to do
MDMA therapy research for my dissertation. And I know that's five
years away or whatever and it's still illegal, but I don't want to get in a
position where I don't mention that to you and that when I get there
after I've done all this work you tell me no. So I'd rather tell you now."

When the last "We regret to inform you . . ." notice arrived in his
mailbox, he went to a secluded room in his house—technically now
his parents' house. "I smoked some pot and I started thinking. And
I was, like, I feel like there's a pattern here and the pattern is that I
want too much too soon. I want to do this psychedelic psychotherapy

research, but the world is not ready for it. It's like relationships with women: a lot of times I want too much too soon. So then it was just, like, all right, well, if the politics is in the way of science, maybe I should study the politics."

And if he was going to study the politics of psychedelics, he figured, he needed to do it in a way that would give him the best mainstream credential possible. That, he decided, would be the world-renowned John F. Kennedy School of Government at Harvard.

Rick remembered a magazine interview with a professor there named Mark A. R. Kleiman who had mentioned the MDMA lawsuit. It wasn't much of a connection, but Rick called him anyway.

"I said, 'You have no idea who I am but I did this stuff that you know, and would you be my mentor?'"

Kleiman encouraged Rick to apply, and this time he got in.

"I think it was just affirmative action," Rick says. "I was the hippie of the year."

The hippie took two years to get his master's degree, then applied for and got a Presidential Management Internship, a prestigious and competitive program for people interested in a career in federal government. The PMI website said it sought "the best and brightest Americans who want to make a difference in the public service" and called the program "a stepping stone to highly visible and respected leadership positions in the federal government."

Rick didn't really want a government career, but he did want to know how to manipulate the levers and pulleys that could move public policy on the issue of psychedelic medicine. When a team from the CIA came to recruit from the PMI recipients, Rick raised his hand. He thought, *What can I do with the CIA?* and the answer that came to him was: *Propose a study on the national-security implications of legalizing drugs.* To Rick, it was obvious that the quarter-century-old war on drugs had wreaked a long list of harms on the country, including unnecessarily swelling prison populations, wasting billions of dollars on ineffective enforcement, providing an inexhaustible source of funding for organized crime and narco-terrorists, and, of course, preventing research into the beneficial uses of marijuana and psychedelics. Would legalizing drugs and putting them under federal regulation ameliorate any or all of the above?

The Agency interviewers must have been impressed with Rick, even if they brushed aside his proposal. Would he be interested in doing psychological profiles of world leaders? they asked.

Um, no.

After he left, Rick thought about the distance he'd traveled: from being, basically, an outlaw, he had arrived at a place where he was exchanging ideas with the likes of the CIA. For Rick, this wasn't just one of life's curiosities but a question of strategic importance.

He asked himself, *Am I more effective from the inside working out or the outside pressuring in?* It depended, he decided. If he had persuaded the CIA to let him study the potential national security benefits of ending the war on drugs, then going inside would be worth it. "I thought, okay, I would be willing to give up drugs and wear a suit to do that."

But that wasn't going to happen. So what other inside job would be worth it? Rick pondered that and came up with answer: he sent an internship application to the FDA.

Once again his timing was uncanny.

For thirty years, ever since the FDA had prevented thousands of horrific birth defects in the United States by refusing to bow to corporate and consumer pressure to approve the sedative and anti–morning sickness drug thalidomide without further testing, the agency had focused primarily on stopping bad drugs from getting to market. But there was a downside to this unrelenting focus on safety: through the seventies and eighties, the time, money, and effort it took to gain FDA approval for new drugs kept escalating. Many helpful medicines were becoming available internationally long before they could be legally prescribed in the United States. The pharmaceutical industry began to push Congress for FDA reform just as the AIDS epidemic created tens of thousands of new victims each year, all desperate for more effective medicines with the clock ticking against them. In 1987, as the pressure to change ratcheted up, a forward-thinking clinical pharmacologist named Carl Peck was appointed to head the FDA's center for drug evaluation with a mission to make drug approval more efficient without compromising the public's safety. Peck created a new staff within the agency, Pilot Drug Evaluation, specifically to find innovative ways to reengineer the drug approval process. To do that, the new division needed some new drug applications to experiment with. Since the FDA bureaucracy had already divvied up all drug categories among existing departments, Pilot Drug would need to wrest some categories from elsewhere.

One of the categories it ended up with—essentially because nobody else wanted it—was psychedelics and marijuana.

Since Rick had founded MAPS, he'd made applications for five small human MDMA studies, each in conjunction with researchers at prestigious universities and each backed by the required animal safety studies. All were rejected. To say that the regulators had an attitude would be no exaggeration. Rick would only learn later, when he wrote his PhD thesis on the subject, that the director of the FDA department responsible for rejecting his applications had once said of the 1960s psychedelic research at the University of Maryland institute where Stan Grof had worked: "It was just an excuse to give people LSD. . . . If I had the power, I would have put the doctor in charge in jail."

The unlikely confluence of events—that the psychedelic portfolio was now being relinquished to a staff specifically intended to break new ground, shake things up, and find ways to help get beneficial

drugs through an obstructionist system just as Rick was blindly applying for an internship—seemed like fate. Rick got a call from the head
of Pilot Drug, Dr. John Harter.

"I went down there and I met with him, and he was, like, 'You're
just what we're looking for.' I'm, like, 'Fantastic.' The thought was that
I would work inside for a couple of years and then I would go back to
MAPS and I would try to bring them proposals."

Here was an opportunity to live inside the belly of the beast and
learn its ways, just as he had hoped. He'd gone through all the high-
level interviews, and Harter was sold. There was just one problem: when
the DEA got wind that the FDA was about to hire Rick, someone senior
gave Harter an earful. "They told him, 'No way can he work on psychedelics and marijuana,'" Rick remembers. "So I said, 'All right, that's
fine, I'll work on any other drugs; I just want to see how you do stuff.'"

Rick was redirected to the bottom of the totem pole, a job that
certainly didn't require a master's from Harvard Kennedy School. The
only remaining interview, with the eight women who would be his
coworkers, seemed a formality. Dr. Harter even invited Rick to spend
the night before the interview at his house. They'd drive in together in
the morning, Rick would do the pro forma interview, and then he'd be
hired.

Harter had apparently forgotten to clue the women in on the plan.
He introduced Rick, expressed his support, mentioned that Rick
wouldn't be working with any psychedelic drug issues, then left them
alone.

"We do a lot of photocopying," one of the women began. "Are you
willing to do photocopying?"

Rick told them he practically lived at Kinko's. Photocopying would
be no problem.

"And then they said, 'Well, how are we going to keep you away from
seeing anything to do with psychedelics or marijuana?'"

Rick tried to soothe their concerns, but he could see where things were headed. When they voted, he lost in a landslide. As it turned out, one of the innovations in Pilot Drug management involved letting the people on the floor have more say in hiring.

Harter, embarrassed about what had happened, offered Rick a consolation job helping to get a computer system up and running. In the end, they both decided Rick would be better off on the outside.

Besides, Rick thought with relief, *now I can still smoke pot and I don't have to wear a suit.*

35.

MICHAEL

(MOTHER IBOGAINE)

Michael had escaped the Peruvian jungle with new insights—and a terrible intestinal infection. On the long trip out, the bugs had been swarming the dugouts and Michael had lathered himself with insect repellent. When he got hungry, mindful of the insecticide still on his fingers, he allowed his hand to drag in the river before reaching into a bag for a handful of almonds. As soon as the nuts hit his tongue, he realized what he'd done. He would have been no worse off if he had gulped water directly from the microorganism-infested current.

Back in Charleston, Michael was sick, lethargic, and depressed for weeks. When heavy-duty antibiotics finally resolved the symptoms, he was once more able to pay attention to what he was supposed to focus on: the needs of his patients.

One patient in particular concerned him. She was an opiate addict who had been through a couple of thirty-day treatment programs, which had done no good.

"She was really a bright woman," Michael says, "but she had this terrible problem. And she'd come to breathwork, but she really felt too self-conscious to get into it."

The woman had been his last appointment of the day, and as he drove home, Michael was still wondering how he might be able to help her. He was only half listening to NPR when he tuned in to a story about a researcher at the University of Miami named Deborah Mash who was using a psychedelic drug called ibogaine to treat cocaine and opiate addictions on the West Indian island of St. Kitts.

Ibogaine had been used for centuries in West Africa. Initiates in puberty rites who took the drug, a bitter white powder derived from a rain forest shrub, were said to enter into communication with "the universal ancestor" and emerge from the two-day experience transformed.

In 1962, in the Bronx, a nineteen-year-old heroin addict named Howard Lotsof was searching for an exotic high when he took some ibogaine he got from a chemist friend.

Lotsof, who died of liver cancer in 2010, told of his ibogaine experience in a 1994 *New York Times* story. More importantly, he described its effect: "The next thing I knew, I was straight."

After taking the ibogaine, Lotsof spent most of a day in a dreamlike state featuring vivid hallucinations when he closed his eyes—almost like watching fantastic movie reels projected on the backs of his eyelids—accompanied by a parade of memories embedded with insights into motivations and effects of past behavior.

When the drug faded, he realized he hadn't had any of the usual heroin withdrawal symptoms during his prolonged ibogaine intoxication. He also emerged with a new outlook. In his altered state, he had realized that he had always viewed the world fearfully and took heroin to dull the anxiety he constantly felt. The answer, and the ability to act on it, simply appeared to him: he didn't have to be afraid; he didn't need heroin.

From that moment, he said, he was a changed man, and drug-free. One of his first acts in a life that would thereafter be devoted to promoting the antiaddiction promise of ibogaine was to persuade six addict buddies to take it. He claimed that five of the six immediately kicked their habits.

Mash, a professor of neurology and pharmacology, at first reacted skeptically to Lotsof's accounts. A chance discovery of a miracle drug coming not from a lab but a junkie seemed suspect on its face. But as Mash looked into an abundance of anecdotal reports and did lab research, she decided there was enough there to merit a rigorous scientific assessment of ibogaine. In lab analysis she discovered that a substance formed when the body's chemistry broke ibogaine down—called noribogaine—and blocked the process that caused opiate withdrawal symptoms. It also appeared that the psychoactive properties of the drug gave addicts an introspective distance and insight into the root causes of their addiction as well as a heightened motivation to break free of it. But she couldn't find any institution willing to fund a study of such a controversial substance, which was classified on the same Schedule I level as LSD and heroin.

Mash persisted, eventually discovering an unlikely partner and an unconventional solution. The government of St. Kitts allowed her to do a clinical trial on the island and pay for it by charging the subjects—something that would not have been permitted in the United States.

Michael learned all this when he got in touch with Mash the next morning. She also gave him a very positive report on the clinical results and the relative safety, which was reassuring, since he'd discovered that people using ibogaine occasionally died within twenty-four hours of administration. Some estimates put the risk of death when ibogaine has been administered to treat addiction at 1 in 300. Far from all of the fatalities were attributable to the ibogaine itself, but the numbers were still scary.

Despite the risk and the unproven benefits, Michael's patient, who felt her life wasn't worth much as an addict, decided to fly to St. Kitts and take the treatment. She asked Michael to come with her.

Michael told her that he wasn't licensed to practice in St. Kitts, but he'd agree to come "on my own dime" as an observer.

She said she understood and agreed to his conditions, so Michael went along.

Ibogaine treatment turned out to be very unlike treatment with LSD, MDMA, or other psychedelics. "There's no talking during an ibogaine session," Michael says. "People are just laid out for a long time. The session lasts ten or twelve hours, and they're not communicating at all, for the most part."

The subjects appeared to be in the middle of a restful sleep, but internally they were having intense experiences of the type Lotsof had described, often seeing their lives pass as if for review, highlighting all the negative events and decisions that led to their addiction. Others had visions similar to what Michael saw on ayahuasca.

"One person there said that this fierce woman he referred to as 'Mother Ibogaine' came to him in his visions and said, *'Stop that shit.'* And he said, 'Okay, whatever you say.'"

Michael found that reports of a personified spirit issuing ultimatums were not uncommon, and often proved effective.

"Mother Ibogaine seems to get people's attention pretty well," Michael says.

The treatment appeared to work for his patient, but only for a time. Back in her former circumstances, she relapsed. Michael knew that, even anecdotally, relapses were not uncommon. Some people did the treatment two or three times before becoming permanently addiction-free, and even then most people required continuing support and therapy.

But ibogaine itself didn't interest Michael as much as Mash's method of getting around the research roadblocks. A light switched on: if he couldn't study psychedelic therapy in the United States, maybe he could do it elsewhere.

36.

NICHOLAS

(DON'T FORGET TO CHECK YOUR GUNS)

After his Humvee got blown up, Nick knew that if he could just survive one more month, his deployment would be up and the 1/6 Marines would be flying home. At least, that's what he thought he knew.

One day in January as they patrolled the city, the voice of the battalion commander crackled over the radio. The lieutenant had the radio on loudspeaker, so they all heard him say, "Be advised we're going to be extended—" The lieutenant lunged to flip the toggle that killed the speaker, but it was too late. When they all began to jabber, the lieutenant told them to put a sock in it. But he knew the damage had been done, so he gathered them around and told them the news: the president had decided to pulse Iraq with elevated troop levels, so they wouldn't be going home soon after all. They'd been extended for three to six months.

"Everybody's hearts just dropped: we lost all those guys and now they tell us we're going to be longer," Nick says. "But it turned out to be worth it. We did that surge and cleaned up that city."

Ramadi became a different place. Between the military penetration into insurgent strongholds and the decision of local leaders to support the coalition, the city went from being the most dangerous in Iraq to one of the safest. In the final months of his deployment, it became rare for Nick to ever have to fire his gun. On Nick's last patrol he was able to do something he'd never dared: stand in his turret waving to the kids running alongside as the dismounts handed out water bottles and footballs.

"It was a chance to show the people we don't just hide in these little vehicles all the time," Nick says. "It felt good."

When they flew out of Kuwait, Nick believed they'd accomplished something. "It meant those guys didn't really die for nothing. I think if we would've left that place and it was still a huge hellhole, it would've been a lot harder."

Spirits were high on the plane, and higher after they'd stopped in Shannon, Ireland, and had time to drain their first beers. Nick, who'd developed a reputation for being the comic relief, came back on board for the last leg of the flight to Cherry Point, sauntered up to the steward-ess, pulled back his sleeve, and pumped his Marines-carved bicep. "Oh, I'm sorry," he said, "I forgot to check these things through customs."

Even the stewardess laughed at that.

And then he was back home. Friends and family waved signs, people called them heroes, and Beverlee embraced him every bit as sweetly as in his most fervid dream.

He found himself doing all the things he'd longed to do the entire time he'd been in Iraq. They went out to a nice restaurant that night, and Bev noticed something odd about Nick's hands.

"They're shaking," she said.

Nick's dad gave her a look. "Shut up, Bev," he said.

Nick glanced up, puzzled, then went back to the almost absurdly delicious food. For that night, and quite a few nights after, Nick thought being home was everything he'd hoped it would be. No issues.

Except, as Nick calls it, "one little problem" that surfaced the first time he and Beverlee and his mom all went to the beach.

Onslow Beach, right on base at Camp Lejeune, stretched alongside an artillery range placed beside the sea so Marine artillery could fire rounds into the water. Nick, Beverlee, and Nick's mom had had a pleasant enough afternoon on the sand and were just leaving, Nick steering the car, when the artillery range went hot. *BOOM! BOOM!*

"Each time one went off, I felt myself, like, back in the vehicle—back in that blast. And I'm trying to drive a vehicle at this time—you know, my mom's in the backseat, and Beverlee's over there to my right. And then it just kept going *BOOM. BOOM.* I think there was one time where they fired, like, three of 'em simultaneously, like *BOOM-BOOMBOOM.* And I just broke down; I didn't know what was going on. I went into tears and pulled the car off the side of the road, and for a moment I was back in the vehicle—in my mind, you know. I just remember saying, 'You motherfuckers. You motherfuckers,' and I was thinking about those Iraqis who had shot at me and all that other stuff. My mom was rubbing my shoulder, and Beverlee was rubbing my shoulder, too, but they didn't say anything. It's like they didn't know how to handle it, and that makes you feel so disconnected, you know? That was the only little problem that I had."

37.

RICK

(MACHINE ELVES)

B ack when he was fighting the legal battle with the DEA, Rick came across a research report on the adverse effects of psychedelics; he was seeing a lot of those as the anti-MDMA forces limbered up. But this particular report caught his eye. The young doctor—only a year older than Rick—who had done the study seemed scrupulously fair and open-minded. His name was Rick Strassman, an associate professor of psychiatry at the University of New Mexico School of Medicine. Rick, always on the lookout for potential allies in his crusade, invited Strassman to a conference he had put together of the leading lights in psychedelic research. It changed Strassman's life. With Rick's encouragement and the benefit of his new associates' experience, Strassman launched a bid for the first psychedelic research project using human subjects on American soil in two decades. He wrote a proposal to study the effects of DMT—the most active ingredient in ayahuasca—on subjects who were already experienced users of psychedelics, figuring that there was no chance the FDA would approve a proposal to introduce psychedelic virgins to the drug.

Strassman had chosen DMT to study for a variety of reasons: it was extremely short acting because of the body's quick breakdown of the molecule. Also, when injected instead of ingested—which was his study's procedure—the major effects, though profound, lasted for only thirty or forty minutes, making it easy to study in a lab setting.

And DMT had nothing like the name recognition, nor did it stimulate a fraction of the knee-jerk resistance, of its three-letter cousin, LSD, or other psychedelics more familiarly abused on the street. Strassman hoped that would make the uphill climb to get a study approved a little less steep.

There was one more reason: Strassman was fascinated by the possibility that DMT, the only psychedelic known to be naturally produced in the human body, might have played a role in mystifying aspects of human awareness, such as "seeing God" in spontaneous religious experiences and the sense some people near death had of leaving their bodies and entering a blinding white light.

Strassman had an even more speculative idea that DMT might actually be the biochemical basis of what some called the human soul—which is why, when he wrote a book about his research, he called it *DMT: The Spirit Molecule.*

But his study proposal didn't mention that kind of thing, just the basics: ascertaining the physiological and psychological responses to the drug at various dose levels. As Strassman put it in his book, "The U.S. government was spending billions of dollars contending with the problems associated with out-of-control substance use. Surely some of that money could fund a human DMT study. Rather than fighting against the government by trying to remove legal restrictions, it made more sense to appeal directly to the scientific thinking that ultimately drives research. We all wanted to know what drugs like DMT did, and how they did it."

Good point.

Until that moment, despite the fact that they had, arguably, been the most studied drugs in history—save for Huxley's poetic but evidence-free speculation that psychedelics somehow got around the brain's reality "reducing valve," which filtered out the unruly awesome-ness of reality—nobody had any clear idea how psychedelics created such dramatic and far-ranging alterations of consciousness.

Not that Strassman's very preliminary study would put even a small dent in that problem, but it would at least be a *start*, the first axe blow in a forest of ignorance left untended for two decades.

Even now, twenty years later, what is known about how psychedel-ics work in the brain is largely conjecture. One researcher described the current state of knowledge this way: "Think crayon drawing, rather than oil painting."

Still, new technologies and clever research methods have begun to shed intriguing light on how psychedelics operate and, by doing so, on no less than the nature of consciousness itself.

From almost the moment Albert Hofmann made his discovery, psychedelics have played a crucial role in the still-nascent quest to understand the links between mind and matter. Just as the first reports of LSD's powerful effects on consciousness were being published, chemists were surprised to discover that a substance called serotonin, which was known to contract the muscle of the small intestine and constrict blood vessels, could also be found in the brain. They had no idea what it did there until, in 1954, a researcher noticed that the chemical structure of serotonin bore an eerie likeness to that of LSD-25. The physical similarity of the two molecules, coupled with the known power of LSD to alter how people think and feel, switched on the light that inaugurated the modern science of the brain.

Serotonin, it became clear, functioned in the brain to mediate the ways we thought and felt, and LSD worked by somehow altering the way the brain processed serotonin. Serotonin turned out to be only one of many body-produced substances that regulated and facilitated brain activity—called "neurotransmitters" because they worked to transfer signals from one brain neuron to the next. In fact, serotonin was far less abundant than other neurotransmitters, but it had outsized impact, involving itself in the regulation of appetite, sleep, memory and learning, temperature, mood, behavior, muscle contraction, and function of the cardiovascular and endocrine systems.

Precisely because the LSD molecule is physically similar to serotonin, it fits into the same neuronal receptors serotonin fits into—like a key in a lock—but with different results. Now the psychedelic experience begins to make a little more sense—the brain with psychedelics mucking around in serotonin receptors becomes a different kind of place.

It's been shown that a psychedelic drug's potency is determined by how adept it is at "sticking" to a particular kind of serotonin receptor. (LSD is much "stickier" than mescaline, for example, and therefore takes effect at a fraction of the dosage.) If you take a drug that blocks that kind of serotonin receptor before you take a psychedelic drug, the psychedelic will not have the usual effects on your consciousness.

The specifics of how psychedelics interacting with serotonin receptors adds up to a "trip" remain mysterious and disputed. The most interesting clues have come from studies using a relatively new technology, fMRI—functional magnetic resonance imaging—which depends on the magnetic properties of blood flow to create pictures of a brain in operation.

In 2012, researchers at Imperial College London published results of a study in which they injected subjects with psilocybin, the psychedelic compound in magic mushrooms, and then observed their brains with the fMRI machine. Given the famous assault on the senses of the psychedelic experience—the flashing patterns, intense colors, enhanced sounds, and overwhelming visions and emotions—they expected to see increased brain activity, which is exactly what some earlier studies using PET scan radiation technology had found.

Instead, their screens registered *decreased* activity, which seemed like a mistake until it was confirmed by a second kind of fMRI scan and correlated with the subjects' reports: the larger the decrease in brain activity, the more intense the subjective experience.

The decreased activity caused by the psilocybin was not uniform throughout the brain. Task-oriented areas of the brain, like the areas associated with seeing and moving, had only nominal decreases. But the more complex areas—those associated with self-image, introspection, and imagining past or future events—showed large decreases. This linked nicely with the reports of the subjects, who did not have significant motor impairment but talked about experiencing a loss of ego, an increased sense that objects outside themselves had unusual significance, and a feeling that the present moment had expanded into a kind of "eternal now." The researchers noted two intriguing connections with other brain activity studies: a brain on psilocybin bore a striking resemblance to the brain of an experienced meditator during deep meditation; and the areas of the brain with decreased activity under the influence of psilocybin were the same regions that showed chronically *increased* activity in people with clinical depression.

Raw activity levels only told part of the story. Even more suggestive results came from looking at which brain areas seemed to be working in concert rather than in opposition. In normal consciousness, when the introspective part of the brain is active, the part that scrutinizes the outside world quiets, and vice versa. But under psilocybin, those areas go up and down in sync. Could this lockstep between the objective and subjective be related to the feeling of "oneness" with the world that is a common feature of the psilocybin experience?

Relating specific experiences to general changes in brain activity is a dicey business, made even more so because the basic reliability of fMRI technology is suspect, at least to some. One critic famously managed to use the instruments to demonstrate brain activity in a dead fish. But, leaving aside for a moment the heated debates that will continue for years to come, the idea that the dramatic psychedelic experience is rooted in the diminishment of the parts of the brain that impose a pragmatic, top-down order on the signals coming in from the world should sound familiar: it was Huxley's sixty-year-old "reducing valve" theory all over again.

The design of Strassman's DMT research project promised only a primitive first step along the path that would eventually lead, two decades later, to the fMRI study. He delivered his proposed study protocol in late 1988. He had no inkling how good his timing would prove to be. Strassman had lofted a shot from mid-court and found the sweet spot: his proposal hit the agency at precisely the same moment Rick had stumbled into the FDA as an intern applicant—a progressive new upper management attempting to lower the barriers to experimental drug research. *Swish!*

Even so, it took two years of serious bureaucratic rat racing to get all the approvals. At one point, as Strassman recounted in his book, he broke down in frustration on the phone. "I'm losing my mind. I'm pulling out my hair. My gums are bleeding. I'm getting on my wife's nerves," he pleaded with the one-zillionth regulator he'd reached in pursuit of final permission.

It worked.

The study began in November of 1990. In all, over its five-year course, he would administer 400 doses of DMT. Although his role in the study was not as a therapist—he wouldn't have been the most qualified therapist in any case—some of his subjects seemed to have emotional breakthroughs as well as mystical-type experiences that profoundly affected them. But it became clear that giving people the short-acting DMT alone, without therapy, was no guarantee of lasting benefit. And some of the experiences it induced were so disturbing, they left the subjects who experienced them with even less certainty about the meaning of their lives than when they began.

This negative consequence would eventually affect Strassman himself.

"There are surprising and remarkable consistencies among volunteers' reports of contact with nonmaterial beings," Strassman wrote. "Volunteers find themselves on a bed or in a landing bay, research environment, or high-technology room. The highly intelligent beings of this 'other' world are interested in the subject, seemingly ready for his or her arrival and wasting no time in 'getting to work.'

"Their 'business' appeared to be testing, examining, probing, and even modifying the volunteer's mind and body. . . . They also communicated with the volunteers, attempting to convey information by gestures, telepathy, or visual imagery."

When Strassman attempted to explain the experiences as dreams, visions, or the obvious and unfortunate consequences of undergoing a highly altered consciousness in an unwelcoming hospital environment ("on a bed in a high-tech room or research environment") and, in fact, being probed by "highly intelligent beings" (i.e., doctors and researchers), "subjects tenaciously resisted . . . because such explanations reduced the enormity, consistency, and undeniability of their encounters. . . . How could their imagination generate a scenario that felt more real than waking consciousness?"

After the study, the participants who had encountered the "beings" created a kind of support group, telling Strassman that others who had had the same experience were the only ones they could talk to. "No one would understand. It's just too strange," one told him. "I want to remind myself that I'm not losing my mind," said another.

"These reports challenge our world view, and they raise the emotional intensity of debate: 'Is it a dream? A hallucination? Or is it real?'" Strassman wrote, broaching the uncomfortable little secret of psychedelic research. The bizarre topology of some psychedelic experiences, coupled with the sense of the experiencers that these visions are revelations rather than fantasies—the "realer than realness" of it—combined to ensure that Strassman wasn't alone in not being able to entirely dismiss the idea that these "alien terrains" have some independent reality, if not in space, then in some inner dimension that isn't simply an artifact of brain function.

The therapists and researchers who wanted to bring back psychedelic medicine had an uncomfortable fact to live with, one that they often shuffled around but that lay not far below the surface of their professional veneer: they often rubbed elbows with, or were themselves, people with at least one toe dipping into the currents of magical realism. Around every conference or gathering of psychedelic researchers one could reliably expect to find a fringe who seemed to be competing to best represent the stereotype of the credulous airheads whose excessive drug history had whipped their brains into an acid soufflé.

And sometimes they weren't so far on the fringe. One of the most influential thinkers in all psychedelia was the writer and psychic explorer Terence McKenna—a full-fledged member of the Esalen ARUPA brain trust that had fought the legal battle against the DEA, and the man who had cautioned Rick Doblin about the consequences of using a synthetic drug like MDMA rather than naturally occurring compounds like DMT and psilocybin. McKenna had written extensively about his experiences with shamanic cultures around the world and his theory that *Homo sapiens* had ascended from its animal origins in large part thanks to the mind-expanding properties of the psychedelic plants our ancestors ingested. These plants, he speculated, were something like messages in a bottle cast into the oceans of the cosmos by superintelligent aliens—rather like edible versions of the monolith in *2001: A Space Odyssey*. He also claimed he had been psychedelically inspired to develop a theory of what he called "timewaves" that predicted that a cataclysmic event would occur on the winter solstice of 2012.

McKenna didn't always take himself seriously, but he never totally disavowed these wild beliefs either. He often said that his underlying goal was to teach people that the universe was a far weirder place than they realized. He once told a journalist named John Horgan that "he called himself a 'visionary fool,' who 'propounds this thing which is a trillion to one shot'—the timewave theory—and then 'gets to live out the inevitably humorous implications of that.'"

In fact, he didn't. He succumbed to brain cancer in 2000 at only fifty-three. (In the end, he admitted to Horgan, "all his psychedelic insights had 'done nothing to mitigate or ward off the ordinary vicissitudes of life.'")

He wrote with erudition and bushels of footnotes, but he also got fairly far out into the psychedelisphere. His favorite drug was DMT, which he smoked. He often described a DMT experience very similar to that of Strassman's subjects:

"If you've taken enough DMT . . . something happens for which there are no words. A membrane is rent, and you are propelled into this 'place' . . . [with] entities . . . things, which I call 'self transforming machine elves,' I also call them self-dribbling basketballs. They are, but they are none of these things. I mean you have to understand: these are metaphors in the truest sense, meaning they're lies! Uh, it's a jeweled self-transforming basketball, a machine elf. . . . That's one metaphor. . . . When I gave [DMT] to shamans in the Amazon, they said, '[t]hese are the ancestors. These are the spirits that we work with. These are ancestor souls.'"

Underlying that entertaining, playful, almost self-parodying passage was McKenna's point: we tend to overvalue Western-style rationality and undervalue the more visionary wisdom of the type accumulated over thousands of years of prehistory, in large part through experiences of the world unlocked by altered states.

Still, machine elves. It's a difficult terrain for scientists to negotiate.

Or, as Strassman put it: "There is intense friction between what we know intellectually, or even intuitively, and what we experience with the aid of DMT."

After a while it began to wear Strassman down. "The reports of contact with invisible worlds and their inhabitants, while utterly amazing, left me grasping at conceptual straws as to their reality and meaning," he wrote. "My attitude toward high-dose sessions started turning from hope for breakthroughs to relief at volunteers emerging unharmed and intact."

His research, begun so optimistically, had left him disappointed and thwarted in a myriad of ways. He'd expected other researchers— ones more qualified to pursue psychedelics' therapeutic potential—to flock to his side and ignite the renaissance he still desired. But that didn't happen. Credentialed researchers who had earlier expressed enthusiastic interest to him backed off or faded away. Despite the approval of his own study, he discovered, psychedelic research remained stigmatized.

And far more difficult than he'd imagined. When Strassman won FDA permission to work with the less debilitating and much longer-lasting psychedelic psilocybin midway through his five-year study, fearing a loss of control of inebriated subjects, his hospital safety committee refused to allow him to conduct the sessions in nearby hospital-owned bungalows that could be made into the kind of peaceful, comforting settings psychedelic therapists had insisted on using for decades. The negatives of the hospital environment, bad enough for the half-hour DMT trips, were magnified to the point of near intolerability for potential subjects who would be delivering themselves into psilocybin's six-hour grip.

Even so, a woman who had been a subject in Strassman's DMT study volunteered to take psilocybin in the hospital room to test the concept.

As Strassman reported in his book, it was an unmitigated disaster. Everything from the placement of the hospital bed in the room to the comportment of a visiting medical student set the woman on edge, and within fifteen minutes of taking a high dose of psilocybin the woman panicked and called her husband on her cell phone. When the call cut off, she blamed it on Strassman's "mind waves." Within minutes her husband came rushing in, scooped her up, and pushed past the attendant with his tripping wife, out of the hospital. It was a horrible no-no, losing control of a drugged test subject. Whatever hope Strassman still had of convincing the safety committee to let him take his research off campus died right there.

That wasn't the end of the bad news. Soon after, he discovered that one of his research assistants had been compulsively taking psychedelic drugs, freelance, with the study subjects. The last straw came when Strassman's former Buddhist monastic community began to criticize his work for attempting to artificially shortcut the path to enlightenment.

What had begun with such promise had descended into a tour of the circles of hell. After five years Strassman threw in the pill bottle. The psychedelic renaissance had dead-ended.

38.

NICHOLAS

(THE MANIAC IN THE MIRROR)

The 1/6 Marines were going back to war, this time in Afghanistan, but Nick only had a year left on his Marine contract—not enough time for another deployment. Like others in his situation, he was temporarily reassigned until the end of his hitch. Some guys got to go to the beach and be lifeguards; other guys got to run around in the woods and tag trees to be cut down. But Nick got sent over to work on the rifle range as a marksmanship instructor. He set up in what was called "the pit," the place where all the targets get pulled down and marked up and sent back to the firing line. He was the man in charge of making sure everything ran smoothly and nobody got shot. Here he was back home, back from the war, but thanks to his new assignment, the gunfire never stopped.

Nick spent his shift in a small booth with windows around it opening onto twenty-five targets to his right and twenty-five targets to his left. Even with earmuffs, Nick could not only hear the blasting of the guns but feel them, like a million blows to the chest. One day, in the middle of a barrage, a man popped up behind the safety line, sighted his weapon at Nick's chest, and opened fire. Once again Nick just

waited for the slap of the bullets that would end his life, his heart gal-
loping and sweat pouring. Then he blinked and the guy disappeared.

"I had heard about guys having flashbacks and all that other stuff,
but I thought a flashback was supposed to be where you went back to
a moment when you were over there and relived it in your mind, not
hallucinating like I was doing. So you don't wanna tell anybody about
that—at all. Then I started seeing guys in my dreams, getting in firefights in my dreams, and getting killed. The nightmares were really
bad. I'd be shot, or I'd be getting shot at, and I'd be back over there.
That's what sucked. All you want to do is have those happy dreams you
had while you were over there of being back home. But Iraq would
always be there whenever I'd go to sleep. You wake up in the middle of
the night just drenched in sweat. And you also wake up sometimes and
don't wanna go back to sleep, because I'd go back to sleep, and I'd go
right back into one of those dreams. So I'd just say, 'Well, I'm just
gonna stay awake.' Then you don't get enough sleep, and that causes
you to be even more cranky and irritable and susceptible to seeing
stuff, and it would just escalate."

He couldn't drive past a trash pile, or over a manhole, without tens-
ing, waiting for a hidden IED to explode. Sometimes he'd even feel it,
that *whoosh* and hammer in the face of a blast wave. In restaurants he
sat with his back to the wall and a view of the door, which he'd watch
compulsively through the meal.

Nick knew he was lucky that he could tell Beverlee now about some
of what happened in Iraq, stuff he never even hinted at in messages and
phone calls when he was going through it. But he didn't tell her everything. "Who can relate to some of these things, you know? Other vets
can, but other vets don't wanna talk about it, or they feel like if you're
talking about it, you're full of shit. Because 'I can't handle talking
about it, there's no way *you* could handle talking about it.'"

One night Nick shot straight up in the bed. "Nick, are you okay?" Bev said.

"Put your hands up where I can see them!" Nick screamed.

"It's me," Bev said, terrified and confused.

"Put your hands up where I can see them!"

His voice was scary, menacing; he sounded unlike any Nick she had ever known.

She put her hands up, crying. "It's me, Nick. Everything is okay."

Nick lay back down and was instantly asleep, but Beverlee knew everything was far from okay.

Whatever came out that night, Nick struggled to keep it in by day, a ragged edge constantly rubbing a raw place in his soul. It seemed like anything could touch the sore spot, igniting a spasm of pain that would make him howl inside like a wounded animal. Even when people tried to connect—or maybe especially when they did—by thanking him for his service or calling him a hero, Nick's inner pain flared. He couldn't even think about it in words, but deep down he knew he was no hero.

If something provoked his rage when he was out with people at a bar or a party, he got good at disappearing instead of risking a meltdown. "I'd go, just get out, because I saw what I was capable of over there, and I don't ever want to unleash that on someone that doesn't deserve it."

And that was the horror. The person who least deserved it, Beverlee, was the one who most often suffered from his rage. He saw it happening and was helpless to stop it.

"When I would lose it sometimes and I would yell, it really felt like I would take this backseat, this third-person perspective, and I would see myself yelling at her and say, 'Why are you doing this? This is your—you *love* her.' But you couldn't get through to yourself. And I would have a thought that said, 'Don't you *dare* say that. Do *not* say that,' and then it would just come out. It was meant to be hurtful and mean, and I just saw how I was treating her, and I knew that it was not going to end up well."

Beverlee could say something as innocent as "I'm starving" and manage to trip the trigger. Somehow the idea that she would use that hyperbolic word in a world of plenty, where food is, if anything, too abundant, drove Nick into a rage.

"I would flip out and say, 'You don't know what starving is! I've seen little kids over there that—' You know, it would be those types of things. I yelled and screamed like a Marine in combat. And we know how to yell over gunfire, and those are very loud situations, so you can imagine me really losing it and yelling at her."

Of course, she cried. And when he'd calmed down, she'd say, "Maybe you should see someone."

But that just annoyed Nick all over again. "I was just annoyed by everybody and everything," he said. "Many times I wanted to just end it because I saw how hateful I was; I didn't think there was any hope for me. I hated everyone in this world, I hated myself, I hated this existence—so much negativity, so much hatred."

He even flipped out on his mother. "I ended up making her cry, and my dad had to yell at me. One of the things that really hurt was he didn't say, 'Don't yell at your mother like that.' He said, 'Don't yell at my wife like that.' That made me feel so, just, disconnected, and I realized what I was doing in that moment. Of course, afterwards they came in to talk to me and I apologized."

But Nick was spooked bad. He thought of the nightmare that had frozen him in his rack in Ramadi, the dream in which he'd screamed at his mother and the creature with the claws grabbed him from behind. It had all come true. The claws had been the shrapnel that got under his skin and was still there. The maniac screaming at his mother was him.

39.

RICK

(EARTHQUAKES AND RAINBOWS)

No one was more disappointed than Rick Doblin that Strassman's breakthrough research on DMT hadn't been a trigger for the explosion of psychedelic research they had both hoped would follow. But Rick wasn't conceding anything. For him, the conflict between the irrational territory to which psychedelics sometimes seemed to point and the rational process of science was no conflict at all. That was the beauty of the reality test, the carefully controlled clinical trial, in which people with psychological issues—measurable deficits in their ability to lead happy, productive lives—would undergo psychedelic therapy and either get better . . . or not.

If only he could put it to the test.

From the moment the DEA overruled the administrative judge in 1985 and declared MDMA a poison with no redeeming value, he'd been trying to play the hand he'd been dealt, pursuing the painfully slow, measured course of the FDA process required to get approval for research with a Schedule I drug.

The problem was not just the background difficulty of getting psychedelic research approved. Since the idea that LSD damaged human genetic material had been discredited, few continued to claim that traditional psychedelics caused long-term harm to brain tissue. But MDMA was different. Even as Strassman was granted permission to study DMT and do a pilot study on psilocybin, MDMA stood out as a potential instigator of brain damage, the real problem child.

For Rick, that was a big problem. He had become convinced that MDMA's potential as a therapeutic drug exceeded any other psychedelic. For one thing, it tended not to induce the kinds of extreme experiences—machine-elf extreme—that had so upset Strassman. Plus the feelings of closeness, connectedness, and fearlessness it so often produced made it seem as if MDMA had been specifically engineered to work wonders in a therapeutic relationship, in which an alliance between patient and therapist was known to be an essential precursor to healing, and an ability to look at existentially threatening realities without turning away in fear preceded almost any significant breakthrough.

To Rick, this wasn't merely theoretical. He had seen it work before his eyes, watched as MDMA and talk had saved the life of his suicidal friend. What's more, he had taken it himself often enough, and with enough friends, that he had a strong intuitive sense that it had done neither them nor their brains any damage.

For the same reason, if it did cause damage, he definitely wanted to know.

What was lacking was any good science on the matter. Basing a judgment on toxicity from results with MDA, a related but entirely different drug, was pointless. The body could react to drugs that were even more similar than MDA and MDMA in radically different ways. (MDMA was also chemically similar to mescaline, and nobody was saying mescaline damaged brain neurons.)

Rick's typically, and somewhat counterintuitively, direct solution to the need for better science on the topic: make common cause with the man who had done the research that had instigated the whole brain damage idea to begin with.

Charles Schuster had since become director of the government's National Institute on Drug Abuse, but Schuster's protégé, the researcher who had done the hands-on work on the MDA rat studies, was the neurologist George Ricaurte, whose research had earlier been cited by the DEA during the court hearings on whether to add MDMA to Schedule I of the Controlled Substances Act. Ricaurte had gone on to do studies with MDMA itself, but still with rats, which were not always a reliable indicator of how humans react. Rick called him and offered to have MAPS buy Ricaurte some monkeys to do MDMA primate studies, the next best thing to testing on humans. Ricaurte was amenable, and the two, about the same age, entered a friendly partnership. Rick even attended Ricaurte's wedding to a research colleague and future collaborator in his MDMA studies, Una McCann.

Ricaurte took delivery of Rick's monkeys, then gave them 5 milligrams of MDMA per kilogram of body weight orally. This would be the rough equivalent of the upper range of what a human heavy user might take recreationally. Tests conducted two weeks after the dose showed that while most brain regions had suffered no damage to serotonin receptors, in two specific areas, the thalamus and the hypothalamus, receptors had been reduced by about one-fifth, without any apparent functional or behavioral consequences.

Since the MDMA dosage Ricaurte had tested was about three times the average therapeutic dose equivalent—1.7 milligrams per kilogram—Rick urged him to do another test at a lower dosage to determine if, at any point above the therapeutic dosage, MDMA would show no long-lasting effect on serotonin neurons anywhere in the brain.

That point came at 2.5 milligrams per kilogram, still 50 percent above the usual therapeutic dosage. Eight doses of that size were administered over four months (one dose every two weeks), after which there was no detectable damage to neurons. Rick was greatly relieved, since that would be the key to persuading the FDA that it would be safe enough to conduct human therapeutic trials.

Unfortunately, Ricaurte had already published the results of the 5 milligram trials that did show some nerve damage, and they had gotten splashy coverage in the press and been incorporated aggressively in campaigns against illicit Ecstasy use—a giant red flag waving in the FDA's face.

Rick says he urged him to publish the new results showing no effect, but Ricaurte refused, saying a single new data point wasn't enough to justify a new publication. Rick says he ultimately persuaded Ricaurte to write a memo to the FDA informing them of the new result. He urged him to conclude the memo on a note he felt the data merited: that it would be safe to move on to human trials. Ricaurte wouldn't go that far.

Once again Rick refused to be discouraged. If they couldn't yet test MDMA on humans in a lab, they could bring humans who had done a lot of MDMA into a lab and test *them*. Rick happened to know people who had done a lot of MDMA, and he could try to recruit them for the study.

Not that that would be easy. At the time, in 1988, the only way to test brain serotonin levels in humans, short of an autopsy, was to remove spinal fluid through a scary spinal tap procedure. To assure himself that he could persuade his acquaintances in good faith, Rick offered himself as subject number one. As he sat on the examination table, his back open in one of those paper hospital gowns, waiting for a gigantic needle to be plunged between two vertebrae into his spinal column, he tried to think of himself as a soldier, a soldier in the War on Drugs, only on the other side—or, rather, on the side of truth and rationality and individual liberty. To anyone who knew Rick, it wouldn't be a surprise to learn he actually thought in those terms. He was fighting for a cause, and soldiers took risks and accepted pain and discomfort. Then, as the needle went in and he felt a disorienting and uncomfortable sensation, he switched to imagining the pain that all mothers go through for the cause of bringing a life into the world; what he was bringing into the world was his spinal fluid so that someday people could legally seek therapy with MDMA.

Anyway, he got through it. Now it was time to persuade friends and acquaintances—heavy MDMA users all—to follow him. Instead of urging them to think of themselves as soldiers or mothers, he incentivized them by promising to fly them to San Francisco and put them up at the luxurious Red Victorian bed-and-breakfast on Haight Street. The procedure would be done at Stanford medical facilities, then they'd all go down to Esalen and sit in the clothing-optional hot tub as a reward.

It worked. About twenty people, mostly friends from New College, all braved the big needle and gave up their fluid for science. None expressed concern that the results would indicate brain damage; all felt in good mental and physical health after years of, in some cases, very heavy use of MDMA and other drugs. On average, each member of the group had taken MDMA ninety-five times.

Ricaurte compared their spinal fluid to levels in a control group that had never taken MDMA. He found that the average presence of serotonin metabolites—what was left after serotonin was excreted and broken down in the body—in the spinal fluid of the user group was 32 percent lower than in the control group.

That was less dramatic than it sounded. For one thing, individual serotonin levels in healthy individuals varied widely; the normal range varied by as much as 100 percent. Still, the 32 percent average was statistically significant: it was very unlikely to be just a coincidence that the MDMA-taking group tested that much lower on average. But it wasn't necessarily due to the MDMA itself. Most of the subjects had also taken many other psychoactive drugs in their lives. So it could be due to one of the other drugs, or the combination.

Or none of the above: about this time, an unrelated study determined that people who had lower serotonin levels also tended to score on the high end of tests for risk-taking behavior. Since drug taking was generally perceived as risky behavior, it would follow that the low serotonin levels could have led to MDMA use rather than the other way around.

There was another factor that Ricaurte didn't explore. No serotonin decrease had yet been linked to any negative behavioral consequences in animal studies, and even years into their frequent MDMA use, Rick and his wide-ranging group of friends were all apparently high-functioning and physically healthy. Beyond that, in a decade of widespread abuse—millions upon millions of recreational doses of MDMA taken in uncontrolled circumstances—no epidemic of any serious brain dysfunction had appeared. Given all of the above, Rick thought looking strictly at serotonin levels would be a myopic waste of resources. As long as he'd recruited this group of willing test subjects, he wanted them to undergo cognitive testing as well to determine how they matched up against a normal baseline in broad measures of brain function.

Ricaurte was collaborating with a team from Yale on an analysis of how frequent MDMA users responded to a drug that challenged the serotonin system, so Rick hired a clinical psychologist from Yale named Charles Opsahl to test the volunteers who had agreed to make another long flight for that study, this time to New York. After suffering through the friendly skies and being injected with the challenge drug—which had a sedating effect—they underwent a battery of written, verbal, and tactile tests. The results were compared to a control group of local volunteers who had never taken MDMA. Opsahl reported the results in a letter to Rick dated July 5, 1988.

"By and large, these results are striking for the fact that most subjects evaluated had IQ scores in the above average range, or higher," he wrote. Well, they were Rick's friends, so . . .

While there was some evidence of impairment in a test of short-term memory as well as a test in which the subjects had to assemble a block puzzle while blindfolded, Opsahl concluded, "It is quite possible [the slightly lower scores] are related to travel fatigue, being in a new environment, or being stressed in some way following the challenge testing that each subject performed."

Rick breathed a sigh of relief. These were people who had been heavy MDMA users for years, and ultimately, regardless of serotonin levels, their cognitive testing results were no worse than what might be expected from people who had just flown across the continent to undergo a medical procedure with a sedating drug. It was another piece of evidence to help persuade the FDA to approve human MDMA studies.

But again Rick would be disappointed—"shocked" is how he remembers it—when Opsahl and his colleagues published their results, the first-ever assessment of MDMA and neurocognitive function. Although the authors concluded that, despite serotonin levels on the low side, none of the test subjects "reported depressed mood or met clinical criteria for an affective disorder at the time of testing," it went on to emphasize the negative.

The cognitive test deficits—which, in his letter, Opsahl said could be no more than the result of travel and stress—instead became "a pattern of mild-to-moderate impairment" which "raise[s] concern about possible detrimental effects of MDMA use on neuropsychological function." The letter contained no mention of the adverse circumstances under which the tests were taken.

Rick struggled with his frustration: everything with MDMA seemed to be an uphill battle. What were basically positive results got reported as negative results, and even if you did take the most negative view, these were subtle dangers under discussion—*potential* subtle dangers—when drugs with far more certain and significant dangers

sailed through FDA approval for clinical trials and became prescription medicines.

Rick had only one gear, and that was forward. If the cloud of potential neurotoxicity couldn't be dissipated, he had to focus on finding a way to test the *benefits* of MDMA that could be set against the
hypothesized detriments. He knew from the therapeutic history of
MDMA before it was criminalized that it had been found to effectively
reduce depression and anxiety and could even make physical pain
more tolerable in patients who were battling terminal disease. Of what
concern would possible long-term serotonin depletion be to someone
who *had* no long term to worry about?

Of course, he'd already tried that argument when attempting to
treat his own grandmother who had been near death. And George
Greer, a plaintiff named in the suit against DEA and one of the leading
practitioners of MDMA psychotherapy before criminalization, had
recently proposed a clinical study on terminal cancer patients and gotten nowhere. He had been told that "even dying people have the right
to be protected against brain damage."

But Rick thought it was time to try again. Of course, he was a
political scientist, not a psychiatrist. He couldn't do medical research
on his own. He needed someone with medical qualifications and credentials to work with, and just as he was struggling with the toxicity
issue, he found one.

Rick noticed a letter in the *Archives of General Psychiatry* pointing
out serious methodological flaws in one of Ricaurte's MDMA studies.
The writer was Charles Grob, the University of California psychiatrist
who would eventually conduct the study of sacramental ayahuasca
users.

Grob had grown up in the sixties and, like so many of his cohorts,
"had modest firsthand experience" in college with psychedelics—
experiences at least impressive enough so that when, after leaving

school, he found himself working as a late-shift technician in a dream research studies lab, he became fascinated with the library of psychedelic literature belonging to one of the researchers. He read to stay awake at night, and soon developed a passionate interest in psychedelic research—enough to motivate him to go to medical school and become a psychiatrist.

"Meanwhile," Grob says in a familiar refrain, "all psychedelic research shut down."

But Grob maintained his interest, and even published a speculative article on how to proceed "if the opportunity should arise to pursue sanctioned clinical research with these unique psychoactive substances."

Of course, Rick Doblin noticed that article too. Rick decided to pay Grob a visit. When he suggested they develop a protocol to present to the FDA on using MDMA to treat cancer anxiety in terminal patients, Grob felt he had come full circle.

The two labored on the protocol, a complex document describing the design of the proposed study that had to be rigorous and overwhelmingly persuasive, both scientifically and politically. It took a frustrating two years to complete; Grob struggled to find the time among his other responsibilities, which kept increasing. Finally, in the spring of 1992, after countless revisions, they submitted it to the FDA for approval.

Once again Rick's timing was impeccable.

Almost immediately, the National Institute on Drug Abuse scheduled a policy summit on the issue of psychedelic research for mid-July, just weeks after the submission of Grob's protocol. NIDA hadn't considered psychedelics (they were still referring to the drugs generally as "hallucinogens" despite the fact that the visual perceptions the drugs provoked were rarely true hallucinations) for fourteen years, largely because there had been little research to consider. Now four currents had converged to change that. First was the fact that, despite ever tougher drug laws, the illegal use of various psychedelics only seemed to increase. Meanwhile, interest in human psychedelic research among researchers—primarily Rick Strassman's DMT study and Grob's proposed MDMA study, both inspired directly or indirectly by Rick— had begun to build. Finally, amidst frustration with the failure to find an effective treatment for opiate drug addiction, impressive reports of offshore success in treatment of addicts with ibogaine were increasingly hard to ignore.

Synchronistically, the FDA, which had neither approved nor rejected Grob's MDMA study protocol, had forwarded it—with a critique and suggested changes—to an advisory committee scheduled to meet the day after the NIDA psychedelic policy review ended.

So, seven years after MDMA had been placed on Schedule I— seven years of unceasing effort on Rick's part—he and Grob boarded a plane to Washington for two meetings in three days that would either open the door to human psychedelic research or nail it shut.

The NIDA and FDA meetings would take place in immense federal office buildings within two miles of each other in North Bethesda, a half hour northwest of the Capitol. Grob and Rick got a hotel room within brisk walking distance of both headquarters. When the NIDA meeting began on July 13, Rick braced for a hostile or at least fiercely skeptical atmosphere.

So he was surprised when the opening speaker, Stephen Szara, the retired chief of NIDA's biomedical research branch, began with a detailed and nuanced review of the history of psychedelic research, including its promise as a therapeutic aid. Szara pointed out that from 1953 to 1973, before the clampdown, the federal government had funded—not even counting the secret military research—at least 116 studies of LSD involving more than 1,700 subjects at a cost of about $4 million. He even spoke about the studies that suggested that psychedelics, given in large doses, produced transcendent, cathartic, and even mystical experiences in subjects ranging from prisoners to priests.

Rick felt as if he had slipped into an alternate universe when Szara reached his conclusion: careful research into the mysterious workings of the brain with these uniquely useful psychedelic tools could yield new discoveries of significant potential.

Rick Strassman, his DMT research still ongoing, made a presentation whose subtext was unmistakable: with caution and proper screening, hundreds of doses of a powerful psychedelic could be safely administered to humans in a research setting.

But the emotional high point for Rick came when Sasha Shulgin, the chemist who had rediscovered MDMA, made a passionate argument for restarting human research. Even as DEA agents looked on, Shulgin didn't shy away from talking about the hundreds of novel psychoactive compounds he had tested on himself and a team of twelve research associates—and not always in a strictly legal manner. If there was one overriding lesson from his decades of research, Shulgin said, it was that the variance in the psychoactive effects of closely related chemical compounds were unpredictable and could be determined only by human testing. He gave specific instances of data from animal studies that had been directly contradicted by human subjects. He referred back to Stephen Szara's talk of psychedelics' ability to produce religious experiences. Did the assembled experts think rats could provide sufficient data on that?

The laughter that followed felt to Rick like the beginning of a new era.

The positive glow followed Rick and Grob out the door as the NIDA meeting concluded. The landscape had clearly changed for the better, as far as they were concerned. But they still faced the trickier of the two meetings. It was one thing for the scientists at NIDA to make general positive noises about human psychedelic research, and quite another for the bureaucrats at the FDA to endorse their specific proposal for MDMA research. The cloud of neurotoxicity still hung over them, and Rick's friend turned nemesis George Ricaurte would be one of those attending the meeting the following day. No doubt he would have his say.

Still buzzing from their NIDA high, and both excited and anxious, the psychiatrist and the psychedelic crusader couldn't sit still in their hotel rooms. They decided to shrug off the on-again, off-again rain and take a hike to the FDA building on Parklawn Drive in Rockville, Maryland, where the next meeting would begin in barely a dozen hours. As they walked, Rick—incorrigible as ever—pulled out a joint and lit it, drawing the sweet smoke into his lungs. He'd always believed the slight detour from normal consciousness that marijuana afforded gave him perspective, allowed him to see familiar terrain in a new way.

Rick recalled what happened next in a report he wrote for the MAPS website:

"As we approached the massive but deserted Parklawn building, where during the day thousands of federal government employees work, we were presented with an amazing sight. Rising over the building, in the watery haze left by a rain cloud, shone a complete rainbow. Though we value rationality as much as the next person, we were sorely tempted to consider it a favorable omen."

It only took until the first speaker cleared her throat the following morning for Rick to feel the omen had been fulfilled. To his surprise, it was Dr. Geraline C. Lin, the woman who had chaired the two-day NIDA meeting that had just ended. Lin got right to the point: NIDA's technical advisors had reached a consensus on the need to conduct human studies with "hallucinogens" both for what that could teach us about the brain and to investigate—in well-controlled, objective human studies—whether the therapeutic benefits of their use, if any, balanced the risks, psychological, cultural, and physiological.

Things got tenser for Rick and Grob when Ricaurte spoke of his now-familiar concerns about MDMA neurotoxicity. But they got some unexpected support from a University of California research psychiatrist named Reese Jones, who called Ricaurte's conclusions alarmist. Given that MDMA-related serotonin depletion in animals had never been associated with any behavioral and physiological problems and that hundreds of human users had reported beneficial effects from MDMA therapy, serotonin depletion, if it even occurred, could as easily be considered advantageous as dangerous, Jones argued.

If a pharmaceutical company produced a drug like MDMA, he said, only half joking, the brain changes that accompanied such positive effects would become a selling point, featured prominently in their TV commercials.

World-renowned pharmacologist Lewis Seiden came to Ricaurte's defense. Along with Schuster, Seiden, fifty-eight, had been Ricaurte's mentor at the University of Chicago. He contradicted Jones, saying that some studies had found cognitive impairments in people with massive serotonin depletion, and that concern over MDMA's neurotoxic potential was not scientifically inappropriate.

There could hardly have been a more uncomfortable moment for the meeting to switch to the closed session in which Grob would present the protocol. "I had never seen him quite so nervous," Rick said.

When Grob had finished, Dr. Curtis Wright, the FDA official directing the review of the protocol, turned to George Ricaurte. He asked Ricaurte's opinion of the risks that the neurotoxic effects of MDMA posed to research subjects.

For Rick and Grob, time slammed to a stop as Ricaurte considered his answer. Finally he spoke the words that Rick had been waiting four years to hear him say: the relatively small doses called for in the experiment would not pose a large risk either to cancer patients or healthy individuals.

The last hurdle had been cleared. Now Rick and Grob were certain their study would be approved. But there was one final twist: the advisory committee said that the cancer study was premature. Studies of whether a drug might be effective for a particular condition were phase two of a three-phase process. Phase three consisted of widespread clinical trials involving scores of clinicians and hundreds of subjects.

But the primary phase was simply to assure that the drug could be given to humans without any acute harm. The committee suggested that Grob begin with that before proceeding with the cancer study.

And, by the way, the committee had decided that, in general, psychedelic research should be handled no differently than any other drug research.

That was all Rick had been hoping for.

The advisory committee endorsement led, finally, to FDA approval—the first ever for a human study with MDMA. But still the process dragged on. It would be nearly two years before the first shipment of Rick's stash of what was now government-approved clinical MDMA would arrive at the Harbor–UCLA Medical Center in the LA suburbs. By then the original simple design of a drug safety study had grown to include a more elaborate one requiring, among other things, background, non-drug research requiring subjects to spend a night in a hospital bed with two dozen electrodes attached to their bodies, faces, and scalps. Once again Rick felt that before he recruited friends and acquaintances, it was only right to volunteer as subject number one.

On the evening of January 16, 1994, he checked into the hospital's clinical research center for an evaluation of his sleep patterns—one way of determining if his heavy MDMA use had any long-term negative effects on his brain. At about eleven p.m., the lights were turned out and Rick managed to fall into a deep sleep, despite being wired up like a Christmas tree. At just after four thirty a.m., violent shaking startled Rick awake. It only took a few seconds to come to his senses enough to realize the center was roiling in a significant earthquake. All he knew about earthquakes was that he needed to get underneath a sturdy desk or table or stand against an interior wall. As he began to push himself off the bed, he realized that all the electrodes cemented firmly to his head prevented him from moving more than a few feet. The researcher in the next room monitoring his sleep patterns tried to come to his aid, but the floor was shaking so much, he fell down.

What became known as the Northridge earthquake lasted for ten to twenty seconds, followed by several thousand aftershocks, some strong enough to shake the building all over again. Casualties in a wide area of Southern California mounted to 57 dead and more than 8,700 injured. Fortunately for Rick, the medical center had been built with a high degree of earthquake tolerance. It stood without significant damage or any serious injuries.

Somehow it seemed appropriate to Rick that the initiation of the first FDA-approved human MDMA study would be such an earth-shaking experience.

The research itself went without a major hitch, and no adverse reactions save for one subject who had a hypertensive reaction to the MDMA: his blood pressure spiked into dangerous numbers until Grob brought it under control. It turned out the man had spent the night before the study with a friend, who had a cat. When he'd begun to have an allergic reaction to cat hair and started wheezing, the friend gave him some of his asthma medication. Asthma medication and MDMA don't mix well. Good to know.

If Grob's first study did little else, it demonstrated that MDMA research was at least feasible—financially, politically, and scientifically. Now Rick was confident they could move forward with their MDMA cancer anxiety study.

But Grob wasn't so sure. By then, he says, "the public atmosphere was pervaded by talk of neurotoxicity and increasing numbers of very young people taking MDMA in mass settings." Every so often someone with underlying vulnerability would take high doses of MDMA in a hot, crowded dance club, overheat, go into kidney and liver failure, and die, which would make all kinds of headlines.

"There was just so much negative press that I backed off of doing more MDMA research," Grob says.

But it was more than that. Rick, in countering the negative publicity, continued to be outspoken in his aggressive, let-the-chips-fall-where-they-may style, a style that began to trouble Grob. It came to a head when Grob saw Rick quoted in a newspaper story seeming to say that their study was up and running, although in fact it hadn't yet begun.

"Rick laughed it off," Grob says. "He was more concerned about my nervousness."

Psychedelic research was professionally risky enough, Grof felt—and MDMA research particularly so—without constantly pushing the envelope by waving your arms and shouting to draw attention to it.

"MAPS was a one-man show, one man's vision and energy," Grob says. "This was a period of time when I was not comfortable working with Rick. My approach was to be relatively quiet, discreet, under the radar, and Rick likes to broadcast everything."

Plus now Rick and MAPS weren't the only game in town. After Rick's decade of activism had managed to restart psychedelic research, some other organizations began to arise. In 1993, David E. Nichols, the Purdue psychopharmacologist with a DEA Schedule I license who had synthesized and safeguarded Rick's supply of research MDMA, founded the Heffter Research Institute, a nonprofit dedicated to "research of the highest scientific quality with the classical hallucinogens and related compounds." Nichols was delivering a message in the organization's name: Arthur Heffter was the first to bring the tools of Western science to the study of naturally occurring psychedelics. His study of peyote buttons led him to identify mescaline as the psychoactive component in 1897. Heffter did not become a psychedelic acolyte, or anything remotely close. He continued to have a long and distinguished career in pharmacology, known for his rigorous scientific method.

By honoring Heffter, Nichols was making clear that the institute would be a science-first sort of place, aiming to remain quietly in the mainstream. Nor was the emphasis on "classical hallucinogens" without implication. The Heffter founding members, which included some in the Esalen group who had distanced themselves from Rick during the DEA lawsuit, had the same queasy feeling about MDMA that Grob did. Plus MDMA wasn't very psychedelic by classical standards. The alterations in perception were much subtler, the experience of Huxley's "other world" fainter. MDMA should be considered an entirely different class of drug, Nichols believed. He suggested the term *entactogen*, meaning, roughly, "touching within," suggesting the ability to reach deep into a psyche's core.

It wasn't that Nichols and his fellow Heffter founders didn't support Rick's efforts: in a letter to Rick, Nichols called MDMA an "outstandingly valuable therapeutic tool." It was simply that, as Nichols explained, "the main thrust of my efforts has been to make these drugs acceptable to the medical community at large, following generally-accepted standards of practice."

If one particular drug in the psychedelic array, or a certain style of splashy activism, made that end more difficult to achieve, the Heffter folks had no desire to push it. They believed in following the path of least resistance—which meant focusing on research with ayahuasca or psilocybin, two psychedelics with a relatively low profile and therefore a good chance of not triggering a panic reaction from the mainstream.

Grob soon got an invitation to join Heffter's board. He accepted and began his studies of ayahuasca, which culminated with his visits to Brazil, where he assessed the physical and mental health of frequent participants in ayahuasca sacraments.

Meanwhile, more years had gone by as Grob and Rick tinkered with the cancer study protocol. The political ground at the FDA had been shifting again as the experimentation of the early nineties petered out and the Pilot Drug Evaluation staff was disbanded. After the great hope of the NIDA and FDA meetings in 1992, nearly a decade slipped away.

"Charlie was slow," Rick says. "He kept getting promoted and distracted by new duties, and he wasn't getting aggressive enough with the FDA. I was like a jockey and Charlie was the horse. I'm riding this horse, crossing a stream, and Charlie decides to throw me off. I felt completely abandoned and betrayed. We could have gotten permission for the MDMA cancer study. He was the researcher I had a decadelong relationship with, and all of it had been for nothing. I was a rider without a horse."

40.

MICHAEL

("ARE YOU A PSYCHIATRIST?")

During his breathwork training sessions with Stan Grof, Michael had heard about MAPS and Rick Doblin. The MAPS mission of promoting psychedelic research naturally appealed to Michael, so he paid to become a member. Aside from getting the MAPS quarterly bulletin—a very impressively produced, glossy publication—mailed to him, he didn't give his membership a lot of thought until, in one of his moments of frustration about not knowing how to advance his desire to work with psychedelic therapy, he noticed a photo of Rick, long-haired and beaming, in the MAPS bulletin. Right then and there he called the MAPS headquarters in Sarasota—Michael had no idea, of course, that the offices were in Rick's old house, the one he'd built himself to accommodate a psychedelic mind-set—and asked to speak to Rick Doblin. Michael thought maybe Rick could give him some suggestions. But the woman who answered said Rick wasn't in and suggested that Michael call back later.

He never got around to it.

Then, in 1999, another MAPS bulletin caught his eye rather dramatically, leaping off the page with the energy of a spectral jaguar. In it was a notice for what was being billed as the first annual ayahuasca conference. After his experience in Peru, how could he ignore this?

Michael showed it to Annie.

"If we go to this conference," he told her, "maybe I'll get some leads about where to do psychedelic research."

They flew out to San Francisco and arrived at the aging Cathedral Hill Hotel in time to attend the opening session on March 17, 2000. Michael glanced around the conference hall and noticed a familiar face: the man in the photo from the MAPS bulletin.

Michael walked over to Rick, who as always was surrounded by people, all of whom had some business to conduct. He waited patiently for an opening, introduced himself, then came right to the point.

"Can you give me some advice on which country would be the best in which to do psychedelic research?"

Rick studied him intently.

"You're a psychiatrist?" he asked.

"Yeah," Michael said.

"And you want to do psychedelic research?" Rick said slowly, as if he wanted to make sure there had been no mistake.

"Yeah," Michael said.

Rick smiled. He'd found a new horse.

"You can do psychedelic research right here," he said. "And we'll help you."

What Rick didn't say was how long it would take.

The study evolved as a trial of MDMA-assisted therapy for subjects suffering persistent posttraumatic symptoms following sexual abuse or rape.

MDMA's apparent ability to allow unflinching consideration of emotionally painful material seemed to match up perfectly with the pathology of PTSD, a condition that had become a specialty in Michael's psychiatric practice and breathwork groups, not to mention ground zero in Rick's psychedelic therapy experience.

By the time Michael had a very preliminary draft of a protocol, eleven months had passed. He flew back out to California to put it before Rick and some of the Heffter Institute people, including Grob and Nichols. Since he'd never done medical research before, Michael needed all the help he could get constructing a protocol that met modern standards. He also managed to persuade Dr. Mark Wagner, an independent neuropsychologist from the Medical University of South Carolina, to do the assessment testing of the subjects before and after their therapy.

Especially since MAPS was sponsoring the study, Michael knew for the trial to be credible to skeptical regulators it was essential to sign on an independent outsider like Wagner—an expert in psychological testing with no prior interest in psychedelics—to, in essence, grade the results.

In some ways his timing for attempting to launch the study couldn't have been worse. Just two weeks after the nearly complete protocol was sent out to colleagues for comment, Alan Leshner, the director of the National Institute on Drug Abuse, spoke before the Senate Committee on Homeland Security and Governmental Affairs to warn them that MDMA use was spreading beyond nightlife into high schools (and middle schools: in 2000, 4.3 percent of eighth graders said they had tried Ecstasy). Scientists, Leshner declared, had reached "across-the-board" agreement that MDMA caused brain damage.

NIDA launched a public service campaign to persuade potential users that MDMA was dangerous, highlighted by PET scan images of blood flow in a "healthy baseline brain" compared to that brain two weeks after MDMA use. The colors indicated drastically reduced blood flow, which Leshner suggested indicated permanent brain damage.

Ironically, what Leshner didn't know was that the "perfectly healthy baseline" image came from a formerly heavy Ecstasy user who had been abstinent for some time, ironically demonstrating the opposite of what he said it demonstrated: that even a heavy user of Ecstasy returned to apparently normal levels in the long run.

The previous year, an even scarier image popped up on MTV and *The Oprah Winfrey Show*: a scan of the brain of a heavy Ecstasy user that appeared to show numerous holes where brain tissue should be. Oprah was impressed. These images "tell the story," she said. But in fact, they didn't. The "holes" were mapping artifacts. They weren't holes at all, but created by coding the computer to represent areas of the brain with a slight decrease in blood flow, which may have been caused by any number of things, as null spaces. But the idea that Ecstasy ate holes in people's brains seized the public imagination.

Inflamed by these frightening images of MDMA's effects on the brain and its spreading illicit use, members of Congress, led by then senator Joe Biden, sprang to action, introducing the Reducing Americans' Vulnerability to Ecstasy (RAVE) Act. The penalties for trafficking MDMA were increased. Rick, Charlie Grob, and Dave Nichols had all gone to Washington in March to testify at the U.S. Sentencing Commission hearing. They weren't alone. The Federation of American Scientists, led by none other than former director of NIDA Charles Schuster, weighed in with statistically loaded arguments against the sentencing changes, which they said was both bad science and bad policy.

"We're still finding out about the risks of MDMA use, especially possible long-term changes in certain brain regions," Schuster said. "No one would say the drug is safe. But treating it as worse than heroin is irrational. Heroin is far more addictive, leads to far more overdose deaths, causes enormous amounts of crime, and helps spread HIV/ AIDS. On any one of those dimensions, MDMA is much less of a threat to public health and safety."

It all was to no avail.

"MDMA is now, dose for dose, punished more heavily than heroin," Rick posted on the MAPS site.

This was the playing field when Michael submitted the protocol to the FDA on October 1, 2001, "a major milestone in the history of MAPS, and hopefully in the history of MDMA research," Rick wrote on his website. Though literally true, Rick's optimism seemed premature, given the black cloud still hanging over MDMA. So it seemed something of a miracle when just one month and one day later he posted this: "It's my pleasure to report some excellent news. About 10 AM, Friday, November 2, FDA contacted me to say that MAPS' MDMA/PTSD protocol was approved. This approval marks the culmination of sixteen years of efforts to obtain permission from FDA for MDMA-assisted psychotherapy research, since MDMA was criminalized in 1985."

Before they could begin recruiting subjects for the trials, they would need to obtain the approval of the institutional review board of the Medical University of South Carolina, where the trial would take place. All human medical research needed not only FDA approval but the approval of an "IRB" as they were called, which served as an ethical and scientific backstop to protect the subjects' rights and welfare.

But after several months Michael got word from a source at the university that the members of the IRB were getting "cold feet about allowing a controversial study."

The source was on target: after six months of stalling, it became clear the university had no intention of housing the clinical trials.

Rick and Michael huddled tensely until they came up with a plan B. They would move the trials to Michael's private office, a 1950s-vintage cottage on the beach road between downtown Charleston and Sullivan's Island, where Michael and Annie lived. It had been tastefully remodeled to create a skylit, high-ceilinged sanctuary scattered with homey landscape paintings and overstuffed furnishings. It felt like your smarter, hipper, better-off friend's house, circa 1976. It may not have been designed specifically to accommodate people tripping on acid, but it was about as mellow a space as you could imagine.

Of course, the new plan had to go back to the FDA regulators, who didn't care about the atmosphere. What concerned them was prompt access to emergency care if the experiment went bad. They put a "clinical hold" on the project until the issue could be resolved.

Michael and Rick ultimately proposed hiring an emergency room doctor and nurse to sit in a spare room in the cottage with a crash cart during all MDMA sessions, just in case. The FDA agreed and removed the hold.

Seven months had passed.

They found a new IRB—the for-profit Western Institutional Review Board, which claimed to conduct the majority of reviews for new drug submissions to the FDA. The application was submitted on June 19, 2002. Less than a month later, it was approved.

Once again they were cooking. "We can now definitely say that the US study will take place," Rick crowed in a web post. Then he went into high gear trying to raise the remaining $90,000 they would need to complete the study. Michael busily began his effort to obtain a DEA license to handle Schedule I drugs. The regulations required that Schedule I compounds be stored in a "securely locked, substantially constructed cabinet." But an agent in the local field office advised him that, "given what you're dealing with," it would be better to have a safe bolted to the floor and an alarm system. Expensive and time-consuming but doable. The agent told him he should have the license in three to five weeks.

Michael formally submitted his application to the DEA on July 3.

After a month he had heard nothing back. He called to check on the application's progress. There had been no progress. Whoever answered the phone told him, "It's not in the system yet," and gave him another person to call, who told him the application was on her desk and she was "getting ready to take it to the reviewer."

Ten days later he called again but couldn't get a live human. He left a voice mail message saying he "hoped to avoid further delays."

He called again in five days and left another message.

Two weeks later, when nobody had responded to any of his messages, he called once more.

This time he got lucky and the woman answered. She told him that the application was no longer on her desk but it still wasn't in the system. She didn't know why.

When Michael asked if it usually took so long for an application to get "in the system," she said, "This isn't a priority." She suggested he call back in a few days.

The trouble with calling back in a few days, Michael told her, "is that I've been calling for three weeks and leaving messages and you never call me back."

She promised to be available all day.

She wasn't. Michael called twice and left messages. When she finally called back, Michael was out. She told Annie she couldn't check on the application unless Michael sent copies of everything.

Puzzled—she'd already told him she was checking on it—Michael called her back yet again. Voice mail.

Michael still hadn't heard anything back from the DEA by the following week, when he got a faxed letter from the Western IRB, which, without notification, had reconvened in a special meeting to reconsider their approval of the study protocol. Rick would report the letter under the headline "Terrible News!" But there really was no easy way to say just how devastating it was. The letter began badly and got worse until it arrived here:

"The Board concluded that MAPS appears to have submitted information about MDMA in a manner that omits significant facts and that uses information in ways that are overly reassuring regarding the risk/benefit analysis. The Board concluded that both the sponsor and yourself appear to lack the scientific objectivity and rigor required to carry out this research and the research presents unacceptable risks to subjects. . . . You are directed to immediately terminate all research activities."

The unexpectedly personal attack almost knocked Michael down. As best as he and Rick could piece it together in a frantic few days of phone calls, an IRB staff member who had taken exception to the initial approval had assembled a brief against it and persuaded the board to reconvene. He attacked Michael's credentials and Rick's motives. But the ultimate ammunition in the dissenter's arsenal turned out to be a phone conversation with some researchers who claimed to have as-yet-unpublished data showing that MDMA was far more dangerous than anyone had previously understood.

It wasn't unpublished for long. Three weeks later, on September 27, an article appeared in *Science*, titled "Severe Dopaminergic Neurotoxicity in Primates After a Common Recreational Dose Regimen of MDMA ('Ecstasy')."

The lead author: George Ricaurte.

The headline is ominous enough even if you don't speak neurosience. But the translation is worse. The $1.3 million federally funded study claimed that MDMA was not only damaging the serotonin system in the brain but the dopamine system as well, and severely. Attributing specific negative consequences to changes in the serotonin system had proven difficult. But dopamine depletion, over time, led to a well-known and disastrous result: Parkinson's, a scary, progressively debilitating disease that can ultimately lead to near paralysis and dementia.

Ricaurte, who had been awarded millions of federal dollars over the years for his MDMA toxicity studies, reported that he had injected squirrel monkeys with MDMA in a regimen he said was "modeled closely" on the way heavy Ecstasy users would attempt to "boost" their high at all-night dance parties by taking another pill as soon as the effects of the first began to wane, and so on for hours at a time.

It was very debatable whether his dosing regimen—three injections of 2 milligrams per one kilogram of body weight, one every three hours—in fact "closely modeled" human users' behavior. The pure amount of the drug given, though not unheard of, would nonetheless represent an extreme dose for a Raver rather than an ordinary one. But the fact that it was injected into the animals instead of given orally, as humans took it, meant that it was far more potent still, as Ricaurte's own previous research had established.

Of the five monkeys, "three tolerated drug treatment without any apparent difficulty. One monkey became less mobile and had an unstable, tentative gait after the second dose, and therefore it was not given the third planned dose. The fifth monkey developed malignant hyperthermia and died within hours of receiving the last dose of MDMA."

When he repeated the experiment on baboons, "again, one of five animals died, this time shortly after receiving only two doses of MDMA. A second baboon appeared unstable after the second dose of MDMA and therefore received only two of the three planned doses."

When the surviving primates were killed and autopsied, Ricaurte found something shocking. Previously, many toxicity studies showed that while MDMA impacted serotonin receptors, the dopamine system remained notably unaffected. But this time was different. The dopamine system in both squirrel monkeys and baboons had been severely damaged.

Alan Leshner, the former NIDA director who had launched the "brain after Ecstasy" campaign with the misleading PET scan images, was now chief executive officer of the American Association for the Advancement of Science, publisher of the journal that printed Ricaurte's study. His statement on the subject played in newspapers around the world: "Using ecstasy is like playing Russian roulette with your brain function," he said. "This study shows that even very occasional use can have long-lasting effects on many different brain systems. It sends an important message to young people—don't experiment with your own brain."

As soon as Rick saw Ricaurte's results, he felt certain something was very wrong with them. If these were doses, as Ricaurte claimed, "lower than those typically used by humans," then the 20 percent death rate should have been a blinking neon question mark on the study's validity: millions upon millions of doses of MDMA had been consumed by humans in uncontrolled circumstances with a multitude of aggravating factors, and yet the death rate was nowhere near 20 percent—it was a tiny fraction of 1 percent. Plus recent human studies, including autopsies of heavy Ecstasy users, not only didn't show massive dopamine neural damage, it showed none at all.

Rick wasn't the only one suspicious.

Dr. Glen Hanson, who was acting director of NIDA at the time of the study—and therefore more or less Ricaurte's boss—questioned the extreme results as soon as he saw them. As Hanson recalled to journalist Thomas Bartlett for a story in the *Chronicle of Higher Education*, when he saw Ricaurte he said, "George, we never see this. Where is this coming from?" Ricaurte responded, "Well, the dosing paradigm is different and there are some subtle differences and maybe there is just this little window that you don't see unless you do it exactly right."

"I really need to see this in more animals," Hanson said he responded, and then added, "And you always like to see it done in another lab."

But the study was published as it was, generating worldwide headlines, including in Spain, where it nailed shut the coffin of a study that Rick had sponsored there—one very similar to Michael's proposed study.

The project in Madrid, led by José Carlos Bouso, a psychologist who had contacted Rick in 1999, had been approved by the Spanish, and it had already begun. The first six subjects—women suffering from PTSD after rape—had begun the double-blinded sessions in a Madrid hospital in late 2000. After national publicity surrounding two deaths attributed to Ecstasy in a drastically overcrowded and poorly ventilated sports arena during a March 2002 rave in Málaga, the hospital where the study was being conducted informed the researchers that its facilities would no longer be available. In July 2002, just weeks after Michael's study had won the initial approval of the Western IRB, the Spanish study was shut down by its IRB equivalent for no longer having a hospital to work with. Before investigators could reassure regulators and find a new facility, George Ricaurte, a Spanish speaker, traveled to Spain to speak about MDMA and dopamine toxicity.

Bouso more or less gave up. "George's talks in Spain definitely have created an impression of the dangerousness of MDMA that has made it more difficult for my efforts to try to restart my MDMA/PTSD study," Bouso lamented. "Perhaps once the MAPS-sponsored US MDMA/PTSD study is fully approved, it will be possible for me to obtain permission to restart my study."

Unfortunately, hope that Michael's study would ever get full approval was fading. It took a month for him and Rick and the MAPS staff to come up with a response to the IRB's "terminate immediately" letter. It included supporting letters from fourteen leading MDMA researchers. Rick had talked to the board's director, who apologized for questioning their motives and credentials, and seemed impressed with their rebuttal arguments. A meeting was scheduled for the day before Halloween to hear their appeal—but a week later it was canceled. Instead the board would meet privately in executive session to decide if the Western IRB should be involved in *any* study of a Schedule I drug.

A month later Michael got a terse letter: "The Western Institutional Review Board, Inc. has made the decision not to provide institutional

review board services for the Multidisciplinary Association for Psychedelic Studies."

Meanwhile, he was getting nowhere with the DEA. The holidays
came and went with nothing to show but more weeks of unreturned
phone messages. Finally, the second week of 2003, Michael managed
to reach someone senior at the DEA who told him, "I have no reason
to drag this out and I can assure you we are not dragging our feet, but
we have some serious concerns and we have given it to somebody else
outside the agency to look at."

As Michael told Rick in an email, "When I asked him if he could
tell me anything about what the concerns were, he would say only that
they had to do with 'safety.'"

Which was odd, and disturbing. It was the job of the FDA and the
IRB to determine if the study was safe, not the DEA. The role of
the DEA in approving a Schedule I license was solely to ascertain that
the drug could be secured from theft and distributed in accordance
with the research protocol.

Rick wrote a letter to the agency reciting the case law, as he explained:
"In 1994, DEA tried to use similar arguments. . . . Fortunately, FDA
Commissioner Dr. David Kessler protested to Dr. Lee Brown, Director,
Office of National Drug Control Policy (the Drug Czar), who wrote a ·
letter to DEA Administrator Tom Constantine reminding him that
DEA has no authority to review scientific matters."

As they continued the struggle with the DEA, they pursued yet
another IRB. It began optimistically. "This IRB has a reputation for
being rigorous but fair, a set of characteristics that inspires confidence,"
Rick reported.

His confidence was shaken in early February when the IRB issued
two conditions for approving the study, both of which would have made
it far more expensive and likely unacceptable to the FDA: (1) Hire an
outside contractor to oversee the study to guard against "unconscious

bias"—in spite of the fact that they already had an independent psychologist who would assess the results (Rick got a quick quote from an outside monitor: $180,000); and (2) conduct the study simultaneously at multiple sites, not just in Michael's office.

Not only would the latter condition multiply the cost, but the FDA usually insisted that a pilot study like this be confined to a single site until effective therapeutic practices could be established.

Rick wrote a despairing post that was characteristically self-revealing:

The IRB's conditions, he wrote, communicated that they were "deeply fearful of approving this protocol":

> *Though I (Rick Doblin) am by nature happy and optimistic (which some friends of mine have teasingly referred to as evidence of MDMA brain damage), the IRC-IRB response resulted in two days of a dark depressive funk, the likes of which I haven't felt for almost 30 years, back when I was working through early difficult LSD experiences. The resolution of the depression came with the decision to throw myself into responding in detail to the IRC-IRB letter.*

This time, no amount of determination could help. The IRB notified Rick it was tabling the application. Rick and Michael got busy preparing an application to yet another IRB, the fourth that had agreed to review the protocol. It took them a month, after which the IRB informed them it had changed its mind and would not consider the protocol after all. By the end of summer, more than a year after the Western IRB had originally approved the protocol, they were applying to yet another IRB, responding to yet another long list of questions and concerns.

Then, in early September, Rick got a call from a source at Johns Hopkins: something big was about to be published concerning Ricaurte's MDMA-dopamine study.

Rick had no idea how big. On September 12, *Science* published Ricaurte's full retraction:

"We write to retract our report 'Severe dopaminergic neurotoxicity in primates after a common recreational dose regimen of methylenedioxymethamphetamine (MDMA)' . . . following our recent discovery that the drug used to treat all but one animal in that report came from a bottle that contained d-methamphetamine instead of the intended drug, racemic MDMA."

Methamphetamine?

The irony wasn't lost on Rick and Michael:

The drug that had been "mislabeled" as MDMA and proven so horribly toxic that it had stopped Michael's study cold—the drug that was far more toxic than actual MDMA, methamphetamine—already *was* a prescription medicine.

Ricaurte's mistake was so spectacular that some claimed it raised questions about his entire fifteen-year history of MDMA research. His critics suggested that in the hunt for millions of federal dollars, he'd been slanting results to give NIDA what it wanted—research that made MDMA look more toxic than it was.

But Ricaurte claimed that, if anything, his retraction proved his *lack* of bias: "Anybody who looks at this current situation would see that here is a scientist who recognized an error and immediately did everything in his power to correct the scientific record as quickly as possible," he told Thomas Bartlett of the *Chronicle of Higher Education.*

He said the drug mix-up was an innocent mistake: the lab that made the drug had accidentally mislabeled it. Lab managers denied they were to blame.

In any case, even while retracting his research results, Ricaurte refused to give ground. "It remains possible," he wrote, without citing any new evidence, "that dose regimens in the range of those used by some humans, but different from those thus far tested, produce dopamine neurotoxicity in primates."

More than a decade later, after countless additional studies, no evidence has emerged that MDMA damages the human dopamine system. Even its effects on the serotonin system remain far from certain. Some studies showed that nerve receptors damaged by MDMA regenerated over time, though possibly not in the original pattern. Other studies had shown evidence of some loss in recall and other cognitive abilities in heavy long-term MDMA users, but those conclusions had been muddied by the fact that heavy MDMA users invariably used many other drugs as well. The search for a population that had abused MDMA but no other potentially neurotoxic drugs seemed like a unicorn hunt.

At least, it did until Rick got a call from a graduate student at the University of Utah. The student, a doctoral candidate and a lapsed Mormon, had come across the research on effects of long-term MDMA use and found it sloppy for ignoring the problem of multidrug use. He told Rick that he knew how to solve the problem: he himself had done MDMA a thousand times—which may have been some kind of record—but hadn't done any other drugs. He didn't even drink alcohol. Not only that, he said, but he could find others like him: young Mormons who strictly obeyed the letter of their religion's law by avoiding drugs and alcohol, but felt free to use anything not specifically mentioned in doctrine. MDMA wasn't on the list.

Rick referred the student to Harvard psychiatry professor John Halpern, who used the Mormon connection to populate a study with 52 Ecstasy-only heavy abusers, comparing them with a demographically similar group of 59 people who used no drugs. His conclusion: "In a study designed to minimize limitations found in many prior investigations, we failed to demonstrate marked residual cognitive effects in ecstasy users. This finding contrasts with many previous findings—including our own—and emphasizes the need for continued caution in interpreting field studies of cognitive function in illicit ecstasy users."

Eleven days after Ricaurte's retraction, on September 23, 2003, the new IRB approved the protocol. Less than a month later Michael was notified that the local DEA would schedule an inspection of his office—the last step before Schedule I licensing approval.

Of course, it wouldn't be that easy: he had to jump through more hoops, place many unreturned phone calls, and wait four months more before he finally had his license. At one point an agent in the Washington office called wanting more information about the therapist who rented an office from Michael on the other side of the wall where the storage safe would be. The agent said they may want to do a background check on the renter to "be sure she's not going to drill through the wall or anything."

Which, when you thought about it, was interesting. The total black-market value of the four grams of MDMA Michael would keep in the safe wasn't much more than $300. Considering the cost of a quality drill and drill bit, it would be barely more expensive, and definitely easier, just to buy the drug on the street.

41.

NICHOLAS

(HAVE A PLAN)

Nick didn't know what to call what was wrong with him. He just knew he didn't want it to be post-traumatic stress disorder. He didn't think he could stand the ridicule.

"It's just part of this thing in the military. We're always taking care of each other, but when you become the weak one in the herd, you bring everyone else down. Whenever there's someone who's hurt or injured and they're complaining, saying, 'I can't stand fire watch,' or whatever, people think, 'Oh, he's just trying to get outta work. I gotta stand fire watch. I just went through the same shit you did.'"

But, desperate now, Nick went to the deployment health center and took a test on the computer that queried him on symptoms and behaviors. When Nick answered yes to question after question, he knew it wasn't good. The clinician looked over the results and said, "Well, you definitely have post-traumatic stress disorder."

When Nick asked what he could do about it, they handed him a prescription for Zoloft, an antidepressant with an armload of side effects. "They set up a thing where I would go in every few weeks and do therapy. Problem with that is you really need to talk to someone, like, every week if not twice a week. They'd push these things out, like,

four weeks, just because they had so many people and not enough
people to man this stuff."

But the treatment offered some help, mainly with his nightmares
and insomnia. The psychologist, who had a particular interest in
dreams, exhibited high interest in Nick's lucid dreaming. That got
Nick to thinking. Maybe he could use his ability to become conscious
inside his dreams to control them. "I realized that when I become
lucid, why don't I just say, 'This is a dream, this isn't real, it isn't happening'?"

And it worked sometimes. One night he dreamed a guy put a shotgun right to his face and pulled the trigger. "I felt every one of those
BBs rip through my skull, shatter the face, rip through the brain—I
felt everything. But I told myself that it was a dream and that I'm still
alive. And somehow my head was still together, and I took that gun
away from him, and I remember hitting the guy, and he went flying
like he was a baseball."

As Nick began to take control of his dreams, the nightmares
stopped. "But the rage and hallucinations, that stuff was still there."

And that was a problem, as Nick would discover one day at the
shooting range.

"It was my job to control all the stuff that's going down. We shoot
at these big targets with this small round; it only makes a small little
hole. The stickers that we have to cover them up so you know which
holes are new and which are old are large—you don't need the whole
sticker to cover up that hole—and they're called pasties. So I'd tell
everyone, 'Look, everybody, come up here. Grab your clipboard for
your target. You need to grab black-and-white pasties for your target.
Do not, do not—*do not*—take a whole roll of pasties to your target
area. Tear 'em off right here in front of my booth, and then you can
even take them and tear them in half, and now you have double,
because *it does not take a whole sticker to cover up a hole.*'"

At the time, the Marines were establishing a nearby base for their own special forces version of Navy SEALs or Army Rangers, "so we had a lot of those thought-they-were-hot-shit guys. Well, one of 'em came up right in front of my booth, right in front of me; he grabs a whole roll of pasties and just tosses 'em right up in the air and catches 'em in his hand and just starts walking. I got on the intercom—he's just on the other side of the glass, but you can't yell through the glass— I got on the intercom and I'm, like, 'Hey! Put those pasties back.' And he's just ignoring me. I said, 'Hey! Hey!' and I'm yelling, and he just kept walking. Well, I'm yelling, and everyone else is poking their head off of the catwalk, I even saw one guy go, 'Hey, he's trying to talk to you.' He just kept walking.

"I slammed the microphone down, and I got out, and I lost it. I went, 'Hey, motherfucker, I'm talking to you!' And he stopped and turned around, like, 'Who the hell you talking to like that?' and I said, 'I *said* you will not take a whole roll of pasties to your target!' He looks at me and says, 'What does it matter?'"

Nick began to sputter. "I said, *'What does it matter? What does it—'* I just couldn't hold it together, and this look on his face, like, the disrespect he'd given me—I thought about what I knew, what I was capable of, and what I did in Iraq, and I saw myself—my mind pieced together how to take him out.

"We had a T-shirt that we wore—it was part of our unit T-shirt—the motto was 'Be professional, be polite, but have a plan to kill everyone you meet.' And it's kind of morbid, but it helped us still be professional to the Iraqi people. But you had to be careful: they could turn on you at any moment. But by doing that, being programmed that way, and going through that whole deployment thinking like that, you cannot disconnect this thing that helps you figure out how to take someone out. It's kind of scary, but I just saw that I could've swooped his feet out from under him, and he would've fell right underneath the target carriage, and I could've taken the target carriage and slammed it at least a couple times and severed his head off. And then I would've been done with him, but then I would've been in a shitload of trouble. And when I realized what I was thinking at that moment, it scared me. I said, 'Go ahead, take 'em.'"

Then he turned his back, returned to his booth, and said, "I'm done."

He told his assistant he was going back to the barracks to get some medication and he walked off the range while it was still "hot," something you are never, ever supposed to do. The whole time Nick pictured the severe punishment he would receive for this outrageous behavior, but he also knew that if he stayed, he was going to kill someone.

As it turned out, the master sergeant in charge of the range heard about what happened and backed Nick up.

Nick returned to his barracks and took more Zoloft. Which didn't help.

"I thought it was kinda like one of those pills that you could take to help you right then and there, but I really shouldn't have taken another one, because it's kinda like doubling your medication, but it was the only thing I could think of. As long as I was taking my pill, I would still be feeling okay. It turned me into a zombie, really. It made me just feel 'blah,' and so whenever I would be really angry, but I was on Zoloft at that moment, I thought, 'Oh, it's not working. I need to be more blah.'"

It was obvious to Nick that the Zoloft did nothing to get at the root cause of all he was experiencing: the hallucinations, the sleeplessness, the rage, the inability to focus, the bad dreams. "It wasn't hitting where I needed it to. And what they do for you is they give you more pills. 'Oh, it's not working? Let's up the medication.'"

Or add another medication. They began giving him Seroquel, a tranquilizing antipsychotic.

"I really felt like they didn't know what they were doing. It was just kinda pump me with drugs or give me pills, and then, 'Go about your way and we'll see you in four weeks for your therapy session.'"

It sure wasn't helping him sleep.

Every night became a miserable, twisting battle. Tossing and turning, night sweats that left him feeling as if he'd been taken out of his room in a brief period of sleep, dumped into a pool, and then brought back to his bed. He'd awake in a puddle.

The medication was accomplishing *something*: It was keeping Nick from getting out of the Marines. It's called a "med hold," allowing the Marines to extend someone's active duty while they are receiving medical treatment. Nick knew someone who had been extended for a full year.

Nick had no interest in living in limbo.

"I told the doctor that I wanted to get off the medicine and I felt like if I could get out of this uniform and get out of these boots and not do this anymore, it would be a lot better."

It wasn't.

42.

MICHAEL

(GETTING CROOKED)

Donna Kilgore was subject number one.

Fourteen years before she found herself on the futon in Michael and Annie's office in Mount Pleasant, South Carolina, on an April day in 2004, a stranger had knocked on her door.

"Is your husband home?" the man asked.

Donna hesitated. Not long but long enough. That was her mistake.

"That was it," Donna said. "He pushed in. I backed up and picked up a poker from the fireplace. I was screaming. He says, 'I've got a gun. If you cooperate, I won't kill you.' He unzipped his jacket and reached in. I thought, 'This is it. This is how I'm going to die.' My life didn't flash before my eyes. I wasn't thinking about my daughter. Just that one cold, hard fact. I checked out. I could feel it, like hot molasses pouring all over my body. I went completely numb."

She dropped the poker.

Afterward she stayed strong. She wasn't going to make the classic victim's mistake of blaming herself for provoking the attack. She had no doubts about that. She'd screamed and screamed until the police came through the door. (They later reported that her attacker jumped up, clutching for his pants, saying, "She said I could!")

And, bottom line, she'd survived. She'd be fine, she told herself. She was wrong.

"It was what it must feel like to have no soul."

She quit all her hobbies. A passion for tennis died. Devastating nightmares woke her in the dark, her heart racing and her palms slick. She dreamed of explosions, tornadoes, bears eating people.

"Psychologists will tell you to go to your happy place," she said. "Well, my happy place had bears in it."

Five years passed. Whatever went wrong, or right, in her life, it felt like it was happening to someone else. She found a wonderful, loving man—she could still recognize those qualities, even though she couldn't respond to them fully—and remarried. She had more kids. But even her family felt alien. It was "almost like going overseas and being an exchange student, living with someone else's family . . . I didn't like being close to people, and my children didn't understand that. Mommy was always busy." She was often irritable and felt an unaccountable anger, which sometimes morphed for no obvious reason into a heavy-breathing, sweat-streaming rage. Almost worse, she couldn't feel the love she knew surrounded her. "I was afraid it was gone—when you look at your child and say, 'I would die for that child in a heartbeat,' I didn't feel it—and I was afraid I would never get it back."

Donna didn't find it easy to talk about how things had been. Her face grew pale as she tried to explain those awful five years: "I would put my finger on my arm," she said, "and it would be like touching a dead body."

Incredibly, she didn't see a connection to the rape. Then one evening she was sitting on her couch, watching a disaster show on TV—she considered her interest in the genre "an addiction"—when her apartment door opened. Something about the angle of the door seemed odd. As she stared at the open door, trying to figure out what could possibly be odd about such an everyday occurrence, the room began to swirl. "It was kind of like a whirlwind, make-you-dizzy moment, and I saw the whole thing, that man pushing through the door, the warm molasses pouring down, my body going numb. I call it 'when I left my body.'"

Finally she understood: she had left her body—and never come back.

The panic attacks began at work one Friday. She felt butterflies in her stomach, then couldn't breathe. "I thought, 'Oh, my God, I'm dying. I'm having a heart attack.'"

It passed, but she was shaken, especially because she'd also been having fainting spells and migraine headaches. She went to a neurologist "sure they were going to find a brain tumor."

The doctor was getting ready to order an MRI scan when Donna just blurted it out: "Things don't feel real to me."

The doctor turned. "Oh? There's a word for that," she remembers him saying. The word is *dissociation*, which happened to be a prime symptom of PTSD.

PTSD is usually triggered by combat, rape, childhood abuse, a serious accident, or a natural disaster—any situation in which someone believes death is imminent or in which a significant threat of serious injury is accompanied by an intense sense of helplessness or horror. Not all or even most trauma victims develop PTSD. In the United States, an estimated 50 to 60 percent of the population are exposed to a significant traumatic event at least once. Of those, one in six or seven—nearly 25 million people, roughly 1 in 12 Americans—have suffered from PTSD symptoms at some point in his or her lifetime. Women who have been raped are especially vulnerable, with nearly half of the victims developing PTSD.

In any given year, estimates suggest, more than 5 million Americans have active PTSD, a costly problem in both humanitarian and economic terms. Drug and alcohol abuse are frequent consequences of

PTSD, as are all the health problems that stem from substance abuse and depression.

Whatever the cause, the symptoms of PTSD are fairly consistent, and Donna's—which rated severe on a standard diagnostic test—were typical. Her prognosis was not great.

The nature of PTSD itself makes therapy problematic. People either block the memories and numb themselves or explode into states of hyperarousal: flashbacks, outbursts of rage, self-destructive behavior. Some antidepressants can diminish symptoms, and various forms of psychotherapy can, over the long term, sometimes untangle the psychological knot at the root of the problem. Some of the most effective treatments involve exposing people to the sights, sounds, smells, and memories of their traumatic events in small, repeated doses over many sessions until they no longer trigger PTSD symptoms. The trick is to prompt patients to recall the trauma with just enough emotional engagement that they can really reexperience it but with enough perspective so that the exposure doesn't trigger the panic reaction. The "window of tolerance" in which the trauma can be successfully reprocessed is narrow and hard to hold open. Although various assessments of exposure therapy judge it to be 60 to 95 percent successful for those who stick with it, a fifth to a third of those who attempt it can't tolerate it and drop out. Even more can't bring themselves to attempt the therapy in the first place. The bottom line is that when people are diagnosed with PTSD, there is better than a 1-in-3 chance that they will still have symptoms several times a week ten years later.

Donna Kilgore was twenty-five when the rapist came to her door, and she was thirty-nine, still suffering, when she heard about Michael Mithoefer and became the first to take one of his little capsules.

In between, she took "every antidepressant you can name" and tried a dozen therapists and an almost equal number of therapeutic approaches. But nothing made that numbness, panic, and rage recede.

"I was getting to the point," she recalls, "where it was either go sit on a mountaintop or go dive off a cliff."

That's when a therapist told Donna about the Mithoefers' experiment. Before she even saw any MDMA, she had three therapy sessions with Michael and Annie, during which they worked to establish a basic level of trust and learn the dimensions of Donna's problem. They also gave her the twenty-page consent form listing all the possible side effects of taking MDMA and spent several hours going over the whole thorny thing—from the possibility of death by hyperthermia or bad drug interaction, to the possible impact on serotonin neurons, to the still unsettled questions about long-term cognitive impairment. Donna took a quiz about it and they went over at length the items she didn't answer correctly.

Finally, at ten a.m. on that April morning, Annie handed Donna the capsule in a small white bowl as if it were a sacrament. Donna took it between thumb and forefinger and swallowed it with a sip of water, then put on a pair of earphones and a sleep mask and lay back on the futon. As a light, soothing piano melody eased through the headphones, she waited for something to happen. For a long time, it seemed, nothing did. Forty-five minutes passed. Still nothing . . . unless . . . was this couch *slanted*? Or futon, or whatever. *It was tilting.*

She hadn't noticed it before, but now she couldn't stop noticing. Like the princess and the pea.

By objective measure, the tilt was negligible—a fraction of an inch—but in her inner darkness the slight tilt magnified, and suddenly she felt as if she might slide off, and that idea made her giggle.

"I feel really, really weird," she said. "Crooked!"

Donna Kilgore laughed, a high-pitched sound that contained both thrill and anxiety. That she felt anything at all—anything other than the weighty, oppressive numbness that had filled her for fourteen years—was enough in itself to make her giddy.

To the sound track of the unfurling piano, behind her eyelids, movies began to unreel. She tried to describe what she saw: cars careening down the wrong side of the road. Vivid images of her oldest daughter, then all three of her children. The all-consuming love that rolled over her—a love she thought she'd lost forever.

"Now I feel all warm and fuzzy," she announced. "I'm not nervous anymore."

"What level of distress do you feel right now?" Michael asked in his deep, mellow voice, just beyond her elbow.

Donna giggled again. "I don't think I got the placebo," she said.

Michael and Annie didn't know if she had or not—that was the point of a double-blind procedure—but they were beginning to get a good idea. And if Donna's hilarity didn't clinch the deal, then the elevating blood pressure and pulse readings Annie kept checking on the monitor that Donna was tethered to by a self-inflating cuff would. It wasn't easy finding a convincing placebo for MDMA's very distinctive psychoactive signature—its ability to make Donna feel "crooked."

They could have chosen another, somewhat psychoactive drug, which would come with its own problems and side effects and, unless it was another psychedelic, wouldn't really feel anything like MDMA anyway.

Or they could have used a low dose of MDMA, which might be difficult to distinguish from a higher dose. But if a low dose were partially effective, it could mask the overall effectiveness of a high dose.

In the end they decided to leave that possibility for a further study, if there were to be one, and stick with a simple sugar-pill placebo, which at least would offer a very clear comparison with MDMA on possible negative side effects. A single sugar pill had none.

And even if they, and Donna, could all guess which pill she got, Wagner, the doctor who would test Donna for improvement four days after the session and then again two months later, had no way of knowing. And that, it could be argued, was the important blind, anyway. It would seem unlikely that, in a condition that had persisted for—in Donna's case—fourteen years at this point, a placebo effect could succeed where all previous therapies had failed; or even if it did succeed in the immediate afterglow of treatment, that it would persist until the two-month retest.

But Michael couldn't worry about any of that now. His job was to focus on Donna, to help support her self-discovery, assisted by whatever forces were working inside her.

The therapeutic theory he had encoded in his treatment manual was that, instead of attempting to direct the session, the therapist should concentrate on creating an atmosphere of safety, openness, and trust in the patient's own "inner healing intelligence," which "the medicine"—the MDMA—somehow activated.

It could all sound a little like hocus-pocus, but Michael could explain it in more earthy terms:

"When I worked in the ER, somebody came in with this big gash on their arm, full of gravel. I don't know how to heal that. My job is to create favorable conditions for the inner healing intelligence to be able to do it—to get the gravel out, bring the sides closer together, irrigate it, and then the body always moves towards healing. What can happen is that things get in the way: infection, not enough blood supply, a foreign body left in there. So in a way, our job in the ER is to remove the obstacles that are blocking the inner healing intelligence.

"I think it's very much the same with the psyche. I think there is this movement towards healing, and there's a lot of shit that can get in the way of that. So one of our principles is, if you have a nonordinary state of consciousness under favorable conditions with the right setting, that allows the inner healing intelligence to be expressed more. Again, that's an empirical finding. People found out that if you get the gravel out and bring the edges closer together, the body heals a lot better than when you just leave it. It's sort of similar with this, I think. And we've just seen it manifested so many times that people end up going towards experiences and making connections that we couldn't have predicted. But they just seemed to, in retrospect, make so much sense that that's what they needed to do to heal. And then, most importantly, we see the way it unfolds in their lives. That things have shifted. That's the evidence that it was a healing process, when you find out that they're able to go to the grocery store by themselves with people in the aisle and not be afraid."

The most acute impact of MDMA in the brain is the massive release of serotonin, but a tide of hormones is also released; cortisol, which is associated with emotional learning; and oxytocin and prolactin, which are also released in similarly large quantities immediately preceding and following orgasm—an event known to engender powerful feelings of intense emotion, security, closeness, and well-being.

Based on the results of recent brain scan studies and theoretical advances, Torsten Passie, a German researcher who is a visiting professor of psychiatry at Harvard, has developed an intriguing theory about how MDMA might help resolve PTSD. It's complicated but worth trying to grasp:

Sights, sounds, scents, and sensations from the sensory organs input into an egg-shaped region at the center of the brain called the thalamus. The thalamus then distributes that sensory data back up to be processed by the more sophisticated and evolutionarily recent brain regions involved with conscious thought. The processed material—sorted for context and assessed for significance—returns to the thalamus, which then deposits it into a tuber-shaped portion of the brain just above the brain stem called the hippocampus, where it is stored as memory.

In the case of a severely traumatic experience, the brain's ability to process is overwhelmed and a more primitive method for storing memory takes over. The sensory information passes through the thalamus and is stored directly in the hippocampus without higher processing. These "raw" memories can bolt into awareness as destructive flashbacks or nightmares. The brain senses that potential as a constant threat, which engages the fear-response system, centered in an almond-shaped structure perched atop the hippocampus called the amygdala. The amygdala acts as a guard, imperfectly suppressing the unprocessed traumatic memory to attempt to keep it from barging into consciousness. It's not a healthy arrangement. The constant tension of having the nasty, poorly kept secret hidden in the brain's basement poisons the psyche, which flails around in pain, creating PTSD's self-destructive symptoms.

Enter MDMA. Brain scan studies suggest that MDMA creates a negative image of PTSD, suppressing the amygdala and stimulating the prefrontal cortex—the planning-analyzing-conscious area of the brain. Passie theorizes that as the amygdala lets down its guard, the traumatic memories can reemerge from the hippocampus to be sent up for the processing the brain never had a chance to do. Possibly assisted by the emotional learning and fear extinction properties of the hormones MDMA releases, the memories can at last be integrated into the personality in a healthy way.

That was the theory. Until MDMA therapy proved to work in real lives, it would be nothing more.

Before Donna took the pill, Michael told her, "We don't want to direct this nearly as much as we want to follow and support the way it unfolds for you. So we trust that your own inner healing mechanism will bring up whatever needs to come up. As we talked about before, we would like to have an agreement that at some point if nothing about the trauma has come up spontaneously we'll bring that up in some way so that we can work with it. But we will let your own unfolding of the process take the lead."

And in Donna's case, it did.

Periodically, Annie or Michael asked if she might want to "go inside" for a time, which meant to readjust the eye mask, lie back, listen to the music on the headphones, and let her mind go where it, and the MDMA, wanted to take her. For a time Michael and Annie looked down on her like loving parents while Donna appeared to simply be sleeping. Minutes rolled past slowly. From the outside, nothing seemed to be happening except that the music shifted from light and relaxing to something more intense, more emotional. No songs with lyrics had been included—"too directive," Michael said.

Behind the eye mask, Donna was riding the crest of an inner current. Images from her life flooded past; realizations bubbled up at a dizzying pace. She began to talk, saying things she'd never said to anyone before, not even herself.

"My husband used to spend a lot of time laughing and cutting up, but things have gotten so serious," she said. "I love him with all my heart, but there just hasn't been that warm fuzzy feeling, how you get excited every time you see him. It's put a damper on it. I don't fully enjoy anything. I don't enjoy my kids. I don't enjoy my dog.

"It's frustrating, just going through the motions day after day after day. I don't get any joy out of it."

She stopped talking. A faint strain of music trickled from her headphones. She took a deep breath. The blood pressure cuff, on a five-minute timer, whirred to life.

"It sucks to just exist, and not live," Donna said.

Donna spent a lot of her time on the crooked couch holding the

Mithoefers' hands, one on each side. She needed that reassurance now that she was recalling the rape.

"I was backed into a corner, nowhere to go, desperate. I kept telling him I wouldn't tell anybody," she said.

"Can you feel that desperation now?" Michael asked.

"A little bit, yeah."

Michael encouraged her to stay with the feeling—"move through it, be curious about it"—instead of fleeing it.

More minutes passed in silence but for the periodic whir of the blood pressure cuff and the amplified sound of her heart thumping faintly on the monitor in the background.

When Donna spoke again, it was as if she were making an announcement.

"I feel protected. I do. I feel completely protected. I don't feel like I'm hanging out there anymore. . . . It feels good to be loved. It feels good to be protected."

Now Donna was absorbed in a vision: she could see herself standing on a ridge, high above a valley shrouded in mist. Down in the valley, she knew, was a battlefield containing all kinds of terrors. Her terrors. She knew they were there but couldn't see their shapes through the fog. Then the fog began to lift. Slowly she could begin to see.

"You're right," she said suddenly, in response to an assertion that hadn't been made. "I am angry. I'm angry at myself. It changed from being afraid to being mad at myself, that I allowed it to happen. . . ."

All this was coming without Michael or Annie saying or doing anything besides gently holding her hands.

"And not just that," she said. "I think that a lot of this baggage I'm carrying around is really stuff that I put in there myself. I stacked the luggage. Either in disappointment in myself or self-blame. Don't get me wrong. Under no circumstances do I think that I deserved it or I asked for it or that I did something to bring that on. I don't feel that way at all. . . . It's like you take your baseline, fear, and you throw some self-doubt on top of that, and then you throw some desperation on top of that, and, before you know it, you got a seven-layer burrito going there. I mean I can feel every one of them. I don't know how to express it, but I can feel them . . . just one right on top of the other, and maybe I've done that for so long, that when the rape happened, that was maybe the straw that broke the camel's back, and my mind said, 'Okay, that's enough, you're cut off, no more.' There's no more room on the pile."

The Mithoefers murmured sympathetic words as Donna continued unburdening herself. Their empathy was so palpable, it could make you think you had never really understood the phrase *murmured encouragement* before.

"It's not just about the rape. It's not just about any one thing. It's so many different things. . . . All I can remember feeling, as far as I can remember, is fear. Heart-stopping, gut-dropping fear . . . I've kept all this inside for so long, and it feels so heavy . . . these emotions—it's like I've been trained to be this way as long as I can remember—to be seen and not heard. Just from that point on, I've tried to make myself as small and inconspicuous as possible. And then the rape happened, and you're headline news. . . . I was ashamed."

The study protocol called for the therapists to periodically ask the subjects to rate their level of distress on a scale of zero to seven.

"Zero," Donna said quickly. Another pause. "No, that's not entirely true. That's a lie. I would say about a two. It's a disturbing revelation, I guess you could say."

Once again she paused.

"I feel calmer, a whole lot calmer," she said. "Kind of putting it all together, rather than just throwing it all in a box."

The acute effects of the MDMA slowly wound down after about four hours. Donna spent the night in the little office bungalow in the company of an attendant, as specified in the protocol. The next morning Donna, Michael, and Annie discussed the session.

Donna said she felt transformed. For the first time in years she could feel herself inhabiting her own body.

"To me, the biggest breakthrough—it meant the world to me to be able to look at the fear, to look at the shame. I didn't know I was ashamed. It was like I'd been wearing the scarlet letter. It was so heavy. When I got out of that session, I felt a hundred pounds lighter.

"Before, I knew the path was through the battlefield, but I just could not get through it."

But under the influence of MDMA, she said, "I knew I could walk through it, and I wasn't afraid. The drug gave me the ability not to fear fear."

Otherwise, she said, "I would have not been able to do it."

Donna's sense that she'd had a breakthrough was supported when she retook the evaluation test on which she'd rated as an extreme case of PTSD just weeks earlier. Her score had declined dramatically—to the point where, if she had been taking the test for the first time, she would not have been judged to have PTSD at all.

Two months later she was retested, and once again the results did not qualify a diagnosis of PTSD.

One subject who followed Donna in the trials—a fifty-year-old woman named Elizabeth—had similar results, but arrived there very differently. Instead of having a logical chain of insights, Elizabeth seemed to reach revelation through an explosive physical release.

"I thought it was supposed to be talk therapy, that I was supposed to talk about things, but it doesn't have to be," Elizabeth said. "The drug itself will do the work."

Her trauma centered on a stepfather who viciously abused her and her brother from an early age. She describes him as "a truck driver, ignorant, uneducated, Southern, moonshine-drinking, swearing, wife-beating idiot. He thought kids were there for his entertainment, amusement, and personal use."

From an early age Elizabeth was stuck in a grim survival mode: "Doesn't matter what you do to me, you will never touch me" is how she described it. "It was a feeling, all self-defense, all self-protection, nobody gets in."

Her whole life evolved, pathologically, from that premise. Running away as an adolescent from the horrors at home, she was raped on two occasions by men who picked her up as she hitchhiked. With no real concept of love or nurture, she got involved in a series of physically and emotionally abusive relationships. When something triggered memories of her abuse, she froze in a nearly catatonic state, caught between fight and flight, unable to do either.

During her MDMA session, Elizabeth remembered that, after her mother divorced her stepfather, she confided to Elizabeth that he had been the best lover she'd ever had.

As she sat on the futon, Michael gently encouraged her to "stay with" the feelings her mother's comment had provoked. To Elizabeth, though, the gentle encouragement felt like a sledgehammer pounding her. "He was pushing me verbally" was how she experienced it. "I was mad, and he was pushing me, provoking me to feel it. I just kept getting madder and madder, hitting the bed. Then the drug just took me and slammed me down. I was sitting one second, then down on my back in the next. I became very rigid, the tension was so powerful. I remember lying on the bed where I slammed down, looking at Dr. Mithoefer . . . like I'm mad at him for putting me through this, and this wave of energy just slammed through me, and it was just a release of a tremendous amount of this negative energy. It was powerful, and it was explosive. I felt like I'd been through something significant. . . . *My mother traded my childhood for sex!*"

In the weeks following the therapy sessions, Elizabeth would be

standing in her kitchen, or just sitting in a chair at work, and without
warning that powerful release would again move through her body.
Afterward she "felt at ease, a level of ease I was not familiar with, just
being comfortable within myself, within my body."

That feeling gave her a new relationship with her life. Difficulties
continued, but a year out from her experience, she said, "I'm not having as much problem with the puzzle. I'm able to just keep slugging
away. I don't feel so much like going to bed and sucking my thumb."

The clinical trial stretched out over four and a half years, included
51 MDMA-assisted therapy sessions, 16 placebo sessions, 337 nondrug
therapy sessions for preparation and integration, and 128 psychological
testing sessions—all without a single serious adverse drug-related event.

"All subjects have told us they found MDMA helpful," Michael
wrote in an article published in a collection called *Psychedelic Medicine:
New Evidence for Hallucinogenic Substances as Treatments*. "Some have
felt the effect . . . was dramatic and even lifesaving: however, others
have reported disappointment that MDMA was not a 'magic bullet' to
remove all their symptoms, or have said it would have been helpful to
have one or a few additional sessions."

One of those was a woman named Amy, in her forties at the time
of the study, who remembered being psychologically and physically
abused by her father "from birth," culminating one winter when he
locked her in the basement for three weeks. Amy had a reaction to
MDMA very different from Donna's instant giggles. MDMA wasn't
always about ecstasy, at least not at first. In a minority of cases, and
Amy was one of them, the onset of sensations could provoke acute anxiety, which, without a controlled environment and expert reassurance,
could escalate dangerously. When the drug started to take effect, she
said, "It just hit me, and it wasn't pleasant. I felt like I was going to
throw up. So I said, 'Okay, when's this happy, lovey feeling going to
happen?' I went to lie down on the couch and waited to go higher, but

the drug took me down instead. Michael was taking notes. I felt like he was drawing circles around me, but he showed me his notes, and they were just notes. That's when I saw that my internal world and external world didn't match up, and I connected with that. I saw myself as a baby wrapped in a white blanket, my family members standing there, and I realized, 'It wasn't my fault. . . .' I was flooded with feelings of peace and safety. 'It wasn't my fault. I didn't do anything,' I kept saying. 'I was a little girl. I was a baby.'

"After the first session, I felt exhausted, like I had a really bad hangover. But everything continued to unfold. I started to make connections. Like going into the grocery store, I used to feel very alienated. I couldn't connect with the other shoppers. But after the first session, I realized I could look at the people, and I wasn't afraid, like they were going to hurt me. I made the connection between the way I was always sizing up my environment, the alienation and the numbness that I felt, and the abuse.

"It felt weird at first, but kind of nice, that I could look at someone, and they would look back, and we'd smile at each other."

But like several other test subjects, Amy also confronted difficult new terrain. "Sometimes to go forward you have to go backwards. I knew that, but it wasn't comfortable to go there, back into the basement, into the abuse, into the beatings. I was apprehensive. I had already started feeling more grounded, but I'd functioned so long on autopilot that feeling things was difficult."

Difficult, but also better in many ways, she says. "Before, I never wore a seat belt. I would look at it but not wear it. It was self-sabotage. But after therapy, without even thinking about it, I just automatically started putting it on."

In the MDMA therapy training manual, Michael warns would-be therapists that in the course of treatment they may encounter reactions that could be considered psychological crises requiring drugs or hospitalization. One of the subjects in the clinical trial suddenly began talking with the voice of a small child.

Conventionally, that would be considered an episode of dissociative identity disorder, which almost always requires medication or hospitalization. But in the altered state induced by breathwork or MDMA, Michael had learned, it was much more likely part of the inner healing process. Especially since the subjects had been prescreened to exclude people with serious mental illness other than PTSD, the manual urges therapists not to push the panic button too early.

In this case Michael and Annie asked the woman the age of the part of her who was speaking. "She immediately said, 'About five or six.' Then we just talked to her about when this had happened before, and what happened at that age. And it had a lot to do with sexual trauma. We explored it."

The next morning, when Michael and Annie found she was still speaking in the child's voice, they were concerned but not panicked. Her husband came to bring her home and Michael and Annie told him what was going on and they all talked about it. They told the woman, "You're probably gonna have waves of this today. Gradually, it's probably gonna just disappear," and to call them if it didn't. But it was gone the next day.

"The fact that we stayed with it and just encouraged her to work with it had a very good result," Michael says. "Instead of having more of that in her life, she stopped having these dissociative periods. If we had responded to that with giving her a lot of medications to stop it, I don't think it would have served her well."

In the end, ten of the twelve trial subjects who had been assigned the MDMA in the double-blind part of the study found dramatic relief. Their scores on the assessment test given four days after their MDMA sessions, and again, two months later, no longer merited a diagnosis of PTSD, a clinical success rate of 83.3 percent after just two therapy sessions. Of the eight participants who initially got therapy with a placebo, only two (25 percent) had similar improvements in their PTSD symptoms, and all but one opted to do an additional open-label session with MDMA. All seven who did the further session responded dramatically and retested below the threshold for PTSD at four days and again at two months.

The single trial, successful as it was, didn't persuade skeptics of MDMA's efficacy, or safety.

Andrew Parrott, a psychologist at Swansea University in Wales who devoted much of his career to studying the dangers of MDMA, shrugged off the positive reports. "MDMA is a very powerful, neurochemically messy and potentially damaging drug," he said. The government "should never have given it a license for these trials. Certainly I would not give it a license for any further trials."

Others pointed at the weak double-blind as a cause to be suspicious.

Scott O. Lilienfeld, an Emory University psychologist, said, "These subjects knew if they got the drug or the placebo. Particularly when you have a very dramatic and powerful intervention, people may change but not in a longstanding way."

Mark Wagner, the psychologist who did the assessments, disagreed. "I didn't know much about the clinical use of MDMA before this," Wagner said, "but I've seen each and every one of these patients, and, just as a clinical psychologist, it is impressive to see the degree of treatment response these folks have had. There are a couple of areas in medicine, like hip replacement, where one day you are bedridden, and the next you're out playing tennis. Or with LASIK surgery, you're blind, and then you can see. Nothing in psychology is like that. But this was dramatic.

"The chance that a placebo effect would last for three months is very slight. And for it to last for a year or more, which anecdotally we believe might be the case here, would be extremely remote."

Wagner would further test that idea in another MAPS-funded study. He and Michael assessed the subjects of the original trial from a year and a half to more than six years after their MDMA treatments. Of the sixteen subjects who were retested, all but four had held on to their significant gains after an average of three and a half years. None felt that the experience had made them want to seek out illegal street Ecstasy or diminished their cognitive abilities. All of the four who had reexperienced PTSD symptoms said they felt another MDMA therapy session would help restore their health.

One of the four was Donna Kilgore. For a full year after her two MDMA sessions, Donna considered herself symptom-free. In the years that followed, problems accumulated. Her husband got laid off from a good job; they had to move; she had a difficult job at a dental practice for children.

One day Donna was doing paperwork in her office when "I started to have catastrophic thinking again." It was a resurgence of the paralyzing, unreasonable fears characteristic of PTSD that she'd had for so many years before the MDMA sessions. "It wasn't in the best part of town. I just started being convinced that someone was going to come in with a gun and start shooting. And then I just couldn't listen to the children screaming in the next room. . . ."

This was three years after her MDMA therapy sessions. She had to quit the job. Speaking about it then, she began to cry.

"I know I can work through it," she said, her voice breaking a little. "I know what I'm fighting now, and I can fight it."

Ten years after the experimental treatment, Donna still struggles off and on with occasional symptoms, but she credits the experience of the first study for giving her the tools to deal with all of it as well as she has. "I can't convey how much hope that gave me, and how much good it did," she said.

In 2012, Michael and Annie got the FDA to approve a new study to gauge the efficacy of re-treating those who relapsed after the first study. It was too late for Donna, who had recently discovered she had clogged coronary arteries, which, though successfully treated, disqualified her from the Mithoefers' relapse study. The three other subjects who experienced some degree of relapse underwent an additional MDMA therapy session. Immediately following the session and two months later, all three tested free of PTSD.

Even given reports of long-lasting positive results from the Charleston MDMA therapy trials, some continued to find reason for skepticism: Michael and Wagner and the study itself were all funded by MAPS. You didn't have to look far to find evidence of a pro-MDMA bias with MAPS. It wasn't all that different from the inherent bias of a pharmaceutical house sponsoring clinical trials for a drug that, if proven successful, the company stood to make millions on—except nobody would ever get rich off MDMA therapy for PTSD. And unlike with some obscure drug nobody had ever heard of, the MDMA research was all happening in a media spotlight.

Rick, who had been so astoundingly successful pushing his unlikely agenda all the way to clinical trials, now was demonstrating a genius for attracting high-profile, primarily positive media accounts in prestige outlets ranging from a Peter Jennings special on ABC, to extensive articles in the *New York Times* and *The Washington Post*, to a major story in *O, The Oprah Magazine*.

O senior editor Jessica Winter spent a year reporting the story. Winter wrote that she initially shared the view of a proponent of a nondrug cognitive therapy for PTSD who she quoted as saying, after watching a video of an MDMA therapy session, "I didn't know what was going on there. I was alarmed. Two therapists, a husband and wife, in very close physical proximity for hours to a patient who looks very drugged.

The patient just talks about whatever he or she wants to talk about, and gets a lot of support. The therapy doesn't make sense to me."

Winter decided she wanted to put MDMA to the test herself. Having cultivated sources among psychedelic enthusiasts, she managed to find an underground therapist, one of a scattershot network of illicit practitioners who had never stopped using MDMA, LSD, and other psychedelics as aids in therapy despite the legal ban. The experience changed her opinion. Her conclusions couldn't have been more enthusiastic:

"In the weeks that follow [the therapy session], I read voraciously, I see more of my friends, I crave exercise. Junk food holds no appeal; nor does Facebook or other online time-wasters. I don't duck away from mirrors. When a colleague seems irritable, I wonder if she's having a bad day, rather than racking my brain for what I've done to upset her. Friends keep saying, 'You're just *different*.' . . . Though I tried MDMA out of professional interest, weeks afterward I feel like the beneficiary of a wildly successful scientific experiment."

Rick's public relations triumphs paid off in several ways. Positive mentions in prestige media outlets attracted donors: donations to MAPS spiked by more than 3,000 percent, from less than $30,000 in 1992 to more than $1 million in 2004, the first year of Michael's clinical trial. The publicity also began to counteract the impression that MDMA was a highly toxic substance with no medical value.

But Rick's ability to get noticed, and his willingness to say what was on his mind, could work both ways.

As Michael's clinical trial had been getting going, Rick had been working with Harvard psychiatrist Halpern to launch another study at McLean Hospital in Belmont, Massachusetts, to test the ability of MDMA-assisted therapy to ease the acute anxiety of terminal cancer patients. Halpern had been an intern on Rick Strassman's DMT study, then spent five years studying the effects of heavy peyote use among

Navajo members of the Native American Church. Sacramental use had been legalized in 1996. Beginning in 1997, Halpern spent months living with church members, observing, and even participating in peyote rituals. When he had earned the community's trust, he conducted medical and psychological testing of church members who had used peyote at least one hundred times and found results very similar to those Grob had observed among sacramental ayahuasca users in Brazil. They were physically healthy and performed as well on cognitive tests as matched controls who had never taken peyote. Many believed that their peyote use had cured them of alcoholism.

Halpern seemed an ideal lead investigator to finally replace Grob and pick up on Rick's quest to study MDMA's ability to ease cancer patients' anxiety and help them cope with the prospect of imminent death. Rick came up with MAPS funds to pay for the study while Halpern, who one reporter dubbed "the anti-Leary," got FDA and DEA approval for the study and began recruiting. The reporter's quip was on target, as Halpern's spotless reputation no doubt helped clear the way for the first study using any psychedelic drug at Harvard since Tim Leary was booted out the door. Rick trumpeted the auspicious symbolism—psychedelic research had finally been redeemed from Leary's excesses—and the story played just as he'd hoped in major media throughout the world.

But still, Leary cast a longer shadow than Rick had anticipated. A change of leadership at McLean brought a new hospital president who suspected that MAPS's sober mission statement about pursuing the best possible science camouflaged a Leary-like enthusiasm for drugs.

It didn't help that the elaborate MAPS home page—alongside a psychedelic research library, the organization's financial statements, elaborate news updates, and notices of psychedelic art for sale—sometimes featured content like a promo for MAPS's "Rites of Passage Project," an extended pitch for the idea that "within responsible limits" parents can sometimes find great benefit in doing psychedelic drugs with their adolescent children. The piece included an archive of testimonials with taglines such as "Mother-Son Peyote Ritual . . . a beautiful rite of passage a mother shared with her teenaged son, strengthening his family connection, his sense of self, and his bond with nature."

It was pure Rick, but just the kind of vibe that raised the hair on the still-sensitive skins of certain Harvard-associated administrators. Halpern was told he could not accept any funding from MAPS.

Rick persuaded the donor to agree to contribute the money directly to the hospital to avoid any MAPS-related stigma, but the study never fully recovered and languished for years.

43.

ROLAND GRIFFITHS

(A HEALING VOID)

Rick, he's had to kind of fight his way through these things,"
Roland Griffiths is saying in his office at the Johns Hopkins
Behavioral Pharmacology Research Unit. "But partly that's a
problem of his own making, because he's so out there publicly that he
tends to . . . I mean, he and I talk about this all the time. I think he's
saying things and doing things that aren't helpful to me and aren't helpful to me persuading the federal government that funding should occur
for this kind of stuff. And you know, that's Rick; I mean, he's transparent and he wants to speak his mind and he's been very effective at doing
that. Well, let's see," he says, chuckling, "he's done a good job—a great
job—of speaking his own mind on this.

Griffiths, a slender man with a thatch of white hair and piercing
eyes, got his PhD in psychopharmacology in 1972 from the University
of Minnesota, then went to the Johns Hopkins behavioral unit, where
he specialized in determining the relative abuse potential of drugs.
Much of his work involved devising ways to determine how much
work baboons or other research animals were willing to do to trigger
an injection of whatever drug was being tested. It turned out that the
substances the primates were willing to, figuratively and literally, jump

through hoops for to get a fix were the same substances that had high abuse potential in humans. He also developed a methodology for rating humans directly. Of course, with humans you could simply ask them to rate the desirability of taking another dose of the drug, but people are notorious liars when no consequences are attached. So Griffiths came up with a scale based on giving test subjects a choice between getting another dose of the drug or receiving money.

"It's 'Would you like the drug you received yesterday or $1, $2, $3, $10, $20, $75?'"

If they chose the money, the participants were actually handed cash. This proved to be far more reliable than a simple survey.

Griffiths became a recognized expert in his field. In fact, it was his work that was cited in the 1985 MDMA Schedule I hearing indicating that, unlike psilocybin or LSD, primates chose to self-administer MDMA and phencyclidine, though less so than cocaine.

Griffiths was happy and successful in his work. In his personal life, he discovered meditation. He'd first tried meditating in graduate school. Although he was training to be a behaviorist, he had a personal fascination with subjective experience.

"It was a question of 'What do we really know about the nature of mind?' And that struck me as being kind of a fundamental and interesting and very personal question."

One that perhaps could be answered in the silence of one's own thoughts.

But his early attempts at meditation were "excruciating."

"Three minutes seemed like three hours, and I didn't know where to go with it. And then almost twenty years ago a friend was doing something with a meditation group here in Baltimore and I tried it again. And I don't know if it was just I was different, if the instruction was different; I heard it differently, I can't tell you what was different, but I got it in a way that I didn't get it before. And that got me really intrigued."

It was more than intriguing. Meditation changed Griffiths in a fundamental way.

"I had remarkable experiences that were unlike anything else I had had. . . . And all of a sudden, for lack of a better descriptor, it opened a spiritual window in the world for me. And all of a sudden I got that there are all these religions out there that are talking about the sacred or God or the beyond or whatever. And I got, yeah, there's a reference to that. And that makes sense to me now. There's more here than meets the eye.

"It raised questions for me about the nature of how I prioritize my attention in my life, both personally and professionally. I mean, here I was doing drug abuse pharmacology and I was well recognized for that and I was well paid for it and I knew what I was doing there, but compared to some of these other kinds of questions it didn't seem all that important."

Still, Griffiths didn't do anything to address the growing split between his research and his ever-deepening spiritual interests until he got a call from Charles Schuster, the former NIDA director who had worked with him and knew of his interest in meditation.

"He said, 'Roland, I went to this interesting meeting in California recently and met this guy Bob Jesse. And I think you'd find you have things in common with him. You should talk to him sometime.'"

On the surface, Jesse had little in common with Griffiths; he was a vice president for business development at Oracle Corporation, the technology giant.

But Jesse, in addition to his engineering major, had studied psychology at Johns Hopkins, and he'd had spiritual awakening catalyzed by California's rave subculture.

"I had personal experiences that led to the loss of duality" is how Jesse cautiously describes it. As a rationalist, he'd lost his religious faith in high school when he realized he was simply mouthing a creed he didn't actually believe. But now he realized that what had been lacking—and the thing that all religious creeds imperfectly attempted to codify—was that personal transcendent experience.

Jesse knew about the community at Esalen and its interest in psychedelic drugs as a means to attaining, or at least glimpsing, that transcendence. In 1993 he learned there would be a meeting there on the subject and asked to attend.

They brushed him off. "They told me, 'Oh, this meeting is just for researchers, and it's going to be held in the living room at the Big House, which has space for only a couple dozen people sitting on the floor.' I said, 'Well, if you need any help pouring the water or setting the table, any way I can help . . .'"

He figured it was a 'Don't call us, we'll call you' situation.

But a few days before the meeting, they did call "and said if you happen to have that time free, and if you are willing to step out if it gets too crowded and sleep in a sleeping bag off-site . . ."

Jesse was willing. When the time came, he found himself sitting in a circle "with all these big shots," talking about what their interests were. "They were saying things like 'receptor binding profile of psilocybin and mescaline,' or 'I'm specializing in treatment of this or that disorder.' Then it was my turn. I explained my job at Oracle, then said, 'I'd like to know what we'd have to change so that healthy, responsible adults could seek this experience using whatever tools are available.' They laughed, but not in a derisive way, in relief that someone had out-and-out said what they'd been avoiding saying.

"Many of the people in this work are born healers," Jesse says, "so it's natural that they'd be looking for ways to help people. But the subtext was that the only way for the field to move forward with the FDA is through clinical trials for pathological conditions, but I never had that assumption. My interest was what can we do to make these experiences more available to more people under circumstances most likely to do lasting good."

Jesse stayed in touch with his new associates but didn't see any movement in the direction he wanted to go. So he decided to take a leave from his job and see if he could move the ball himself. The leave became permanent. He called his aspirational organization the Council on Spiritual Practices. Its mission, he says, was "to make primary religious experience more available to more people and create social structures to maximize the benefits. Notice what's not mentioned: drugs. A variety of techniques bring people there. Practices that take years of discipline."

Psychedelics, which he calls "entheogens"—meaning "generating the god within"—are "a crash course," he says. "But they may not be easy and may be destabilizing. It's not just the revelations, it's the context they occur in."

Since he had no scientific or religious credentials, Jesse might have been dismissed as a crackpot. But his ability to communicate his vision proved remarkable. When he was looking for a beyond-reproach, hard-to-ignore board of directors, he decided to go after a most unlikely get, former NIDA director Schuster, who he saw at a conference on drug abuse.

"I had no idea where he stood and had a little trepidation," Jesse says.

The trepidation was not misplaced. Schuster had once warned a young protégé, a physician named Juan Sanchez-Ramos, whose entire reason for becoming a researcher was his interest in the LSD experience, not to ever admit that in public "or it would ruin your career."

But Jesse introduced himself and explained his idea. "Let's understand this phenomenon, look at hypothesized benefits, but at the risks as well," he told Schuster, who, incredibly, ended up agreeing to serve on his board, as did Huston Smith, one of the country's leading religious scholars.

Schuster told Jesse the same thing he told Roland Griffiths: the two seekers should meet.

"At some point, Bob Jesse came out here and we just had lunch together," Griffiths says. "I was asking lots of questions about meditation and religious practices and comparative religion. And he was the one that really said, 'You're a psychopharmacologist. You could actually study some of this.'"

When asked why it required Jesse to point out the obvious—that, as he puts it himself, "this is an excuse, if you will, for me to bring together my professional expertise in pharmacology and clinical trials with this burning interest I had in understanding the nature of some of these kinds of experiences"—Griffiths pauses before answering.

"I grew up in a scientific culture that had just ruled out doing research with these compounds," he says finally. "It just seemed unlikely that we could ever get approval for that. But as I just contemplated more deeply and really thought where my interests lay, I thought, 'Well, why not?' And I was a skeptic. I mean, my meditation practice was going well and I saw all these potential ways of deepening spiritual practice, none of which included taking drugs, because in the circles I was traveling in, that certainly wasn't an acceptable option."

Together they developed a protocol aimed at assessing the pharmacological impacts of psilocybin on healthy humans. But the subtext—their joint interest—was assessing if psilocybin actually produced authentic religious experience.

With Griffiths's ties to the federal drug research establishment and Jesse's networking skills—and a drug less controversial than MDMA—they quietly navigated through the permitting process and began their study in Griffiths's offices at Johns Hopkins, which they'd taken care to make as comfortable and soothing as possible, avoiding the harsh institutional setting that had marred Strassman's DMT trials.

Over the course of the study, which began in 2001 and was published in 2006, three dozen people lay on the comfortable couch in the architecturally challenged building on Johns Hopkins's Bayview campus in north Baltimore and took psilocybin.

"What I wasn't prepared for," Griffiths says, "is people would come in two months later and I would say, 'Well, so what do you think of the experience?' And they'd say, 'God, it was big.' What does that mean? And they'd say, 'It was one of the most important experiences in my life.' And when they say that, my initial response was kind of disbelief. It just doesn't sound right, does it?

"I've been involved in hundreds of studies with many, many different kinds of psychotropic compounds, given lots of questionnaires, talked to people after several days, asking them about their experience. And you don't have someone saying, 'Oh, that experience, oh, that's among the most important of my life.' Some actually said, 'That's the single most important experience I've ever had in my life.' What kind of life have you led? What does that mean? And they would say, 'Well, when my daughter was born, it changed my entire worldview. I was totally changed. Because it's kind of like that.'"

The sophisticated psychological assessments Griffiths conducted at two and fourteen months following the psilocybin sessions backed up the claims. In an article in *Scientific American* Griffiths coauthored with his fellow Heffter board member, Grob, he reported that "the data showed that participants experienced increased self-confidence, a greater sense of inner contentment, a better ability to tolerate frustration, decreased nervousness and an increase in overall well-being. Ratings of their behavior by friends, family members and work colleagues uninformed about the drug experience were consistent with the participants' self-ratings."

More than 70 percent of the participants self-rated the experience as one of the five most important in their lives. Perhaps even more astoundingly, nearly a third rated it the *single* most important experience.

Acutely aware that some would criticize the study as inspiring increased illicit use of psilocybin and other psychedelics, Griffiths makes sure to always highlight the risks involved. In the *Scientific American* article he said this:

> *Hallucinogens can sometimes induce anxiety, paranoia or panic, which in unsupervised settings can escalate to accidental injuries or suicide. In the Johns Hopkins study, even after careful screening and at least eight hours of preparation with a clinical psychologist, about a third of participants experienced some kind of significant fear and about a fifth felt paranoia sometime during the session. But in the supportive, homelike setting provided in the research center and with the constant presence of trained guides, the Johns Hopkins participants encountered no lasting ill effects. Other potential risks of hallucinogens include prolonged psychosis, psychological distress, or disturbances in vision or other senses lasting days or even longer. Such effects occur infrequently and even more rarely in carefully screened and psychologically prepared volunteers.*

A strong sign that times and attitudes were changing came when Dr. Herbert D. Kleber, the director of the division on substance abuse at the New York State Psychiatric Institute and former deputy director of the White House's Office of National Drug Control Policy, wrote this commentary on the publication of Griffiths's study:

> *The positive findings of the study cannot help but raise concern in some that it will lead to increased experimenting with these*

substances by youth in the kind of uncontrolled and unmoni-
tored fashion that produced casualties over the past three
decades. . . .

Any study reporting a positive or useful effect of a drug of abuse
raises these same concerns. In this Internet age, however, where
youth are deluged with glowing personal reports in chat rooms and
web sites as well as detailed information about the various agents
and how to use them, it is less likely that a scientific study would
move the needle much.

Discovering how these mystical and altered consciousness states
arise in the brain could have major therapeutic possibilities. . . . It
would be scientifically shortsighted not to pursue them.

This kind of reception by serious people—a sober parsing of risk and benefit emerging on the side of benefit—was exactly what Griffiths and Jesse had hoped for. But it also demonstrated why Jesse's dream of focusing on the spiritual benefit of psychedelics in healthy people was still a tough target to hit. The thinking, and the funding, always bent toward "therapeutic possibilities."

And they would have to bend with it—although in the end, the therapeutic and the spiritual would become hard to distinguish.

Even as Griffiths was completing his initial study with healthy volunteers, Grob had been conducting a Heffter-sponsored pilot study at the Harbor–UCLA Medical Center involving twelve terminal cancer patients. Very similar to the abandoned study he had been planning with Rick, this one substituted psilocybin for MDMA. The number of subjects in the study, or the size of the dose of psilocybin given, was too small for the results to reach statistical significance, but the patients reported diminished anxiety and improved mood, even months after their psilocybin sessions.

Griffiths embarked on his own psilocybin-cancer study, only on a much larger scale—eventually forty-four people will participate—at Johns Hopkins. Because Grob had struggled to find "healthy dying people"—i.e., both sick enough to meet the definition of *terminal* but healthy enough to undergo the intense psilocybin experience—Griffiths got the FDA to approve a shift in the protocol, allowing him to include those with cancer considered life-threatening but not necessarily terminal.

A retired psychologist named Clark Martin saw a mention of the study online in 2008. His cancer had been first diagnosed in 1990, when he was forty-six, the same year his daughter was born. He had a kidney removed. Then, four years later, doctors discovered extensive lung cancer, for which he had surgery and eleven months of chemo, followed by the discovery of three more metastatic tumors. He threw himself into researching his illness, and fighting it took over his life. He had been a passionate sailor but lost interest in that, and almost everything else, even to the point where "I was much less available to my daughter—just day-to-day kind of availability, both timewise and being present with her, just being alert to things going on with her. I kind of got into this very narrow sort of life space," Martin said.

But his obsession led him to the Johns Hopkins website, and Martin called the number he found there. Griffiths himself answered the phone and seemed eager to fly him out for screening.

"I have always been interested in doing psilocybin but never considered doing it off the street," Martin said. "So it seemed like a nice opportunity."

Nice didn't quite cover it.

After taking the drug in the comfortably appointed space reserved for psilocybin sessions, the first thing Martin noticed was that the music on his headphones annoyed him. He wanted to turn it off or down. But before he could act on it, the music disappeared. *Everything* began to dissolve. The psilocybin swallowed him whole. The ceiling began to swirl above him, as if he were drunk on alcohol, only it wasn't a room spinning on its axis but reality itself.

He felt a clutching panic as simple everyday constructs began to melt down and evaporate. He envisioned falling out of a sailboat and treading water helplessly as the boat disappeared out of sight. And then the water disappeared. And then *he* began to disappear.

Martin had always been about maintaining control in his life, pegging the world in neat, rational categories, everything in its place. Now he was flailing. "There was this desire that I'd never experienced before. It's like my entire body, my entire psyche, just wanted to get everything to fall back into place, to gel again.

"I knew what I needed to be doing in terms of meditating and relaxing and trying to go with it, but the more that I relaxed into it, the worse it seemed to get."

He thought that if he could get up off the couch, *do* something, touch something solid, maybe he could regain a sense of normality. At one point he sat up and became aware of the presence of his two sitters. They weren't there as therapists, like the Mithoefers, but to offer security and reassurance as needed. Martin didn't take off his eye mask, and the sitters didn't talk to him, but one of them put his arm around his shoulders. He felt that presence as a touchstone, a link to a more soothing reality, without which his panic might have accelerated. He lay back down and went to a place that demonstrated the bizarre variability of the psychedelic experience. No hallucinations, no thoughts, no visual images, no sense of self—a yawning, diamond-cut void where he disappeared entirely. Except something remained: an unadorned awareness, thoughtless yet present.

The panic faded into tranquillity. The hours that passed in the study room he would later describe in a journal entry:

There was no experience of any "things" and the mind seemed lucid and alert. It was very comfortable and somehow familiar. There was no drugged feeling. If there were any words to describe it, they might be curiosity or awe, perhaps similar to that of a young child within a new experience.

And then he had the sense he was beginning the long journey back to the familiar reality, an experience, he wrote, "of being midway between the perceptual void and everyday consciousness, in which neither was dominant."

He felt he had a choice: return to everyday reality or remain in that void. He found himself reluctant to leave the simple clarity, so he practiced allowing himself to slip out of it toward normality, then return to the void.

"I did that, I don't know, maybe a dozen times, because I wanted to sort of bake that into my muscle memory, so to speak, so that I could voluntarily return to that state."

As he emerged he began to marvel at the steady presence of the sitter who had put his arm around his shoulders, and the fact that it was his presence alone—no words, no actions other than that one touch— that had meant everything to him in his panic. And he realized that he had been missing that simple fact in his most important relationship: with his daughter.

"I had an insight that my primary role as a father was to maintain a rock-solid attunement with my daughter. That is, no efforts to influence her development should sacrifice her experience of my attunement or of her being loved. . . . The significance of this for me was that personal relationships do not need to be managed. Therefore, there is no need to present a false self and, in fact, doing so will severely limit the joys available naturally in relationships."

When he finally fully came back—left the study office, returned to his hotel room—he was shaken. "I was scared to go to sleep because I was fearful that I would drop back into the study stage and there wouldn't be anybody there."

He continued in a kind of daze, but in the coming days and weeks the experience kept working on him. It was as if a kind of gravity kept tugging at him until, eventually, he fell into a new way of being.

A year after his psilocybin experience he wrote:

> *I am surprised with the on-going fallout which has occurred with no conscious intent. There has been a shift from trying to micro-manage life to trusting intuition and spontaneity. . . . I'm more focused on values and process and less likely to feel long range goals are set in stone. I am again involved professionally and socially. Most significantly, life has continued to open up, a move away from the depression and what felt like a downward spiral. Somehow, the psilocybin re-engaged a fullness of function that had been lost.*

He had a new relationship with his daughter: instead of an arm's-length, role-dominated father-daughter relationship, "we're two people who share what's going on in our lives in a very real, sponta-neous kind of way."

Another breakthrough he hadn't considered possible came in his relationship with his father, who lived in a nursing home in an advanced stage of Alzheimer's. Before the psilocybin, Martin had visited him out of obligation.

"I wasn't really present. I was there being the son but figuring out in my mind how I should be responding and what's this and what's that, and what should we do next, and how long will it be before I leave?"

After his psilocybin experience, he found that he didn't worry about any of that stuff. When he was there he was just . . . *there.* "I con-nected with him at the level that he was functioning. And he just really cranked it up—not that he can maintain a conversation, but he attempted it. It's hard to imagine that with an Alzheimer's patient, but the quality of our time together . . . it's pure merit."

He began to see things through his father's eyes and felt his frustration at being so constrained, day after day, by four walls. On impulse, he gathered his father up, got him in the car, and went driving for hours in the wide-open ranchland that surrounded the home, something he never would have considered doing before.

Now his father "just lives for those drives. He thrives on it. He's actually gotten better physically and mentally. And I know it sounds odd, but I've never felt closer to him."

44.

NICHOLAS

(THE VICIOUS CYCLE)

Nick used the 50 percent disability payments—for his PTSD, his knee and back injuries, the shrapnel in his butt, and the ringing in his ears he'll hear the rest of his life—plus his GI Bill benefits to move to Summerville near Beverlee and to enroll at Trident Technical College in North Charleston. But he wasn't able to focus. During a test in a history class, a question on ancient Sumer triggered something worse. "I thought about where that was, and I was there. And all I know is that I was starting to get kind of panicky." When he looked down at his watch, thirty minutes had passed, during which he had done nothing.

He never knew when he'd suffer some kind of episode. One day as he was driving into a Taco Bell, his attention focused on the glass storefronts across the street. As he watched, the glass came crashing down.

"It looked like rounds were getting shot into the window, like .50-cal rounds. And then a guy—it was really weird: he was in all white, and he had a red little smock thing on his head and a military duty belt on, with canteens, like we wear. I couldn't believe that I was actually seeing this." The rounds were hitting the window, and the glass was shattering, and then the guy in white came out into the doorway. He lifted up an

RPG launcher and fired it straight at Nick, who watched the incoming rocket hit the windshield, shattering it. Once again he was engulfed in those slow-motion flames. He looked over to Beverlee. Her flesh was melting up to her face, and her hair was starting to frizz up.

"Do you want any sauce with that?" the guy in the Taco Bell take-out window asked.

"Are you okay?" Beverlee asked. She had her hand on his leg and a concerned look on her face.

"No, I don't need sauce, thank you," Nick said. The tires squealed as he pulled away and he felt tears pouring from his eyes. He pulled into a parking spot and tried to stop crying. He told Beverlee what he'd seen.

"You know what? Fine," Beverlee said. "You just had a bad vision. It's not real."

"And I was, like, 'But it felt real.' You know, I can't go the rest of my life seeing those things. You can't explain those things to other people. You can't be comfortable around other people. You don't know when it's gonna happen, when am I gonna see something like that again, you know? And it was very vivid, very real. This felt like it got bigger the more I fed into it, the more my fear manifested it. I said, 'Man, I've gotta have some kind of help.'"

This time he went to see doctors at the Veterans Administration hospital, who prescribed the same drugs he'd been given at Camp Lejeune. He tried them again for a few months, with no better results.

Nick had been planning to study psychology, hoping that someday he'd get clear enough to be able to help other vets in his situation. But first he would have to survive, and with no help in sight he couldn't feel confident that was going to happen.

"When I'd think I was getting better in a certain area, like the dreams, something else would just get even worse. I'd have moments sometimes where—like a month or so—when I'd actually be fine.

Things would be going great. And then outta nowhere, these feelings come up inside—you don't know why. You have no reason to be sad, or upset, or angry. Everything's going great for you. And then it's just something inside is eating away at you."

He thought about the last time he'd felt any real peace. Oddly enough, it had been in Iraq, after his Humvee had gotten blown up. Another Marine had asked him if he wanted to smoke, and Nick told him he'd just finished a cigarette. "No," the guy said. "I mean *smoke* smoke."

Nick had been scared; he'd never smoked pot before, and he didn't want to get in trouble—not that there was much chance of that: there were no urinalysis tests over there. The guy led Nick down to an abandoned bunker dominated by an old, broken-down antiaircraft gun. Nick figured the bunker had been built by Saddam's people. It was dark, and filled with silhouettes Nick couldn't make out, and didn't want to. He just wanted to get out of there. But someone handed him a joint. He took a drag and passed it. It came around several times. Nick felt nothing.

Nick decided that either he didn't respond to marijuana or the joint they passed around was oregano or some other counterfeit. Then he lit a menthol cigarette, and the first rush of menthol rolled in and kept rolling. It came in like a tide, lifting him off the shoals he'd been grounded on. Dusk had become darkness, and he looked out at the city over the base walls as if seeing it for the first time. And in a way it was: the first time he'd been able to consider it with some kind of distance, rather than just right up in his face in a constant clench. He felt his body relax, and the release was astonishing. He was able to think, to actually process, for the first time since he'd flown in there holding tight to his fear. "I felt peace at that moment, and I really didn't feel like it was the marijuana making me feel peace. I felt like I was able to comprehend and realize what peace was and it felt really good."

He remembered that feeling now in his desperation, and thought, *Well, maybe that's what I can do. Maybe I can medicate myself with that.*

He started researching it online and found that while a few states allowed marijuana to be prescribed medically, "the only one that was doing it for PTSD was New Mexico, and there was no way I was gonna move to New Mexico. So I just figured I'm gonna have to get it myself and try to do it that way. I was very uneasy about having to do it that way, but it was either that or fall apart."

He bought some pot, and it helped. Kind of.

"If there were times where I'd feel like I was about to lose it on Beverlee, I would much rather go in the bathroom and have a little smoke, even if I didn't want to, to keep myself from blowing up. I was able to think about why I was feeling that way, just sitting on the toilet, having my little smoke, and just contemplate and release it."

His grades went up. He was able to sit down and focus on his homework. "It's like I would smoke, and then the gunfire and all that crap in my head would stop, and I could focus and do my work. I could do my artwork. I could sit there and focus and pay attention to detail and do all those things. I was able to do them."

He smoked off and on, but despite the relief, he realized it wasn't helping the PTSD, not really. "I knew it wasn't treating it, it was helping me with the symptoms, so it was kind of like a quick fix in those situations. But then I thought to myself, 'I'm not getting better, because after it wears off, I go back to being depressed again. That's not gonna work. I can't keep doing this. That's just gonna cause me to have a drug problem. There's gotta be something else.'"

Nick was losing faith that there actually was anything else. "I was heading for a brick wall. I knew how it was gonna end, and it wasn't gonna end pretty."

He began to think about that more concretely. He'd reach under his mattress and pull out the .45 revolver he never wanted to be too far from. He felt the weight and the cool metal in his hand, then sat on the edge of his bed studying the gun as if it were some fragile machine whose workings he had to decipher. As he sat there, arm limp, the gun on his lap, his head filled with the hot mess that wouldn't leave him alone. He raised the hand gripping the handle of the gun until he felt the cold hardness of the steel pressing against his temple. He imagined the bullet rocketing out of the barrel, blasting through his skull, taking all that hopeless mess with it. Now pressed against the thin membrane between being and not being, he imagined the small twitch of a nerve and flex of a muscle that would break through that membrane and end this. All he had to do was press down on that trigger, go cyclic on himself.

45.

MICHAEL

(THE PEACE DRUG)

When Donna Kilgore began her experimental therapy for rape-related PTSD in Charleston in the spring of 2004, awareness of another kind of PTSD crisis was beginning to emerge 531 miles to the north, in the labyrinthine halls of the Pentagon. Just as wars in Afghanistan and Iraq—wars destined to last most of a decade—got going, military planners were startled to discover that the number of veterans receiving compensation for PTSD had grown nearly seven times as fast as the number receiving benefits for disabilities in general. According to an accounting by the Veterans Administration, more than 200,000 veterans would receive PTSD-related payments that year, at a cost of $4.3 billion.

And that wasn't even the scariest part: the huge increase in vets needing assistance was fueled primarily by those who served in Vietnam, still suffering the effects of PTSD *three decades after that war ended*. The toll from the wars in Iraq and Afghanistan, which ultimately would suck in more than two and a half million American men and women in uniform—almost precisely the same number that had served in Vietnam—had barely begun to be felt. One in five returning Iraq-Afghanistan vets would be diagnosed with PTSD, which, if scaled ·

up to the entire number of deployed forces, would eventually work out to 500,000 vets with PTSD to whom the public, and the U.S. Treasury, would owe lifetime health care. A Congressional Budget Office study determined that costs related to care for PTSD patients would be particularly stubborn: 80 percent were still seeking treatment four years after diagnosis, an even higher percentage than those with traumatic brain injury. The direct costs from treating the PTSD itself are only the beginning. People diagnosed with PTSD have proven to be considerably more likely to suffer from a wide range of other costly maladies, including diseases of the heart, the lungs, and the digestive and reproductive systems, and arthritis, not to mention alcoholism and drug abuse.

"The VA has increased its annual budget from $40 billion to $140 billion in the past decade," says Linda J. Bilmes, the Daniel Patrick Moynihan Senior Lecturer in Public Policy at the Harvard Kennedy School. "One of the main drivers is the enormous number of cases of PTSD."

Bilmes calculates that the country is already committed to paying Iraq and Afghanistan veterans disability payments and health benefits in excess of $1 trillion just until they turn sixty-five. "That's not counting that we know over time that people apply for additional benefits, and it's not accounting for the fact that they will have increasing health care needs as they age," Bilmes says. It also doesn't include loss to the country's productivity of so many people in their prime earning years. Bilmes points out that even vets who come back from war as double or triple amputees could make a full functional recovery if it weren't for their PTSD. "The prosthetics are so good now, it's not the prosthetic that keeps them from functioning," she says. "It's the PTSD."

This grim calculus would seem to make the development of a drug/therapy combination that might all but cure PTSD in a handful of administrations a critical priority. Yet, despite the enormously promising results of Michael's MAPS-funded study, the federal government— which continued to spend millions on studies that, after decades, still failed to definitively demonstrate any severe long-term hazards of massive MDMA abuse—had contributed exactly nothing to MDMA-therapy research.

It seemed clear to both Michael and Rick that their work would be more difficult to ignore if its potential to treat veterans with combat-related PTSD were tested directly. The new study ultimately would include twenty-four participants at a projected cost of $1.25 million, of which MAPS had raised less than half.

The FDA approved the protocol in 2010, and as Michael waited for the DEA to approve a new Schedule I handling license—a much smoother process this time around—he posted recruitment notices.

"What I got out of the notice," Anthony Macie says, "is pretty much 'You got out of the military, you know something's wrong with your life, but you can't figure out what the hell exactly it is.' Also, there was something about not conforming to taking antidepressants. They don't work."

The ad might as well have had Macie's name, rank, and serial number stamped on it.

He'd been a forward observer in Army airborne, serving nearly fifteen months southeast of Baghdad in 2006 and 2007, during the American "surge." He'd been in firefights nearly every day, learned how a bullet vibrates the air when it passes a fraction of an inch from your head, missed a devastating truck bombing of his base by sheer luck, and had to live with the knowledge that one of the men who had been killed—the man who won a posthumous Silver Star for standing up and firing his machine gun at the incoming truck, causing it to swerve at the last minute, vastly reducing the death toll—had been standing right where he would have been standing if he hadn't been called off on a mission. He existed in a landscape of trash and litter, any one piece of which could kill you. He once kicked a plastic bottle that exploded. It knocked him down and almost out, but he escaped serious injury. While moving in on a house that supposedly harbored a high-value target, wearing night vision goggles and a forty-pound pack with the platoon's radio, he vaulted a three-foot stone wall only to discover a ten-foot drop on the other side. He pitched forward face-first onto his goggles and felt a bolt of pain in his back. Adrenaline got him up and moving to complete the mission, but the next morning he had to be helped out of bed. He finished out his deployment in "the Talk"—the computerized communications center where he helped direct combat operations remotely—and never knew until he got home that his back had been fractured by the fall.

He'd been diagnosed with PTSD after returning from Iraq: he'd lost his temper at a higher-ranking Veterans Administration chiropractor who said there was nothing he could do to help him. Macie felt he'd been brushed off and he said so.

"I wasn't showing respect. Like, in the military you're supposed to show respect with rank."

He was in the "Warrior Transition" program at the time, which means he had a caseworker who saw the whole thing and sent him to a counselor to have his "stress level" evaluated.

"Well, I mean, it probably wasn't just that one event. They probably just saw that I was stressed-out in general. At first it was adjustment disorder for like a week, and then I looked at my military records and it had been switched to PTSD. I was adamant that that was bullshit and I was fine, blah, blah, blah. Because to me, at that time, that was, like, disrespectful. He was calling me . . . I don't know how to describe it. When I was in the military, that's, like, the biggest blow to your ego you could ever get is being told that, because that's weakness."

Okay, so he *didn't* have PTSD. Just to be clear.

But something wasn't right.

When he started back at college at Clemson University, in South Carolina, he found he just couldn't sit still for the length of a class.

He'd revved his motor so long and so hard in Iraq and now it just wouldn't stop revving.

Just like Nick, in restaurants he'd choose the seat against the wall so he could keep his eye on the entrances and exits. Driving, he'd swerve all over the road just to avoid a fluttering piece of trash or a crushed can, any one of which, in his mind, was primed to explode.

He had friends and family waiting for him at home, but their well-meaning gestures mostly irritated him, making him frustrated and angry. He'd returned home, but he couldn't *come* home. "I was on a whole different level," he says. "Nothing they could do would satisfy me. I was just frustrated because I was frustrated. There's no making veterans like that happy. They'd be pissed off at you if you did what they're thinking they wanted you to do. It's as if they *wanted* to be miserable, almost."

He tried smoking pot a few times, and it only made him feel worse—more anxious, more out of control, more paranoid. So he began to drink. In high school he'd been a social drinker, but now he found himself drinking heavily—vodka, whiskey—every night.

"At the time I wouldn't have admitted that I needed it to sleep, but there's no other reason I'd drink every night before bed."

Not that it helped much. And his back pain was relentless. After a few months he started taking prescription pain pills and stopped the drinking only because "I couldn't really drink a fifth of vodka and take painkillers too. I'd be dead."

After he'd been taking them for about six months and his prescription ran out, he discovered that the pills had become an even bigger problem than his back. Withdrawal hit hard.

"It's like your body thinks you're going to die from not having it. My back was worse than ever. Constant anxiety. Just thinking about the pills over and over and over. I went to VA and told them what I was going through and they gave me a shot of Demerol and a new prescription.

"It was, like, 'Oh, here you go.' So then I talked to the doctor and he told me, 'This happens when you take it for that long.' They're telling me you're *supposed* to be dependent on it. So I'm hearing 'Oh, it's okay.' That's all I need to hear when I have an addict mentality: a doctor saying it's okay."

Every month, with military precision, he'd get 120 more pills in the mail. And when he started taking more pills more frequently, no problem. "It'd be, like, a week before I was supposed to get my refill, and they'd refill it."

Aside from the pain pills, "they had me on every type antidepressant you could think of. And after a while I wouldn't take them. They didn't work; they'd make me sick. And I never felt depressed. They always told me I was depressed, but I was, like, 'No, I feel like I just got out of war and I'm back here and I'm trying to be a civilian.' Like, I mean, yes, I'd have things that don't make me happy, but you do too."

Macie was an ideal study subject. He'd had PTSD for nearly four years—an unusually severe case, according to the diagnostic test—and had tried all those drugs that hadn't helped. Long-term, treatment-resistant, combat-related. Check, check, and check. And Clemson was less than a four-hour drive from Charleston—no expensive plane tickets required.

In January 2011, at the low point of his life, Macie began a periodic commute to the Mithoefers' office in Mount Pleasant.

"They took really good care of me. They paid for food and gas, put me in a nice hotel. They actually even let me bring my dog into their office with them."

In the early meetings he was surprised that Michael and Annie mostly just listened to him. "They were smart by letting me think I was in control, because I realized that was my biggest thing."

After a handful of preparatory meetings over several months, he came in for his first "experimental session" in April. As soon as he swallowed the pill, he wished he hadn't. What had he done? What was this new drug going to do to him? It was too late to stop it now, and as he waited on the futon with the earphones and eye mask on—fifteen minutes, thirty minutes—his anxiety began to spike. He could barely suppress a desperate desire to jump up and flee. After he had spent an interminable hour lying there, fretting and regretting, waiting to feel whatever he was going to feel, Annie left the room to take his dog out. He was saying something to Michael, who was sitting right beside him, when "all of a sudden, it just took over."

Knocked back into the futon, Macie barely managed to construct a sentence: *"What the hell is this?"*

"And Michael's, like, 'It's MDMA. We talked about this.' And suddenly it was like when you look at an image, and it's like your brain switches, and you see something completely different."

Everything changed in an instant. *I don't feel anxious,* he realized. "I laid back and I was, like, 'Oh, my God, okay, I get this.' I think I mumbled, 'This is amazing.' And Dr. Mithoefer was, like, 'Are you feeling anxious?' I was, like, 'No, I feel good.' And he was, like, 'Okay,' and he started laughing."

The tremors of anxiety had transformed into a wave of warmth that swept through his entire body, from the top of his head to his toes. The pain in his back, a constant presence for so many years, ceased, as if someone had flipped a switch. His entire being exhaled an enormous sigh, and relaxed.

"I just let go and accepted that whatever was going to happen, I was safe with who I was with, and felt fine. Just then, Annie came back in and asked me to rate my anxiety, and I was like, *'What anxiety?'"*

At first he didn't want to talk. He didn't want to do anything. He just wanted to sit there and feel the relief, the blessed relief, at the absence of fear. It had been so long. Or maybe it had been his whole life.

For a half hour he didn't say a word, didn't even think, he just glowed—an inner brilliance coursing through him, radiating outward from his center. In this completely novel state, without effort, things began to come clear.

Over the next three or four hours, he says, "the medicine showed me that always being anxious over things does nothing. Once I dealt with why I was anxious, then I felt really good. That's the message my body was teaching me. Every time some memory would come up and I wouldn't think I was ready to talk about it and I'd try to suppress it, I'd get anxious. Then, as soon as I'd just say it, I'd get like a wave of pleasure and feel fine. And I'd be, like, 'That issue wasn't a big deal at all.'"

What came up surprised him. The things he expected to be the toughest—the violence he witnessed and participated in, the friends who'd been injured, his own injuries—faded. Instead his mind played scene after scene dominated by his impotent rage and frustration over the impossible position the military, the entire war, had put him in. Like the times he saw an Iraqi with a shovel digging a hole for an IED but couldn't shoot because a shovel wasn't a rifle, only to learn the next day that a buddy got blown up by a buried bomb; or when insurgent mortars and bullets rained down on them, but they couldn't return fire because they didn't know exactly where it was coming from; and all the other times he idly waited to get shot at or blown up, expecting to die, *knowing* he was going to die, unable to respond because nobody really knew for sure who he was supposed to be helping and who he was supposed to be killing.

And the times he had to make horrible choices. Like deciding to refuse a request for medevac helicopters from soldiers trying to retrieve their comrades who had been, literally, blown to bits. He had to save the choppers for those who had only been injured and still had a chance to survive. He remembered telling the soldiers over the radio to collect their friends' bodies, piece by scattered piece, and carry those bloody, torn pieces back by hand. And he remembered how they wouldn't talk to him after that, and not blaming them for it.

As each of these memories arose from the dark hole where he'd buried them, he'd feel the charge of shame and guilt that had been torturing him for so long, making it impossible to relax or rest or trust. For four years he'd been sacrificing his health, any chance at happiness, any chance for even a few moments of peace, all to make sure those memories stayed buried, as if his life depended on it. Now that unrelenting focus on repression simply evaporated. "I was completely in the mode where I was totally okay with things, so it came up. I feel like whatever was buried in my subconscious could come up, because it was okay."

That night, watched over by a paid attendant, he slept dreamlessly until morning.

"For two or three months after, I was just euphorically happy," Macie says. "I went to the other side of the spectrum. All the bad feelings became good feelings. It was like all that fear and anxiety—I didn't even know how to think like that anymore."

When he got home, he went into his medicine cabinet and threw out his bottles of pills. The withdrawal came as a minor annoyance. "I mean, I felt my body ached and stuff, but before, I'd sit at my house and not do anything, lie on the couch. Now I was active. I was optimistic about my life, so I didn't really think about it. I was actually kind of proud of it."

There was only one underlying minor chord: Was it too good to be true? When it came time to do his second session with MDMA, he asked Michael and Annie if they could talk first. He told them he was thinking of dropping out of the study. He wanted to prove to himself that his improvement was real, and not simply owing to some chemical still floating around in his system. Although Michael explained to him that all chemical traces of MDMA were long gone, in Macie's mind the principle still held. He told them he felt he was still processing all the things that had come up. He needed more time.

"I talked to them, like, two or three times and just came to the conclusion that for me it was probably better to talk about how to progress without more MDMA."

More than a year later he believed he'd made that progress. He still felt healthy, still at peace with himself, and when he returned for the one year follow-up with the study psychologist, his PTSD symptom scores remained very low.

But because he didn't complete the rest of the treatments in the study, as far as the Mithoefers' primary statistics are concerned, the therapy he received will not count as successful.

46.

NICHOLAS

(THE WEB OF LIFE)

Nick couldn't figure out "his shrapnel," the slivers of metal he had carried around in his buttocks ever since his Humvee blew up. They were uncountable, except on an X-ray, and unremovable. Sometimes he could sit on them fine, no problem. Then, out of nowhere, they'd begin to burn, searing-hot splinters shoved into his flesh, just like the day it happened, the day Seabass bled to death.

And when that happened, he knew a panic attack was coming.

"Me in a corner, screaming at the top of my lungs—extremely loud. Clawing at myself. Just wanting to rip my thoughts out of my mind if I could. Just a mess. Hysterical. I'd start laughing really loud, and then I'd go back to freaking out. It was just this wave, a roller coaster. Just no control at all."

If Beverlee was around, she pushed down her fear and rushed to his side. "All thoughts of myself just kind of went out the window. I just did whatever I could to be there for him, but I knew there's nothing you can say that's gonna get through. I could say all the wisest things in the world but he wouldn't listen. He'd just say, '*I can't, I can't, I can't.*'"

When she tried to hold him, he'd scream and push her away, as if her touch caused him physical pain.

There were times Beverlee would call her mom and say, "I don't think I can do this."

But how could she abandon him now? He had written her from Iraq—long, heart-wrenching letters, whenever his friends' wives or girlfriends left them or cheated on them. It made her ill to think about doing it to him. He'd told her so many times how her love was the only thing that made living worthwhile. So she did what she could to comfort him, to love him, and waited for it to pass.

In his good moments, Nick was sweet and loving and sometimes even seemed overprotective. He worried about her health. He noticed something in the way she walked. An odd wobble. She was always running into things, tripping or falling for no apparent reason.

"I've always been a klutz," she'd tell him.

"There's something wrong," Nick insisted.

He kept at her until she agreed to see a neurologist. The doctor ordered a raft of tests. They pricked her and paced her and hit her with little hammers. Nothing.

Finally the doctor said, "Well, we have one more test we can do."

He didn't say for what, but whatever it was required ten tubes of blood drawn from the vein in the tender tissue on the inside of her elbow.

A couple of weeks later Beverlee got a call: the doctor wanted her to come in to discuss the results. Nick went with her.

"You have Friedreich's ataxia," the doctor said. He told them it was a rare (1-in-50,000) genetic neurological disorder and, unfortunately, degenerative. There wasn't any cure, not even much in the way of treatment. He suggested they might want to do their own research.

None of it sank in until Nick got on the computer.

From the Friedreich's ataxia fact sheet on the National Institute of Neurological Disorders and Stroke web page:

The first symptom to appear is usually gait ataxia, or difficulty walking. The ataxia gradually worsens and slowly spreads to the arms and the trunk. There is often loss of sensation in the extremities, which may spread to other parts of the body. . . . Generally, within 10 to 20 years after the appearance of the first symptoms, the person is confined to a wheelchair, and in later stages of the disease individuals may become completely incapacitated.

Beverlee was sixteen when her symptoms became clearly noticeable. She was twenty-five at diagnosis. It had already been nine years.

All they could do was make sure her diet included loads of antioxidants to combat the free radicals that were steadily attacking and destroying her nerve endings, and ensure that she kept exercising to maintain muscle tone as long as possible.

And try to stay positive.

"I felt like if I lost her, I'd end up killing myself," Nick says. "That's pretty much the only thought I had on it as far as myself, but like I did with all the other stuff, I just sucked it up and pushed it down and focused on her. But I guess, in hindsight, doing that caused some of the problems of me blowing up on her and everything."

They tried to avoid situations that might set him off. He drank, but always stopped before he got drunk. If he felt a fit coming on, he'd smoke his pot and hope it damped the fire. They were both broken now, both being consumed from the inside by a malignant, corrosive force. They needed each other.

They got married in the fall of 2010 at a romantic, marble-columned hilltop mansion overlooking one of New York's Finger Lakes—the lake where Beverlee had spent some of her happiest childhood days.

It was luxury they couldn't afford, but Beverlee's mom told the wedding booker the whole story—about the wounded combat veteran whose young bride had just been diagnosed with a degenerative disease—and a $30,000 package turned into a $5,000 package.

When the day came, Beverlee radiated from a form-hugging white satin gown as Nick stood straight and strong at her side in his Marine dress blues, heavy with overlapping medals—two beautiful young people whose handsome, unlined faces, glittering eyes, and dazzling smiles suggested a long, happy, procreative union.

And then the wedding was over and they were back in South Carolina, shuffling again and again through the lousy hands they'd been dealt, as if somehow a two of clubs might magically transform into an ace of hearts. If possible, Nick loved Beverlee even more now. But no matter how grateful he was, no matter how hard he loved, the panics came, the rages came, all fueled by a crushing fear that forced him to the brink of some cataclysmic explosion.

"I'd tell myself, 'You've got a wife. You've got this going for you. You've got friends and family. You're loved.'

"Nothing would sink in, because everything I would say would get thrown back at me. 'You've got nothing. You're gonna lose this because you've seen how everything gets lost. You've seen how one minute everyone's happy and laughing, and the next minute guys are dying.' And I'd always have that. It was more powerful than the truth that I was trying to speak to myself."

Even the one thing that sometimes helped became a trap. "I didn't want to get attached to the marijuana, I didn't want that to happen, so I was, like, 'Okay, I'm not gonna smoke.' And then I'd start dealing with my feelings, and things would start coming up, and I was, like, 'I'm not gonna smoke, I'm not gonna do that, I'm just gonna try and deal with it.' Oh, man, it would get horrible. And then I'd find myself going and grabbing the pistol and seeing if I had enough courage to do it this time. And then I remember one time the voice in my head said, 'Instead of smoking, *why don't you just smoke yourself out?*'

"There were times when I would completely unload the pistol and just put it at different points on my head and dry fire it, just thinking about what it might be like the moment it happens."

He believed he knew what it would be like, and that was a problem. "Because I was blown up, and I had already tasted death, I knew that it wasn't going to be painful on the other side. The voice inside of my head was, like, 'Just do it. Get it over with. Remember what it was like when you got blown up? Don't you want to go back there, see more of what you saw, and try and really comprehend it?' That stuff started getting into my head, and it was a battle."

In desperation he searched the Internet for some alternative kind of healing. "I thought it would be amazing if I could somehow find some shaman or something, climb some mountain in Tibet, meet some monk, and have him give me some herb that would help me go into a trance. That's the kinda thing that I thought."

He didn't find a shaman, but he did find a friend who told him about the alleged power of psilocybin mushrooms to rearrange your perspective, and how you could buy spores online and grow them yourself.

He knew he was taking a chance—not so much because he worried about the risks of taking the mushrooms, but because he thought the website could be some kind of sting operation.

"I didn't know what I was doing. And it wasn't really smart of me, but I was trying to find help; I had no trust in the VA, so I was trying to find other ways. The way my PTSD was—it sucked how it made you do stuff like that, but you kinda weigh it in your hand and . . . I thought about it, I did, and I thought about how I could've ruined things in life, made 'em worse for me than they even were, but I was trying to live. I was trying to stay alive. And I was willing to try whatever was possible.

"So I blended mine up with some orange juice and drank it, and then we just went walking out in the woods, and we just got to talking. I don't even remember when I realized that it had kind of kicked in. It felt very, very peaceful, very enlightening. It was like I was wearing a different pair of glasses. Not necessarily making me see actual hallucinations; I was seeing the same things but perceived them differently, understood them differently. I would touch a tree and feel like I saw its whole life flash before me, it falling to the ground as a little helicopter seed and then growing superfast, and then the clouds going by superfast, like time going by superfast, and then here I am touching it now and it was just, like, 'Whoa, how could I get all of that information?'

"It did help, but I felt like I wasn't doing it the right way, because I was always talking with my friend and moving around. I really just wanted to sit still and go inward."

Except when he did that "it got rough. I had to open my eyes and get out quick. I saw the web—I don't know how to explain it—the web of, like, life. I saw birds flying in the sky with a connection, a light between them, and that kind of scared me, just being revealed to me like that. Then I started seeing white lines connecting me to everything else; I saw them connect into my chest and my legs, and where my feet were going off into the earth. I saw these tunnels and these geometric shapes and patterns. Sometimes I would go down these little wormholes, and they'd get so fast, it'd scare the crap out of me. . . . It just feels like 'Am I gonna drift off to this and never come back?' I would get scared that I would stop breathing or I'd die and forever be lost."

The fear passed and his familiar unlivable reality returned, but the vivid experience stayed with him. "I started realizing that there's more to reality than I'd thought. So that kind of made me get a little bit of excitement for life again. I was, like, 'Well, I want to discover what these things are. I want to know what this is.'"

That curiosity led him back to the Internet.

What he saw was, literally, a sign.

It said: "Experimental treatment for PTSD: Ecstasy."

It was a link to a CNN special. He saw an interview with "a blond-haired girl" who had volunteered in an experimental trial. On camera, a woman named Rachel Hope, who'd had debilitating PTSD that no other therapies had been able to touch, said of her MDMA therapy experience: "It felt as if my whole brain was powered up like a Christmas tree, all at once." Following her sessions, she said, 90 percent of her symptoms disappeared.

Nick felt his own resurgence of hope, but remained hesitant at first: this was a man-made drug, like the ones the VA had given him, not natural like the mushrooms. But that blond-haired girl, the way she said, "I felt a hundred pounds lighter"—that struck a chord. "I thought to myself, 'Well, maybe this is it. Let's figure it out.' So I got on the MAPS-dot-org website and they just happened to be doing a research study in Charleston, South Carolina, where I was."

In fact, Summerville, where he had been living, was a twenty-five-minute drive from Michael's office.

But when he clicked on the link for information, he discovered that the study wasn't enrolling subjects yet.

He meant to keep on top of it, but "I kinda lost track of it for a while." When he got around to checking the site again in November, "they had a new little advertisement, and I realized that they were accepting people. I thought, 'Oh, no, I've gotta get in! I know they're only gonna take a certain number of people.' I called, left messages, tried for the longest time."

He feared he'd blown his chance, until one morning when he was eating in a Cracker Barrel restaurant, his phone lit up with a Charleston number. He went outside to take the call. It was Annie Mithoefer.

Pacing on the restaurant's front porch, ignoring the old-fashioned wood rocking chairs lined up there as if the patrons might want to "set a spell" after a hearty meal, he told her the three-minute version of his story.

"Well, you definitely sound like a candidate," Annie said. "But you'll need to go through a screening process."

He drove down to Charleston and "took more psychological tests than the military gave me."

Just like Tony Macie, he was a shoo-in.

Nick made the drive to Mount Pleasant once a week, attending all the preparatory sessions required by the protocol. He loved the low-key, peaceful vibe of the skylit office, which to him was a novelty. "It's set up real nice," he says. "I mean, there's holes in the ceiling; regular light can come in."

He also appreciated the contrast with the psych appointments he'd had at the VA. "There, it's 'Your hour's up and we need to see our next patient, so we'll see you in four weeks.' Michael and Annie would let you just talk as long as it took. Never interrupted you and just really listened."

Nick responded to the sympathetic vibe. "I opened up to them," he said. "But it's really hard for them to get to you. I mean, they could say the things they needed to, to help you out—you know, comforting things. But you're already at the point where you don't listen to anybody—not even yourself, 'cause you've already tried."

Which made the first, nondrug sessions difficult. It's no fun believing you're a hopeless case.

"When I come here I always feel anxious and nervous," he told Michael on his last visit before he was to take the MDMA. "I'm outside and I'm, like, 'I don't want to go in there.'"

But on the morning of April 16, 2011, almost four months since Annie's call had lured him out of the Cracker Barrel, he came through their door in his jeans and olive USMC sweatshirt with something approaching eagerness. With his close-cropped hair, neatly trimmed brown beard, cupid-bow lips, and cheeks smooth and rounded as a child's, he looked heartbreakingly young and clean-cut, like some nine-year-old's favorite summer camp counselor. He settled onto the futon and smiled shyly.

"This morning I wasn't as nervous as I usually am when coming here," he said. "I felt like in Ramadi when I had to go out on a mission. You're nervous, but once you get on the truck and get your gear on, this calm comes over you. I don't know if it was just because everyone else was feeling the same way, but when we'd get on the truck we'd all be laughing and joking; you'd know you weren't alone."

"Well," Michael said, "you're not alone here either."

Nick had been briefed on the design of the study, which aimed at resolving the unsuccessful double-blind attempt of the first go-round. This time subjects would be randomly assigned one of three different doses of MDMA: 125 milligrams, the full active dose from the previous study; 75 milligrams, a milder dose, but still considered a possible catalyst for therapy; and 30 milligrams. The hope was the lowest dose would be felt enough to keep everyone guessing about who got what, but not enough to actually create a therapeutic effect that could obscure how effective the higher doses had been. In other words, it was kind of a Hail Mary pass at fulfilling the FDA's idea of rigorous drug research in a situation that inherently resisted that approach.

He kicked off his shoes and pulled off his sweatshirt, revealing a white V-neck undershirt and a braided rope necklace with a stone pendant.

"Is that your shark's tooth?" Annie asked.

"To be honest," he said, "it's an arrowhead I found when I was doing mushrooms." Nick told them the story, about how he'd always dreamed of finding an arrowhead as a boy, and how during his psilocybin mushroom journey he'd found himself staring down at the same patch of ground he'd searched so futilely so many times only to see the pointed end of a stone pointing straight at him. At first he thought it couldn't be real—either it was some kind of hallucination or maybe just a naturally sharp rock. But as he picked it up and began cleaning off the caked mud, a perfect arrowhead emerged, which he took as "a sign that I was going in the right direction."

Michael took his cue.

"Are you ready to take your capsule?"

Nick gingerly plucked the pill from the bowl Annie handed him and swallowed it with a nervous smile and a swig of water, then sat back against a cushion propped against the wall. Minutes passed. He wasn't certain how many, but it seemed like quite a while. He chattered nervously.

"Would you like to try the eyeshades?" Annie asked a half hour in.

He put on the green foam eye mask and the large noise-canceling headphones she handed him and lay back. A gently tinkling piano, like a sleepy spring rain, played over the headphones. The piano gave way to a plaintive violin and then to a flute that sounded at first almost human, then like the lonely cry of a wolf. There was something vaguely Native American about the sound of the music. Nick suddenly remembered one of his friends in Ramadi, a part-Indian guy named Ellis, who always carried a medicine bag. Before a mission once, he invited Nick to participate in a Native American prayer. Ellis lit some tobacco, offering the smoke to the four directions. And then he pulled something out of his medicine bag and handed it to Nick—a bear claw. It seemed like such a precious and extravagant gift to Nick, and yet, until this instant, he'd forgotten it. After Ellis had finished the little ceremony, they'd climbed onto the truck, which rolled outside the wire.

They found themselves in a particularly intense firefight that day. Ellis had seen something in a building and fired first. Nick hopped on his gun, shooting in the same general direction. The hostile fire ceased immediately, but they kept shooting. Nick held his finger tight against the trigger. What he remembered now was the sea of red rage he'd floated in as the gun bucked and the *BLAM-BLAM-BLAM* beat to the rhythm of the tidal surge of hatred and discontent rushing through him. Odd, he thought, that a memory like that would come up with such quiet, peaceful music.

Nick was lost in that memory when he felt a touch on his shoulder. It had been an hour since he'd swallowed the pill.

"Just checking in," Michael said.

Nick pushed up the eye mask, blinked, and said, "It's brighter out here than I thought."

"Are you feeling anything, Nick?" Annie asked.

Nick squinted. "Not really. Not anything more than usual when I close my eyes and let my mind wander."

He shifted the shades over his eyes and lay back, once again letting his mind idle. Twenty minutes later he'd still not felt anything out of the ordinary when, like a clap of thunder on a sunny day, his heart leapt in his chest and began to pound so hard he could hear it chug.

I didn't get the low dose, he thought.

The strange feelings and sensations kept coming, kept building. A wall of heat rose up and crashed over him.

Oh, my God, he thought. It had to be the high dose.

His skin tingled. His heart kept beating as if it intended to leap from his rib cage. He felt sweat trickling from his temples and could feel that familiar panic gathering, ready to clamp on and not let go.

Then something odd happened. He heard a voice inside his head say, *Breathe! You're too tense.*

In the prep sessions, Michael and Annie had warned him that some people got anxious when the drug effects began, and told him to try to take deep, slow breaths if that happened. He tried that now. He visualized the tension in his body and directed his breath into the tension, just as they'd told him to. As his lungs drew in the air, the tension vanished like fog before a rising sun. He could feel it evaporating through his skin, leaving a warm, evanescing glow, as if he had been lathered in Vicks VapoRub.

Now the MDMA had his attention.

Just as he was marveling at how quickly the anxiety had disappeared, another wave of unease began to build. He breathed into it: gone. Then again. Each time the anxiety dissipated, it returned with diminished force. An image came into his mind of wading into the ocean through the surf.

"You hit a little wave, hit a little wave, but In order to get out there to where it's nice and calm, you've gotta break that big wave and then go through a few small waves, and then . . . you're there. And that's kind of exactly how MDMA was—it's like wading into the ocean."

Nick shot up from the futon and yanked off his eye mask. "Ohhh, I have to tell you something! I breathed when I had anxiety, and it just vanished."

"Just do that every time," Michael said, "and let us know if you need any help with anything. Would you like to go back inside?"

"Oh, yeah," Nick said. "Let's go back."

"And then I started seeing things," Nick remembers, "digital things and stuff like that. I didn't remember how it started, but I remember going on this journey. I see a tree with a little hole cut in the bottom of it, so I open up the little hole in the tree, just like *Alice in Wonderland*, but the forest I was in was all covered in moss—beautiful. I crawled into that hole, and I go falling down like Alice. And the cool thing was, I could feel the fall—the sense of falling. And I've been skydiving before, so I know what that feeling's like, and I was just falling into it. And then I felt like I had stopped, and I'm in a black room."

Nick had used visualization techniques before, when he tried meditating on his own. In his earlier visualizations he had gone down the rabbit hole to the black room, descended a spiral staircase cut into a stone wall. At the bottom of the staircase, past a flaming bonfire, he entered another room. Inside, he found a horrible, snarling dragonlike creature straining against the heavy chains that kept it tethered to the wall.

Now, with the MDMA fully engaged, this visualized world seemed real, *present*, beyond his conscious control. He explored the dark space until he came to a door, but it was guarded by an old man with long white hair and beard—like a sage, Nick thought, a wise man. The sage opened the door and led Nick to the stone wall's ledge. They descended the spiral stairs together, but the fire at the bottom had burned out. Nick followed the old man to the second door. The old man gestured at the door and Nick opened it. Inside, the chain was lying on the ground. The dragon was gone.

Then the scene changed. Nick was now the sage, and chained in the dungeon was not a dragon but a human, a man dressed in Marine fatigues, hanging his head in sadness or despair. As he crept closer, the Marine looked up. His face, contorted with rage or pain, had glowing red eyes, like a demon's, and fangs protruding from his mouth. But what most horrified Nick was that the monster's face was his own.

He wanted to turn away, to run, but the sage him refused to budge. Nick stood there forcing himself to look at the monster he had become. As he held that demonic gaze, something unexpected happened. His revulsion faded, then melted away, replaced by a swirl of other emotions; pity, regret.

"I went up to him, and I took off the chains, and I remember saying something like 'If you want to rip me apart, I would understand, because I put you here. It was very wrong of me.' I remember the face melting, and us hugging each other—the sage me and the warrior me. It was just, like, this forgiving moment. I was inwardly forgiving myself. It was just so profound, like, 'Oh, my God.' It lifted me up to that point of ecstasy. It was when I finally found the ecstasy they talk about from the drug. I had achieved that."

Now nearly two hours had passed since he'd swallowed the pill, and Nick's thoughts raced by. He had the sensation of thinking a dozen things at once without any confusion, almost like the times when the world slowed down and his mind speeded up in the middle of a fire-fight. Only now there was no fear, only insight after insight. He struggled to relate them all to Michael and Annie, completely losing his sense of time until a new visualization seized him. "It was like being two different places at once. I would sit there and be, like, 'Whoa, this is a very strong visualization, but I know I'm on a bed right now. I can hear the music in my ear. I know there's eyeshades on. I can *feel* Michael and Annie. They're out there.' But when I would go back to my visualization, you just kind of forget it all. The outside world kind of disappears. You can sit there and stare at that chair and feel that chair and your mind starts going down to the fundamental level of what everything is made of, and you're, like, 'Well, if it's all made of the same stuff, then we are all pieces of the same thing,' and it just hits you, like, 'Whoa,' and you can feel it. I don't know how to explain it, but in those sessions, I felt . . . eternity. It blows your mind. It's just like a quick glimpse, and when you try to rationalize it and understand it or articulate it, it goes away. But when you can feel that connection with everything, it's really beautiful.

"When you go to these other inward worlds, there's no form of communication; our form of communication is for this outside, conscious world. And so some of these things that we experience on the inside, there's no language for it. All I can say is they would click, and I would understand them inside.

"One of them was actually about my body. I had realized that the only thing that I came into this world with, that I started off with, was my body. And that within my body were all the answers that I needed. I was communicating with this inner healer inside—you know, I felt this source that was within."

Whatever that source was, it kept taking him back to Iraq. At one point he began to replay the mission where his Humvee got blown up by the insurgents' rocket-propelled grenade, remembering details he hadn't brought to mind since the moment they happened. He took off his eye mask and began narrating, his voice barely more than a whisper. As he talked, his eyes darted rapidly around in their sockets, as if he were really seeing what he described. He remembered the confusion, shooting blindly at an unseen enemy, staring at his reflection in the still pool of Seabass's blood. He talked about standing in the shower, his butt aflame with shrapnel, his knee twisted and torn, but feeling nothing except guilt and shame for failing Seabass, for absently taking the magic gum out of his mouth, violating his promise to keep praying.

Michael and Annie leaned in as his voice became fainter but didn't falter. "I cried, told him I was so sorry about the gum, sorry that I didn't stop it, didn't see it coming. Now I can totally forgive myself. It's not my fault; it was his time to go. I can really accept it now. But I always think about what it must have been like for him, what it felt like. I always thought back to that moment when he was slumped over, what was going through his mind. Everything happened the way it happened and there's no point in thinking about what you could have done, but part of me wishes I could have helped him when the firefight was going on, gone in and held him as he was leaving, because he seemed so scared.

"I know some things in this world we're not in control of. Part of it is letting go and trusting that no matter what happens, it's all for the better somehow. When you come home people tell you you're a hero. They come up and shake your hand, offer to buy you drinks or meals. I used to not like that—maybe because it made me think of all those things I did, and I didn't feel like a hero—but thinking of it now, I really feel a lot more comfortable with that. I didn't feel like no hero and killing somebody was just ridiculous, but when I think about those scenarios, either I let someone shoot me and I die or my friends die. It was just the situation we were in: it was cruel, it was hateful, everything that disgusts me about man sometimes, but it is what it is, and I feel like I shouldn't take away the bad things, that I should be grateful . . . really thankful that I'm still alive. . . ."

Michael and Annie both murmured approving sounds as Nick went on.

"I'm not done. I still have things to do. I survived all those miraculous situations for a reason. I shouldn't feel like I should be punished or punish myself. I guess there's really just this part of me that really understands. It's like talking out loud, I feel like I am communicating with that self, I just feel the understanding kind of float through me."

It just kept spilling out. Michael sat to his right on a blue-leather office swivel chair, in his jeans, this-is-who-I-am ponytail, and gray Mister Rogers sweater; Annie to his left on a wide, neutral-colored armchair, her thick, curly brown hair held off her broad, strong face by a hair clip. Annie said that the main thing she learned about being a therapist from watching tapes of her sessions was *Why are you talking?* and she'd learned her lesson well. Nick's flow of words were self-directing. You could almost see his brain turning these new ideas over, shuffling them, tilting them at different angles.

"I always wondered before I got into combat how I would handle those things when they came at me, how I would handle making the decision to pull the trigger on somebody. I remember being in the turret, squatting down and looking through the front window. I would

see them firing at us and jump up in the turret and return fire so fast I
don't know how I did it. I was always being so anxious, like, where is
it going to come from? And when it happened I just did it so fast, and
I think about having locked up in a cage that part of me that kept my
friends alive. I don't think he had a face of evil, it's just something I put
on him. I don't feel separate from him right now; it was something
innate within me the whole time, this warrior, this protector, even
when I say it in my mind: 'I'm so sorry I caged you up.' I thought it
would be hateful but . . . I was just scared and . . . honestly, I never
thought I'd come home from the desert. I felt like I was lost over there
and I'd never come home. But I wasn't lost, and I took that person and
caged him up. Coming back, I felt really disconnected, I felt no one
could relate to what I was going through, I felt angry at everyone. It
sounds silly now, because they were back here living their lives and I
was over there dying. I created the disconnect. I couldn't escape the
feeling that someone was going to come out of nowhere and I'd have to
get in a firefight. . . ."

On and on he went. As the hours passed, the MDMA still afloat in
his psyche became less apparent. His voice regained a more normal
timbre. He got chilled and put his Marine sweatshirt back on, gestured
with his hands to make a point. To all appearances he was a man lying
on a futon, talking. But his eyes still skittered around, and the thoughts
emerged with a comfort belied by their enormity.

"Maybe I was angry at myself for participating in something like
that," he said at one point, trying to understand why he'd allowed
himself to become so disconnected from those close to him, so "afraid
to live."

"I think that . . . I really think that I was punishing myself for . . .
being . . . you know . . ." His eyes closed and his chest heaved; for the
first time he seemed to be struggling to get words out. ". . . a . . ." A sob
started in his throat, but he choked it off. ". . . a . . . killer."

He sank deeper into the pillow, his eyes searching the ceiling as if something important were streaming in through the skylights. When he began to speak again, his voice was soft, shaken. "I would . . . I don't . . . you know whenever I shot people I didn't . . . I don't know, I didn't really feel anything. I didn't feel excited. I didn't feel bad. I just kind of felt numb, and that scared me. And when I got back here and think about those things, I don't know, I feel bad for doing those things and acting the way I did."

"Are you feeling some of that sadness now?" Michael asked.

Nick's eyes traced an arabesque on the ceiling. After a minute he said, "When I think about it now, the same thoughts come to my head that normally do, but now I'm not really bothered by them. I understand. Like, normally the feelings that rush up to me and make me all teary-eyed and emotional, now I think I understand why I cried and why I felt the way I did, and now the past is the past. Those things are always going to be with me, carved into my soul, scars on my soul. Whenever I thought about those scars, I got really emotional, I wanted them to go away, wished I never had them. Now I realize they're never going to go away, I'm always going to have them. . . . It's like a splinter in the mind, but it's not going to come out. I've just got to file it down and smooth it out. Those things are just part of my life, part of my experience, and I should just not look at those scars in the mirror and get sad but just come to them and pat them down. . . . I don't know how to describe it."

"If there's a splinter," Michael said, "it's important to get the splinter out, but there may be a scar; that is part of healing. It's still there, but it's healed. I don't know if that resonates."

"I still feel like there's something there that's . . . that's . . . kind of lurking around in the background."

Michael's experience told him it wasn't up to him to talk whatever it was out in the open. It was up to the MDMA.

"Now might be a good time to go inside again with the music and just see what might be there," he suggested. "Does that feel right? Then come out and let us know."

Nick went back into Native American chants and wispy space music. The face behind the eye mask revealed nothing. Michael would later use the video of Nick's session to make the point to would-be therapists that in MDMA sessions it could often look as if nothing were happening when in fact worlds were being created or destroyed.

Ten minutes later Nick pulled off the eye mask. He'd visualized sitting around a campfire at night, he told them. "I had a powerful vision of something rustling around in the bushes," he said. He was there in his two incarnations, warrior and sage, but try as they might, they couldn't get the shadowy presence to reveal itself. "I don't know if it's bad, but I had this overwhelming feeling that I'm supposed to confront it. . . . Makes me feel like I did when I was a kid. When you think there's something under your bed, part of you wants to look, and part of you doesn't want to see something scare the crap out of you, but if you don't look, you have to lie there wondering."

It had been almost four hours since he'd taken the MDMA, and the acute effects of the drug were winding down.

"Everything else that's come up, I've been able to take care of it," he told Michael and Annie. "All those things that seem to be taken care of and resolved, I can't tell you how tremendous I feel."

But the last vision had been disturbing, and it lingered, suggesting unfinished business.

Over the next few weeks Nick felt he was exploring a strange new country. He told Beverlee to picture a feather falling from outer space, moving inexorably toward recovery, but spinning and twirling unpredictably with the currents.

It wasn't all easy. Beverlee, who at least had been used to Nick's icy, silent rages, found it difficult to adjust to him needing to be alone even when he was feeling perfectly fine. He was so different, it made her wonder if he was still going to need her. After an awkward first night, they both sat down with Michael and Annie, who helped her see that it wasn't that Nick was upset with her or that they'd lost their connection. "It was just that he still needed to go within himself to finish the healing. But I noticed a huge difference," Beverlee said. "Like, things that I would say or do that would cause him to blow up before, he would just laugh it off or he would just calmly talk to me. He wouldn't blow up at me anymore."

In the end, her main problem was envy: all the talk of transformative visions made her wish that she'd gotten to experience it too.

Nick felt guilty about that, but much more so about his fellow Marines. The one thing he'd embodied most passionately from his training was that you never left a wounded man behind. And yet, so many of his friends were still suffering—some worse than he had been—but hadn't been lucky enough to find this ladder out of hell. He had to tell himself that his participation in this study would help them all if it helped prove the therapy successful and MDMA became a prescription medicine. But that was a thin thread—a far-off glimmer against the dazzling sunlight he was basking in.

Not that there weren't some dark clouds. Sitting in class one day a week out of the therapy, he felt the first cold fingers of depression grip his heart. Instead of clenching tightly, anticipating the usual descent into a panic attack, he reacted as Michael and Annie had suggested, with curiosity, trying to trace what it was that had set him off. Transitory depression following treatment had been one of the possible side effects listed on the informed consent form he'd studied with Michael and Annie. He'd learned that MDMA, which flooded the brain with serotonin during the session, could leave a hangover of serotonin depletion for a few days, which might be associated with depressed feelings. Oddly though, in Michael's first study, the subjects who took only the sugar pill reported more depressed feelings following the sessions than those who got the MDMA.

Nick had brought up the depression at a follow-up visit a few days after it happened. He told Annie, "When I felt it, I heard your voice telling me not to push it away, to just feel like what it is to be there, but it's easier to do that on MDMA. It's a new thing to me . . . to just try to be."

"Hopefully you'll have a different relationship to your feelings now," Annie told him. "That's the whole point of therapy. Just watch the feelings come as if you're watching from above, witnessing them as they roll through."

"I like that," Nick said. "It's such a radical way of thinking compared to how I was thinking. There's a strangeness ever since—same life, same me, but things seem different. I find myself getting this strange smile coming on; reminds me of being a kid, happy for no reason. I'll be taking my trash out to the Dumpster and I'll just start noticing how beautiful the trees are, same way I used to. I can't help but feel happy about that. But part of me fears that I'll forget all these profound things I've experienced."

Michael reassured him: "It is helpful to refer back to it, to reconnect, have a daily practice of some kind, whether it's getting out in nature or doing artwork or any other way, but at the same time it can turn over into grasping and worrying about losing it. It's about letting things happen, not grasping. You can trust that the same inner healing intelligence that gave you that experience, if you create space for it, it will keep working for you. Stan Grof liked to say it's about changing life from a boxing match to surfing: you still might wipe out in the impact zone, but you're not constantly getting punched in the face."

Nick took the Mithoefers' advice to heart and took a drive into the country, to a place he knew where he could park the car and walk into the woods. As soon as he'd left the parking spot behind and could hear the wind sighing through the branches and see the leaves flashing silver in the sun, everything got clearer and all the insights he'd had during the MDMA session echoed in his mind. He was deep in thought when he heard the distinctive high-pitched cries of a hawk. He looked up and saw not one hawk but three circling on the currents directly above him. He looked away and the birds' cries grew more insistent, as if they were demanding his attention. When he looked up again, they went silent, sailing on the currents in lazy circles high above. Part of him wanted to believe that this avian trio was all about him and his journey back to health. The cynical adult in him scoffed at that narcissistic impulse. He kept watching, thinking the birds would drift off, go find another human to soar above. But they just kept circling above him. Suddenly he felt that same lurking, invisible presence he'd felt in his vision. Something about the hawks, but what?

Then he had a thought: there were three hawks, a trinity of sorts. He'd discovered two parts of himself, one of which he'd locked away in a dungeon. Maybe, it occurred to him, there was a third part, buried even deeper than that.

Nick's second session with MDMA came a month after the first.

"Any intentions for today?" Michael asked as Nick settled back into the futon.

"I guess this time will be different," Nick said, "but I don't know how, and it's making me a little nervous. I feel like there has to be something else. I can't get rid of this too-good-to-be-true feeling about how good I've been feeling. I told myself that I'd figure it all out while I was under, when I got that clarity."

Once again he popped the pill into his mouth, this time with a brisk flip of the wrist, and swallowed. Once again he put on the earphones and varieties of space music emerged. Once again he lowered the eye mask and settled back, awaiting those strobe flashes of insight.

An hour later, no insights had appeared.

"The only thing that was coming to my mind was being a kid, just kind of being apart from everyone else, feeling significantly different," he said when he pushed the eye mask up. "I just feel connected to how I did when I was younger, out of place."

"Just be with it," Annie said. "Try not to move away. It's coming for you to see and feel it."

He settled back down and tried to do what Annie suggested. Memories rushed through him, things he hadn't thought about in years. It was as if his entire childhood appeared before him, like a village in a snow globe, comprehensible in a single glance—all the things that had been lying around in the dark recesses of memory but never before fully seen and understood. Now it was all so clear. His problem was all those odd things he saw that others did not. That led to the withdrawal, the bullying, the feeling of isolation that even his parents' love couldn't diminish.

On the futon in Mount Pleasant all those years later, his eyes closed and voice barely a whisper, Nick appeared to be in a trance as he tried to relate all this to Michael and Annie.

"All the anger had just built up and built up. I just felt because I had built so much anger up I had desensitized myself to things that were gruesome. I'd imagine the kids picking on me, just beating their face in until there was no more, and not feeling anything. And when I got into combat and saw all that stuff, it didn't bother me. It felt wrong not to feel more. . . . I felt like the military was the path in which God was leading me, but I also know deep down inside that I was just trying to prove myself, do something strong and tough and get some confidence. Being a Marine was huge confidence builder. I don't like saying it, but part of me wanted to go over there and shoot someone."

Michael leaned in closer. "It makes sense that there was a part of you that wanted to," he said, his voice calm, low, as if wanting to kill was the most natural thing in the world. "But it's just a part. It's not all of you."

Nick's eyes moved, rippling the closed lids.

"I feel bad that I wanted to do that," Nick said, as if Michael's words hadn't quite registered.

"We all have those kinds of feelings," Michael said. "What matters is that's not all of you. Your heart is much different than that."

"I don't like how I cannot feel," Nick continued. "That part right there seems not human. I just blamed it on the PTSD."

"You're exploring another level of it," Michael said.

Annie, who'd been taking this all in from the other side of the futon, gave Michael a glance. "Seems like maybe this would be a time to go inside, if it feels right to you," she said.

"We'll be right here," Michael said.

A half hour later, Nick pulled off the eye mask.

"I realized that I'd come to believe because I got picked on and was an outcast that I believed I was supposed to be, so I pushed people away too."

"Sometimes," Annie said, "these stories we tell ourselves about our childhoods need to get rewritten."

Nick nodded. "I had a vision of me now telling the young Nicholas, 'When you're older you'll have better friends than you have now, and people will like you,' but that young Nicholas wasn't getting it; it wasn't sinking in."

"Sometimes that's what it takes with our young parts," Michael said, "to bring them into the present. Anything that young part wants to show us or you before he's ready to come to the present?"

Nick stared at the ceiling, slowly rubbing his thumb against his middle finger. When he spoke, his voice was vague, distant sounding.

"Just a lot of fear," he said. "Being alone in the world. I felt haunted when I was a kid; that's why I felt scared."

"Tell us more about that," Annie said.

"Seeing the things I saw, I felt haunted."

"What were the things that you saw?"

Nick wanted to tell them about the fuzzy dots that put him to sleep, the crazy self-propelled clock radio, the mutating Teenage Mutant Ninja Turtle. He stared at the ceiling a long time.

"All I can get now is things that weren't there. Just because that's what I was told, that it's not really there. Things happened all my life and I just don't acknowledge it."

"What is it about it that's uncomfortable?" Annie asked.

Nick searched the ceiling again.

"Part of it is just how it sounds. It was so real, it's scary. . . . I just care too much about how the world views it."

Michael had seen scores of psychotic and schizophrenic patients in his career. They also reported seeing and hearing fanciful things that seemed real. But Nick bore little in common with them. He'd had inexplicable experiences, but he clearly understood that they didn't meet the usual definition of reality and felt appropriate chagrin about the dilemma they presented in a society defined in stark rationalist terms. In fact, on the prestudy screening tests he'd been asked if he'd ever seen things that others said weren't really there. He'd been afraid that answering honestly might disqualify him, but he told the truth anyway. Even so, the screening tests showed no indication that he was psychotic. If it had, he would have been excluded from the study.

"I think it is true that a lot of people don't understand these things and might label them as crazy and psychotic," Michael said. "But it's very clear that's not what this is. A lot of people have a lot of these experiences, and we understand that."

Michael wasn't just saying that to be reassuring. As he well knew, one of the underlying challenges of embracing the psychedelic experience in Western medicine is that its very nature can seem at times to run counter to the rational, scientific viewpoint. He'd learned from Grof, and the entire history of psychedelic therapy, that what was important wasn't if they were "real" but if they could help heal.

In the therapy training manual Michael was writing for future MDMA therapists, he put it this way:

> Such experiences can be difficult to interpret, and in some cases may challenge the therapists' own belief system. The therapists are not required to understand or even have an opinion about the onto-logical status of these experiences, but it is essential that they accept them as real and important aspects of the participant's experience and convey respect for and openness toward the participant's own view of them without dismissing or pathologizing any experience based on its unusual content. If necessary, the therapist should help the participant integrate these experiences into their ordinary lives. These experiences may provide the participant a perspective beyond identification with their trauma and even beyond their usual sense of self, affording the participant the opportunity to foster awareness of an innate ability to integrate their traumatic experiences and move forward with their lives.

Now Nick was putting that theory to the test.

"Ever since I've listened to my heart in life, it's just let me know that I'm not crazy," Nick said. "But it still scares me."

"What scares you about it?" Annie asked.

"I don't want it to be true. It's hard for me to talk about it. I don't want to bring it to the surface. I know how it sounds. . . ."

He stumbled to a stop, closed his eyes, considered whether to go on. When his eyes opened again, he'd made his decision.

"There is something that happened to me. I really wanted to write it off as a dream. I know deep in my heart that it wasn't, that it was me in some other realm, it was beyond real and I had never been so afraid in my entire life, and I went through all that combat and stared at death and nothing has scared me as much as . . ." Nick glanced at the video camera standing on its tripod, pointing in his direction, then shut his eyes again and sighed. "Part of me doesn't want to say it, but I know you'll have to keep it rolling for the study. . . ."

"Do you want us to turn the camera off for a couple minutes?" Michael asked.

"I think I would talk about it if . . ."

Michael turned off the camera, and Nick told them what was haunting him.

When he got out of the Marines he took care of some business in South Carolina, then went home to Paducah for six weeks, to his parents' house, built on the site of the trailer he'd lived in as a kid. In fact, the bedroom he was staying in occupied precisely the same point in space as his childhood bedroom in the trailer, the place where he'd seen the fuzzy dots and self-propelled stuffed animals.

One night during the six-week stay, sleeping in that room, he dreamt that he woke up in the middle of night, sensing something odd in the room. He couldn't move except for his eyes, which he swiveled to his left. As soon as he did, he saw a hand reach up to touch his. As the bony, elongated, four-fingered hand touched his, he went numb. He could feel the presence of the hand but not its texture. Now he could see the rest of whatever it was standing there. A human shape covered in blue-grayish skin that shimmered like an oil slick on water. But it was the eyes that filled him with terror. They were huge, almost like holes in a mask, but when he looked into them, their glossy depth pulled him in like a tractor beam. The creature, or whatever it was, straddled him, rolled him off the bed, and slung him facedown over its shoulder as easily as if he had been filled with down instead of bone and muscle. As it carried him out the bedroom door, he could only watch helplessly as his bed receded. The last thing he remembered from the dream was a growing glare, as if someone had switched on a powerful Klieg light.

Only now, as he relived it under MDMA, he remembered more. As the creature passed into the hall with him slung over its shoulder, the being turned to reach for the door to shut it, and Nick saw two more creatures standing by the door and a third one down the hall in the kitchen. The one holding him laid Nick down on the floor, and the two that had been standing by the door came over to where he lay, paralyzed, feet stretching back toward the bedroom. They began to prod his legs as if they were inspecting them. He sensed intense confusion, not just on his part, but on theirs. He felt that he wasn't supposed to be awake. Every time Nick would try to look down toward his legs, one of the two—the one Nick somehow knew was female—looked right at him, through him, with those all-consuming bottomless eyes. When he looked into them, he felt a calm spread through him.

As the MDMA brought him deeper into the memories, the images began to waver, like a TV flipping between two stations. The creatures' faces shifted from alien to almost human. He wondered if it was simply his fear—the paralyzing, all-consuming fear—that had made him see the creatures as alien.

When Nick finished his account, Michael turned the camera back on.

"It was just so hard to get it to come out of my mouth," Nick apologized. "I realized that I was fighting the medicine. My combat experiences, I always have been able to talk about those—they were a lot more gruesome—but the other was just so unusual."

He said he felt it was all connected to those odd experiences he'd had as a child, as if all those things he had seen were really interpretations of the same thing. For some reason he'd been prone to having these unacceptable experiences that everyone else said couldn't have happened, and as a result he learned to deny them, to push them down and disconnect from other people because he couldn't share their sense of reality and they couldn't accept his.

"I have those moments where I don't feel emotion; it's because I started cutting everyone off when I was young," he said.

Michael and Annie encouraged him to explore those feelings and go back inside.

When Nick put the eye mask back on, the space music amped up, leading off with a fanfare of electronic tones, reverberating. This was no accident: Michael and Annie had programmed the music to become more active and dramatic just as the MDMA would be reaching its peak.

Nick came out thirty-eight minutes later, transformed.

"It's bright out here!" he said, laughing.

"I don't even know where to start," he continued. "I started letting myself feel all the things I needed to feel. I think I was depressed because last time my inner self came to me so quickly and guided me and was able to provide clarity I needed, and this time I wasn't getting it. I think I just expected that once the drug was in, I'd get the clarity again and be able to reconnect. I realized that I stumbled upon it the first time by blessing, and this time I needed to develop a route to connect with it so I wouldn't need the MDMA next time."

So he'd done what he'd always done when he prayed or meditated: just offered himself up, tried to let go of himself, and began to visualize the door in the base of the tree and falling down the rabbit hole into the subterranean world.

Suddenly he'd found himself as both the warrior and the sage aspects of himself around the campfire where the shadow lurked. "I caught a glimpse of that thing poking out of the darkness, shadowlike, and I got scared," he said. "But then I had a visualization of it coming out, and it wasn't a creature at all, it was little Nicholas, the true me, whoever we are inside. The best image my mind gives it is me as a little boy, blond, green-eyed, a brilliance that outshone fire. And it felt like a completion of a trifecta, Little Nicholas in tune with my true self, at the top of the pyramid, branching down to the warrior me and sage me. I thought I was just being imaginative, but it felt so real and so right."

Feeling that release made him want to go deeper. Again he visualized himself at the cave where the dragon and the dungeon had been, and there he saw a stone staircase leading to a platform poised precariously above an abyss. On the platform was a cross inside a circle, like a gunsight. He walked down the stairs and stood at the center of the cross, "and all of sudden I felt like a tube of energy all around me. Next thing I know, I'm in clouds, orange and pink like when the sun's setting. . . ." His mother and father were there, and he told them, "It's a dream," and they said, *"No, it's real."*

And like that, he knew what that lurking shadow had been; he knew that the most terrifying thing about his "dream" of the entities had been that, deep down, in the core of his being, he didn't believe it was a dream.

Still engaged in his vision, he walked through a grand gate into a courtyard. On one side was a boulder with water spouting from the center: water from stone. In the middle of the courtyard he saw a golden door with rune-like symbols carved in it around the indented outline of a human figure. He remained aware that this was all a visualization—that he was lying on the futon, Michael and Annie sitting patiently beside him—but at the same time he felt a connection to the vision, as if it had a reality independent of his imagination.

"I pressed myself up against the indentation, just kind of floating in this place of peace, and started asking questions of myself and got the clarity I was looking for. I kind of understood the situation—I don't know what to call it, 'my experience'—better. I didn't see it as threatening, more as protective. It was like my higher self told me that I had visualized the beings to look that way because I was afraid, and that I could see it another way if I chose to. . . . It was almost as if it were telling me that, as bizarre as all the things sound and seem in my life, I should be accepting of them because they are who I am and denying them or trying to rationalize them is just going to create more confusion. Then this voice came to me and said, 'Now you know how to get here,' and that made me feel so good. I am too hard on myself. I should stop worrying about what sounds weird or not. I'm not that little kid anymore who needs people to accept him."

Nick seemed lighter now. Hours in, the effects of the MDMA in his system had passed their peak. He asked for a snack and ate it, chatting amiably about his tattoos. In high school he'd been desperate to get some. "My mom said, 'No way.'"

Once he became a Marine, of course, tattoos were nearly part of the uniform. He pulled up his shirt and showed off the one on his torso: a reproduction of his dog tags inked above his ribs. Marines called them "meat tags" and wore them so if they got rendered into separated body parts, someone would still be able to make an identification.

After he'd finished the snack, he went back under, earphones and eye mask in place. Twenty-four minutes later he pulled off the eye mask.

"Violent images keep flashing through my head," he said. "Eyes bursting out and blood and all kinds of different things—someone grabbing the back of a head and peeling flesh off the body—something out of a horror movie. People in butchers' gowns stacking body parts up. I feel no emotion, I'm desensitized to it. Like it was nothing. If anything is attached to it, it's just like confusion—why I'm not grossed out or disgusted. Why those things even came up I don't know."

Michael watched Nick's face carefully before speaking.

"I'm thinking about the fact that before you went back inside you showed me your tattoo with the dog tag info," Michael said. "The fact that they are called 'meat tags' and you're wearing them, and all your buddies are wearing them, must harden you in a certain way."

"We just kind of viewed ourselves as robots or whatever," Nick said. "'Meat suits,' we called them. . . . I viewed my body as an organic mechanized robot that I used to fight in combat. Just patch you up and get you back in the fight. Seabass, he just sprung a leak that couldn't be fixed. Doesn't feel right, just feels cold to think that way. I see how everyone squirms, turns their head, and averts their eyes when I express that."

Michael knew that Nick's breakthrough in the first session—the vision he'd had of letting the warrior part of himself out of lockdown—had only been the first step in a long process of accepting himself and all that he'd done in the war, but he'd been waiting for Nick to let him know when he was ready to go further. Now was the time.

"It's not about having that part in charge," Michael told him, "but acknowledging that we all carry parts that have rage and potential for violence. You know that's not who you are."

"I can't hear that," Nick said. "It's like it won't sink in. This is like the part of me when I have my episodes that just won't let anything in."

"I'm wondering if it was the part of you that was a protector. You needed that at times. You were in the middle of a fight and your truck got blown up and you had to keep going. You didn't just murder people. You were in Iraq, in a war. You had your name on your chest because that might be the only part of you that was recognizable. How could you not protect yourself in some way from all that, from how all that feels?"

"I just thought I was going to go over there and die, I didn't . . ." Nick started, and then stopped short, as if he were surprised by what he'd been about to say.

Michael waited a long time, and when he finally spoke, he chose his words with care.

"Is that what part of you wanted, to go over there and die?"

Nick lay flat against the futon and stared at the ceiling. His mouth began to quiver; his eyelids flickered, then closed.

"I think so," he began, choking it off.

"You think so?"

Nick nodded, closed his eyes again.

"Is it okay to feel that?" Michael asked.

"There's just no way for me to feel like that," Nick said.

"Just be with that part that feels like that for a few minutes," Michael said. "If it's okay, just stay with that."

Nick clapped his hand to his forehead and his chest heaved.

"Let it come," Michael said.

Now Nick let it pour out: deep, loud sobs rolling though his convulsing body. Michael lightly touched his shoulder. "Let it come, um-hmm, um-hmm."

Nick gasped for breath between the sobs.

"I just wanted to be done."

Michael patted Nick's shoulder as he continued to sob and sniffle. "This part of you has been carrying a lot of pain," he said. "It really needs to be heard."

"It's like every time I opened my eyes I was in a nightmare. Every time I woke up from a dream, I was in a nightmare."

The sobs began to quiet and the gasps came further apart.

"How do you feel toward this part of yourself that has been carrying all this pain for so long?"

"I'm ashamed of myself for feeling like I wanted to die," Nick said.

"Can you ask those parts that are ashamed to give some space?" Michael said. "Would that be okay?"

Nick turned to look at him, wiping tears from his eyes.

"This is very confusing. I just don't know where it came from. I don't know why . . ." he sniffled. "I guess I was just lying to myself.

When I was over there I always thought that I wanted to just get back home, when there was this part of me that just wanted to die over there."

"Were there other parts that did want to get back home?"

"Just the part of me that loved life and loved everyone and loved Beverlee and my mom."

"Those parts are real also," Michael said. "Would it be okay to bring your attention to that part of you that wanted to die for a few minutes and see what you can discover from a place of curiosity, for those parts of you that judge it?"

Nick stared back at the ceiling for a long time.

"It's 'cause I wanted to quit, like everything was too hard."

"How do you feel about that part of yourself right now?"

"I think it's wrong of me to want to quit."

"I hear that there's part of you that doesn't want to quit, but can you ask that part to give a little space and to bring some curiosity and compassion to the part that did want to quit? Just take your time and see if you can picture just being present with this part with some curiosity and compassion for what it's experienced."

It wasn't clear Nick was listening. His eyes raced around on the ceiling, chasing after the cascading thoughts.

"It's like I didn't want to be here anymore. This place, this life, just didn't seem enjoyable. . . . Like when I was a little kid and I knew I couldn't make it stop, the bullying, and not feeling comfortable here, and I just wanted to leave."

"Just being here with this part and how painful it's been—is it okay to feel this?" Michael asked. "Let this part know that if it doesn't take over completely, you can be there with it, give it a chance to express its feelings; you can be with it so it doesn't have to be alone anymore."

"I'm having trouble with that," he said.

Michael read Nick a short poem by the thirteenth-century Persian poet Jalal al-Din Rumi. One verse in particular seemed to apply:

The dark thought, the shame, the malice,
meet them at the door laughing and invite them in.

Be grateful for whatever comes
because each has been sent as a guide from beyond.

"Remember when you said earlier that you needed to just cry, but the feelings were blocked?" he asked. "So maybe this is a part of the healing, that the tears are coming."

"I feel like my self is way too hard on this part of me," Nick said. "I can't justify it at all. It feels weak and selfish and all the things that I . . ."

"This is a young part of you," Michael said. "So it's not very strong. But you're not young anymore. You have some really strong parts, and also parts that think it's not okay to let this part be felt and expressed, and they're just trying to protect you too. They just don't realize that, actually, this is healing. There was a time when you couldn't afford to feel this and those parts of you that protected you from that deserve a lot of respect. The parts that protected you from being overwhelmed by those feelings served you well. They got you through, and that allowed you to become strong and confident in the Marine Corps and survive all that. It's just now coming up to be healed because it doesn't serve you for it to be shut off anymore. It's hard for the protective parts to realize this is not only okay but helpful. Does that make sense or is it more confusing?"

Nick looked at Michael again. "That makes sense," he said. "I'm just realizing I have a lot of baggage. I'm just a scared kid, not only of being bullied, but of the otherworldly stuff that just doesn't make sense."

Once again he sobbed out loud.

"Let these feelings come now," Michael said. "You don't have to hold that in anymore."

"I just want to sit up," Nick said.

Michael helped him to sit. Nick put his forehead on his knees and his hand on top of his head and cried.

"You want me to put my arm around you?" Annie asked.

Nick nodded.

"Me too?" Michael asked.

Nick nodded.

Michael and Annie sat on either side, wrapping their arms around him protectively.

"I always thought there was something wrong with me," Nick said.

"It's so frightening to feel that," Michael said.

"I'm sorry you had to go through that," Annie said. She handed Nick a Kleenex and he blew his nose, then sighed heavily.

"You're going to be okay," she said.

"I just don't know why that . . . that I'm so different than . . . the weird things that just . . ."

"Nobody knows why," Michael said. "But certain people have these kinds of experiences. We know a psychiatrist named Judith Orloff who has written books about this. She had experiences growing up and her mother told her they were not real, and later as an adult, after suffering and becoming addicted to drugs, she accepted it, and then realized her mother had had similar experiences. She eventually learned to see it as a gift, but it took her thirty years. She's certainly not crazy."

Nick sighed again.

"Take your time with this," Michael said. "It's a very important part of the healing process."

"I wish it had come up earlier," Nick said.

"I hear what you're saying, but I trust your inner healing intelligence," Michael said. "As we've said—I can't emphasize this enough—the process isn't just the six hours when you take MDMA. We know that some of the most important stuff happens in the hours and days that follow, and sometimes the unfolding is difficult."

"I just didn't like that stuff so much that I didn't want it to come forth, but it needed to," Nick said. "I just liked the idea, the insight, that I had the first time. But I had the idea that there were still some pretty dark rooms to go through."

"In a way you have to get to a safe enough place and a strong enough place to allow you to expose them," Michael said.

"We had to wait to get back to base before we could shed tears over our fallen guys."

"And there was a good reason for that," Michael said. "What you did earlier today and in the first session is what made this possible—a tremendous healing shift."

Nick lifted his head off his knees. "I can see that," he said.

When the study's blind was removed, it turned out that Nick had been given the 75-milligram medium dose of MDMA in each of his first two sessions. When he retook the PTSD test in the weeks following his second session, his score had dropped from a severe 74 rating to a nonexistent 6, a 68-point decline to a level at or below any mentally healthy person off the street. When the study reached the halfway mark in the fall of 2013, the PTSD scores of the six participants who had taken the 125-milligram high dose had dropped an average 30 points after two sessions, while the three who took the medium dose, including Nicholas, had dropped an average of nearly 60 points—compared to a drop of merely 6 points for those who took the 30-milligram low-dose placebo. Michael and Annie suspected that the superior performance of the medium-dose therapy over the high-dose one probably was an anomaly caused by the extraordinary circumstances surrounding one participant, whose score actually increased from 110 to 115 after two high-dose sessions. The subject had learned two weeks prior to his post-treatment retest that ten members of his old unit had been killed in Iraq. In fact, he arrived to take the retest directly from one of the funerals. After a third, open-label treatment session with 125 milligrams, his score dropped from 115 down to 33.

But the scores were just numbers. What impressed Nick were the changes in his life.

"I was communicating with this inner healer inside—you know, I felt this source that was within. I came to this conclusion that I wasn't treating my body right: I wasn't eating my vegetables right, I wasn't eating the things I needed to eat right, and I wasn't taking care of my body the way that I needed to. And my taste actually changed. Like, literally changed."

Beverlee couldn't believe it. She'd always loved broccoli, and Nick gagged at the sight of it. After one of his sessions, he'd said, "Man, I could go for some broccoli."

"I just about passed out," she said.

"It wasn't just that I knew it was good for me," Nick said. "It was like my body agreed with it—like, 'Yes! We want you to be on board with this thing.'"

The changes went way beyond food choices. "You'd have to jump in my body and see the world through my eyes to really understand. It's just . . . the colors seemed brighter. There was more life in everything. Dreams were amazing. It was like I was still processing stuff that was going on, and it was just beautiful."

The panic attacks, the explosions at Beverlee: gone.

It wasn't that Nick didn't ever get irritated, but when he did, instead of blowing up, "I'd find myself thinking, 'Calm down, breathe, don't do it.'

"Then I'd talk to her calmly, and I noticed that when I would talk to her like that, it was getting through."

He discovered that, almost at will, he could go into a meditation and "feel like I have MDMA in my system without having to actually take it. I'll be able to completely drift off and get in touch with that inner healer again and have those communications—be able to talk about what I'm dealing with right now, you know. 'This is stressing me out, this is stressing me out, I've got this going on.' And it will just speak some profound things to me, like, 'Why are you worrying about these things? None of that stuff truly matters. You're worried about it so much that you don't get it done like you need to. You just create even more negativity by not just getting it over with.' And it's just, like, why didn't I think of that? But I did."

Nick had begun taking art classes around the time he discovered he'd been accepted for the Mithoefers' study. He remembered the powerful feeling he got after he'd sketched out a profile of Beverlee when he was so in need of her in Iraq, and now he wanted to see if he had any real talent. He bought a sketchbook and had been slowly filling it with sketches, spending ten or twenty minutes on each. The images, typical subjects for a beginning art student—a pinecone, a table setting—had gradually become more refined with each attempt, but remained clearly the product of a novice.

For his first project after his therapy breakthrough, he chose something more ambitious. As he scratched his pencil across the paper, something about the work caught hold of Nick. His usual anxieties about not finishing the project, or failing, disappeared. It felt as if he were getting himself out of the way, letting his hands do the work. The sketch turned into a drawing, and the drawing into something more.

He kept at it intently for hours—a feat of focus and concentration that would have been an impossibility just weeks earlier.

When he finished, he'd created an astonishingly lifelike portrait of himself staring searchingly into the empty orbits of a human skull held in the palm of his right hand. It was a level of work wholly apart from

the sketches on the pages before it. The face on the rag paper seemed
to radiate a soft light, a willingness to look death in the eye without
pretense or denial.

Nick had never read *Hamlet,* nor had he watched any productions
containing the scene in which the prince contemplates the skull of
an old friend. But he had once seen a parody on TV in a *Gilligan's
Island* episode in which Gilligan asked the musical question "To be, or
not to be . . ."

It was a question Nick now felt he could answer, without fear or
ambivalence.

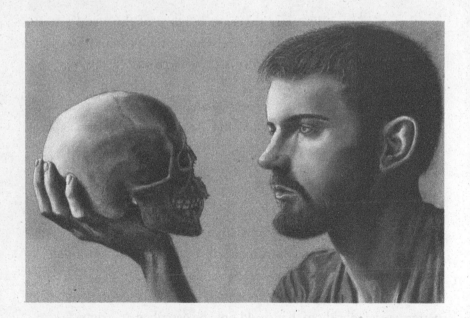

47.

RICK

("OUR LIVES AND TIME")

I n the spring of 2013, more than one hundred of the world's most prominent psychedelic scientists convened at the Oakland Marriott City Center hotel to present their latest research on LSD, psilocybin, ketamine, ayahuasca, ibogaine, MDMA, and other exotic psychoactive drugs. The 1,900 paying attendees included an eclectic assortment of therapists, journalists, academics, and New Age enthusiasts, along with a smattering of rainbow-hued, patchouli-scented spiritual descendants of Wavy Gravy, apparently launched into the psychedelisphere in the Woodstock era and still spacewalking. When sessions were completed on April 19, day one of the conference, many of the attendees ferried across the bay to San Francisco to dance all night at a party in honor of the seventieth anniversary of "Bicycle Day," Albert Hofmann's first experimental LSD experience. Two nights later, diners at the conference's culminating dinner were entertained by a combination dance performance/light show that could only be described as "trippy."

But the talks themselves were straight-up science. The plumes of incense and hemp necklaces in the cheap seats contrasted with the business suits and conceptually challenging charts and graphs at the podium. Rick Doblin, whose nonprofit was sponsoring the event, had insisted that all MAPS personnel wear business attire. In a conference-opening presentation, wearing a dark suit and carefully knotted tie himself, he described his thirty-year odyssey as an attempt to dislodge psychedelics from the fringes of society and plunge them into the mainstream of medical science.

To make the point, a slide of a bearded, long-haired, shirtless eighteen-year-old Rick was projected on the large screen on the stage beside the soberly suited Rick of today.

"I identified myself as a counterculture, drug-using criminal," he told the large gathering at the conference welcome, "and I felt that that was really a mistake. It was the mistake of the sixties, the acceptance that we were part of a counterculture."

The alternative was embodied in the list of conference presenters, top scientists and scholars with the names of elite, mainstream institutions scattered liberally through their résumés. Their remarks were delivered with all the caution and reserve honed by years of navigating radical programs through a conservative culture. And in that they had been astoundingly successful.

Follow-up phase II studies of MDMA therapy for PTSD were under way or planned in Colorado, Canada, Israel, Great Britain, and Australia. Human research on the physiological mechanisms underlying MDMA's positive effects were ongoing in Switzerland, England, and the Netherlands. A pilot study testing the ability of MDMA therapy to improve the social interactions of people with autism had been approved by the FDA in the fall of 2013. A small Russian study on the use of ketamine to assist in the treatment of heroin addiction had been completed with promising results. At Harvard, John Halpern was investigating the use of an LSD derivative that appears to defuse debilitating cluster headaches, often called suicide headaches because sufferers find the pain so unbearable. Two studies using psilocybin to treat anxiety in cancer patients continued at Johns Hopkins and New York University.

Johns Hopkins's Roland Griffiths and his associates conducted a pilot study to test whether psilocybin therapy can help addicted smokers quit tobacco—which would be especially important given that existing drug-assisted therapies have success rates of well below 50 percent and some serious potential side effects. Of the fifteen heavy smokers who volunteered to be in the trials, twelve were verified smoke-free after six months. For the first time in forty years, LSD itself would soon make headlines as a therapeutic drug. A MAPS-sponsored Swiss pilot study of twelve subjects with advanced-stage life-threatening illness published in the *Journal of Nervous and Mental Disease* showed statistically significant reductions in the patients' anxiety levels after therapeutic use of the drug.

Even as government-approved psychedelic research programs mushroom around the world, producing consistently promising results, widespread legal use of these therapies remains a distant goal.

The frustration that is normally hidden behind the mannered and measured language of medical research bobbed to the surface in one of the scores of presentations over the three-day conference when Andrew Feldmár, co-therapist in the Canadian MDMA-PTSD study, began his remarks by noting that after the study had been fully approved by all required governmental bodies, it took no less than two and a half years to obtain a measly 9 grams of legal MDMA and get it delivered to the approved safe in his office. "From Ottawa, the capital, *three times* two people were flown out to inspect the pharmacy to see if it's safe," he said. "This is really not science. I mean, give me a break. This is politics. All this stuff is what power does to cover its ass and to make those who want to do something that they don't want to do squirm. This is rubbing the helpless nose into the ground."

A surprised but sympathetic tittering rippled through the audience. He wasn't done.

"I have worked in this field since 1967. We have worked aboveground and underground and to the right and to the left. . . . If these rigorous procedures we are about to do came out proving MDMA is not an effective adjunct to psychotherapy, would I believe it for one moment? We are not discovering something. We are proving something that we very well know. There is absolutely no doubt in our minds."

Some of his colleagues on the panel of researchers conducting similar studies elsewhere—all with their own tales of frustrating, Kafkaesque delays—winced at Feldmár's departure from scientific sangfroid, but out in the hall the cathartic laughter became an ovation.

Annoying as the bureaucratic difficulties have been to researchers in the field, with each successfully completed study the regulatory obstacles have receded. What remains will be an even higher hurdle: the drug approval process itself, a gauntlet that challenges the resources of giant pharmaceutical conglomerates and may seem insurmountable for a coalition of tiny homemade nonprofits.

In 2000, Doblin had spoken of MAPS's "$5 million five-year plan" to make MDMA a prescription therapy drug. In his introductory talk at the 2013 conference, he admitted "we've had a $5 million five-year plan for about fifteen years, then we've had a $10 million ten-year plan for the last ten years."

Now it's a ten-year, $20 million plan.

But this time the ten years could be for real. Rick has hired a full-time director of clinical research named Amy Emerson. Emerson previously managed research for the multinational pharmaceutical conglomerate Novartis, which, Rick gleefully points out, is the descendant by merger of Albert Hofmann's old company Sandoz. Emerson estimates that the current phase II studies will be completed by the end of 2015, giving MAPS data on treatment of nearly 100 subjects usually required before the FDA will approve the launch of phase III trials. Phase II trials are baby steps compared to phase III—which will consist of two separate studies involving a total of thirty to forty treatment sites and four hundred to six hundred subjects. In order to treat all those subjects, as many as 250 new therapists must be trained, which includes giving them the option of undergoing MDMA therapy sessions themselves. As the MAPS-sponsored phase III studies proceed, Emerson said, the organization will seek FDA approval to provide expanded access to the therapy to 2,000 additional subjects, who would pay for their treatment at cost—thereby expanding the reach of the therapy without increasing the cost hurdle. Emerson estimates that the entire phase III program can be completed before 2021.

This timetable, though arguably not as unrealistic as some of Rick's earlier timetables, nonetheless depends on things moving smoothly, according to plan—which would be a first in the history of psychedelic research. First, the phase II studies must be completed with positive final results, and with continued safety. Adverse outcomes unseen in studies so far—such as psychotic breaks or attempted suicides during the course of the therapy—could complicate matters should they occur. Assuming the results mirror the impressive ones achieved thus far, phase III will begin when MAPS and the FDA can agree on a protocol for administering the therapy and measuring the outcomes on a large scale. If the phase III trials then follow the same successful pattern as phase II, the FDA will deliberate on whether to approve MDMA as a prescription drug. Simply reaching a decision on that could take as long as eighteen months. If all that goes perfectly, MDMA will have to be rescheduled from Schedule I to Schedule II to permit medical use. To prevent abuse of MDMA prescription writing, MAPS's plan calls for the drug to be administered only in licensed clinics with specially trained therapists, as is done with methadone treatment for heroin addiction. Nobody foresees doctors handing scrips directly to patients to be filled at the pharmacy counter in Walgreens or CVS.

And then there's the question of money. Emerson's estimate for the total cost of moving MDMA through phase III trials is just under $20 million, a figure that could easily be optimistically low. As all patents on

MDMA have expired—meaning sale of the drug will not generate huge profits—investors are unlikely to rush in to provide that money, leaving MAPS dependent on private donors. MAPS's current rate of donations of well under $2 million a year—which must be stretched to cover all of the organization's projects and expenses—will not be enough by itself.

In 2011, a MAPS board member and possibly its most enthusiastic donor, Ashawna Hailey, died at age sixty-two. That mean, among other things, the loss of MAPS's largest single annual donation. But in her will, Hailey bequeathed MAPS an estimated $5.5 million. Hailey was an American original, a computer software genius whose many software innovations—from a launch sequencer for an antiballistic missile system to major advances in microprocessor design—formed the basis of a great personal fortune. She was born Shawn Hailey, but in midlife underwent a program of hormonal therapy and began living as Ashawna. Rick said Hailey told him she wasn't interested in becoming a woman but rather obtaining the nurturing and empathic characteristics of femininity so she could try to possess the best traits of both genders.

In recognition of Hailey's passionate support for the use of MDMA therapy to treat PTSD, MAPS earmarked almost all of her bequest to fund phase III studies, which still leaves at least $10 million to raise from other sources.

Considering the spectacular preliminary results of the Mithoefers' most recent study—and the moral and financial debt owed to the estimated half million servicemen and -women returning from the wars in Iraq and Afghanistan with PTSD—the most obvious possible alternative source of funding is the Department of Defense or Veterans Administration. The $10 million or so needed for phase III could probably be found lost in the cushions of Pentagon sofas, given that the military's annual budget approaches $700 *billion*.

The VA has an additional budget of $140 billion. And although the number of veterans receiving treatment for PTSD and other mental disorders reached 1.3 million in 2012, with an average of twenty-two veterans a day committing suicide, the VA has yet to contribute a dime to researching MDMA-assisted psychotherapy.

For some years now, even though there has been enthusiasm for the promise of MDMA therapy among middle-ranking psychiatrists in the VA or DOD, any proposal to contribute to research got kicked upstairs to die. But that may be changing.

Rick's networking connected him with another major donor: Richard Rockefeller, the great-grandson of the oil tycoon John D. Rockefeller and cousin of then–West Virginia senator Jay Rockefeller. Richard, a physician and philanthropist, was introduced to Rick by a mutual friend and soon became a major supporter of MDMA-PTSD research. As the former chair of the U.S. advisory board of Doctors Without Borders, an international association of medical providers who minister to people caught in armed conflicts and other disasters, Rockefeller had seen more than his share of suffering resulting from war. As a result, he said, the development of MDMA therapy had become the centerpiece of his extensive philanthropic efforts.

"We need to know how to treat the trauma that afflicts most of the world or we're screwed," he said.

Rockefeller underlined his seriousness by committing $1 million to MAPS for MDMA research over the next five years and pledging to raise $9 million more, which will supplement a surprise bequest of $1.9 million from a longtime MAPS donor who died in 2012.

Rockefeller, who would tragically die when the small plane he piloted crashed on Friday the thirteenth of June 2014, made a contribution that went well beyond raising money. He worked his connections to get meetings for Rick and Michael with senior officials at the DOD, including assistant secretary of the Navy for manpower Juan M. Garcia III and Navy surgeon general Vice Admiral Matthew L. Nathan. Rick offered MAPS funding for an MDMA/PTSD study at the Naval

Medical Center in San Diego, under the direction of Dr. Robert McLay, the chief psychiatrist there.

Rick reported in an email, "We thought we'd made progress and that the message would be communicated that if the Admiral [C. Forrest Faison III, the Naval Medical Center commander] wanted to go forward with the study, he would not be punished professionally."

But in the fall of 2013, after six months and despite the support of Richard Rockefeller's cousin, Senator Jay Rockefeller—a West Virginia Democrat who wrote the assistant secretary of defense for health affairs, Dr. Jonathan Woodson, urging him to be open to the idea—Rick's sources inside the military reported that the project was "dead in the water."

Senator Rockefeller had also met with secretary of Veterans Affairs Eric K. Shinseki, the former Army chief of staff, alerting him to Michael's promising work with veterans, which resulted in discussions between MAPS and the executive director of the VA's National Center for PTSD, Matt Friedman, about possible research. By the end of 2014, Rick and Michael were working with VA-associated psychiatrists to develop protocols for MAPS-funded studies involving veterans and their spouses using MDMA in combination with a variety of therapies, including those already in use within the VA system. This in itself would not get them any closer to the goal of completing phase III studies and gaining prescription status for MDMA, but it would at least finally get the federal government involved collaboratively in the research. Also, VA treatment centers around the country have been making inquiries about becoming testing sites when MDMA treatment for PTSD moves into the final phase III studies in the coming years.

But there is still a formidable stigma around the idea of psychedelic medicine among our military's senior leaders. After the hardcover publication of this book, when National Public Radio's *Diane Rehm Show* producers were looking for a high-ranking Pentagon official to discuss psychedelic research on the air, an intermediary relayed a negative response to the invitation from a general: "Too dangerous for folks in uniform." Nonetheless, Rick has continued to have contact with highly placed officials in the Department of Defense. "The DOD—specifically the office of the Assistant Secretary of Defense for Health Affairs—is supportive of MDMA/PTSD research," Rick said in early 2015, "but wants the initial studies to be conducted in veterans rather than in active duty soldiers. The DOD is trying hard to enforce a policy of no illegal drug use and doesn't want to directly endorse research with a 'drug of abuse' until there is more proof that it can be effective in military-related PTSD."

After the 2013 Psychedelic Science conference, Rick made a pledge to himself that he would stop traveling quite so much. His three kids, ages nineteen, eighteen, and fifteen, were all on the verge of going off on their own, and it had been weighing on him just how much time with them he'd sacrificed for his crusade to bring back psychedelic medicine. The kids had grown up in the ramshackle four-bedroom house in Belmont—not far from Harvard—that Rick shared with his wife, Lynne, who he'd met when they were classmates at the Harvard Kennedy School and Lynne sought his thoughts on a powerful psilocybin experience she'd had in college. (Ironically, Lynne, with a background in civic activism, now manages a family foundation that donates about $12 million a year to philanthropic causes around the Boston area but is "totally firewalled to MAPS.")

The cluttered hominess of the house, a very well-lived-in three-story gray clapboard structure, is a sharp contrast to the soaring, inspirational space of the house Rick built in Sarasota. The only slight architectural echo is a small roof deck with a hot tub off Rick's attic office. The office, decorated with a late-sixties *Acid Test*–meets–*Animal House* vibe, is where Rick holes up, endlessly working the phone and his email correspondence, a Sisyphean endeavor that a MAPS employee now helps him navigate. At least, that's where he is when he's not traveling—which he hasn't been able to curtail as much as he'd hoped, what with psychedelic conferences to attend, proposed study sites to inspect, potential donors to court, and the walls of the Pentagon and the VA to scale.

In late fall of 2013, he made a trip back to the Florida West Coast, where he's planning to repurchase the Sarasota house from his parents. He sees it as a future retirement home for him and Lynne. He imagines setting up an MDMA/PTSD clinic there and becoming what he's always dreamed of becoming: a psychedelic therapist.

Now sixty, Doblin knows there's no guarantee MDMA will become a prescription drug even by the time he's in his mid-seventies. He also understands that there's a real possibility it won't happen in his lifetime.

"It doesn't really matter," he said in his remarks at the Psychedelic Science conference. "The question is: Is it a worthwhile project to invest our lives and time in. And I think it is. The struggle itself is nourishing. That's the only way I've been able to continue this for such a long period of time. . . . How lucky I was that that eighteen-year-old was able to pierce through all the propaganda and have an experience with LSD that brought me a life's mission, and that all these years later still seems to be exactly what I should be doing."

NICHOLAS

(SEMPER FI)

After the completion of Nick's therapy, he and Beverlee moved to Paducah. In Iraq, the dream of once again walking the woods and fields of his hometown had helped sustain him, and the appeal had only grown stronger since his MDMA experiences. The couple found a duplex off the town's main highway, just a few miles from the land Nick's grandfather had farmed and the woods where he'd played paintball as a kid. Nick enrolled in the local college and talked about looking for a job. Before he'd gotten around to doing anything about it, he got a call inviting him to an interview at Lowe's hardware; Beverlee had filled out the online application in his name.

"Of course I wasn't going to say no," Nick said.

Nick found a pair of black pants and a dress shirt. He had never had a job interview before and he didn't own a tie. "But I figured, hey, it's Lowe's," Nick said. When he got to the interview, the interviewer didn't give his attire a second glance, but he kept asking him questions about his experience dealing with customers. Flustered at first, Nick finally said, "From here on out in the interview, whenever we say 'customer,' can we just understand that we're talking about the Iraqi people?"

That seemed agreeable, but Nick was convinced he'd blown the interview anyway, because when the interviewer asked, "Was there ever a time that you couldn't do anything to help a customer?" he recounted an experience he'd had when his platoon scrambled into the city to restore order after an Iraqi suicide bomber drove an explosives-laden car into a building to kill the leader of a rival faction. When Nick's Humvee arrived at ground zero, bodies lay scattered like broken dolls and moans rose from beneath the rubble. A man carrying a torn and bleeding child staggered to their truck. The corpsman jumped out and started trying to patch the boy up. Nick desperately wanted to climb down from his turret to tear through the rubble to try to free the trapped. But he knew he couldn't leave his post at the gun.

As he had been trying to find words for the frustration he had felt, tears just started leaking out of his eyes. A sure interview killer, he figured.

He got the job anyway. "I think they got a huge tax credit for hiring me," Nick said.

He woke up each morning at three a.m. to begin his shift at four. On his third or fourth day he was unloading a huge semitruck, stacking goods on pallets and then putting the pallets on pallet jacks and pulling them out onto the floor. The store had a wide center aisle intersected at right angles by a series of narrower aisles.

"It just reminded me of whenever we'd be parked on the street in Ramadi, and you'd look down an alleyway, and you've just got all these intersecting roads. I just got to thinking about if someone were to pop out with a gun. So I kind of daydreamed a person popping out real quick and then . . . *BAMBAMBAM!*"

Suddenly Nick no longer was controlling the daydream. He saw himself getting hit as he pulled on the pallet jack and fell to his knees. Instead of blood pouring out, his wounds gushed sand. He tried to catch the sand with his hands and got so caught up in it that he hadn't noticed that he'd pulled the jack several aisles too far. He came to himself and brought the pallet back, but his heart was pumping and he was dripping sweat. He kept telling himself that this was a daydream, not a hallucination, but he felt a panic attack coming on.

"I was breathing deeply and calmly as I could, saying, '*Not now, not now, not now.*' Then there was just a stronger voice in me, saying, '*No, now!*' I started getting choked up and running faster to get to the bathroom. I remember before I finally got to the bathroom, tears were starting to come out of my eyes. By the time I slammed the door, I just went straight to the corner and curled down and put my hand over my mouth so people wouldn't hear me screaming. Just screamed into my hand. Cried. Splashed some water on my face and stared in the mirror and told myself to pull my shit together. Went back out there. Walking back, I remember talking to the guys and saying, 'Oh, stomach problems.'"

He had to run to the bathroom again, and again—five times within a couple of hours.

"My boss finally came to me and said, 'Is everything okay?' And I wanted to say to myself, 'Suck it up,' but that booming voice came into my head and said, 'Tell him!' So I said—I whispered it to him, 'cause all the other guys were standing behind him, and they were staring at me too—I was, like, 'I'm having panic attacks.'"

The boss sent him home, and the next day he came back and admitted to everyone what had happened.

"If it happened again, I wanted them to know," Nick said.

As soon as he told them, he realized that his real problem had not been the daydream but that he had tried to suppress it rather than letting it come up, as he'd done in the MDMA sessions. "After that," he said, "I could have the same kind of rush of anxiety without manifesting it where I'm actually in a corner crying and screaming. Now I can meditate and just get back in touch with that inner healer. I can relive it, bring back that voice: 'Hey, you need to relax, this isn't something you should be worrying about.' Afterwards I'd feel this huge relief— like vapors just coming off my body."

After that, when things came up, they no longer seemed so threatening. "I'd think of them like bubbles," Nick said. "They'd float up there, and I'd just look at them, and then they'd come to the surface and just pop, poof, gone."

He says he became so mellow, and felt so comfortable talking about what he'd been through, that "guys at work, they'd say, 'You don't seem like you're a Marine,' and that's when I'd tell them about the therapy that I went through and stuff. I said, 'Hey, they gave me Ecstasy in these sessions, so it loosened me up and turned me into, I guess, a softie, you would say, so that's why I don't mind talking about these things, and I see the benefit in talking about it.' I learned how to keep the warrior without having to always have my shield up, my guard up, you know? Without having to have my head on a swivel, thinking something's always trying to kill me."

Nick eventually left Lowe's to take a master carpentry trade course. His father had always been able to build or fix just about anything, and as a kid Nick had held tools for him but never expressed any curiosity about the work itself. Now that he was learning those skills, he asked his father all sorts of things he'd never thought to ask, and not just about carpentry. They communicated with a kind of ease they'd never known.

In 2013, when Nick, now twenty-six, completed his college degree, he lost his GI Bill educational stipend. He and Beverlee, who was working a cash register at a retail store, could no longer afford the $650-a-month duplex. A friend of Nick's sister sold them a trailer for $11,000; it had been damaged in a storm, then fixed up like new with insurance money. Nick and Beverlee moved it to a small plot on the family land a few hundred yards from the house his parents had built there. Nick used all his new skills to fix the place up. Each morning he'd wake up and take a short walk—or a quick ride on the gas-powered cart his parents kept in their garage—from the tree-fringed cornfield where, especially after a heavy rain washed away the topsoil, he often found the ancient arrowheads that seemed to pop out of the earth like good omens.

Living on his own land, being steps away from deep woods, seemed to Nick like a continuation of his therapy. "There's something about it—something that's in the trees, in the earth—that just makes you feel whole. I learned that from my MDMA sessions. When you start feeling scared or freaked out, to ground yourself, just visualize—well for me, I'd visualize that my body was made from the same material as the earth, you know, that it came from the earth, so that I had that connection and that it's always there."

Nick had been doing more and more artwork, much of it involving the intricate geometric formations and vaguely hieroglyphic symbols that he'd seen in his MDMA visions, punctuated by mysterious figures that bore a completely coincidental but powerful resemblance to images of the bird god Abraxas he'd never encountered. He carved a beautifully engraved cane for Beverlee who, despite an ambitious program of physical therapy, was having increasing difficulty keeping her balance; and he built a kitchen table for his parents using a blowtorch to burn symbols of his father's career as a firefighter into the wood surface.

His work appealed enough to inspire commissions from people who came across it, including several who asked him to design tattoos for them. Nick, now in the habit of listening to his inner voice, realized that what he really wanted was the freedom granted by the military disability payments he had earned in war, and his good luck in inheriting a home place, to devote himself to becoming an artist.

For quite some time after the revelations of his therapy sessions, he still had trouble feeling completely comfortable with his conviction that his experience of being visited by strange beings was no dream. It was difficult and frightening to perceive the gaping chasm between the completely rational part of him and the common wisdom of the world he inhabited, with this belief that defied reason. But then, he realized, this had always been his problem. In some way, he felt certain now, the fuzzy dots of his childhood and the entities of his visitation were aspects of the same thing, a thing that, in its ultimate reality, he guessed, had little to do with either dots or beings with saucer eyes. Maybe it was some alternative kind of awareness or an unexplored kind of connection to the subconscious—he didn't know, and now he knew he didn't have to know. He had had a powerful experience, one that he no longer felt the need to judge except to see it as an invitation to view the world as a bottomless mystery—which, for an artist, after all, could be a great gift.

As Michael had predicted, in the two years following the sessions, the scars of war, both emotional and physical, though always with him, seemed to heal over. Unlovely as they were, they no longer seared him or posed an existential threat. His knee would never be what it once was, and the slivers of shrapnel in his butt would periodically announce themselves as burning embers. Even the constant ringing in his ears from the blast that killed Seabass—a constant high-pitched hum that lurked in every silence and could get so loud, it would drown out the music in his headphones—he managed to use to his advantage. Whenever he wanted to fall into the now-familiar reassurance of meditation, he needed no mantra, no droning *"om."* He just listened for the hum and used it to take him away to that place of peace he had learned to find.

But the war, and his wounded psyche, weren't quite done with him. Late one night in the fall of 2013, he was working on a piece of art in his new home when an enormous blast thudded through the foundation and shook the walls. Before he could conceive what had happened, he heard a woman's scream, so shrill and full of pain that it sounded as if it came from that animal lurking deep beneath our humanity that knows only suffering and death.

His heart froze in his chest. He was sure he was having one of those awful hallucinations he'd thought he'd left behind. But the screaming kept on and on. Maybe it was real.

He ran out the door. There, in the highway just yards from his front door, he saw a still-spinning, steaming wreckage of two cars now rendered into a field of debris. The screaming was coming from somewhere among the twisted bits of metal, shattered glass, and splattered blood. Suddenly Nick was back there, back in Iraq, back in the darkness that had nearly killed him.

That night, after the injured had been rushed to the hospital, he lay awake until dawn, hearing that awful scream over and over. It tore at him, reminding him of when he couldn't escape his thoughts. He kept telling himself, *I'm okay now. I'm healed*, but it didn't help, and that terrified him.

In retrospect he realized that stresses had been building up to the crash. Beverlee had been falling more and more often, which stripped away any possibility of denial about the course of her illness. And now that he'd committed to being an artist, he found that it was harder not to be anxious about working too slowly or to avoid the gut-clenching fear of failure.

It didn't help, either, that he couldn't go on the Internet without seeing news blurbs about Fallujah and Ramadi falling back into the hands of Al Qaeda. "My heart aches, as do the wounds I received while fighting in those streets," he wrote on his Facebook wall. "So much blood was sacrificed. Now it feels like a waste. This world is like a joke."

After witnessing the wreck at his doorstep, he began to have scary lapses. He'd be at his drawing table and drift away for thirty minutes at a time, as he had done in school before his therapy. Once he was trying to work on deadline, listening to rap music he liked to get himself charged up, when instead of the rap he began to hear Seabass's voice as loud as if he were sitting beside him, that exact timbre and accent coming in so clear. It was only afterward that he realized that some of the tunes he'd been listening to were the ones he'd listened to in Iraq.

He was painfully aware that when these unwanted thoughts and memories came up, he was unable to simply watch them pass as he had been able to do for so long after his therapy. One night he awoke out of breath and shaken. In his dreams, he'd been trapped in a full circle of flames that were engulfing him.

Beverlee woke up, saw what was going on, and reached out to him. "You brave, brave man," she said. But she knew courage could only take Nick so far. When she gingerly asked if he thought he might be regressing, that made Nick more anxious still. Yet, he knew this wasn't quite the terror it had been before.

"I slayed the demon that was always tempting me to take my own life," he said.

He still felt that way, still wanted to believe that his therapy sessions had given him the tools he needed to deal with whatever life threw at him, but it scared him that, for the moment at least, he'd lost his path to that place of peace.

He thought often how reassuring it would be to know that, if he really needed it, he could have another session on that futon with Michael and Annie beside him, the medicine showing the way.

But he knew that wasn't likely to happen. His part in the study was over. And MDMA therapy was still illegal.

Meanwhile, life would keep happening, throwing challenges and opportunities his way. When the hardcover edition of this book was published in the fall of 2014, Nick fielded a variety of invitations to speak to reporters and at various events, including a large gathering at the New York Horizons Conference before a paying audience that filled the six-hundred-seat auditorium. It wasn't an easy invitation for Nick to accept. He'd never been to New York, and he wasn't looking forward to it.

"I have this thing about cities that makes me very uncomfortable," he said. "There's just too much concrete in cities and not enough trees. . . . I don't think I would enjoy being in New York City any longer than I would have to be."

But with the video cameras rolling and floodlights giving his hair, now long and flowing to his shoulders, a halo-esque shine, he spoke with a surprisingly calm intensity about his obligation to his Marine brothers, who still suffered without the same chance he'd had to undergo therapy with the Mithoefers.

After three days in the city, and some classic New York wandering that brought him all the chance encounters with colorful characters (including a protest rally of bare-breasted women in support of women's rights) that a flawless fall weekend so often provides, Nick was at least partially converted, able to see venturing out into Manhattan as a sort of psychedelic experience in itself.

By then he knew that, despite Beverlee's worsening ataxia symptoms, she was pregnant with their child—a girl they intended to name Freya LeeAnn. Though this ignited in him a blissful energy he'd never imagined himself capable of, he wasn't immune to fears about the unusually challenging future he faced.

When toward the end of the year, with the baby's due date just a month away, Nick had to ask to postpone an appearance on a webinar sponsored by MAPS, he explained to me in an email:

> The day before, I went running out in this shitty cold weather and must have picked up a bug. I don't normally get that sick but lately I've been stressed out and that probably lowered my immune system.

The whole "I'm about to have a baby and I'm not prepared" thing has been weighing me down and I'm unable to shake it. I feel as if weeks ago my inner strength was taken from me in my sleep. It was as if I woke up one morning and everything turned back to dull, it had lost its brilliance or something. I seem to have lost that pivotal connection that gave me focus. Almost as if that Well of Fortitude that used to give me so much strength . . . had somehow run dry. Yet, I know that my well is bottomless but for some unseen reason I can't seem to pull from it.

I know this is probably just a wave that I'm passing through and that whenever Freya is born I'll kick into high gear; just as I used to when I would leave the gates of Hurricane Point and roll into the arena of Ramadi. It's just that . . . well, the beast within me doesn't settle down easy once all my compound stress factors begin to swarm. My breathing techniques don't work when I'm unable to find room to breathe. I just don't want that beast to cause any damage that I'll have to repair later.

I've never been in a storm that lasts forever, so I know the clouds will part soon.

On the last morning of January, in the brand new year of 2015, Nick drove Beverlee to the Paducah hospital. At 12:15 p.m., Freya Lee-Ann emerged into this scary, beautiful, unfathomable world.

Nick, who has long since learned not to fear letting his poetic instincts roam free, wrote in his first Facebook post as a father: "Love, which was once just a word between us, is now made flesh."

AFTERWORD

A s I researched this book, I couldn't help but wonder: it had been thirty-five years since my last psychedelic experience. Given decades of encounters with life's sometimes difficult realities, how would I perceive such an experience now? The more I discovered about the work that's being done using psychedelics in clinical studies and the scientific investigation of their potential to provoke life-changing mystical experience, the more I realized that I needed to find out.

With a good deal of trepidation—possession of psychedelics is still a felony—I managed to obtain a plastic bag of dried *Psilocybe cubensis* mushrooms, stiff, sticklike things instead of the soft, fleshy specimens of my memory.

From my research, I knew that the physiological danger of ingesting mushrooms was minimal. I do not have high blood pressure or heart disease—two potential risk factors. Also, my lack of any history of mental illness and my past positive experience with psychedelic drugs limited the psychological risks.

I had one advantage over my youthful exploration: I had never known what dosage the mushrooms we boiled up represented, or even what dosage was desirable. Now I knew that Roland Griffiths, the lead psilocybin researcher at Johns Hopkins, had found that a dose of 20 milligrams per 70 kilograms of body weight was the "sweet spot," tending to bring subjects in his experimental sessions most of the positive experiences and all but eliminating the negative fear/anxiety responses higher doses sometimes triggered. In further research I discovered that each gram of dried *P. cubensis* equaled approximately 6 milligrams of psilocybin (though some sources said it varied greatly from batch to batch), which meant the 3.5 grams of the dried stuff I possessed contained about 21 milligrams of psychoactive ingredient—and hit that "sweet spot" almost exactly.

Now it was merely a matter of when—and how—to do it.

In my experience decades before, I had never planned to do a psychedelic drug alone—though I had inadvertently ended up being alone while tripping once or twice. But I had a strong sense that another person's presence would only distract me from the deeper experience I was hoping for. So with some small twinges of anxiety, I decided to go solo. At first I thought maybe I should wait until my wife, Lisa, was out of town. Then I considered the long, solitary days I often spent working at home while she was at her office. Knowing that the effects of psilocybin would wind down after just four hours, and pretty much vanish in six, I was able to calculate with confidence that if I ate the mushrooms immediately after Lisa left in the morning, I'd be past all but possibly the post-trip afterbuzz and perhaps a headache by the time she returned home ten hours later. When Lisa told me that on an upcoming Wednesday she'd be staying slightly late to go for drinks after work, and I saw that the forecast was predicting a partly sunny day with a high just around eighty and low humidity (it had been hot and sticky up to that point), I decided that was the day.

In the morning, I had coffee but didn't eat anything, keeping my stomach as empty as possible for the mushrooms to exert maximum effect.

Lisa left at about seven thirty. I straightened up the kitchen, then got out the wood cutting board and a sharp knife. I retrieved the baggy of dried mushrooms from my sock drawer and began to chop the dozen or so shriveled shrooms into pieces. They were tough to chop, particularly the sticklike stems, and very unappetizing in appearance. But after about ten minutes I had a board full of finely minced shards. I poured a half bowl of granola, sprinkled in the shards, and topped it with plain yogurt. It tasted pretty much like a bowl of cereal, with only a tiny aftertaste that may have been more faint scent than actual taste. But it went down fairly easily as long as I didn't think about what I was eating. I looked at the digital clock, which read 8:09 a.m. I put the bowl in the washer and went out back to water the garden.

As I held the hose on the hydrangeas, my thoughts raced pleasantly, due I was pretty sure more to anticipation than to any drug effect. It was only when I began to skim the leaves out of the pool that I began to feel it. It's hard to describe what "it" was exactly. My visual sense perked up. The light took on a more bristly, electric quality. The water and leaves swirling in the wake of the skimmer basket began to form patterns, which seemed to have some unnamable significance. My mind wandered and the task I was performing began to recede— though I wanted to stick with it as long as possible. I hurried as I felt the onward rush and managed to finish at just about the moment when I no longer could summon the focus or interest to continue.

I put the skimmer away and thought that now I was ready to let the shrooms take me wherever they would. Still, though, there was something I wanted to do before I got too distracted. I climbed the porch steps and walked into the house. In the enclosed space, the room began to swirl around me. By "swirling" I don't mean the kind of dizzy spinning as when drunk. I wasn't dizzy, just awash in the sense that everything— furniture, walls, paintings, decorations—had a nearly animate presence, as if breathing or simply exuding energy. It took an effort of focus to walk straight and stay on task: I fished my iPod out of the drawer, put in the earbuds. The illuminated words on the iPod's tiny screen throbbed and the multistep process of programming took a force of will to complete. I wanted to hear some new songs from Regina Spektor, an artist I'd been drawn to recently, but barely managed to press the right prompts: Music—Artists—Spektor—Play All.

I hit play and went upstairs to my room, where I kept my computer. I debated whether I should look at my e-mail messages. I decided it wouldn't hurt to glance. The larger screen almost stopped me cold. Its vivid colors began to mix and swirl, far more interesting to me than the content of the text, which I read with great detachment and a dawning sense that I was no longer a part of the same world they came from.

Now I was beginning to feel physically overwhelmed. "It" came in great waves. The bed, made as always with a white quilt spread over three levels of pillows, beckoned. I lay down and sank deeply. It was such a relief to let go and not have to struggle against the currents that were roiling over me. The comfort was stunning, and not just physical. I felt a powerful security and refuge in this spot, my normal position in the bed in the bedroom of my home overlooking a quiet residential street. I closed my eyes, savoring the peace, and the music took over.

In interviews Regina Spektor has said she doesn't write confessional songs, that lyrics about crazy things just pop in her head, having nothing to do with her or her personal feelings. But as I listened to a song called "Fidelity," it seemed obvious in her voice that, at least in this case, that wasn't true. This was as confessional as it was possible to be. I didn't consider it speculation. I could *hear* how private and close to her core those lyrics were. She wasn't acting or emoting for the microphone. This was real, and painful. The emotion in her voice was overpowering as she sang the chorus:

I hear in my mind
All these voices
I hear in my mind all these words
I hear in my mind all this music
And it breaks my heart

I felt I understood her perfectly. I felt she understood *me* perfectly. As the chorus came around again her voice soared up the register of feeling and shot out the top. It surprised me much later, when I looked up the lyrics, that she was singing about "voices, words, and music," because what I was hearing so clearly was: *I see in my mind, all this beauty, and it breaks my heart.* I felt a deep communion with her; felt so keenly what had been haunting me most of my life—this overpowering connection to the beauty I saw and experienced all around me and the devastating knowledge that all of it was fleeting, ephemeral, impossible to hold on to. My hand brushed my cheek. To my surprise, it was wet.

From this point on, all of this recounting is horribly flawed and incomplete. So much of the experience defies description; nothing was linear or just one thing. Everything happened on multiple tracks, splintering kaleidoscopically in a way that can't be rendered accurately into narrative. But I do remember losing myself in the softness of the bed and the bittersweet sound of the music, feeling an intense bond with the singer, eyes sometimes closing, sometimes opening, images strobing, Regina's voice pouring into my brain and squeezing my heart. I was being swept away with sensation; images and half-formed thoughts ricocheted in my mind. At one point I looked down at my bare feet. They were no longer the feet I was so familiar with. The toenails appeared thicker and yellowed, an old man's feet. I had a vision of my body aging around me, melting around the self that has been so unchanging from when I was a child and a teenager and a young man. This vision wasn't horrifying or even particularly upsetting to me. I didn't enjoy it, but there was no denying it was simply the way things were, or would be.

I felt I could stay collapsed in that bed and let the experience continue to roll over me like waves across a beach, but that suddenly seemed too limited. With resolution I stood up, and my scattered self seemed to reassemble within the limits of my body. Walking down the stairs felt oddly mechanical, but I plodded forward to the back door and opened it.

As I stepped beyond the threshold, I entered another world—like Dorothy walking into Oz. A slight breeze swirled the leaves and branches and blossoms of the garden, brushing the skin on my arms. Soft air and clear light caressed my face. Just then, the music stopped. It took me a moment to realize that the music in my head was actually in my iPod, and the iPod had run out of power. I took out the earbuds and a far more fantastic music flooded in, leaves rustling, birds chirping, insects buzzing, the distant shoosh of tires on the road invisible behind the trees. I sat at the wrought-iron table and put my feet up. The crystalline light astonished me. The air, neither hot nor cold, invigoratingly dry, caressed my skin. I felt energy radiating from my body, mingling with the visible radiations emanating from all the life surrounding me. I scanned the backyard. The ornamental grasses had begun to shoot out golden tufts; the crepe myrtle, hydrangeas, stonecrop, petunias, and geraniums all had covered themselves in blossoms. Figs grew large and heavy on the fig tree, which exploded tropically in one corner of the yard, and fat red tomatoes swelled on the still-leafing vines in another. Tendrils of Virginia creeper and wild grape dripped from the pines across the back fence; persimmons hung from the persimmon tree like Christmas ornaments. I had seen all this the previous morning, and many other mornings before that. But now I had stepped into a page from an illuminated fairy tale. Just as that thought entered my mind, three large yellow butterflies appeared, flitting in spirals around me. I laughed aloud: I was in Oz after all.

And just as suddenly, the witch appeared, in the form of a dead pine tree that seemed to leap into the scene, leaning in from a neighbor's yard. I didn't normally notice this tree, as it blended in behind all the other leafed-out trees that formed a wall of green at the back of the yard. But now its black, rotting limbs vibrated with a sinister presence. The significance of this as a memento mori was immediately apparent to me—death had reared its head in the garden. I knew this was not only a symbol but a real threat, as a pine, struck by lightning, had crashed across our fence earlier in the year and caused significant damage. I looked around, newly alert for any other discordant notes, and sure enough, I noticed that among all the glitter and flutter of the tree canopy, the leaves of a huge old tulip poplar had a shriveled look, as if something was sucking the life from them. I wanted to think it was just the impending fall: tired leaves getting ready to brown and descend. Or maybe it was a mild hallucination. But I sensed I was seeing something real. This was a sick tree, an even more serious threat, towering a hundred feet above my yard. I climbed down the porch steps a little unsteadily into the yard. The tree rose in the far corner beyond a small brick patio where I'd put a wrought-iron porch swing. Stacked in front of the swing were split logs from a chunk of the tree that had fallen on the fence. I looked up the twisting trunks of the tulip tree, which threaded dizzyingly among those of the persimmon, a maple, and a wild cherry. The trees seemed to twine around one another like a giant caduceus. I couldn't separate one from the other, and the harder I tried, the more they began to snake and swirl. I brushed some dead leaves off the seat of the swing, which was rarely used, and turned around to sit. Then I looked up and . . . everything changed.

This was still my backyard, but it was something else entirely. Time cracked wide open and the present moment expanded endlessly like a series of trapdoors. I looked up at the sky, somehow *seeing* the multilayered reality. I saw that in normal life we lived as if moments were beads rolling by on a string, but that in fact, the awful sense of time fleeing was an illusion. Each moment had its own unfolding expanse. It was *obvious*; I could see it: a timeless space extending in all directions in a way I knew even then I would never be able to put into words. I was astonished and amused to think of humans tunneling through this infinite reality with our heads down, eyes locked straight ahead, completely blind to the truth. And though this was completely novel to me, I had a haunting sensation that it was also familiar, as if I'd experienced this before.

As I've said, the act of writing this is creating a false sense of conventional sequence. In the event, it all mixed together. I can't say which happened "first," my sense of time splitting open, or a sudden awareness that the split logs, lined up at my feet, glowed from within. My son had left for school abroad just the previous morning. The fact that he'd come out without a word and chopped and stacked them on the eve of his departure now struck me as an overwhelming expression of love. His whole life appeared to me in an instant: the blue-eyed infant, the towheaded little boy, the sensitive teenager, and now this soulful and gentle young man. I touched the logs and felt an almost painful surge of affection. It welled up and burst out in a rush and I heard myself exclaiming his name. I hadn't meant to speak aloud, but it came out. I looked around. The boughs and bushes and flowers swayed and swirled in the breeze. I noticed that the pool, though rippling liquidly in the sun, had pine needles scattered on the bottom, and the cracks between the cement blocks of the patio sprouted a lacy green weed. Garden tools and a broken-down wheelbarrow were scattered near a wall by the vegetable plot. Self-planted wildflowers overgrew some geranium pots at the base of the fence. But all these imperfections, even the dead and dying trees, had a beauty of their own. Everywhere I looked, the sometimes haphazard way I planted or maintained the yard seemed as if it had been strategic, working only to add to an overall perfection. Nothing seemed damaged or out of place or less than ebulliently and fulsomely alive, dancing in the cool breeze and sparkling sunshine, an absolute Eden. The angle of view from the swing gave me an unusual perspective on my home—as if I were seeing it from some unaccustomed middle distance. As I watched, I felt myself flooding with love for my family. Images of them came to me one by one, not just images but entire perceptions of the nature and features of our individual relationships and flashes of insight into how each of them saw me, as if I could look from their eyes. At the same time I was aware that this footprint of land, the house and garden, the imperfections and the beauty, were all the manifestations of this love I felt, that this small created space, this patch of time and earth, was the physical expression of my life, of our lives together, and the love and labor we all shared. I saw it not only as it was but as it had been over the years, and all that had gone into it, the panorama of often tedious and taxing effort we had put into creating and maintaining this little acre. I was looking now not just at my home but at the truest self-portrait.

It struck me that, consciously and unconsciously, I had been preparing for exactly this moment for weeks, months, or even years. It was no accident I had planted and weeded and mowed all that grass, clipped all those hedges just days earlier. It was no accident that the morning was as fresh and clear as a mountain spring or that I had caught the garden at its golden end-of-August peak; or that the dogwood was gently nodding in the breeze and the ivy curling up the trunk of the cherry tree. I had planned it all, on some level of consciousness of which I hadn't been aware until now, to reach this very moment. I stood up and stepped out of the shade into the light.

I can't think of any other way to put this but to say the sky opened, and grace poured down all around me. Light itself had transformed into a palpable substance, spilling down as if from a fountain. But it was more than light. It was blessings of every kind, goodness incarnate, flowing inexhaustible and immutable from above. I didn't say to myself, "What is this?" I didn't guess. I knew. A radiant energy enveloped me, filled me up. But it wasn't just energy; it was a presence. I was not alone.

I said, or shouted, "Okay, I am *definitely* not an atheist," but God was mute. This wasn't a God with whom I could have a conversation, at least not two-way. I understood, or perceived, that the only response God would make was the boundless bounty of beauty cascading over me.

I understood that this gift absurdly overmatched anything I could possibly have deserved. I thought, and said aloud, "Why me?" Instantly, that seemed too self-satisfied. I could just look at this phenomenon that confronted me, this Niagara Falls of beauty pouring down, and know that I hadn't been "chosen." I was no one special. This was just what God was, a permanent condition that somehow had remained invisible to me until this moment.

I was keenly aware that this left a primal puzzle: What about people living in trash heaps, caught in the crossfire of wars, wasting with disease? I could "see" that this fountain of bounty was infinite—in any case, it clearly didn't stop at my property lines. So where was the blessing in the lives of all those so afflicted? And what if tomorrow I was struck by a truck or someone close to me fell deathly ill? How did that fit into this apparently universal cascade of good? I didn't have an answer, or even sense one. All I knew was what I saw.

As I stood there, my arms out, caught in the most miraculous sun shower, all the ways I'd been almost absurdly fortunate when I could have been unfortunate, all the times I had felt spared from disaster, or led to a good outcome, spooled through my mind's eye. "Why me?" I said again. Why had I been granted such consistent good fortune in a world containing so much misery? I saw myself as others might, raving in a psychedelic trance, pacing alone in my backyard talking to an invisible God; I was amused by the thought.

Once again, a coterie of butterflies flitted around me. It was all too gorgeous to bear, and I felt tears streaking down my face. "Tears of joy," I thought, and then I felt the pain in the joy, the unbearable beauty of the world, and fell to my knees. I wondered if this was what mystics and prophets through the ages had seen, and if Jesus's real suffering came not from torture or the burden of the world's sin, but his realization of the untenable infinitude of this unstoppable grace.

I found my way to a reclining chair on the porch under a green umbrella. I'd searched for years for the perfect reclining chair and just happened on this the previous spring—a perfect fit for my head and back that tilted to a balance point which felt like floating. Again, it struck me that it was no accident that this chair was here at this most astonishing time. I lay back and felt my body dissolving into the surroundings. My eyes felt heavy, and at times I couldn't tell whether they were open or closed. I made an effort to look up to the porch, where I was surprised and comforted to see my dog, a yellow Lab–hound mix, lying with her chin on her paws, a touchstone of my ordinary reality fifty feet and a million miles distant. I kept going away, disappearing into this indescribable timeless enormity, and then what seemed like days later looking back to the porch, surprised to see her still there. I felt my breath come slowly, a long exhale, then a moment of void, a moment that seemed like it could stretch on forever, followed by a deep sob of intake. I wondered if this was what dying would be like. "No *way* I can ever describe this," I said aloud. I think I yelled it. I had never expected anything like this. I was gobsmacked, overmatched, overawed into a throbbing puddle of being, who for some reason had been made privy to . . . all *this*. Again I thought, "Why me?"

"Who am I?" I asked God. *"Who the fuck am I?"*

The waves of light just kept coming.

It's odd that I can't remember when that sense of being inundated by a sacred presence ended. I know that at some point, I had the realization that it was gone, and that the ineffable sense of *knowing* was gone too. I understood even then, still undeniably feeling the effects of the psilocybin in my brain and body, that the most magical portion of my journey was irretrievably past. I could only "remember" a two-dimensional version of what had been a four-dimensional experience. It is the two-dimensional approximation that I have recounted here.

Maybe the turning point came when I was shocked by the first unambiguously negative feeling of the day: here I was having such an astonishing and significant experience, and I hadn't even told my wife what I'd intended. In fact, I'd more or less hidden my plans from her by omission—out of fear that she'd worry or object. Now a thought hit me with sickening force: I'd betrayed her. Here she was going off to work at a job that at times oppressed her, staying long hours, while I was lolling around in our backyard doing drugs! I had a vision of her working so hard and humbly, giving so much of herself to our family, so unselfishly and so lovingly. I say it was a vision because it wasn't a verbalized thought but an image that embodied all of those qualities which I experienced as revealed truth. I knew I would tell her what I'd done, and what I'd seen, as soon as she got home, and I'd apologize for not telling her in advance. I was so lucky to have the freedom that I enjoyed, and now I knew that I wanted to use that freedom to give my wife something. It came to mind instantly: just that morning she was saying how much it bothered her that we had let our housekeeping slide recently, and that she didn't have the time or energy to do anything about it before our daughter came over on the coming weekend. Well, I had the time. And I was determined to muster the energy. I'd seen God. Now it was time to clean the house.

I looked at the clock: it was 12:39, just four and a half hours since I had eaten the mushroom shards, though it seemed a timeless eternity. I was once again firmly in the coils of linear time: I had six hours before she came home. I felt driven to get it all done before then.

I began by fetching the laundry from the dryer and trying to fold it, but I kept getting distracted. The towels were so plush and beautiful! I'd never really noticed them before, but now I saw in them all the time and effort my wife had spent to find just the right towels, and just the right furniture, and just the right décor—filling our lives with comfort and beauty that would be almost totally absent if it had been left to me. As this revelation reverberated, I realized I was sitting down, stroking the soft fabric of the towel, and not actually doing any cleaning. I forced myself forward, which took great concentration at first, but soon I was just cleaning, going through the whole routine I'd learned from helping her. I wasn't hungry, but I was noticing the start of a headache, so I tentatively nibbled some fruit, then ate some more. I drank some water, then decided to try a beer, hoping to take the edge off the physical tension that was beginning to manifest now. The cold hops tasted okay but did little to diminish the tension.

By the time Lisa arrived home, the house was clean, and I was almost completely in a normal state of mind. I told her what had transpired. She raised an eyebrow but wasn't upset. We went out to dinner and sat at an outside table, talking until dark.

The next day I considered the implications of the dramatic nature of my trip. It seemed obvious to me that, had I any serious psychological issues, the power and profundity of the experience could have had a lasting positive impact. As it happened, I'd gone into it without any unusual problems, reasonably happy with my mental state. On the morning after, perhaps the only surprise was that nothing much had changed. I knew I would never forget what I had experienced, and that it would always be a source of inspiration I could draw on, reminding me that the world was filled with inexpressible beauty and goodness. But it was largely consistent with the beliefs I already held—admittedly, beliefs that were in no small part shaped by the psychedelic experiences I'd had as a young man.

Of course, I hadn't expected to "see the light" so literally, or to be shaken to the core of my self, but there were no new sets of beliefs or goals that emerged. I knew I had room to wonder if what I'd seen was nothing more than a drug-magnified version of the appreciation I've always had for the natural wonder of the world, combined with a chemical riot in the receptors of my brain.

On the other hand, the universe inarguably *does* shower us with all we need to live in a spectacular existence, and physicists insist that time clearly *does* expand in all "directions," with no one "present" point that is in any way more real than any other point in the "past" or "future." So what I *saw* that morning is arguably more in keeping with the best, most current cosmological understanding than what we think of as a "normal" way of looking at things.

Nonetheless, I was still just myself, pretty much as I had been . . . except, as the days passed, and for quite some time, I felt an out-of-ordinary calmness and centeredness. I found it was easier to "be in the moment" consistently. Neither anxieties about the future nor regrets about the past jostled me into that jumbled state I'd so often fallen prey to.

So after thinking about it, I would have to say that if I had indeed arrived someplace that afternoon, it was a place I could describe only as "here and now."

I can only hope it will stick.

ACKNOWLEDGMENTS

This book would have been impossible without the honesty, courage, and openness of those involved in the various drug therapy trials, including Nicholas Blackston, Anthony Macie, Donna Kilgore, Clark Martin, Lori Reamer, and others unnamed in this book.

Rick Doblin, Michael Mithoefer, and Annie Mithoefer were unstinting in permitting access not only to their work but their personal lives. Roland Griffiths, Robert Jesse, Charles Grob, Richard Rockefeller, John Halpern, and Jessica Dibb all provided invaluable insight, as did much published work. Of special importance were the collected works of Stan Grof; *DMT: The Spirit Molecule* by Rick Strassman; *The Doors of Perception* by Aldous Huxley; *The Psychedelic Explorer's Guide: Safe, Therapeutic, and Sacred Journeys* by James Fadiman; *Psychedelic Psychiatry: LSD from Clinic to Campus* by Erica Dyck; *LSD: My Problem Child* by Albert Hofmann; *Ecstasy: The MDMA Story* by Bruce Eisner; *The Varieties of Religious Experience*, by William James; *The Psychedelic Future of the Mind: How Entheogens Are Enhancing Cognition, Boosting Intelligence, and Raising Values* by Thomas B. Roberts; and *Esalen: America and the Religion of No Religion* by Jeffrey J. Kripal.

My agent, Gail Ross; my publisher, David Rosenthal; and my editor, Sarah Hochman, all provided warm personal encouragement as well as expert professional guidance. No writer could be more fortunate than to be associated with that triumvirate.

Finally, I was lucky to have access to the advice of those kind enough to read all or significant portions of the first draft of this book, notably Lisa Shroder, Gene Weingarten, David Klein, Eric Estrin, David Presti, and Torsten Passie.

INDEX

Page numbers in *italics* indicate artwork.